D0801420

PEDRO MENENDEZ DE AVILES.
Natural de Avilés en Asturias, Comendador de la orden de Santiago, Conquistador de la Florida, nombrado Gral. de la Armada contra Inglaterra. Murió en Santander Aº. 1574. á los 55. de edad.

THE SPANISH SETTLEMENTS

WITHIN THE PRESENT LIMITS OF THE UNITED STATES

FLORIDA 1562-1574

WITH MAPS

WOODBURY LOWERY

NEW YORK
RUSSELL & RUSSELL · INC
1959

The Library of Congress has cataloged this book
as follows:

Lowery, Woodbury, 1853–1906.

The Spanish settlements within the present limits of the United States. Florida, 1562–1574. New York, Russell & Russell, 1959.

xxi, 500 p. illus. 24 cm.

1. Florida—Hist.—Spanish colony, 1565–1763. 2. Florida—Hist.—Huguenot colony, 1562–1565.

F314.L91 1959 973.16 59–6234 ‡

Library of Congress

Printed in the United States of America
by Hallmark Lithographers, Inc.

PREFACE

THE principal sources for the history of Pedro Menéndez de Avilés and his conquest of Florida are: 1. A collection of letters written by and to him, memorials, royal cédulas and patents, instructions, relations, and other documents covering the period from 1555 to 1574, but chiefly relating to the conquest of Florida. This collection is published in E. Ruidíaz y Caravia, *La Florida su Conquista y Colonización por Pedro Menéndez de Avilés*, Madrid, 1893, volume ii. 2. Memorial que hizo el Doctor Gonzalo Solís de Merás de todas las jornadas y sucesos del Adelantado Pedro Menéndez de Avilés, su cuñado, y de la Conquista de la Florida y Justicia que hizo en Juan Ribao y otros franceses. This forms volume i. of the *La Florida* of Ruidíaz. 3. Vida y hechos de Pero Menendez de Auiles, Cauallero de la Hordem de Sanctiago, Adelantado de la Florida: Do largamente se tratan las Conquistas y Poblaciones de la Prouincia de la Florida, y como fueron libradas de los Luteranos que dellas se auian apoderado. Compuesta por el maestro barrientos, Catredatico de salamanca. This work is contained in *Dos Antiguas Relaciones de la Florida publícalas por primera vez Genaro García*, Mexico, 1902, pp. 1–152. 4. The account contained in the *Ensayo Cronologico para la Historia General de la Florida*, por Don Gabriel de Cardenas z Cano (anagram for Don Andreas Gonzales Barcia), Madrid, 1723, pp. 36–151.

The second volume of Ruidíaz's *La Floridà*, containing the Avilés correspondence, is published as an appendix to the Memorial of Merás in the first volume. In place of following a chronological arrangement the editor has grouped his material under the headings of "Letters of P. Menéndez de Avilés." "Letters addressed to Pedro Menéndez de Avilés," "Memorials of Pedro Menéndez de Avilés," "Royal Cédulas," "Royal Patents," "Instructions," "Relations," "Illness Testaments and Act of Translation of the Body of Pedro Menéndez," "Various Documents," etc. This artificial grouping has caused him to overlook certain obviously erroneous dates given in the titles of some of the documents and to leave unsolved the conflicting statements of Barcia, Merás, and Vigil as to the dates of the second and third voyages of Avilés to the Indies, to which a more logical arrangement would have directed his attention.

In justice to Sr. Ruidíaz it should be stated that the work is said to have been prepared hurriedly in anticipation of his admission into the Royal Academy of History, and although his introductory matter exhibits some traces of this haste, the collection is of primary importance to the historian and bears witness to an extended and painstaking investigation among the Spanish archives. With the exception of six documents,[1] which are reprinted from other collections, and seven letters of Avilés, which

[1] These are:

Real Cédula, March 22, 1565, Ruidíaz, *La Florida*, tomo ii., p. 351; Buckingham Smith, *Colección de varios Documentos para la Historia de la Florida*, tomo i., p. 13. Mendoza's "Relación" in Ruidíaz, *ibid.*, tomo ii., p. 431; *Col. Doc. Inedit. Indias*, tomo iii., p. 441. Letter of Toral, April 5, 1567, Ruidíaz, *ibid.*, tomo ii., p. 295; *Cartas de Indias*, p. 238. Vandera's "Relación," January 23, 1569; Ruidíaz, *ibid.*, tomo ii., p. 481; *Col. Doc. Flo.*, tomo i., p. 15; *Col. Doc. Inedit. Indias*, tomo iv., p. 560; B. F. French, *Hist. Col. Louisiana and Florida*, 2d series, "Historical Memoirs and Narratives," p. 289. "Disposición de quatro fuertes que ha de haber en la Florida," Ruidíaz, *La Florida*, tomo ii., p. 566, where it is wrongly dated 1566; *Col. Doc. Inedit. Indias*, tomo xiii., p. 307, dated 1569. "Diligencias hechas en Sevilla con motivo de la venida de Esteban de las Alas de la Florida," Ruidíaz, *ibid.*, tomo ii., p. 568; *Col. Doc. Inedit. Indias*, tomo xiii., p. 309.

are extant in an English translation, the volume consists entirely of material then for the first time published.

Barrientos finished his account in December, 1568.[1] He was professor of Latin in the University of Salamanca, and the little that is known of him is given by García in the preface to the above-mentioned work. Barrientos derived the material for his history from at least three independent sources. On p. 147 he relates that Avilés on his return from Florida to Spain in 1567, "presented this relation to the King," a statement which admits of the inference that Barrientos reproduced either in whole or in part the original relation written by Avilés himself. In addition to this he has apparently consulted parts of the Avilés correspondence[2] and finally he mentions several incidents which are omitted by Merás and Barcia.

The Memorial of Merás terminates with the return of Avilés to Spain in 1567 and his arrival at Court. Ruidíaz in his introductory remarks ascribes no date to the work. The year "1565" appears on the title-page which precedes the Memorial. Barcia says[3] the history was written at the time. Merás, who was the brother-in-law of Avilés, accompanied him to Florida, and both Barcia and Ruidíaz are under the impression that he went in the capacity of historian to the expedition. It is to be noted, however, that Merás relates various occurrences at which he was not present, and which he must have learned either from an eye-witness or from a document. The manuscript published by Ruidíaz is torn and illegible in several places. As the Memorial is silent upon a variety of subjects in the career of Avilés which are related by Barcia, the editor has supplied the omission by interpolating into the body of the text extensive extracts from the *Ensayo*

[1] *Dos Antiguas Relaciones de la Florida*, p. 149.

[2] *Ibid.*, p. 106, lines 2–5 from the bottom of the page, which are found in the letter of Avilés of October 15, 1565, in Ruidíaz, *La Florida*, tomo ii., p. 94.

[3] *Ensayo Cronologico*, p. 90.

for the purpose of presenting a more detailed and consecutive narrative, indicating the interpolations by reference to foot-notes.[1] There is nothing to indicate that Merás had access to that part of the Avilés correspondence which has been printed by Ruidíaz and which, as previously noted, appears to have been in part consulted by Barrientos.

On comparing the Merás and Barrientos relations they are found to contain numerous parallel passages in which not only are the events related in the same sequence, but the same phrasing and even words are employed in an identical arrangement. Many sentences are absolutely the same in both, while others differ only in the tense of the verb, or else employ the same words in a slightly different order.[2] The supposition that one writer copied from the other is precluded by the occasional occurrence in one of the accounts, either in the body of a sentence common to both writers, or at the end of the same, of a qualifying word or clause relating to a detail which does not occur in the other, as well as by an occasional difference in a number, which Barrientos, as a rule, spells, while Merás employs the Arabic numerals. It follows that these passages in Barrientos and Merás were obtained from the same original, for they present all the appearance of an abridgment following very closely the language of the original document. It also seems probable, from the variance in the numerals referred to and an ocasional variance in the readings, where the words employed still remain identical,[3] that the two

[1] See tomo i., p. 10, note ; p. 39, note and elsewhere.

[2] Compare Merás, pp. 74–77, and Barrientos, pp. 44–45.
" " 111–126, " " " 63–69.
" " 151–156, " " " 87–90.

[3] See the varying account of the answer of the sailor. Barrientos, in García, *Dos Antiguas Relaciones de la Florida*, p. 63, and Merás in Ruidíaz, *La Florida*, tomo i., p. 111 ; of the tying of Ribaut's hands, Barrientos, *ibid.*, p. 69, and Merás, *ibid.*, p. 125.

abridgments were made from different copies of the original, or that one of the accounts has been less carefully edited than the other.

The question arises at once—What was this original document from which both of these writers have derived so large a part of the incidents which they relate? The statement of Barrientos, above quoted, that Avilés on his return from Florida to Spain in 1567 "presented this relation to the King," points with much probability to the conclusion that it was the original relation of Avilés himself. The possibility of this being the case is borne out by the fact that the Memorial of Merás, who had returned to Spain in July, 1566, terminates with the arrival of Avilés at Court in 1567, and also by the statement of Barrientos that he finished his account in December, 1568, which was subsequent to the same event.

Barcia's account is largely taken from the Memorial of Solís de Merás, a manuscript copy of which was in his possession.[1] On pp. 85–90 Barcia gives a lengthy extract from it and distinguishes the quotation from his own text by reference to the original and by printing it in italics. The quotation corresponds to the Merás account given by Ruidíaz on pp. 110–131 in volume i. of his *La Florida*, which includes parallel passages in Barrientos. These two versions are not absolutely identical. There are occasional differences in certain words used in both accounts, in the tenses of the verbs, and there are a few unimportant transpositions and omissions. From all this it appears probable that Barcia and Ruidíaz had access to two different copies of the Merás Memorial. Several other short extracts from the Memorial are also given in italics, and the major part of Barcia's text is merely a condensation of the Merás narrative. Barcia also states that he had access to the papers of Avilés.[2]

[1] *Ensayo Cronologico*, Introduction, ¶ 6b and p. 90.

[2] *Ibid.*, Introduction, ¶ 6b.

In addition to the matter taken from the Merás Memorial he gives a number of details which do not appear in Barrientos, or in the documents published by Ruidíaz.[1] Barcia was aware of the existence of the Barrientos manuscript, but was unable to obtain access to it.[2] The curious result arrived at is that all three of the published accounts appear to have been largely derived from a common source,—the as yet undiscovered relation of Avilés himself.

This conclusion, if correct, has an important and obvious bearing on the value of the three narratives, since it reduces to a single source the evidence for the greater part of the events which they record in place of accepting them as three concurrent and independent sources of testimony. It follows that the reliability of the three narratives ultimately reposes upon the unsupported statements of Avilés except in so far as the latter are verified by the correspondence of the French and Spanish ambassadors and by contemporary French accounts. Assuming the above conclusion to be correct, the effort has been made to present the character of Avilés in such a light, not palliating his faults, nor yet belittling his virtues, that the reader may form for himself an independent estimate of his sincerity unbiassed by the confidence which the writer is disposed to place in his unsupported statements.

This confidence is founded upon the concurrence of the Avilés correspondence, extending over a period of several years, with the substance of the Avilés relation given by the writers above referred to; the absence of any reasonable motive for a misrepresentation of the facts on his part; the fact that Fourquevaux nowhere impugns his

[1] See *ibid.*, Año XLVII., p. 125, where names of vessels and of persons are given which do not appear elsewhere, and the date of the departure of Avilés for Carlos, March 1st, not mentioned by either Merás or Barrientos.

[2] *Ensayo Cronologico*, Introduction, ¶ 1c.

veracity; that Avilés does not appear to have been of an intriguing disposition; that he was too continuously, variously, and actively employed to have sustained successfully a prolonged deception; and that his letters betray, as a rule, the curt and frank bearing of a soldier rather than the place-seeking suavity of a courtier.

In recent years but two works of importance have appeared which treat at any length of the Florida episode. The first is Mr. Parkman's *Pioneers of France in the New World*, of which the first edition was published in Boston in 1865. The incident of the French colony in Florida occupies about one-third of the book. Mr. Parkman informs us that he had access to some of the Avilés correspondence entitled *Siete Cartas escritas al Rey, Años de 1565 y 1566*, MS., a copy of which was procured for him by Mr. Buckingham Smith,[1] that distinguished and indefatigable investigator for material relating to the history of Spain within our country. Unfortunately Mr. Parkman made but a very slight use of them, citing only three letters.[2] In 1875, M. Paul Gaffarel published his *Histoire de la Floride Française*, in which his only knowledge of the Spanish side of the story was apparently confined to that given by Parkman and to an exceedingly cursory reading of Barcia. He gave us, however, our first knowledge of the diplomatic correspondence which arose between France and Spain on the subject of their respective claims to Florida, confining himself entirely to that of M. de Fourquevaux, the French ambassador at Madrid, of whose unpublished letters he printed some interesting

[1] *Pioneers of France in the New World*, Boston, 1893, pp. 6, 104, note 1.

[2] Parkman cites only the letters of September 11, October 15, and December 12, 1565, which is dated December 25th in Ruidíaz. The remaining letters are those of August 13, December 5, December 16, 1565, and January 30, 1566. Mr. Henry Ware has given an English translation of all of them in the *Massachusetts Historical Society Proceedings*, 2d series, vol. viii., pp. 416–468.

extracts. In 1893 Mr. Parkman published his revised twenty-fifth edition of *The Pioneers* in which he made some reference to the extracts of the Fourquevaux correspondence printed by Gaffarel, but with no addition to the Spanish side of the story. Of shorter recent essays on the subject there are but two deserving of special mention. These are "Un glorieux épisode maritime et colonial des Guerres de Religion" by Maurice Delpeuch, published in the *Revue Maritime*, tome clv., pp. 1882, 2150, October and November, 1902, and the concise chapter on the "French and Spaniards in Florida" in "Spain in America," by Professor E. G. Bourne, volume iii. of *The American Nation: A History*, published in 1904.

Since the appearance of the histories of Parkman and Gaffarel, not only have the two Spanish works previously referred to been published, but the first volume of the letters of M. de Fourquevaux has also appeared, extending over the period embraced in this present volume. In addition to this new material, the importance of which cannot be underestimated, a careful search in the archives of Seville, Madrid, Paris, and London, and in collections in New York and Washington, has revealed the existence of unpublished documents of much value bearing upon this period, such as letters and reports exhibiting the Spanish attitude towards French colonisation in Florida; the Spanish accounts of the depredations committed by the Laudonnière colony, and the correspondence of the Spanish ambassador at Paris with Philip II. during all of this period, which fills out the Fourquevaux correspondence and throws an interesting light on the relations of Catherine de' Medici and Philip in their contest for supremacy in the peninsula of Florida. A liberal use has been made of all this material in the preparation of the present volume, rather with the view of bringing out the true attitude of the Spaniards than that of retelling the story of the French colony, which has already been done with so much ability.

In conclusion it may not be amiss to make some reference to the ponderous quarto manuscript history of Florida by Pulgar, MSS. 2999 in the Biblioteca Nacional, Madrid, the title of which is as follows:

Historia general de la Florida/diuidese en tres partes/ La primera Parte / contiene sus descubrimiento, description (*sic*), y los / successos temporales y Espirituales, assi / de los Espanoles, como franzeses, ingleses / y Las Missiones de Religiosos / dominicos, de la compania y / franciscos / La segunda Parte / Contiene el descubrimiento de los franzeses desde / el año de 1669 (*sic*), y sus suzesos, y la Relazion de los / viajes, q̄ los Españoles han hecho al Seno Mexi / cano desde el año de 1683 (*sic*) asta el de 1673 y / la description de la Bahia de s^{ta} Maria / de galve, y otro de la empalizada / La tercera parte / pone la Relazion de el Alvar nuñez cabaza de Vaca / enteramente. y La historia de Hernado (*sic*) de Soto / continuada, compilada de las decadas / de Antonio de Herrera / Escribiala/ El D^{or} D. P^{o} Fernz de Pulgar Canonigo de La / ss^{ta} iglesia de Palenzia, y Coronista /mayor de indias / dedicasse./

This manuscript history appears to be a development of certain chapters on Florida referred to in the Preface to Book IV. and also in the Index to volume iii. of Pulgar's *Historia General de las Indias Occidentales*, Decada Nona, continua la de Antonio de Herrera desde el año 1555 asta el de 1565 (Bib. Nac., Madrid, MSS. 2796–2799), but which do not appear therein. It consists of 776 closely written pages in a small and cramped caligraphy rather difficult to decipher, and is divided into two parts of two and three books respectively. The first book has six chapters, as follows: 1. The discovery of Florida. 2. Its coast. 2 (*sic*). Its people and customs. 5 (*sic*). Spanish discovery, De Leon, Ayllon, etc. 6 (*sic*). French discoveries, Ribaut, Laudonnière, etc. 7 (*sic*).

What remains to be discovered. The second book is entitled "Spanish Expeditions to Florida" and contains ten chapters on De Leon, Ayllon, Narvaez, De Soto, Fr. Luis Cancer, the fleet lost on the Florida coast in 1553, and Arellano. The third book entitled "French Expeditions and Menéndez de Avilés," consists of ten chapters on Ribaut, Avilés, the Jesuit missions, and Gourgues. The fourth book consists of six chapters on English expeditions to Florida, and the second Franciscan mission. All of these chapters are divided into numbered sections. The second part is in four books. The first book is a description of Louisiana in three chapters. The second book treats of Spanish discoveries since 1685 in two chapters. The second (*sic*) book contains the relation of Cabeça de Vaca and the second (*sic*) book relates the De Soto expedition in twenty-nine chapters.

The work is unfinished and the chapters are frequently incomplete, many of them being represented by a short paragraph of one or two pages only; others are very long, and still others have merely the title of the chapter written in, the page below being left blank. The material is unorganised, the same subject being sometimes repeated two or three times under different headings. The text consists very largely of extracts from and abstracts of published histories and accounts of the events related, the abstracts from two or more writers on the same subject being arranged in successive sections under the chapter heading.

The authors whose works have furnished the material for the history, and to whom constant reference is made, appear to cover all the literature on the subject in Spanish, French, and Latin extant at the time of its composition. The list includes in Spanish: Herrera, Torquemada, Las Casas, Castellano, Gomara, Padilla, Rivas, Garcilaso, Nieremberg, Remesal, etc.; in French: De Thou, Le Challeux, Laudonnière, De Laet, etc.; in

Latin: Algambe, Ribadeneyra, Camargo, Schott, Montanus, De Bry, Le Moyne, etc., and, in Italian, Benzoni.

In a word, the history is a vast and ill-digested compendium of all of the published material extant at the date of its writing, and the inference of Dr. Brinton, who had never seen the manuscript, that "it was not probable" that it "would add any notable increment to our knowledge"[1] is largely justified.

In conclusion the author wishes to express his obligation to Dr. José Ignacio Rodriguez, Librarian and Chief Translator of the International Bureau of the American Republics, for his kindly assistance in the deciphering of some obscure passages in the Spanish documents which have been consulted.

WOODBURY LOWERY.

WASHINGTON, D. C.
February, 1905.

[1] *Notes on the Floridian Peninsula*, Philadelphia, 1859, p. 36.

CONTENTS

BOOK III. THE GUALE AND VIRGINIA MISSIONS
CONDITION OF THE COLONY

APPENDICES

ILLUSTRATIONS

BOOK I

THE FRENCH COLONY

CHAPTER I

THE SPANISH TREASURE FLEETS AND FLORIDA

WITH the opening of the year 1562, the eastern coast of the continent of North America from Pánuco to the St. Lawrence was still untenanted by the white man. To the north the region discovered by Cartier and Roberval had become the seat of short-lived colonies, which had been abandoned in despair, and France appeared for the time being to have withdrawn from the unequal contest with the wilderness. To the south the persistent efforts of Spain to take possession of the vast region to which she laid claim had proved equally abortive, although they had brought her some acquaintance with the interior of the country and with the nature of its savage inhabitants. She, too, had become discouraged by her vain attempts, her useless sacrifice of life and treasure, the stern reception given her by the warlike natives, and her failure to discover those sources of the precious metals which had so amply rewarded her conquests in Mexico and South America. She no longer feared the intrusion of another power within this part of her domain, where she herself had so signally failed, and in September of the previous year Philip had proclaimed that no further attempt should be made to colonise the eastern coast.[1]

It was true that she professed it to be her desire to bring into the bosom of the Church the natives of her vast transatlantic dominions, but she felt herself fully equal to the gigantic task, and would brook no interference in her mission, even from foreigners of her own faith. Moreover, the greater portion of the continent was hers by right of discovery, conquest, and papal patent, and its boundless treasures furnished the sinews for her incessant European and African wars. Although she had now abandoned a small part of her Atlantic coast, her unparallelled success in other regions had soon awakened jealousies and stimulated competitors, lured by other incentives than the cure of souls, and she was determined to defend the pathway to the New World against the intrusion of all her rivals. Portugal, France, and England watched with envious eyes the extension of her possessions and the uninterrupted stream of gold that flowed into her coffers. As the route by which this wealth reached her ports of Cadiz and Seville had a direct bearing on her policy with regard to Florida, we will now proceed to consider how vast this wealth was, the path by which it crossed the Atlantic, and the risks to which it was exposed on its way.

Whether 1497 or 1501 be fixed upon for the inception of commercial relations between Spain and the Indies, the establishment of the Casa de Contratación in Seville, by cédula of February 14, 1503, through which all business with the Indies was compelled to pass, with the appointment of its governing board consisting of three officers, agent, treasurer, and accountant, indicates that

[1] *Spanish Settlements*, 1513–1561, p. 376.

even at that early period a trade of considerable magnitude was already in existence.[1]

The bulk of the exports from the mother country consisted chiefly of grain and provisions, arms, ammunition, and clothing, for the colonists were still comparatively few in number, and their warlike occupations gave them little leisure to indulge in luxuries. Horses and cattle, seed, plants, and instruments of agriculture occasionally formed a part of the cargo of the outgoing vessels, and slaves, both black and white, as we have seen in a previous volume. These exports were encouraged by an absolute freedom from duties during the first half of the sixteenth century and by the opening of other ports of the realm to the West India traffic.[2] The vessels returned from the Indies loaded with brazil and other native woods, dye-stuffs, medicinal herbs, cotton, hides, gold, and silver, and articles of native production.

It is difficult at this distance of time, and with the limited data at our command, to determine with any approach to exactitude the value of the precious metals exported from Spanish America to the mother country during the first half of the sixteenth century. Moncada states that by 1595 two thousand millions of registered gold and silver had entered Spain from the Indies since their discovery,[3] and Navarette, writing in 1626, asserts

[1] D. Rafael Antunez y Acevedo. *Memorias Históricas sobre la Legislación y Gobierno del Comercio de los Españoles con sus Colonias en las Indias Occidentales*, Madrid, 1797, pp. 1, 3.

[2] Antunez, *ibid.*, pp. 21, 24. The cédula of January 15, 1529, opened nine ports in addition to that of Cadiz. This privilege appears to have fallen into disuse, owing, among other reasons, to the necessity of sailing in convoy and the imposition of export duties. It was revoked in 1573. *Ibid.*, pp. 11, 13, 20, 22. The cédula is given in full, *ibid.*, Appendix, p. 1. See E. G. Bourne, "Spain in America," New York, 1904, in *The American Nation: A History*, vol. iii., pp. 282–284, for Spain's colonial commerce during this period.

[3] Sancho de Moncada. *Restauración Politica de España, Primera Parte, Deseos Publicos al Rey Don Filipe Tercero nuestro señor.* Madrid, 1619. "Discurso Tercero," cap. i., fol. 21b.

that during the century comprised between the years 1519 and 1617 this imported wealth amounted to 1536 millions.[1] As the new country became known and the mines were discovered and worked, the annual importations of the precious metals, though comparatively small at first, increased rapidly. It is reported that during four years of the period which we are now considering (1564, 1566, 1567, and 1568) something like thirty and a half million dollars found their way into Spain, an estimate which does not include quantities of jewels and precious stones. This was an enormous sum, when we consider that its purchasing power was perhaps fourfold what it is to-day. What may have been the total value of the unregistered wealth surreptitiously introduced into the kingdom from the same sources through the connivances of interested and dishonest officials, it is naturally impossible to determine. Unquestionably it must have been very great when we consider the facilities that were offered for defrauding the revenue.[2]

Spain quickly recognised that her increasing prosperity could not be displayed with impunity before the greedy eyes of her less fortunate neighbours. Neither was she slow in taking the necessary precautions. "*En boca cerrada no entran moscas*," says the Spanish proverb, and in two different directions did Spain strive to exclude these buzzing flies from her succulent morsels, that she might close to them every channel of information concerning her West Indian possessions. In the first place, she sought to prevent the publication of all charts and maps which could indicate the way thither. This did not arise from any absence of information concerning her distant domains. As the discoveries progressed the mass

[1] Pedro Fernandez Navarette, *Conservación de Monarquias*, Madrid, 1626, p. 143. And see Humboldt, *Ensayo Politico*, tomo iii., p. 316; E. G. Bourne, "Spain in America," p. 301.

[2] See Appendix A. Registered Gold and Silver imported into Spain from the West Indies.

of geographical material accumulated by Spanish mariners and explorers became accessible to the map makers, for masters of vessels and pilots were required to keep a record of their journeys for the purpose of facilitating the navigation of the Atlantic.[1] A register was kept of all the islands, bays, shoals, and ports, their contours and locations, and the distance of the voyages to the Indies, which was deposited in the Casa de Contratación in Seville there to be "well guarded and concealed"[2]; every precaution was taken to see that pilots and masters of vessels were thoroughly equipped with all the nautical knowledge and the instruments pertaining to their art, and discoverers were ordered to forward a full and complete relation of all they had done to the Council of the Indies.[3]

As early as 1511 it was forbidden to supply foreigners with charts or maps,[4] and in 1527 Charles V. enacted that even pictures and descriptions of the Indies should not be sold or given to them without special licence.[5] Such was the secretiveness of the authorities that no official map of the western discoveries was published in Spain until the year 1790, and it has been thought that this reticence on the part of the Government may have led to the suppression of Peter Martyr's *First Decade* and of the La Cosa Map, which was in some of the copies.[6]

[1] Herrera, *Historia de las Indias Occidentales*, Madrid, 1730, tomo ii., dec. 4, lib. ii., cap. vi., p. 32, 1527.

[2] *Recopilación de Leyes de los Reinos de las Indias*, Madrid, 1841, lib. ix., tit. xxiii., ley 12, tomo ii., p. 303.

[3] *Ibid.*, lib. iv., tit. i., ley 14, 1542, tomo ii., p. 95. For early regulations of this description see *Final Report of Investigations among the Indians of the Southwestern United States, Carried on Mainly in the Years from 1880 to 1885*, By A. F. Bandelier, part i., p. 45, note 1. See also Henry Harrisse, *The Discovery of North America*, pp. 11–17.

[4] Winsor, *Narr. and Crit. Hist. Am.*, vol. ii., p. 113, note 3.

[5] *Recopilación*, lib. ix., tit. xxiii., ley 14, tomo iii., p. 303; Kohl's essay on the Ribero Map in *Maine Hist. Col.*, 2d series, vol. i., p. 302.

[6] J. C. Brevoort, in his "Notes on the Verrazano Map" (*Journal of the Am. Geographical Soc. of New York*, 1873, vol. iv., p. 240,) and in

The other precaution taken was the total exclusion of foreigners from the crews of vessels sailing to the West Indies. Masters of vessels were required to be natives of Castile, Aragon, or Navarre, and no foreigners were permitted to hold the office.[1] No foreign sailors were allowed in the armadas and fleets sailing to the Indies, and officers were commissioned with authority to visit the outgoing vessels in order to assure themselves of the due execution of the law and to prevent their embarkation.[2] Finally the exclusion of foreigners from the Indies in any other capacity except under licence was rigorously enacted.[3] But the sheen of the gold was too dazzling to be hidden in this ostrich-like fashion, and in a hundred different ways the story of Spain's newly acquired wealth reached the outer world, and the knowledge of it spread. The French ambassador at Madrid, M. de Fourquevaux, kept his Most Christian Majesty fully informed of the expected treasure fleets from Peru and Mexico and of their arrival.[4] The banks at Lyons were also advised of the same.[5] Portuguese agents sought to bribe Spanish pilots to show them the way.[6] French pilots went to Seville and se-

Verrazano the Navigator, New York, 1874, p. 102, cited also in *Narr. and Crit. Hist. Am.*, vol. ii., p. 113, notes 2 and 3.

[1] *Recopilación*, lib. ix., tit. xxiii., ley 4, 1527, tomo iii., p. 303.

[2] *Ibid.*, lib. ix., tit. xxv., ley 12, 1553, tomo iii., p. 317, *ibid.*, ley 14, 1554.

[3] *Recopilación*, lib. iv., tit. ii., ley 1, 1501 and 1526, tomo ii., p. 96; *ibid.*, tit. i., ley 3, tomo ii. p. 93, and lib. ix., tit. xxvi., ley 1, 1560, tomo iv., p. 1. Instructions given to Ovando, September 17, 1501. Instructions given to the Casa de Contratación by Ferdinand and Isabella in 1510. Antunez, *Memorias*, pp. 41–42, 268 *et seq.* E. G. Bourne, "Spain in America," New York, 1904, in *The American Nation: A History*, vol. iii., p. 245, instances some of the exceptions.

[4] *Dépêches de M. de Fourquevaux Ambassadeur du Roi Charles IX. en Espagne 1565–1572*, publiées par M. l'Abbé Douais, Paris, 1896, pp. 97, 124, 126, *et passim.*

[5] Alava à Philippe II., Lyon, 22 Juillet, 1564, MS. Arch. Nat., Paris, K, 1502 (10).

[6] Herrera, tomo i., dec. 1., lib. vii., cap. iii., p. 197.

cretly made the voyage to the Indies as sailors on Spanish vessels.[1] Shipwrecked mariners and unsuccessful colonists rescued by passing vessels brought their knowledge to the country of their rescuers, while paid spies and informers were employed by the countries interested in obtaining such information.

With the rapid extension and increase of this traffic the high seas were soon filled with vessels of other nationalities preying upon it. To these France and England contributed the greatest number. During the first half of the century France and Spain, it is true, were almost continually at war with each other except for brief intervals of peace in which to recover breath. England was ostensibly at peace with Spain for the entire period. But the piratical subjects of both countries, acting apparently in defiance of the wishes of the home Government, were in reality often in secret connivance with interested officials of the most exalted position. The French corsair, Jean Florin, identified by some authorities with the explorer Verrazano, captured the treasures sent home by Cortés[2]; French pirates sank Spanish vessels which were coming from Peru,[3] or made a bold descent upon Havana[4]; the announcement was made of the fitting out of a

[1] Christobal de Haro to Charles V., April 8, 1541, MS. Arch. Gen. de Indias, Sevilla, est. 143, caj. 3, leg. 11.

[2] *Narr. and Crit. Hist. Am.*, vol. iv., pp. 5, 21, 1523. E. G. Bourne ("Spain in America," New York, 1904, in *The American Nation: A History*, vol. iii., p. 143, note 3) says the identity of Verrazano with Florin has been disproved by Peragallo, *Bull. of the Soc. Geog. Ital.*, 3d series, vol. ix., p. 189, and had never any documentary evidence to rest on.

[3] "Réponses du ministère de France à diverses réclamations présentées au nom de l'Empereur par Jean de Saint Mauris, son ambassadeur (1545, avril ou mai)." Sans date. *Papiers d'État du Cardinal de Granvelle d'après les manuscrits de la Bibliothèque de Besançon*, publiés sous la direction de M. Ch. Weiss. Paris, 1841, vol. iii., p. 140.

[4] "Relación de lo subcedido en la Habana, cerca de la entrada de los Franceses en ella." In *Colección de varios Documentos para la Historia de la Florida y Tierras adyacentes*, By Buckingham Smith, Londres (1857?), tomo i., p. 202.

fleet in England for the purpose of sacking the island of Madeira.[1] The cutting out of a treasure ship of the fleet returning from the Indies[2] became of such frequent occurrence that as early as 1541 Spain sought to obtain from the English Government a statute forbidding the sailing of any armed vessels from its ports for Brazil or the Indies without security being given by their commanders that they would not molest Spanish subjects.[3]

Particularly exposed to depredations of this nature were the many vessels which, shipping hides, sugar, and cassia in the islands of Puerto Rico and Hispaniola, threaded the Gulf of Mexico to carry their merchandise to Tierra Firma, Honduras, and Spain. These vessels were unwilling to sail home in convoy with the fleet which gathered at Havana for that purpose, because it would involve them in serious delay; and thus, compelled to return unattended with the money which they had obtained in exchange for their merchandise, they fell an easy prey to the pirates infesting the Gulf of Mexico.[4]

Necessity soon pointed the way to a method of self-protection, and very early in the course of the century it became customary for the vessels going to and arriving from the Indies to sail together in company in order to

[1] "Copia de carta de Su Majestad al Conde de Feria, fecha en Bruselas a 24 de Abril de 1559" in *Colección de Documentos Inéditos para la Historia de España*, por el Marqués de la Fuensanta del Valle, D. José Sancho Rayon y D. Francisco de Zabalburu, tomo lxxxvii., pág. 176.

[2] "Capitulo de carta del Obispo Quadra á S. M. de 16 de Agosto de 1561," in *Col. Doc. Inédit. Hist. España*, tomo lxxxvii., pág. 364.

[3] Eustace Chapuys to the Queen Regent, Jan. 2 (4), 1541, London, in *Calandar of State Papers, Spanish*, vol. vi., Pt. I., p. 304.

[4] Pero Menendez (de Avilés) sobrel Remedio, pa. q̄ haya muchos nabios (undated), Brit. Mus. Add. MSS. 28, 366, fol. 299b. The letter appears from internal evidence to have been written at some date between July, 1561, and the spring (?) of 1562, prior to any Spanish knowledge of the French occupation of Florida, Avilés being then in Spain, having returned from his second voyage to the Indies.

afford one another mutual protection.[1] It was one of the duties of the *visitador* of the Casa de Contratación not only to see that the vessels were properly equipped with a crew and supplies for the long voyage, but also that they carried arms and ammunition with which to encounter the sea-robber.[2] But as the sailing together of the vessels was not compulsory, individual ships or a small company of two or three would set out under a special permit and meet their fate at the hands of the pirates, to whom they could offer no effective resistance. A stop was at last put to this by royal cédula of July 16, 1561. It was enacted that in January and August of every year two expeditions should sail from the *rio de Sevilla*, the one called the Fleet of New Spain, with destination for the Antilles and the Gulf of Mexico, and the other called the Fleet of Tierra Firme for Carthagena. The two fleets were to proceed together under the command of an admiral, and on arriving off Dominica, the vessels destined for New Spain were to divide from those destined for Tierra Firme, with the General of the fleet in command of the one and the Admiral of the other.[3]

Another danger to which the merchant fleet was exposed arose from the selfishness of individual captains who endeavoured to save themselves at the expense of their companions. On an attack of the pirates the vessels would disperse like a flock of frightened sheep, those that were swift and light abandoning those that were slow and more heavily laden to the mercy of the enemy; and the rumour of the presence of a pirate in the neighbourhood of a port would inspire them with such terror that

[1] Antunez, *Memorias*, pp. 83, 84, thinks it dates from the beginning of the commerce of the West Indies.

[2] *Ibid.*, pp. 59, 61, 69, and see also the cédula of Feb. 13, 1552, *ibid.*, p. 16.

[3] *Ibid.*, p. 85; *Disquisiciones Náuticas*, por Cesareo Fernandez Duro, Madrid, 1877, p. 169.

it would delay the sailing for days. To this danger the fleet was particularly exposed in time of war, and in 1521 an armada was sent to protect the merchantmen arriving from the Indies, owing to the presence of French vessels off the coast of Andalusia and of Algarve.[1] The following year an armada was sent as far as the Canaries to convoy the outgoing India fleet. In 1532, fearing the revival of a war with France, an armada was raised to protect the vessels arriving from the Indies. In 1552 it was provided that an armada of four galleons and two caravels should escort the fleet, a second be raised in Santo Domingo for the protection of the coasts, and a third be stationed off Cape St. Vincent in Spain to guard against pirates.[2] Finally, under the cédulas of July 15, 1561, which regulated the sailing of the fleets, and another of October 18, 1564, arose the *Armada de las Carreras de las Indias*,[3] whose duty it was to escort the fleets on their way to the Indies. It then awaited in Havana the gathering of the various vessels and treasure ships from Tierra Firma and New Spain, and accompanied the treasure fleet and the merchantmen, who sought its protection on their return passage across the ocean.[4]

The fleets sailed twice a year from Havana during the summer season, passed northward through the Straits of Florida, or the Bahama Channel as it was then generally called, until they reached the neighbourhood of Bermuda, when they set their course for the Azores and from thence to Seville.[5] The passage through the Channel,

[1] Herrera, tomo ii., dec. 3, lib. i., cap. xiv., p. 23.

[2] Duro, *Disquisiciones*, pp. 167, 168; Antunez, *Memorias*, pp. 20, 178.

[3] Antunez, *Memorias*, pp. 15, 16; *Recopilación*, lib. ix., tit. xxx., ley 55, tomo iii., p. 49.

[4] Pero Menendez (de Avilés), sobrel Remedio, pa. q̄ haya muchos nabios, Brit. Mus. Add. MSS., 28, 366, fol. 299b; Duro, *Disquisiciones*, p. 168.

[5] *Pero Menendez* (*de Avilés*) *sobrel Remedio, fol. 299b.* Derrotero y señas de tierra y sondas de la costa de la nueua españa y de tierra firme y buelta de las yndias a españa . . . por fran^co manuel . . . empesose a 15 de

discovered by Ponce de Leon [1] in his first expedition, was considered a dangerous one [2] on account of the prevalence of violent storms at certain seasons of the year, the roughness of its waters, and the ever-present peril of the reefs at its entrance, the Martyr Islands of the early maps. In its narrowest part it is but thirty-nine miles wide, and from the earliest times that its blue and tepid currents were ploughed by the keels of the Spanish galleons the wreckage along the Florida coast attested its terrors to navigators. So fatal was the Channel to merchantmen and treasure fleets, that in the course of the following century the assistance rendered to Spaniards cast away on the Florida shore, the large number of lives rescued, and the watch kept upon the passing vessels by the coast Indians, subject to the Spanish rule at St. Augustine, were perhaps the most powerful of all the arguments presented by the Spanish inhabitants of Florida against the abandonment of the colony. Even prior to the Spanish settlement at St. Augustine, and shortly after Menéndez de Avilés returned from his second voyage to the West Indies, he had begun to urge upon the King the necessity of locating and establishing ports of refuge in the neighbourhood of the Channel, where vessels disabled in its passage and in the region of the "still vex'd Bermothes" could put in for repairs, and thus avoid the long and perilous return to Puerto Rico.[3] It is not difficult to conceive with what apprehension the Government viewed the possibility of the establishment of a piratical band in

abril año del señor 1583 as. Brit. Mus. Add. MSS., 28, 189, and see earlier maps. J. C. Brevoort in his "Notes on the Verrazano Map" (*Journal of the Am. Geographical Soc. of New York*, 1873, vol. iv., p. 239,) and in *Verrazano, the Navigator*, New York, 1874, p. 101, gives a good note on the routes to and from the West Indies. Gomara, *Histoire Générale des Indes Occidentales*. Ed. Fumée, Paris, 1587, liv. vi., chap. xxvi., p. 479 *et seq.*

[1] Herrera, tomo i., dec. 1., lib. ix., cap. xii., p. 250.

[2] Antunez, *Memorias*, p. 91.

[3] *Pero Menendez (de Avilés) sobrel Remedio*, fol. 300b.

some stronghold along the shore, within easy reach of the golden flood which at stated intervals flowed through the Channel, or the passing of the Floridian Peninsula and the territory to the north of it into the grasp of another nation with as keen an appetite for the yellow metal as its own, even though it might be a Catholic power and friendly for the time being.

Another and very imminent danger attendant upon any settlement by a foreign power in the vicinity of the West Indies and of the route of the treasure ships arose from conditions peculiar to the population which at that time occupied the Spanish colonies, a danger which pointed more particularly to France. As early as 1514 the rapid increase of the negro slaves in Hispaniola had already become a source of fear to the white population, and measures had been taken to prevent it;[1] this as well as the slave insurrection in Aylon's colony,[2] probably the first of its kind within our country, indicate but too clearly the treatment to which the negro population was subjected at the hands of its masters. By 1560 the natural increase of that prolific race, coupled with the constant inflow brought by the slave-traders, had created a most alarming preponderance in their number over that of the whites. Says Menéndez de Avilés in his letter to the King, previously referred to:

"In the Island of Puerto Rico there are above 15,000 negroes and less than 500 Spaniards, and in all of the Island of Hispaniola there may be 2000 Spaniards and there are over 30,000 negroes, . . . the same is the case in the island of Cuba and in Veracruz, Puerto de Cavallos, which is in Honduras, and in Nombre de Dios, Carthagena, Santa Maria, and the coast of Venezuela, where there are twenty negroes to one white man, and with the lapse of time they will increase to a great many more."

[1] *Spanish Settlements*, 1513–1561, p. 112.
[2] *Ibid.*, p. 167.

And then he points the moral and lays bare the danger.

"In France no negro is a slave, neither can he become one by law of the realm. Were France to arm three or four thousand men they would be masters of all these islands, and ports of Tierra Firma; for the city of Santo Domingo, which is the strongest, is easily taken, in spite of the fort, bulwarks, and artillery; and 500 harquebus men—for the honour of the city I do not say fewer—could take it with ease, and by freeing the negroes, most of whom are *ladinos*[1] and natives of the land, and by liberating them, so that they be no longer slaves, they would kill their own masters, and put all their faith in the French, because the French had made them free."[2]

Menéndez was wise and timely in his warning against French aggression, as we shall soon see.

France, England, and Portugal had all turned their eyes on the New World, were spying out its possibilities, and seeking to reap what advantage they could from the knowledge so obtained. Of the three powers mentioned, England was, for the time being, the least to be dreaded. Although the Cabot expedition had called forth a protest from Spain, the charters for discovery and colonisation granted to him and others were "without prejudice to Spain and Portugal," and respected the papal bull of demarkation. The early part of the sixteenth century was spent in building up the English navy as a distinct service, and the country was largely occupied with its revolt from Rome, the final success of which was instrumental in breaking down the respect for the papal bull which had stood in the way of England's discovery and colonisation

[1] A ladino was a slave who had served over one year.

[2] *Pero Menendez (de Avilés) sobrel Remedio*, fol. 300. "Memorial de Pedro Menéndez de Avilés," undated [1561–62?] in E. Ruidíaz y Caravia, *La Florida*, Madrid, 1893, tomo ii., p. 322. "Vida y Hechos de Pero Menendez de Auilés," por Bartolomé Barrientos, in *Dos Antiguas Relaciones de la Florida*, Genaro García, México, 1902, p. 29.

in more favourable climates of North America than those visited by the Cabots. It was this infant navy which became the cradle of the Stukeleys, Hawkinses, and Drakes, who were to carry her flag in triumph over seas.[1] The period in the era of Spanish enterprise in our country which we have now reached (1560–62) was but the dawn of their energy before which the older Spanish naval supremacy was destined finally to succumb, and Spain's watchful jealousy of English aggression in America can be best considered when the English colony in Virginia began to arouse her active resentment. For all that, Spanish vigilance was in no wise relaxed, and her ambassadors at the English Court kept her faithfully informed of all rumours and designs upon her West Indian possessions.[2]

Portuguese pretensions and Spanish distrust began with the return of Columbus from his first voyage.[3] Pope Eugenius IV. had granted Portugal the right in perpetuity to all heathen lands that might be discovered beyond Cape Bojador on the African coast, including India. This grant had been solemnly confirmed by succeeding popes, and Spain, by the treaty of 1479, had pledged herself not to interfere. But the return of Columbus from his first expedition aroused in the suspicious mind of King John of Portugal the fear lest he might have been trespassing upon these rights, although Pope Alexander VI. had issued his second bull of May 4, 1493, with the express intention of avoiding any such conflict between the

[1] Froude mentions as an important element of the success of the English navy the boat with sails trimmed fore and aft, which could work to windward, invented by Mr. Fletcher of Rye. *English Seamen in the Sixteenth Century*, by James Anthony Froude, New York, 1895, p. 12.

[2] *The Discovery of America*, by John Fiske, Boston and New York, 1892, vol. ii., p. 17. *The Genesis of the United States*, by Alexander Brown, Boston and New York, 1890, vol. i., p. 2, note.

[3] Herrera, tomo i., dec. 1, lib. ii., cap. viii., p. 47 and cap. 10, p. 49 (1593).

two powers.[1] King John threw out hints of an immediate rupture to the Spanish embassy sent to announce to him the departure of Columbus on his second expedition, and appears to have contemplated seriously the sending of a small fleet to take possession of some point in Cathay or Cipango, and then to dispute the Spanish claims. But a vigilant eye was kept upon his movements, the equipment of the fleet was delayed by diplomatic means, and in the following year by the treaty of Tordesillas the line of demarkation was advanced westward 370 leagues beyond the Cape de Verd Islands, which secured Brazil, accidentally discovered in 1500, to the Portuguese Crown.[2]

The progress of Spanish discovery and the wealth which it brought to light did not tend to lessen the envy of Emanuel I., King John's successor, and so persistent were his efforts to learn the path followed by the Spanish adventurers that in 1510 Charles V. sent him word by Alonso de la Puente that he was to make an end of stealing Spanish pilots.[3] The following year, Portugal seized the Moluccas, and in 1514 an expedition to Darien was only stopped by the timely protest of Spain.[4] Disputes were soon rife between the rival powers as to the longitude of the Moluccas in respect to the dividing line at the antipodes, which Pope Alexander had failed to define. On account of the intensifying of these disputes Spain postponed the proposed Gomez expedition of 1523, and in the following year (1524) the Congress called at Badajos to settle the question, broke up after two months

[1] Fiske, *Discovery of America*, vol. i., pp. 325 and authorities there cited, 441, 445, 453; *Ferdinand and Isabella*, by William H. Prescott, Philadelphia, 1869, vol. ii., pp. 174, 175.

[2] Herrera, tomo i., dec. 1, lib. ii., cap. v., p. 43 *et seq.;* Fiske, *Discovery of America*, vol. ii., pp. 97, 98, 453, 459; Prescott, *Ferdinand and Isabella*, vol. ii., pp. 176, 177, 181.

[3] Herrera, tomo i., dec. 1, lib. vii., cap. xiii., p. 196.

[4] *Ibid.*, tomo i., dec. 1, lib. x., cap. x., p. 282.

of wrangling, each party still holding to its own opinion.[1] Only six years later (June 20, 1530) was a peaceful conclusion reached by Spain's relinquishment to Portugal of all her rights thereto under the bull of demarkation.[2] But Portuguese sailors still passed westward in Spanish ships and studied the waterways of our Atlantic coast, probably in search of a westward passage to the Moluccas. As late as 1562 Menéndez complains that in Villafañe's expedition to Florida, as well as in that of the Moluccas,

"there were many Portuguese fighting men and very good pilots, and two [of them] who had been captains of caravels of the King of Portugal's armada, who, it appears, were sent there by their king or by his council to understand and learn those navigations and lands and their secrets and of what matters the captains of your majesty treat with the peoples of those lands,"

and he urges upon the King the exclusion of all foreigners.[3] For many years after, the ships and adventurers of France and England drew an unfailing supply of skilful pilots from the little kingdom, sometimes enlisting them by cunning, sometimes by force, and not infrequently finding in them ready and willing servants to conduct their most hazardous enterprises.

In January, 1548, while present at the Diet of Augsburg, Charles V., believing his end near at hand, had, among other instructions advised his son, Philip II.,

"In respect to the Indies, have a care to be ever on the watch if the French wish to send an armada thither, secretly

[1] Herrera, tomo ii., dec. 3., lib. iv., cap. iii–viii., pp. 178–188.

[2] *Ibid.*, tomo ii., dec. 4, lib. v., cap. x., p. 93 *et seq.;* Prescott, *Ferdinand and Isabella*, vol. ii., pp. 180, 182 and authorities in note 29; *Christopher Columbus*, by Justin Winsor, Boston and New York, 1891, pp. 589–591.

[3] *Pero Menendez (de Avilés) sobrel Remedio*, fol. 303.

or otherwise, and to notify the governors of those parts to be on their guard and where and when necessary in conformity therewith, to resist the said French; for though they have often undertaken to go there, it has been observed that their armadas have not endured and more than that, when resistance is offered them, then they weaken and go to pieces; and thus it is of much advantage to be ready to hand against them." [1]

The Emperor's advice was based upon no vague prejudice concerning a neighbour with whom he was constantly at war; whose intrigues were for ever fomenting fresh trouble for Spain, and whose King had said of the Indies that "God had not created those lands solely for Castilians." [2]

Breton fishermen had been familiar with the Newfoundland fisheries for many years before Verrazano's much-disputed expedition to America in 1524 first gained for him the notice and favor of Francis I., by whom, indeed, it is said to have been authorised.[3] We have no knowledge of any interference of Spain with the first and second voyages of Jacques Cartier in 1534 and 1535; but in 1537, while the war was still in progress in which Francis I. had revived his pretensions to Italy, and only a few months after Cartier's return, in July, 1536, from his second expedition, Charles V. was considering whether some article ought not to be introduced in his instructions to Los Cobos and Granvelle for treating with the Grand Master of France to prevent King Francis from any

[1] "Instrucciones de Carlos Quinto á Don Felipe su hijo," Augusta á 18 de enero, 1548, *in* Ch. Weiss, *Papiers d'État du Cardinal de Granvelle*, vol. iii., p. 295.

[2] Herrera, tomo ii., dec. 3, lib. vi., cap. ix., p. 189.

[3] Shea's *Charlevoix*, vol. i., p. 107; cited in *Narr. and Crit. Hist. Am.*, vol. iv., p. 5 and note 1; Henry C. Murphy, *The Voyage of Verrazano*, New York, 1875, p. 163, and B. F. Da Costa, *Verrazano the Explorer*, New York, 1880, p. 25.

undertaking in the Indies.[1] In the following year the King and Queen of Portugal were informed of the Emperor's intention in this respect and of King Francis's answer thereto[2]. Three years later (1540) Spain was urging the "slow-moving Portuguese" to take action against France in view of certain licenses granted by Francis to his subjects to sail for the East and West Indies;[3] and in November of the same year Los Cobos wrote Louis Sarmiento de Mendoza, Spain's ambassador to Portugal, that while there was no fear of a French expedition against the Indies during the winter, "it must be borne in mind that when the Spring sets in, and the weather is fine and the winds are favourable they may all of a sudden be tempted to carry out their bad intentions."[4]

The Emperor did not wait for the French to act in order to ascertain their designs. . Following the advice he had given his son, to forestall any attempt on their part to invade the Indies, he dispatched a secret agent, Don Pedro de Santiago, during the winter to see what the French were doing, and on Santiago's return he was sent a second time to visit the entire French coast from Bordeaux to Brittany and Normandy to learn what ships were arming in the different ports, their number and equipment, and if they were designed to rob or injure the shipping that came from the Indies. No port, however insignificant, appears to have been overlooked, and the agent, having ascertained that a fleet of thirteen sail,

[1] The Articles discussed with His Majesty at Monçon with regard to the instructions to be given to Cobos and Granvelle for treating with the Grand Master of France, 1537; *Calendar of State Papers, Spanish*, vol. v., Pt. II., p. 407.

[2] Luis Sarmiento (de Mendoza) to the Emperor, July 30, 1538; *Calendar of State Papers, Spanish*, vol. vi., Pt. I., p. 5.

[3] Cardinal Tavera to the Emperor, Madrid, Oct. 11, 1540; *Calendar of State Papers, Spanish*, vol. vi., Pt. I., p. 279.

[4] High Commander Cobos to Luis Sarmiento (de Mendoza), Madrid, Nov. 16, 1540, *Calendar of State Papers, Spanish*, vol. vi., Pt. I., p. 291.

with ammunition and artillery for a two-years' cruise, was being fitted out at St. Malo in command of Jacques Cartier, sought an interview with him and learned that his intention was to people a country called Canada.[1]

The conclusions of the Councils of State and of the Indies, based upon Santiago's report, are particularly interesting in view of what actually occurred twenty years later; they find that the intention of the French is "to place themselves near the Bahama Channel, which is the best position they could take, when the war with France shall brake out, to harm the ships of the Indies, for most of them come through the said Channel of Bahama, and not a single one could pass without their seizing it."[2] They also advise that in place of the single caravel which the Emperor had ordered to follow Cartier's fleet three should be sent, and recommend that, on learning where the French intend to colonise, a person of capacity be appointed Captain General, who should publicly appear as its discoverer and apply for the right to conquer and colonise it, which should be done, however, at the cost of the royal treasury. Although the Cardinal of Seville did not accept the conclusion of the Councils as to the object the French had in view,[3] the two caravels were dispatched,

[1] Carta de Cristoval de Haro al emperador Carlos 5d, fecha en Burgos á 25 de henero de 1541, MS. De samano [Juan de Samano, secretary of Charles V.], traslado de una ca q̄ se escriuio a xpobal de haro, de Madrid, MS. (undated). Copia de la carta q̄ escriuio xpōual de haro a su maḡ. en ocho de abril, 1541, MS. All of these three letters in Arch. Gen. de Indias, Sevilla est., 143, caj. 3, leg. 11. An extract of this last letter is printed with out date or reference in *Una Expedición Española á la Tierra de los Bacallaos en 1541*, José Toribio Medina, Santiago de Chile, 1896, p. xxv. "Relación de lo que dice la espia que el Consejo de las Indias embió á Francia para saver lo de las Armadas que se preparaban allí," Buckingham Smith, *Col. Doc. Flo.*, tomo i., p. 107.

[2] "Lo que se acuerda en el Consejo de Estado y de Indias sobre lo que se presenta tocante al intento de la Armada de Francia, en respuesta á Su Majestad," Buck. Smith, *Col. Doc. Flo.*, tomo i., p. 109.

[3] In his letter of June 10, 1541; Buck. Smith, *Col. Doc. Flo.*, tomo i., p. 111.

the one sailing from San Lucar, and the other from Bayonne in August of the same year, and but a few days apart.[1]

In 1545 came official complaints concerning certain ships from Peru reported to have been sunk by two French vessels[2]; neither did the proposed Roberval expedition of 1547 escape the sharp eyes of the Spanish authorities.[3] In 1549 Simon Renard, Charles V.'s ambassador at the French Court, was advised to inform himself "if vessels are being armed to go to the Indies, or to await on their passage near Seville ships of subjects of the said Emperor arriving from the Indies."[4] In 1555 the French pirate, Pedro Beaguez, visited Santa Martha, and Jacques de Soria made a descent upon the island of Margarita, where the pearl fisheries were, seized the town through the treachery of one of its inhabitants, by the freeing of the negro slaves, and caused it to pay a heavy ransom. He next visited Santa Martha, where he betrayed what Pulgar calls his "Lutheran perfidy" by pillaging the church, and then burned Carthagena, and burned and sacked Santiago de Cuba and Havana.[5]

At last Charles V. and his son Philip, "King of Eng-

[1] Medina, *Expedicion á los Bacallaos*, pp. xxvii.–xxxv.

[2] "Réponses du ministère de France à diverses réclamations presentées au nom de l'Empereur par Jean de Saint Mauris, son ambassadeur" (1545, avril ou mai). Sans date. In *Papiers d'État du Cardinal de Granvelle*, vol. iii., p. 140.

[3] "Copie de ce qui a esté escript de Paris à l'abbé de Sainct Vincent touchant (le) Canada," 1547; Brit. Mus., Add. MSS. 28,596, fol. 154.

[4] "Instructions à Simon Renard, ambassadeur à la cour de France." Sans date (Bruxelles, janvier, 1549), *Papiers d'État du Cardinal de Granvelle*, vol. iii., p. 343.

[5] "Memorial de Pedro Menéndez de Avilés," undated, [1561–62 ?] Ruidíaz, *La Florida*, tomo ii., p. 322; *Historia General de las Indias Occidentales*, *Decada Nona*, continua la de Antonio de Herrera desde el año de 1555 asta el de 1565, Doctor D. Pedro Fernandez de Pulgar, tomo i., fol. 69, Bib. Nac., Madrid, MSS. 2796. And see the versified account of Juan de Castellanos in *Primera Parte de las elegias de varones illustres de Indias*, Madrid, 1589, p. 314.

land," succeeded in imposing the long-contemplated restrictions upon French activity in the Indies. In the truce of February 5, 1556, signed at Vaucelles and which was to last for five years, Henry II. agreed that "the subjects of the said Sir King of France or others at their behest shall not traffic, navigate, or trade in the Indies belonging to the said Sir King of England, without his express leave and license; otherwise, doing the contrary, it shall be allowable to proceed against them as enemies; the said truce remaining none the less in force and vigour."[1] The ink of the treaty of Vaucelles was scarcely dry when, four months later (June, 1556), the Neapolitan Pope, Paul IV., who had invoked the aid of the Turk in his struggle with Philip over the temporalities of the Church in Sicily and Naples, induced Henry to break it, and the three-years' war with France began which terminated with the treaty of Cateau-Cambrésis in 1559.

To the last moment of the truce Spanish vigilance continued on the alert. Villegaignon had sailed for Brazil the previous year under the auspices of Admiral Coligny to found a Protestant colony there, while Dona Juana, widow of Don John of Portugal, was Regent of Spain during Philip's absence in England and the Netherlands. Renard, who had a secret agent in Normandy giving him information of ships under construction and their destination,[2] wrote to the Regent in July, 1556, that Villegaignon,

"having seized a port in the passage of the Indies, is fortifying it and has advised the King of France, that if he will send him four or five thousand soldiers he will conquer a part of the

[1] *Corps Universel diplomatique du Droit des Gens*, J. Dumont, Amsterdam, La Haye, 1726, vol. iv., Partie III., p. 84. "Additions de quelques Articles au Traité de Vaucelles, etc."

[2] L'Ambassadeur Renard à Philippe II., Paris, 7 juillet, 1556; *Papiers d'État du Cardinal de Granvelle*, vol. iv., p. 622.

Indies for him and prevent the navigation of that part. . . . And as the French are arming vessels in Normandy and Brittany," continues Renard, "although they may be for another object, it appeared to me that I should not fail to give this advice, in order that your Highness may warn and advise those whom it concerns; for they could easily molest travellers and navigators to the said Indies."[1]

In 1559 the treaty of Cateau-Cambrésis was signed between Philip and Henry II., by which France disgorged an accumulated plunder of years, said to have equalled in value one-third of the kingdom.[2] No reference was made to the Indies in the treaty itself. There appears, however, to have been an understanding that, while the French pirates and privateers were to be duly punished, and while France agreed that she would not interfere with Philip's West Indian possessions, she still insisted that the freedom of the sea was hers, as well as of those regions which did not belong to Spain, and that she would not "consent to be deprived of the sea and the heavens."[3]

Be that as it may, the Duke of Alba in a subsequent conversation with Fourquevaux, the French ambassador to Spain, implied that the omission in the treaty arose entirely from the absence of any adverse occupation of the Indies by the French at the time of its signing.[4] In June of the same year Philip was married by proxy to the French Princess Isabella of Savoy, and in January, 1560, shortly after his return to Spain, he met her for the first time at Guadalajara. The close bonds now estab-

[1] L'Ambassadeur Renard (à la princesse de Portugal?). Sans date. (Commencement d'aout, 1556); *ibid.*, vol. iv., p. 658.

[2] *The Rise of the Dutch Republic*, John Lothrop Motley, New York, 1859, vol. i., chap. iii., p. 202.

[3] Unsigned and undated note, 1564-1566, MS. Arch. Nat. Paris, K, 1503.

[4] Lettre au Roi, 24 décembre, 1565, *Dépêches de M. de Fourquevaux*, p. 17.

lished between himself and France, which had been one of the main objects of the last treaty, were insufficient to quiet Philip's ever-suspicious spirit. Hardly had the marriage by proxy been performed, when the Duke of Alba, who had represented Philip at the ceremony, was writing to the King from Paris regarding the prohibition which the French King was to proclaim in respect to the navigation of the Indies.[1]

In August of the same year Chantone arrived in Paris as Philip's ambassador, and began his complaints against the French piracies. During November and December Rouen citizens were arming vessels at Havre de Grace to plunder the Indies,[2] and December 24th Philip wrote directing him to oppose the granting by the French King of licences to go to the Indies, "because if they sought to conquer territory, it could only be on the same coasts which we already hold, or in our provinces, which we have discovered in those parts, and because they would not be able to maintain them." [3]

Early in January of the following year Chantone protested in open council against the equipment of the vessels already referred to. Admiral Coligny replied that none of them would be permitted to sail from Brittany or Normandy, where he commanded, either for the Indies or to their harm or that of any of the Spanish King's subjects.[4] A few months later, again importuning the Cardinal of Lorraine in respect to suspicious vessels arming in the same ports, he received the curt reply that the French "were under no obligation to hold their vessels at the will of their neighbours, nor to be prevented from

[1] Letter of July 22, 1559, MS. Arch. Nat. Paris, K, 1492 (60).

[2] Letter of Nov. 15, 1559, Blois, MS. Arch. Nat. Paris, K, 1492 (77); and Dec. 2, 1559, *ibid.* (82), fol. 5.

[3] Letter, Dec. 24, 1559, Paris, MS. Arch. Nat. Paris, K, 1493 (12).

[4] Letter, Jan. 17, 1560, MS. Arch. Nat. Paris, K, 1493 (30).

sending them where it best suited their convenience, and if the Spaniards suspected their actions without reason, the French saw no way of undeceiving them." [1]

Everything aroused Chantone's suspicions, from the rattling of an anchor chain to the laying of a keel; and his eyes were never off the ports of Normandy and Brittany, hotbeds of "Lutherans" and breeding-grounds of pirates. Early in the year 1561 reports of the arming of a fleet of ten galleys, manned by seventy "Lutheran" sailors, carrying fifty pieces of artillery, and provided with a launch for shallow water, for the purpose of pillaging the shores of the Indies and robbing the returning Spanish vessels, called for special remonstrance on the part of Philip.[2]

This was followed by a convention of ship captains held in England to which the captains of Normandy and Brittany were summoned, and whose action awaited the return of Coligny from Châtillon, where he had gone to spend Easter. "This junta of vessels has awakened my suspicions," writes Chantone, "and I was anxious for some days, because the Admiral is a friend of novelties, and of seeking his own advantage. . . . It is also reported that the said ships are bound for the Indies." [3] In May he forwarded to the King a report of the ships in the various French ports.[4] Coligny again readily promised that he would do all that was in his power, and what was just, to stop the piracies.[5] Meanwhile the plundering, by corsairs, from Normandy and Brittany of Spanish vessels returning from the Indies and the slaughter of their

[1] Chantone to Philip, Nov. 20 and 22, 1560, MS. Arch. Nat. Paris, K, 1493 (107), fol. 2b.

[2] Letter, 1561, MS. Arch. Nat. Paris, K, 1495 (1) and Philip to Chantone, March 23, 1561, Toledo, MS. *ibid.*, K., 1495 (26).

[3] Letter, April 7, 1561, MS. Arch. Nat. Paris, K, 1494 (73).

[4] Letter, May 1, 1561, MS. *ibid.*, K, 1494 (84), forwarding the Report dated April 20, 1561, MS. *ibid.*, K, 1494 (80).

[5] Letter, Nov. 9, 1561, MS. Arch. Nat. Paris, K, 1494 (107).

crews continued,[1] until Chantone, in justifiable indignation, writes his King under date of January 13, 1562, "with the robberies committed in the route of the Indies during the past days, all those of Normandy and Brittany are so possessed of greed, that there is not a man of those that follow the fleets who does not seek to own a ship or to have one built, although they would have to sell their inheritance to attain it," and he adds, "that all those who were engaged in this matter were heretics, and of those regarded with the most favour."[2]

[1] Letter, Aug. 11, 1561, MS. Arch. Nat. Paris, K, 1495 (62); letter, 1560 or 1561 (?), MS. *ibid.*, K, 1494 (17).

[2] Letter, Jan. 13, 1562, MS. Arch. Nat. Paris, K, 1497 (5).

CHAPTER II

THE FIRST FRENCH COLONY

IN the same letter of January 13, 1562, Chantone, after expressing his desperation in the terms just cited, informs Philip that "the three ships which I wrote Y. M. were preparing to sail for Florida have come to be six, and a number of people will go in them, and they will leave after the close of this month with the first fair weather. . . . The said six vessels go under the command of Jean Ribaut. . . . I will not fail to have a word about it with the Queen, although they deny that they are bound for those parts, but the thing is very certain, and it would be well, if it please Y. M., to mention it to Limoges."[1] Ten days later he saw Catherine de' Medici and handed her a memorandum on the subject, which she retained in order to show it to Coligny and to answer it by letter, while she assured him at the same time that nothing would be done to the detriment of Philip's interests.[2]

A week later Chantone, whose suspicions were thoroughly aroused, wrote Philip that an effort was being made to obtain the pardon of a certain Portuguese pirate, who had been implicated in robberies of the India fleet,

[1] Letter, Jan. 13, 1562, MS. Arch. Nat. Paris, K, 1497 (5). "Limoges" was Sébastien de l'Aubespine, Bishop of Limoges, French Ambassador to Spain at the time.

[2] Chantone to Philip II., Jan. 23, 1562, MS. Arch. Nat. Paris, K, 1497 (6).

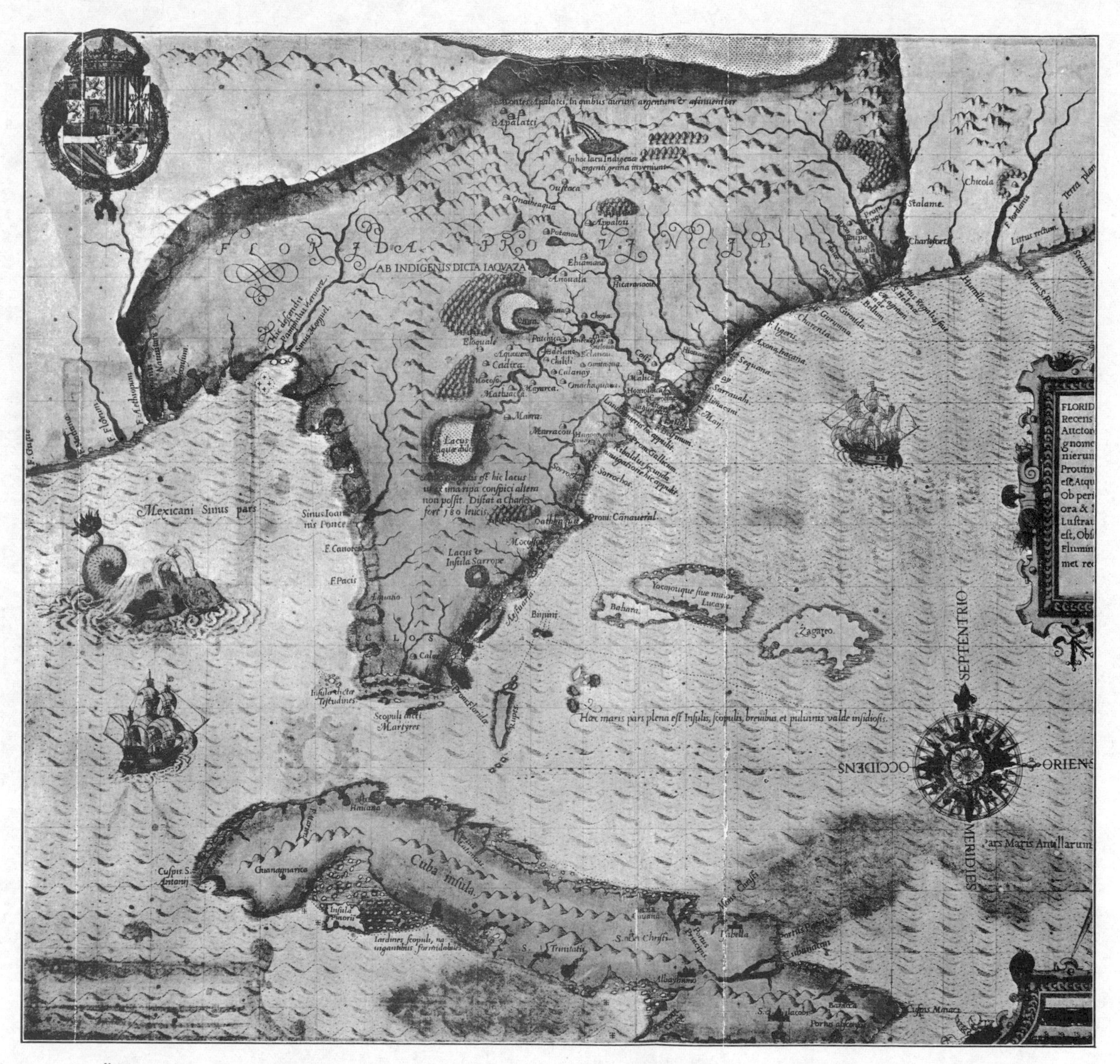

"FLORIDÆ AMERICANÆ PROVINCIÆ RECENS & EXACTISSIMA DESCRIPTIO," BY JACQUES LE MOYNE DE MORGUES, PUBLISHED BY DE BRY IN 1591.

in order that he might accompany the vessels destined for Florida; that he had complained about it to the Queen; that she professed to know nothing about the matter, but would inform herself; that it was evident from her written answer that the expedition was fully determined upon, and that a Spaniard had been secretly conveyed by night to the Admiral's apartment, and was secretly brought back, with the object, as Chantone surmises, of giving information about the Florida coast, or of acting as agent for the Spanish heretics.[1] Philip at once referred the letter to the Council of the Indies for their consideration, urging haste in the matter of the ships bound for Florida, concerning which he asked for their advice, whether it were best to take some immediate action or to await further developments.[2]

The decadence of France at about this period was most profound. Within her own bosom she was torn asunder by civil war arising from religious intolerance. Her armies had almost disappeared, her navy had lost its former glory, and she was deserted by her allies. Gaspard de Coligny, lord of Châtillon-sur-Loing and Admiral of France, a staunch patriot, a brave soldier, and an earnest Huguenot, had dreamed of restoring her to her lost greatness. In pursuit of this object his eyes turned longingly to Spain's transatlantic possessions, and he thought that by depriving her of those he could hope to weaken her world supremacy, for he hated her both as a Frenchman, with whom she had been almost continually at war, and as a Protestant, against whose religion she was persistently intriguing. As early as 1555 he had sent to Brazil the unsuccessful expedition of Villegaignon already referred to. Undismayed by this failure, he determined to renew his enterprise, and in 1561 called for a gathering of

[1] Letter, Jan. 30, 1562, MS. Arch. Nat. Paris, K, 1497 (7).

[2] Endorsement in the King's hand on the letter of Jan. 30, 1562, MS. Arch. Nat. Paris, K, 1497 (7).

volunteers, at Havre, without respect to religion, and announced that an expedition would soon sail from thence for Florida.[1]

On the 16th of February, 1562, the expedition set out.[2] The fleet consisted of two Dutch three-masters, small vessels of one hundred and seventeen and sixty tons respectively,[3] and a large sloop, besides two smaller ones which were carried aboard the large vessels while at sea.[4] It was commanded by Jean Ribaut of Dieppe, a skilful sailor, a devout Protestant, and a man of some diplomatic experience, for in 1559 he had been sent to Scotland in the French interests, where he had fulfilled his mission with credit to himself. His lieutenant characterised him as perhaps a little obstinate in his opinions with "deuises of his owne braine, which sometimes hee printed in his head so deeply, that it was very hard to put them out."[5] Of his entire crew of one hundred and fifty men, half of them were arquebusiers, and for the most part old

[1] *Histoire de la Floride Française* par Paul Gaffarel, Paris, 1875, pp. 1–9.

[2] Histoire notable de la Floride située es Indes Occidentales contenant les trois voyages faicts en icelle par certains Capitaines et Pilotes François descrits par le Capitaine Laudonnière qui y a commandé l'espace d'un an trois moys, Paris, 1586 ; sec. xv., reprint in Gaffarel, *Hist. de la Floride*, p. 354. This French version is usually known by the name of its editor, Basanier. English version entitled "A notable historie containing foure voyages made by certaine French Captaines into Florida : Wherein the great riches and fruitefulnesse of the Countrey with the maners of the people hitherto concealed are brought to light, written all, sauing the last, by Monsieur Laudonniere, who remained there himselfe as the French King's Lieutenant a yeere and a quarter. Translated out of French into English by M. Richard Haklvyt." In *Voyages of the English Nation to America*, collected by Richard Hakluyt and edited by Edmund Goldsmith, Edinburgh, 1889, vol. ii., p. 417.

[3] Relación e información de los Franceses que han ido á poblar en la costa de la Florida. San Cristóbal de la Habana, 9 julio, 1564 ; MS. Arch. Gen. de Indias, Sevilla, est., 54, caj. 1, leg. 15, pp. 18, 19 ; Gaffarel, *Hist. de la Floride*, p. 14.

[4] Lescarbot, *Histoire de la Nouvelle France*, Paris, 1611, p. 42.

[5] "A Notable Historie," *Hak.*, vol. ii., p. 523 ; Basanier, p. 114 ; Gaffarel, *Hist. de la Floride*, p. 13.

soldiers. There was also an Englishman in the party, and several gentlemen, one of whom, René de Laudonnière, was destined to play an important part in subsequent events.[1] The pilot was a Portuguese "than whom there was none more competent to show them the way," writes Chantone.[2] As most of the men were Calvinists a preacher accompanied them. The vessels carried twenty-five pieces of artillery all of bronze,[3] and were well equipped with ammunition and supplies for a long period. Chantone, who had ample means of informing himself, writes his King that besides Coligny, who was obviously the soul of the enterprise,[4] the Queen Mother, Vendôme,[5] the Prince of Condé,[6] and Madame de Cursot[7] had contributed to the enterprise. Among the crew itself the rumour ran that the Queen and Vendôme had each of them given a thousand ducats, and that the fleet was bound directly for Florida, to settle at Santa Elena, and to learn if it was a good location from which to enter the Bahama Channel in order to seize the fleet of the Indies.[8]

Although it was too late to run any danger of encoun-

[1] Basanier, *Histoire Notable*, Paris, 1586, p. 8 ; *Hak.*, vol. ii., p. 417.

[2] Chantone to Philip II., Jan. 24, 1563, MS. Arch. Nat. Paris, K, 1500 (43), written after the return of the survivors of the expedition. The *Relación e información de los Franceses*, etc., p. 20, says there was also a Spanish pilot named Bartholomew, from Seville.

[3] *Relación e información de los Franceses*, etc., pp. 14–19.

[4] Chantone to Philip II., Jan. 24, 1563, MS. Arch. Nat. Paris, K, 1500 (43).

[5] Antoine de Bourbon, of the Vendôme branch of the Bourbon family.

[6] Louis I., Prince of Condé and brother of Antoine de Bourbon.

[7] Spelled "Corosot" in the MS. of the Navarrete Collection, and probably intended for Madame de Cursol, who became Duchess of Uzais, and whose name is mentioned by Brantôme among those of the court ladies of Catherine de' Medici.

[8] *Relación e información de los Franceses*, etc., p. 19 ; see the opinion of the Venetian ambassador, written in 1573, as to the quality of the French colonists and the object Ribaut had in view (Ruidíaz, *La Florida*, tomo i., p. cxl., footnote).

tering the outgoing Spanish fleet, and too early for the returning one, Ribaut, anxious to escape the observation of the Spaniards and conceal from them his exact destination, pursued an unfrequented course, by which he avoided the Canaries and the Azores, the customary route of the Armada.[1] He cut across the current of the Gulf Stream, and in place of making the coast of Canada, where France was now in undisputed possession, struck the eastern shore of Florida in 29° 30′ north latitude on April 30th, off a headland which he called French Cape, and which was perhaps a little above the present site of St. Augustine.[2] He had taken two months and a half to cross the Atlantic and during his prolonged trip had met

[1] "The true and last discoverie of Florida by Captain John Ribaut," reprint in *Hist. Collections of Louisiana and Florida*, by B. F. French; 2d series, "Historical Memoirs and Narratives," 1527–1702, New York, 1875, chap. i., p. 166; Basanier, *Hist. Notable*, p. 8; *Hak.*, vol. ii., p. 417; Gaffarel, *Hist. de la Floride*, p. 14. Ribaut's first English account appeared under the title: "The whole and true Discoverye of Terra Florida (Englished, The Flourishing Land), conteyning as well the wonderful straunge Natures and Manners of the People, with the merveylous Commodities and Treasures of the Country; as also the pleasant Portes and Havens and Wayes thereunto, never found out before the last year, 1562. Written in French, by Captain Ribauld, the fyrst that whollye discovered the same, and now newly set forthe in Englishe, the XXX. of May, 1563." This was first printed by Hakluyt in his small black-letter volume of 1583, but not in the folio collection, under the title of "The True and Last Discoverie of Florida, translated into Englishe by one Thomas Hackit." The French version, entitled "Historie de l'expédition Française en Floride," was published by Ribaut in London, in 1563; Shea in II., *Narr. and Crit. Hist. Am.*, p. 293; Brinton in *Notes on the Floridian Peninsula*, p. 28.

[2] "The true and last discoverie of Florida," reprint, *ibid.*, p. 169; Laudonnière (Basanier, *Hist. Notable*, p. 8; *Hak.*, vol. ii., p. 417) and Le Moyne (*Brevis Narratio*, Plate I.) say 30°. Laudonnière (Basanier, p. 36; *Hak.*, vol. ii., p. 445) says that the second expedition landed "neere a little riuer, which is 30 degrees distant from the Equator, and 10 degrees aboue Cape François drawing towords the South, and aboue 30 leagues aboue the Riuer of May." This he named the River of Dolphins. The marginal note to the above paragraph is: "Cape François between the riuer of Dolphins and the Riuer of May, maketh the distance 30 leagues about which is but 10 leagues ouer land." Gaffarel in his *Hist. de la Floride*, p. 15, places the

with but one vessel, a Spaniard returning from the Indies, which he encountered off the Bermudas.[1] Coasting north Ribaut struck the St. John's River, which he named the River of May, having discovered it on the first of that month.[2] He remained there the following day, entered into friendly relations with the Indians, and erected on a

landfall "at the point of land north of the City of St. Augustine." *The Territory of Florida*, by John Lee Williams, New York, 1837, p. 169, places the landfall "about the latitude of St. Augustine." Guillermo Rufin, in *Relación e información de los Franceses*, etc., p. 20, says: "La primera tierra della que vieron oyo dezir al piloto que hera el cavo de la florida junto a la canal de bahama." Parkman in his *Pioneers of France in the New World*, Boston, 1893, p. 36, says it was probably one of the headlands of Matanzas Inlet.

[1] *Relación e información de los Franceses*, etc., p. 20.

[2] *Hist. Notable*, Basanier, p. 10; *Hak.*, vol. ii., p. 419; Le Moyne, "Eicones" in *Brevis Narratio*, Plate II. "Copie d'vne lettre venant de la Floride, enuoyée a Rouen, et depuis au seigneur d'Eueron; ensemble le plan et portraict du fort que les François y ont faict." A Paris, pour Vincent Norment et Ieanne Bruneau, en la rue Neufue-Nostre-Dame, à l'Image Sainct-Iean l'Euangeliste, 1565; reprint in *Recueil de Pièces sur la Floride*, par H. Ternaux-Compans, Paris, 1841, p. 238. In Laudonnière's account (*Hist. Notable*, Basanier, p. 8; *Hak.*, vol. ii., p. 417) the first place discovered beyond the landfall is "a very faire and great Riuer" where Ribaut sets up the pillar on which "the Arms of France were carued and engraued. This being done hee embarked himself againe, to the ende always to discouer the coast toword the North which was his chiefe desire. After he had sayled a certaine time he crossed ouer to the other side of the riuer," evidently of the river already mentioned, where he is entertained by the Indians. It is evident from the context here and from the location of Cape François, mentioned in the preceding note, that the River of May was the first river visited by Ribaut according to this account. In Laudonnière's history of the second expedition (*Basanier*, pp. 36, 37; *Hak.*, vol., ii., p. 445) he describes the River of Dolphins, but makes no reference to having previously visited it with Ribaut. Le Moyne, who was not with Ribaut on the first expedition, appears to have confused the two accounts. In Plate I., after having described Cape François in "about thirty degrees from the equator," he continues: "Coasting thence to the northward, they (Ribaut and his companions) discovered a broad and beautiful river, at whose mouth they cast anchor in order to examine it more in detail next day. Laudonnière, in this second voyage, called this stream the River of Dolphins," etc. See Appendix B, The River of May.

sand-hill near the mouth of the river a stone column, on which were engraved the French arms, the date, and the name of the commander of the expedition.[1]

Continuing his discoveries along the coast to the north, Ribaut passed nine rivers in a distance of sixty leagues, to which were given familiar names of the rivers of his own country: the Seine, the Somme, the Loire, the Charente, the Garonne, the Gironde, the Belle, and the Grande. Their identity it is now well-nigh impossible to determine, as the names given them by Ribaut "were altered by the Spaniards in their geographical tables; and if some be found where the names are given, we owe it to the Hollanders," complains Lescarbot.[2] Ribaut had evidently some acquaintance with Spain's discoveries in North America, for in a parley with the natives on the St. John's River, he inferred from their signs that he was but twenty days distant by water from Cibola and its great treasure.[3] In the hope of a still more promising harbour than any he had yet found he determined to seek for the "River Jordan," "one of the fairest of all the North," writes Laudonnière.[4]

Following the coast to the north he came at last upon a great river, three leagues wide at its mouth, and into which at flood tide the largest of French ships could enter, which he named Port Royal, and sailing three leagues up the stream, he anchored his vessels. Ribaut thought it was the River Jordan[5] and Parkman identifies

[1] See Appendix C, The Pillar Set up by Ribaut.

[2] Lescarbot, *Histoire de la Nouvelle France*, Paris, 1611, sec. v., p. 45; *Hist. Notable*, Basanier, p. 10; *Hak.*, vol. ii., p. 420; Gaffarel, p. 18. And see Appendix D, The Rivers between the River of May and Port Royal.

[3] "The true and last discoverie," etc.; *Hist. Col. Louisiana and Florida*, pp. 174–175.

[4] *Hist. Notable*, Basanier, p. 11; *Hak.*, vol. ii., p. 420.

[5] "The true and last discoverie," etc., *Hist. Col. Louisiana and Florida*, p. 185; Laudonnière in *Hist. Notable*, Basanier, pp. 12, 16; *Hak.*, vol. ii., pp. 421, 425, thought the Jordan was more to the north.

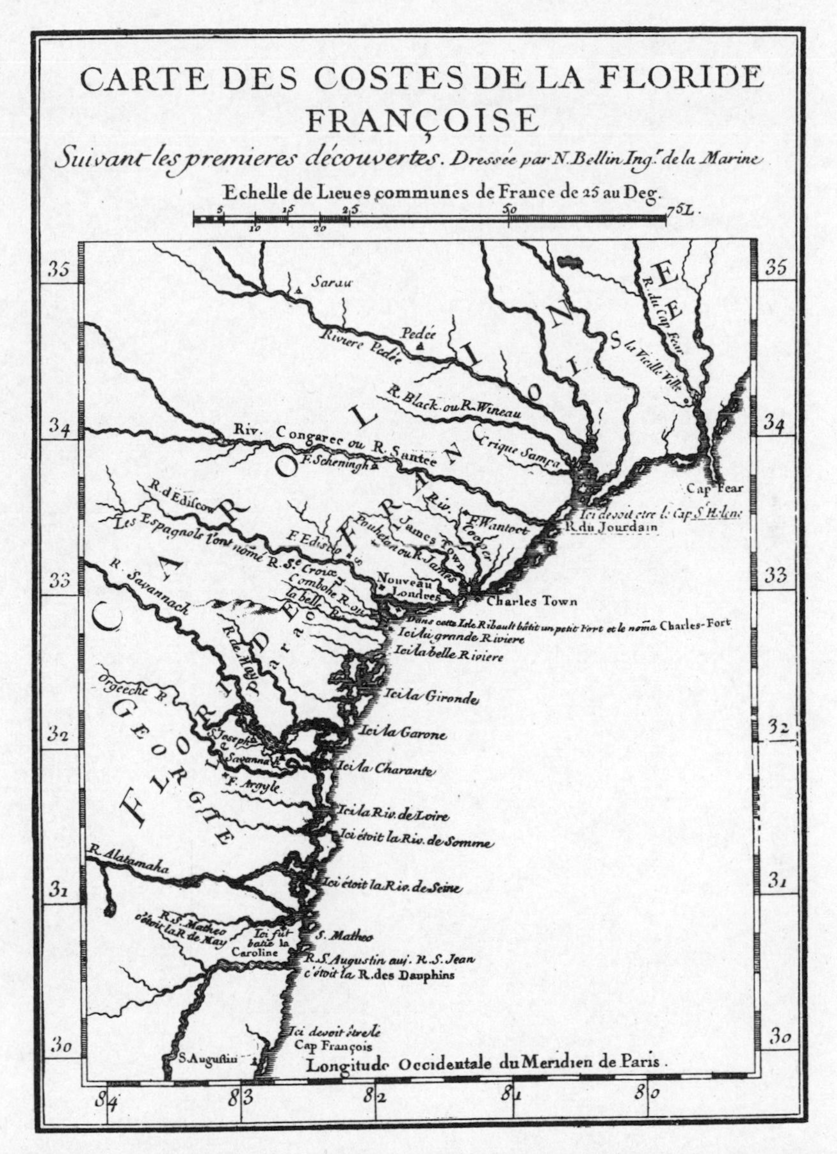

MAP OF THE FRENCH FLORIDA COLONY OF 1562-65, BY NICOLAS BELLIN, IN "HISTOIRE ET DESCRIPTION GÉNÉRALE DE LA NOUVELLE FRANCE," PAR LE P. DE CHARLEVOIX, PARIS, 1744.

it with the Broad River.[1] Ribaut, who was soon on a friendly footing with the savages, explored for some distance its lower affluents, erected another column to indicate that the country was a French possession, and finally gathering his people together, made them an address in which he recalled to their memory the importance to their young King of the enterprise upon which they had all embarked, and asked for volunteers to remain behind and hold Port Royal for their sovereign. Most of the soldiers eagerly offered their services for the new colony. Of these he selected twenty-eight,[2] appointed as their captain a certain Albert or Aubert de la Pierria, and constructed for them on a little creek, which he named Chenonceau, a house of logs and clay, thatched with straw, and surrounded with a bulwark for its defence. He armed it with eight pieces of artillery, stored it with ammunition and provisions for several months, and named it Charlesfort, after his King.[3]

On June 11th, Ribaut took leave of his colony, which saluted his departure with a salvo of artillery, and sailed away for France, having promised to return within six months with more ships and supplies. Ribaut carried away with him a few pearls, a little silver which a sailor had "rescued" from the natives lower down the coast, some deer-skins, and native mantles as evidences of his discoveries,[4] and on July 20, 1562, arrived safely in

[1] *Pioneers of France in the New World*, p. 39; and see Appendix E, Port Royal.

[2] *Hist. Notable*, Basanier, p. 20, says twenty-eight; *Hak.*, vol. ii., p. 429, says twenty-six; Chantone, letter, Jan. 24, 1563, says there were twenty-five men; Rufin, in the *Relación e información de los Franceses*, etc., p. 21, says there were twenty-six men.

[3] Chantone to Philip II., Jan. 24, 1563, MS. Arch. Nat. Paris, K, 1500 (43); also a copy in Direc. Hidrog., Madrid, *Col. Navarrete*, tomo xxi., doc. No. 81; *Relación e información de los Franceses*, etc., p. 21, and see Appendix F, Charlesfort.

[4] *Relación e información de los Franceses*, etc., pp. 21, 23.

France, "having reconnoitred in six weeks more than the Spaniards had done in two years," observes Laudonnière.[1]

He had reached home at a most unpropitious moment for the future of his little colony. Civil war, fomented by England and Spain, each ostensibly in the interest of religion, was raging between the Catholic and Huguenot parties, and the unity of his country was in imminent danger.[2] Coligny, the original promoter of the colonial scheme, was immersed in the fratricidal struggle, and could give Ribaut and his enterprise but passing attention, and so the settlement at Charlesfort was left to its fate. Ribaut is said to have taken an active part in the war[3] and at the conclusion of the peace of Amboise, which was signed in March, 1563, betook himself to England, where in the summer of the same year he published the results of his Florida expedition.

Ribaut, however, did not confine himself to the arts of peace alone, for the experience and knowledge he had acquired in Florida were more than sufficient to secure him a ready admission into the circle of adventurers who were just beginning to display their activity and to lay the foundations of the English navy. It is evident that he was in no wise discouraged by Coligny's failure for the time being to assist the colony in Florida and was seeking eagerly about him for resources to further the enterprise. Through what channel his presence in England became known to Queen Elizabeth we have no present means of knowing, but he had probably been but a short time in the country before he obtained an audience with the Queen. Ribaut set before her the importance and wealth of Florida and urged her to assist him in its conquest. Elizabeth, after listening to his relation, began

[1] *Hist. Notable*, Basanier, p. 21 ; *Hak.*, vol. ii., p. 430.

[2] *Ibid.*, p. 32 ; *Hak.*, vol. ii., p. 441 ; Gaffarel, *Hist. de la Floride*, p. 26.

[3] Haag, *La France protestante*, Paris, 1861, vol. viii., p. 313, cited by Gaffarel, p. 27.

to refuse him her immediate help "so that if Philip should complain she would be able to swear that nothing had been done by her order"; however, she encouraged Ribaut to undertake the adventure himself, promised him half of all that he found, and added that even were the country not as good as she had been told, it was on the way of the ships from New Spain, Peru, and elsewhere, which Ribaut could safely seize.[1] But the temptation proved to be too great to be long withstood, even by Elizabeth's tender conscience, and she ended by offering him a pension of three hundred ducats and a house as an inducement to undertake the discovery. At a later period, when the incident was closed, Ribaut disclaimed ever having accepted the bribe.[2]

However this may be, it appears that in May, 1563, the notorious Thomas Stukeley was arming a fleet consisting of five vessels, one of which had been contributed by Ribaut and another by Elizabeth. The crew was three hundred strong, and the fleet, which was well equipped with supplies, ammunition, and artillery, flew the royal standard presented by the Queen herself.[3] There were three French pilots aboard, who had previously accompanied Ribaut to Florida. Quadra, Philip's ambassador in London, was himself inclined to attach some credit to the current rumour that it was designed to attack Florida,

[1] Silva relates this on the authority of Stukeley; see Guzman de Silva to Philip II., London, Oct. 22, 1565, in *Correspondencia de Felipe II., con sus Embajadores en la Corte de Inglaterra*, 1558–1584, tomo ii., p. 214; English translation in *Spanish State Papers*, 1558–1567, I. Elizabeth, p. 495.

[2] Quadra to Philip II., London, June 26, 1563, *Correspondencia de Felipe II.*, tomo i., p. 527; see also Guzman de Silva to Philip II., London, March 30, 1566, *ibid.*, tomo ii., p. 292. English translation in *Spanish State Papers*, 1558–1567, I. Elizabeth, p. 536. This account of Ribaut's experience in England has been previously printed by the author in the *American Historical Review*, vol. ix., p. 456, April, 1904, under the title of "Jean Ribaut and Queen Elizabeth."

[3] Quadra to Philip II., London, June 19, 1563, *Correspondencia de Felipe II.*, tomo i., p. 525.

but it was also said that its object was to assail the Spanish vessels returning from the Indies.[1]

Stukeley, who had sought and obtained an interview with the ambassador, gave Quadra to understand that he was urged on in the undertaking by the Government, but notwithstanding this assurance Quadra was indisposed to trust his revelations. Stukeley then became most profuse in his protestations of friendship for Spain, telling Quadra that he was leaving England dissatisfied and desperate, but with the intention of going into the service of Philip; that he had risked all of his property in the enterprise, and he requested Quadra that on his arrival in any Spanish port or elsewhere in Spanish possessions he should be recognised as a servant of the King. Quadra met his advance with caution, and replied that the thing was impossible in view of the friendly relations existing between England and Spain, unless his destination were for parts not included within the Spanish lines of demarkation. And at last the true object of the expedition became apparent, as well as the importance of the part which Ribaut was expected to play, for Stukeley answered that no one had visited the country where he was going except a few Frenchmen a short time before, and that it was but three days distant from Cuba. Quadra then told him roundly that in such case the thing was an impossibility, because the land fell within the lines of demarkation.

Quadra's suspicions had been in no way allayed by Stukeley's apparent frankness, which he regarded merely as a cunning device on his part for safeguarding the expedition from Spanish attack. In the letter relating these circumstances, which he wrote to his King, he expressed his opinion that the enterprise was really due to French

[1] Quadra to Philip II., London, May 1, 1563, *ibid.*, tomo i., p. 512. English translation in *Spanish State Papers*, 1558–1567, I. Elizabeth, p. 322.

as well as English intrigue, adding: "I have no assurance that he carries a commission; it seems to me that his project is a result of the determination . . . reached by the Admiral of France [Coligny] and of those who govern here to harass that commerce [of the Indies] and to conquer Your Majesty on the Ocean Sea." "I expect to talk about it to the Queen," he continues, "although I know what answer she will make me, which is the same answer she has given me on former occasions, and which she has also written me."[1] A week later Quadra wrote that the fleet was not only destined for Florida, but for the very spot where Ribaut had founded his colony, and that Ribaut had promised to turn over to Stukeley the fort he had built there, together with its small garrison.[2] The affair was brought to a sudden and most unexpected termination, so far as Ribaut was concerned, by the discovery that he and the three French pilots had planned to escape to France with the ships and hostages. The outcome of it was that Ribaut was seized, thrown into prison, and threatened with hanging, while the three pilots were put into chains and kept to conduct Stukeley's fleet.[3]

In the light of contemporary events it is permissible to doubt if Ribaut had at any time intended to betray the Florida colony into English hands. Havre was still occupied by the English, and only on the 29th of July of this very year, 1563, was it finally returned to France after fierce fighting under its walls and after the plague had decimated its English garrison; while Calais, which Elizabeth was most anxious to recover was still held by the French. Ribaut was a brave, cool, and determined man, as subsequent events fully proved, and, moreover, he was

[1] Quadra to Philip II., London, June 19, 1563, *Correspondencia de Felipe II.*, tomo i., p. 524 *et seq.* English translation in *Spanish State Papers*, 1558–1567, I. Elizabeth, p. 334.

[2] *Ibid.*, June 26, 1563, *Correspondencia de Felipe II.*, tomo i., p. 531.

[3] *Ibid.*, June 26, 1563, *ibid.*, tomo i., p. 527.

a Frenchman, which means that he loved his native soil with the devotion that pre-eminently distinguishes his race and which has made of it the most home-loving of people. This dramatic incident in his career occupied less than two months, and it may well be supposed that the hardy Dieppois, who, like the French of to-day, probably looked upon all foreigners as outside barbarians, was not at all averse to practising a clever trick on Stukeley and his English Queen, and had entered into his engagements at the very outset with this end in view.

The Frenchmen left behind at Charlesfort at once turned their attention to completing their defences, working day and night upon them, and then began roaming about the rivers and swamps and forests, visiting the chiefs of the neighbouring Indian villages. Like some of their Spanish predecessors they appear to have mistaken the names of localities or tribes for those of individuals; for among those whom they visited we hear of one called Audusta, whose country Captain Albert reached by water.[1] It is not impossible that we have here a chief of the Edisto Indians, whose name under another form, that of Orixa, Ayllon's Indian Chicora had rattled off so glibly among those of other South Carolina provinces.[2] Laudonnière himself, shortly before Ribaut's departure, had been beguiled with tales of Chiquola, the greatest lord of that region, a foot and a half taller than any of his subjects, and his memory promptly reverted to the Chiquora of Aylon, and perhaps the legend of the giant race; but the story which the Indians told him of Chiquola's great city lying to the northward, swarming with men, and where gold, silver, and pearls were in such abundance as to be of no account whatever, did not kindle his imagina-

[1] *Hist. Notable*, Basanier, pp. 21, 22; *Hak.*, vol. ii., p. 431.

[2] See Mr. James Mooney's identification of Audusta with the Edisto, in *The Spanish Settlements in the United States*, 1513–1561, Woodbury Lowery, p. 452.

tion to the point of inducing either him or his companions to visit it.[1] It seems not at all improbable that the Frenchmen were now treading the country reached by Ayllon's abortive first expedition in 1520.

In blissful ignorance of their impending doom, and of the internal dissensions which were raging in their country at home, the colonists planted no maize, perhaps because it was already too late in the season, and took no precautions against the non-arrival of the expected relief from France. Like thoughtless profligates, they followed the example of the Spaniards before them and lived on the bounty of their Indian friends, who generously supplied them with maize and beans and squashes as long as their own stores lasted.

On the return of the colonists from a reconnoitring expedition up the River Belle, and while they were peacefully asleep under their thatched roof, a fire broke out at Charlesfort, which consumed nearly all their possessions. The loss of their shelter was soon made good. Then their food supplies began to diminish and again the natives came to their rescue. At last internal dissensions broke out among them. A drummer was hung by Captain Albert for a very insufficient reason, according to the colonists. Another soldier named Lachère was for some unknown cause exiled to a neighbouring island, where he was left to die of hunger, although the Captain had promised to keep him supplied with provisions.[2] Finally the soldiers, seeing the violence of their Captain constantly on the increase, and fearing for their own lives, rose against him and killed him.[3]

Cupidity prompted by the hope of a speedy return to

[1] *Hist. Notable*, Basanier, pp. 15, 16; *Hak.*, vol. ii., p. 425.

[2] *Ibid.*, pp. 26, 27, 29; *Hak.*, vol. ii., pp. 436, 438.

[3] Guillaume Rufin, the sailor left behind by these colonists, says that a soldier, whom Albert had beaten, killed him with a sword. *Relación e información de los Franceses*, etc., p. 21.

France may also have furnished a motive for getting rid of Albert. Several years later M. de Fourquevaux, the French ambassador in Spain, wrote Charles IX. that a Spaniard was on his way to Florida to discover a treasure of some four hundred thousand ducats, said to have been hidden there by six of the soldiers in Ribaut's first expedition. While roaming about the country they had come upon a party of twenty Indians, who, in fear of the French, were flying from the neighbourhood, and were carrying along with them great lumps of gold and silver stamped with the mark of the Spanish mint, which they had gathered from the wreckage of vessels along the coast. The soldiers, having possessed themselves of the treasure, buried it in the earth, and bound themselves by oath not to reveal its hiding-place either to their Captain or to any other person.[1]

Having made away with their commander, the soldiers rescued the starving Lachère from his island, and elected another captain, one Nicolas Barre, who proved himself an efficient leader, quieting the dissensions and restoring peace among them. As the days sped by and the promised reinforcements did not arrive, their eyes turned longingly to France, and the desire to escape from their dreary exile grew upon them. There was not a man of the party who was familiar with the building of a ship, but desperation lent them daring, and with the aid of the forge left them by Ribaut they began the construction of a small vessel of about twenty tons. They caulked the seams with grey moss gathered from the forest trees and with pitch collected from incisions made in the pines. Sails were manufactured from shirts and bed coverings. The Indians, glad to be rid of them, furnished them with ropes and cordage twisted from the bark of trees. They

[1] Advis d'Espaigne au Roy par le s^r de Fourquevaulx. Aout, 1567. *Dépêches de M. de Fourquevaux, ambassadeur du Roi Charles IX. en Espagne, 1565–1572*, publiées par M. l'Abbé Douais, Paris, 1896, p. 263.

next loaded the boat with the guns which had been left for their defence, the forge, and what ammunition remained to them, stored it to the best of their ability with provisions obtained from the Indians, and in their eagerness to depart, set sail for France without thought of the fickleness of the winds, the meagreness of their supplies, or the fact that there was not a member of their party who understood the art of navigation.[1]

They had barely travelled one-third of the distance which separated them from their homes, when they were overtaken by calms so prolonged that in three weeks they made but twenty-five leagues. In the meantime their provisions began to fail them, and their rations were cut down to twelve grains of corn a day. Finally even this slender sustenance was exhausted and death by starvation and thirst stared them in the face. The miserable Frenchmen were now reduced to eating their leather shoes and jerkins, and to slaking their parched throats with the waters of the surrounding sea and their own urine. In this extremity their frail vessel began to leak at every seam, and in their enfeebled condition they were compelled to keep bailing it continually to escape being devoured by the sea. Then a contrary wind arose and threatened to swamp them. Some of their number died of hunger, and at last, having gone for three days without food or drink, but one supreme expedient remained, and the unfortunate Lachère, who had barely escaped with his life from starving to death on the island near Charlesfort, was sacrificed to furnish food for his perishing companions.[2] At last land was discovered, and, driven crazy

[1] *Hist. Notable*, Basanier, pp. 29, 30; *Hak.*, vol. ii., p. 439; *Relación e información de los Franceses*, etc., p. 22.

[2] Meleneche, in his deposition, says that two members of the party suffered the same fate. "Carta escrita al Rey, por Juan Rodriguez de Noriega, fecha en Sevilla á 29 de Marzo de 1565 sobre lo que convenia proveherse en el remedio de la nueba población que hicieron franceses en la Florida," etc., MS. Direc. de Hidrog, Madrid, *Col. Navarrete*, tomo xiv., No. 33, fol. 3.

by the sight, they allowed their boat to drift hither and thither upon the sea without an effort to reach it. In this pitiable condition they were spied by an English vessel on board of which was one of their own countrymen, who, in a preceding voyage, had himself visited New France, and through his instrumentality the survivors were rescued.

As the peace of Troyes was not yet signed, and England and France were still at war, part of the survivors were put ashore at Corunna, where they were allowed to go free; but the leaders were carried away to England. Some of them managed to escape to France, but their trials were not at an end, for it would appear that certain of their number were ultimately seized and thrown into prison for the murder of Captain Albert.[1] Such was the miserable ending of the first attempt of France to plant a colony on Spanish soil in the immediate neighbourhood of the pathway of the West India treasure fleets.

Philip meanwhile did not relax his efforts to secure from Catherine some definite reply concerning Ribaut's Florida expedition, and only two months after its sailing Chantone wrote him that, as the Queen still delayed her answer, he had advised her categorically that his master "would adopt measures for getting possession of those who had gone there in order to chastise them."[2]

With the opening of the following year (1563) Chantone sent Philip full and accurate details of the force Ribaut had left in Florida, of the places where the columns had been set up to denote French possessions,[3] and

[1] *Hist. Notable*, Basanier, p. 30; *Hak.*, vol. ii., p. 440 *et seq.* Deposition of Meleneche in letter of Noriega to Philip II., MS. Direc. de Hidrog., Madrid, *Col. Navarrete*, tomo xiv., No. 33, fol. 3.

[2] Chantone to Philip II., May 7, 1562, MS. Arch. Nat. Paris, K, 1497 (29).

[3] Chantone to Philip II., Jan. 9, 1563, MS. Arch. Nat. Paris, K, 1499 (7), and Jan. 24, 1563, MS. *ibid.*, K, 1500 (43). It is interesting to observe that in his letter of Jan. 24, 1563, Chantone gives the *Spanish* names of the

of the high personages who were interested in the undertaking. On the receipt of Chantone's letter the King promptly proceeded to have the question of safeguarding his Florida territory properly discussed[1] and to take advice as to the best means of fortifying the Florida coast, and of "expelling the French who had gone to settle there, and to avoid the robberies to which the fleets and single vessels coming from the Indies were exposed by the nearness of such settlements." [2] A royal cédula was also dispatched to Don Diego Mazariegos, the Governor of Cuba, giving him the information contained in Chantone's letter, and directing that a vessel should be sent along the Florida coast, to remove and destroy the columns Ribaut had erected, to visit Santa Elena where the French had settled, and if, after a careful reconnaissance, circumstances should seem to justify it, to expel the settlers, destroy the fort, and bring all of the artillery, with what prisoners might be taken, to Cuba.

In the latter half of May, 1564, Don Hernando de Manrique de Rojas, commander of the expedition, set sail in the frigate *Nuestra Señora de la Concepción* with a company of twenty-five men to carry out the above orders. He struck the Florida coast below Cape Cañ-

localities visited by Ribaut in Florida. As Chantone must have obtained his information from French sources, it would seem to indicate that the French had used Spanish charts, as well as having a Portuguese or Spanish pilot with them, and were therefore fully aware of having entered on territory previously discovered by Spain. It is also possible that Chantone, or some one for him, had identified the French names given by Ribaut and Laudonnière with those on a Spanish chart. The remarkable feature is that the identification was sufficiently correct to enable at least one of the localities to be found.

[1] Philip II. to Chantone, Feb. 14, 1563, MS. Arch. Nat. Paris, K, 1499 (17).

[2] "Memorial de Pero Menéndez de Avilés respecto á las medidas que sería conveniente tomar para la segura posesión de la Florida y evitar que los franceses é ingleses pudieran causar perturbación en aquellos dominios." Undated [Feb.-July, 1562?]; in Ruidíaz, *La Florida*, tomo ii., p. 320.

averal in 27° 30′. Sailing only by day, and as near as possible to the shore, he reached the Rio de la Cruz, in 29°, probably Mosquito River, on the 22nd of the month and searched the neighbouring shores for the French pillars in conformity with his instructions; but he found nothing whatever, and being without an interpreter, he could learn nothing from the Indians. The same experience was repeated at Matanzas Inlet in 29° 30′, where he arrived on the 25th. On the 26th he was in the Rio de las Corrientes, probably the mouth of the St. John's River, and though no pillar was found,[1] he learned from the natives that three vessels manned by Christians had been there and had left for the Cape of Santa Elena to the north. The discovery of a wooden box and other objects of Christian make in the hands of the Indians along the river confirmed Manrique in the belief that he was at last on the right track. May 29th he left the Rio de las Corrientes, and on the last day of the month entered the river of Santa Elena in latitude 32°. Both the northern and southern shores were thickly settled with native villages, the Indians indicating by signs as many as seventeen communities, among them a town on the southern bank named Yanahume, and another called Guale on a stream on the north bank of the Santa Elena. Both of these he visited, and in Guale he again found indications of the presence of white men who wore beards, but who had gone farther to the north, according to the report of the Indians. But he searched in vain for the fort of the French settlers.

Although Manrique had now fully complied with his instructions by visiting all of the localities which they

[1] B. R. Carroll, in *Hist. Col. South Carolina*, vol. i., p. xxxiii, note, says: "The most indefatigable search has been made to discover this pillar. Dr. Holmes (the author of *Holmes's Annals*), wrote to many of his friends upon the subject, but after the most diligent investigation of the subject they were none of them able to arrive at anything like certainty."

specified, he was so encouraged by the reports gathered from the Indians in the two harbours which he had last entered, that he determined to push still farther along the coast to the north. June 7th he again sailed away, and in the course of a few leagues, perhaps twelve or fifteen, he visited six different harbours. June 11th he reached a harbour in 32° 20′. The Indians here informed him that a vessel with thirty-four white men aboard had been there and sailed away, leaving a member of the company behind who was living at the time in a village called Usta in the interior. Manrique at once sent him an Indian bearing a wooden cross, to signify that Christians had arrived there. The following day the white man came down to the ship. He was in Indian dress, and proved to be a French lad, seventeen years old, Guillaume Rufin by name,[1] who had come over with Ribaut and had been left with the garrison at Charlesfort. A French sailor aboard of Manrique's ship served as interpreter, through whom Rufin gave a remarkably detailed and accurate account of the expedition. He told them that the fort and one of the pillars was in 32° 15′, according to the reckoning of Ribaut's Spanish pilot, and 32° according to that of the French, and could be reached by ascending the river without going to sea. And he explained that he had remained behind, not daring to trust himself in the company of the escaping soldiers, knowing their ignorance of seamanship. After his examination, Rufin was detained aboard the ship to be carried a prisoner to Cuba.

The next day Manrique left his frigate in charge of his pilot with strict injunctions to allow none of the crew to go ashore during his absence, and ascended the river, taking with him a notary to attest the proceedings and Rufin to show the way. This time the search was not in

[1] See Laudonnière's attempt to find Rufin on his return in 1564, in *Hist. Notable*, Basanier, p. 74; *Hak.*, vol. ii., p. 484.

vain. At a distance of three leagues from the harbour where Manrique was anchored the party came upon the thatched hut which had sheltered the little garrison. It was still standing, but empty and deserted, and was situated upon a stream which fell into Port Royal Sound. The party landed and Manrique gave directions to have the frail edifice burnt to the ground, then they re-embarked and went in search of the column. This, too, was discovered on a knoll, where Ribaut had erected it. It was some distance back in the forest, not far from a stream which flowed into the Broad. The column was dug up in the presence of the notary and witnesses and transported to the frigate. Satisfied that he had fulfilled his duty, Manrique set sail on the 15th of June for Havana, which he reached in good season, taking with him, as evidence of his success, the Frenchman Rufin, and the vain emblem which France had erected to bear witness to her supremacy in South Carolina.[1]

[1] Relación e información de los Franceses que han ido a poblar en la costa de la Florida, San Cristóbal de la Habana, 9 Julio, 1564. MS. Arch. Gen. de Indias, Sevilla, est. 54, caj. 1, leg. 15.

CHAPTER III

THE SECOND FRENCH COLONY—THE TIMUQUANANS

IN September, 1561, Philip was already of the opinion that Florida presented no sufficient inducements to justify the founding of a settlement. Menéndez de Avilés had reported that even the point of Santa Elena was not practicable because of the absence of a safe harbour, owing to the strong currents there; and the results of Villafañe's reconnaissance in that vicinity had substantiated the King's conclusion. He had been informed of the poverty of the region in its vicinity and that there was no fear that the French would set foot in it, or take possession of the country. But before reaching a final conclusion he directed his Viceroy of New Spain, Don Luis de Velasco, to report to him upon the subject after consultation with persons who had had some experience in the country.

In March of the following year, the Council of New Spain had reached the same conclusion, after consultation with Villafañe and his captains and some of the companions of Don Tristan de Luna. The country in the vicinity of the river of Santa Elena was very low and sandy, subject to inundations and uninhabited, the harbour insufficient, and the region was wholly unsuited for a colony. To the north of it, as far as Villafañe had sailed, the country was quite as inhospitable, neither gold nor silver was to be found, and the Council recommended that no steps be taken in that direction until the coast had been discovered farther to the north.[1] Alarming as was the report of Ribaut's settlement in the very country which the Viceroy had so relentlessly condemned, Chantone's assurance of its utter failure must have come as a relief to the royal mind, and as a final confirmation of the correctness of the opinion rendered by the Council of New Spain. But disquieting rumours of expeditions destined for Florida continued to reach Philip from France, and of the continued depredations of the daring French pirate, Jacques Le Clerc, surnamed Pie de Palo by the Spaniards on account of his wooden leg.[2]

In the midst of these contentions for the possession of a continent came the last echo of the early discoverers. Lucas Vasquez de Ayllon, son of the Ayllon in whose first discovered territory Ribaut had made his abortive settlement, asked for an extension of the date set for his sailing to settle in Florida, because of the difficulties he had encountered in securing colonists for his undertaking. Disheartened by his fruitless efforts to organise the expedition, it is probable that his failure preyed upon his mind and he ultimately died of melancholia at Hispaniola.[3]

[1] "Parecer que da á S. M. el Consejo de la Nueva España, en virtud de su Real Cédula (fecha en Madrid á 23 de Septiembre de 1561) que sigue, sobre la forma en que estava la costa de la Florida, y que no convenia aumentar la Población." México, á 12 dias del mes de Marzo de 1562 años. MS. Madrid, Direc. de Hidrog., *Col. Navarrete*, tomo xiv., doc. No. 29. There is also a copy of the Parecer in Buckingham Smith, *North American MSS., 1561–1593*, p. 11.

[2] Chantone and Alava to Philip II., Jan, 18, 1563, MS. Arch. Nat. Paris, K, 1500 (4); same to same, Feb. 5 and 8, 1563, MS., *ibid.*, K, 1500 (48); Philip II. to Chantone, Feb. 14, 1563, MS., *ibid.*, K, 1499 (17); Chantone to Philip II., June 7 (1563?), MS. Direc. de Hidrog., Madrid, *Col. Navarrete*, tomo xxi., doc. No. 81, fol. 50.

[3] Memorial de Lucas Vasquez y Ayllon pidiendo la prorogación de la salida para el descubrimiento de la Florida. (The scrivener's certificate is dated "Sevilla doze dias del mes de junio de myll e quinientos e sesenta y tres.") MS. Arch. Gen. de Indias, Seville, Patronato, est. 1, caj. 1, leg. 1/19, Ramo 3. *Ensayo Cronologico*, Año MDXXV., fol. 9.

The peace of Amboise, and the successful termination of the suit against him for complicity in the assassination of Francis de Guise, at last set Coligny free to renew those aggressions on Spain's West Indian commerce on which he had set his heart.[1] "I seek new means of traffic and profit in strange lands," he writes,[2] and his attention promptly reverted to Florida and his plan for weakening Spain across the Atlantic. The result was that a second French expedition had been on the Florida coast for several days when Manrique de Rojas set sail from Havana to drive out the last remnants of Ribaut's colony. Indeed if Manrique carried out his instructions as thoroughly as his report would lead us to believe, it is extraordinary that the Frenchmen should have escaped his attention.[3] He must have passed their settlement at some point in his northward coasting, and it is not improbable that the three vessels heard of at the River of May may have been their fleet.

As Ribaut was still languishing in an English prison,[4] Coligny had selected for the commander of the new venture René de Laudonnière, one of Ribaut's companions in the first attempt. He, too, was a skilled sailor, but he lacked the latter's firmness of character and presence of mind, and, notwithstanding his previous experience in Florida, he showed so little talent in adapting himself to the new conditions of the colony, that it is to his ill-advised policy in dealing with the natives that the

[1] Quadra to Philip II., July 15, 1563, *Col. Doc. Inedit. España*, tomo lxxxvii., p. 352.

[2] *Pièces sur l'Histoire de France*, tome viii., année 1865; quoted by Gaffarel, *Hist. de la Floride*, p. 46.

[3] Laudonnière struck the coast above St. Augustine, June 22, 1564, and Manrique de Rojas set sail in May of the same year.

[4] Noticias de la población que habian hecho los Franceses en la Florida, segun declaración que dió en Cuba, Stéfano de Rojomonte natural de Paris (1564). MS. Arch. de Indias, Seville, Patronato, est. 1, caj. 1, leg. 1/19; Ramo 14, p. 3.

calamity which ultimately overwhelmed it may in part be attributed.

Coligny supplied him with funds with which to equip a fleet,[1] and at Havre de Grace, of which Coligny was now governor,[2] the future colonists, three hundred in number,[3] assembled. Of these, one hundred and ten were sailors, one hundred and twenty soldiers, and the balance artisans of every description, besides a number of servants for the soldiers, and pages, and four women, one of whom went in the capacity of chambermaid and housekeeper to Laudonnière.[4] There were a few gentlemen, such as Ottigny, Erlach, and La Rocheferrière, who went as officers and volunteers.[5] There were four members of the party which had made the disastrous voyage across the Atlantic[6]; there was also an artist named Le Moyne de Morgues, to whom we are indebted for one of the relations and a series of interesting pictures of the country and of the natives. And in addition to the sailors there were a few foreigners, an apothecary, an artificer, and carpenters, "so that I may assert that there came to the undertaking of that navigation men greatly expert in all

[1] De Laet, *Hist. du Nouveau Monde*, Leyde, 1640, liv. iv., chap. x., says 150,000 francs ; De Thou, *Hist. Universelle*, Londres, 1734, tome v., p. 490, says 100,000 francs. Rojomonte in his deposition says the Queen also assisted him ; *Noticias de la Población*, etc., p. 1. Meleneche says in his deposition : "El autor della fué el Almirante de Francia y el Cardenal Xatillon, su hermano, aunque al tiempo que la Armada se hacia se dió la voz en el Pueblo que la mandaba el Rey hacer." "Relación del suceso de la Armada Francesa que fue á poblar la tierra de la Florida," etc., annexed to Noriega's letter to Philip II., March 29, 1565, MS. Direc. de Hidrog., Madrid, *Col. Navarrete*, tomo xiv., doc. No. 33, fol. 4.

[2] Gaffarel, *Hist. de la Floride*, p. 47.

[3] Hawkins, in his relation in *Hakluyt*, vol. iv., p. 242, says 200 men ; Rojomonte in *Noticias de la Población*, etc., fol. 4, says 300.

[4] Deposition of Meleneche in Noriega to Philip II., Mar. 29, 1565, fol. 4 ; *Hist. Notable*, Basanier, Paris, 1586, p. 102 ; *Hak.*, vol. ii., p. 512.

[5] "Los mas de los soldadas son cavalleros y jente principal," Rojomonte in *Noticias de la Población*, etc., 1564, p. 1.

[6] Meleneche's deposition in *Noticias de la Población*, etc., fol. 3.

the arts," says Le Moyne.[1] Curiously enough, there was no clergyman in the party. With that shortsightedness which seems to have been the bane of all first attempts at colonization, farmers and field hands were also wanting, for it was not to the laborious planting of the soil that the colonists looked to increase their wealth, but, from the Spanish view, at least, to other and more questionable sources. The majority of the adventurers were Protestants, but there were some Roman Catholics among the number,[2] and it may well be imagined that with the recent conclusion of the civil war no small part of the various elements which gathered for the enterprise consisted of turbulent and unruly men but ill-fitted for the peaceful occupation of the soil.

The fleet consisted of the *Isabella*, the *Little Briton*, and the *Faulcon*,[3] small vessels of sixty, eighty, and three hundred tons,[4] the largest being a man-of-war. It was well armed to resist attack by sea, and to afford protection for the future settlement, and two pilots, the one a Basque, the other a Portuguese, accompanied it to point the way.[5] Although its destination was Florida, its mission was ostensibly not directed against Spanish interests. "The Queen has charged me very expressly," wrote Laudonnière "to doe no kind of wrong to the Kinge of Spaines subjects, nor anything whereof he might conceiue any ielousie."[6]

[1] De Bry, *Brevis Narratio*, p. 6.

[2] Noriega in his letter to Philip of March 29, 1565, calls them "muy finos Luteranos," and makes this statement on the authority of the French prisoners.

[3] "Coppie d'une lettre venant de la Floride, 1565," *Recueil de Pièces sur la Floride*, p. 234.

[4] Rojomonte says 80, 200, and 300, tons, *Noticias de la Población*, etc., p. 1; Meleneche says 80, 125, and over 200 tons, the largest being a man-of-war. Noriega to Philip II., Mar. 29, 1565, fol. 4.

[5] Alava to Philip II., June 7, 1564, MS. Arch. Nat. Paris, K, 1501 (85).

[6] *Hist. Notable*, Basanier, p. 64; *Hak.*, vol. ii., p. 474.

The colonists set sail April 22, 1564,[1] and after an adventure off the English coast, in which they mistook a Flemish fleet for a band of English sea-robbers,[2] they turned south, made the Canaries and after cruising among the Bahama Islands struck the low-lying Florida coast on Thursday, June 22,[3] in the neighbourhood of St. Augustine.[4] As with Ponce de Leon the first impression was full of charm, for "we perceived a sweet perfume of several good things because of the wind which blew from the land," wrote one of the company to his father.[5] Laudonnière reconnoitred the entrance to the harbour, called Seloy by the natives, and named by him the River of Dolphins,[6] but, finding it unsuited to his purpose, set sail on the following day and two days later reached the River of May, the St. John's. Here he went ashore and was received with rejoicing by Saturiba,[7] an Indian chief whom he had met there on the occasion of Ribaut's first visit, and who conducted him to a sand-knoll where stood the pillar erected by Ribaut,[8] and which Manrique had

[1] *Hist. Notable*, Basanier, p. 33 ; *Hak.*, vol. ii., p. 442.

[2] "Coppie d'une lettre venant de la Floride, 1565," in *Recueil de Pièces sur la Floride*, p. 235.

[3] De Bry in *Brevis Narratio*, Francoforti ad Moenum, 1591, p. 7 ; Laudonnière in *Hist. Notable*, Basanier, p. 36 ; *Hak.*, vol. ii., p. 445, and the author of "Coppie d'une lettre," etc., in *Recueil de Pièces sur la Floride*, p. 236, all say June 22nd. Meleneche in Noriega to Philip II., March 29, 1565, fol. 3, says in the month of June. De Laet in his *Hist. du Nouveau Monde*, Leyde, 1640, liv. iv., chap. x., p. 119, says June 20th.

[4] *Hist. Notable*, Basanier, p. 36 ; *Hak.*, vol. ii., pp. 444–445 ; Parkman, *Pioneers of France in the New World*, p. 50 ; Gaffarel, *Hist. de la Floride Française*, p. 50.

[5] "Coppie d'une lettre venant de la Floride," in *Recueil de Pièces sur la Floride*, p. 236.

[6] *Hist. Notable*, Basanier, p. 37 ; *Hak.*, vol. ii., p. 446.

[7] Variously called Satouriona, Saturiova, Satirova by the French ; Satourioua in Hakluyt ; Sotoriba, Saturiban, Saturiba by the Spaniards. Merás calls the chief Saturiba, the form adopted in the text.

[8] "Coppie d'une lettre venant de la Floride," in *Recueil de Pièces sur la Floride*, p. 239.

failed to discover. "Being come to the place where it was set vp," says Laudonnière, "wee found the same crowned with crownes of Bay, and at the foote thereof many little baskets full of Mill," placed there probably as an offering to the mysterious emblem of the foreigners by the superstitious natives, for "when they came thither they kissed the same with great reuerence and besought vs to do the like, which we would not denie them, to the ende that we might draw them to be more in friendship with vs." [1]

The following day Laudonnière visited Saturiba, whose village of the same name, consisting of twenty-five large huts with a population of about two hundred Indians with their families, lay a short distance to the south-west of the mouth of the St. John's,[2] and then explored the river for some distance. On St. John's Bluff, some five miles up the river,[3] he rested and sent Ottigny to examine the interior. He had selected a delightful spot in which to await his lieutenant, and even the horrible scene which he was destined to witness in the near future did not suffice to blot out the recollection of its beauty from his memory. The bluff was crowned with palms and "ceders red as blood" and "Baytrees of so souereigne an odour, that Baulme smelleth nothing like in comparison." "The sea may be seene plaine and open from it, and more than six leagues off . . . the medowes diuided asunder into Isles and Islets enterlacing one another"—a place "so pleasant, that those which are melancholicke would be enforced to change their humour." [4]

Ottigny presently returned with a marvellous story. He had seen two men of very great age, and had enquired of the younger of the two how old he might be.

[1] *Hist. Notable*, Basanier, p. 37; *Hak.*, vol. ii., p. 446.

[2] Barrientos in García, *Dos Antiguas Relaciones de la Florida*, p. 43.

[3] Parkman, *Pioneers of France in the New World*, p. 52.

[4] "Coppie d'une letters venant de la Floride," in *Recueil de Pièces sur la Floride*, p. 242; *Hist. Notable*, Basanier, p. 41; *Hak.*, vol. ii., p. 450.

"Then the olde man called a company of Indians, and striking twyse vpon his thigh, and laying his hands vpon two of them, he shewed him by signes that these two were his sonnes; againe smiting vpon their thighes he shewed him others not so olde, which were the children of the two first, which he continued in the same manner vntil the fift generation. But though this olde man had his father aliue more olde than himselfe . . . yet it was tolde them that they might yet liue thirtie or fortie yeeres more by the course of nature; although the younger of them both was not lesee than two hundred and fiftie yeeres olde,"

according to the Frenchman's generous reckoning.[1] Neither was this a solitary example of extreme old age which the credulous Frenchman found among the Indians. On a subsequent occasion one of their inferior chiefs informed Le Moyne "that he was three hundred years old, and that his father, whom he pointed out to me, was fifty years older."[2] But this gift of longevity was apparently unattended by a corresponding growth in morals. "They were the greatest thieves on earth," says one of Laudonniére's companions, "for they steal as well with the feet as with the hands."[3]

On returning from his pleasant retreat on the bluff to the mouth of the river, Laudonnière again met the chief and "forgot not to demaud of him the place" from whence had come a wedge of silver which Saturiba had presented him on the previous occasion. He learned that it proceeded from a region named Thimogoa,[4] several days dis-

[1] *Hist. Notable*, Basanier, pp. 40, 41; *Hak.*, vol. ii., pp. 449–450. "Coppie d'une lettre venant de la Floride" in *Recueil de Pièces sur la Floride*, p. 239. Le Moyne in his *Eicones*, Plate XII., mentions a sorcerer 120 years old.

[2] Le Moyne in his *Eicones*, Plate XXVIII.

[3] "Coppie d'une lettre venant de la Floride" in *Recueil de Pièces sur la Floride*, p. 240. Le Challeux in "Histoire Mémorable du dernier voyage en Floride," Lyon, 1566, reprint in Gaffarel, *Hist. de la Floride*, p. 461.

[4] Timuqua. Le Moyne in *Brevis Narratio*, p. 14, says that "Thimogoa"

tant up the St. John's, and with whose people Saturiba was at war. Pleased with the near prospect of such wealth, Laudonnière readily promised him his aid against his enemies, and then proceeded on a short reconnaissance up the coast, during which he assembled his company and set before them his plan for the settlement. He pointed out to them how the report of the first expedition showed that if "they passed further to the north to seeke out Port Royall, it would be neither very profitable nor conuenient . . . although the Hauen were one of the fairest of the West Indies. . . . And that for our inhabiting it was much more needefull for vs to plant in places plentifull of victuall, then in goodly Hauens," and that they had found the River of May, "the same only among all the rest to abounde in Maiz and corne, besides the Golde and Siluer that was found there" with its promise of further happy discovery in time to come.[1]

As his proposition met with general consent the expedition returned to the River of May, and after some exploration a spot was selected for the erection of the fort. It was on the right bank of the river, where it narrows to less than half a mile in width, at the head of the sand-bars which obstruct its entrance, and in the neighbourhood of a small stream, which empties into the St. John's. It was almost unapproachable from the seacoast, owing to intervening streams and marshes, and stood not far from the bluff, which commanded the wide prospect that had so entranced Laudonnière. The fort itself was located on a broad, flat knoll, raised a few feet above the marsh and the river.[2] Having selected the site the company was assembled at daybreak at the sound of the trumpet, and after singing a psalm the men set to work on the

signifies an enemy, for which reason he understands Saturiba to refer to his "enemy" Outina, who lived some distance up the St. John's.

[1] *Hist. Notable*, Basanier, p. 43; *Hak.*, vol. ii., p. 452.

[2] See Appendix G, Fort Caroline.

fort. It was built in the shape of a triangle, with a trench and turf battlements on the land side, which was towards the west; on the south side there was a bastion built of fagots and sand, in which was a magazine for the ammunition, and it was enclosed on the river side by a palisade of planks.

Laudonnière erected his own lodging within the fort on the river side, with one door towards the river and another opening on the court of the enclosure; covered galleries extended from it; on the south was the *corps de garde*, and another structure was built towards the apex to the north. With the assistance of Saturiba's Indians, who had come to watch the proceedings, the buildings were thatched with palm leaves in the native fashion. Seven pieces of artillery were transported to the fort and placed to command both sides of the river.[1] It was named Fort Caroline in honour of Charles IX. A meadow stretched inland to the edge of a pine forest, which was distant but a quarter of a league, where lay the spring, reached by a narrow pathway across the field.[2] In this field, around the exterior of the fort, there gradually arose a small collection of buildings consisting of the bake-oven, a storehouse, and other outhouses.[3]

Laudonnière had chosen a thickly populated region to plant his settlement. He was in the midst of the Timuquanan Indians, whose affiliation and language extended through the centre of the peninsula as far south as Lake Miami, where they touched the confines of the Caloosas to the south-west, and of the Tegestas on the south-east. They were hemmed in from the Atlantic to the east by the Ays Indians, who lived on the shores of the long

[1] Le Moyne in *De Bry*, p. 8; *Hist. Notable*, Basanier, pp. 45, 46; *Hak.*, vol. ii., pp. 454, 455; Rojomonte in *Noticias de la Población*, etc., p. 1; Le Moyne in his *Eicones*, Plates IX. and X. These plates, however, do not correspond to the description given by Laudonnière.

[2] "Hist. Mémorable" in Gaffarel, *Hist. de la Floride*, p. 460.

[3] *Hist. Notable*, Basanier, pp. 46, 93; *Hak.*, vol. ii., pp. 455, 503.

lagoon stretching southward from Cape Canaveral and now known by the name of Indian River; but about the mouth of the St. John's they came down to the coast, and occupied some of the coast islands to the north,[1] such as Talbot and Amelia Islands. Their western boundary extended as far as the north-eastern angle of the Gulf of Mexico, where they came in contact with the Appalachians. Their northern boundary may have extended into Georgia. The Timuquanan tribes had their most populous settlements on the St. John's River, along whose banks, and those of its tributaries, lay scattered many villages, each with its petty chief. On one of these was situated the village of Thimogoa,[2] from which their name Timuqua is derived, and in the vicinity of Cape Canaveral lay the village of Tucururu, one of the southernmost of their habitations.

Laudonnière in his *Histoire Notable*, as well as Le Moyne in many of the drawings in his *Eicones*, with their accompanying legends,[3] has left us a vivid description of their

[1] Laudonnière (*Hist. Notable*, Basanier, p. 57; *Hak.*, vol. ii., p. 467) mentions the Paracoussy of Alimacany, whose river is identified with the Somme by Gourgues. *La Reprise de la Floride*, Larroque, Bordeaux, 1867, p. 48. The name is variously written Allimacany, Alimacany, Halimacany, Alicamani, and his country was probably Fort George Island. See Le Moyne's map, where the name is placed in this locality and Las Alas to ————, March 23, 1568. *Brooks MSS.*, Library of Congress, Washington. Barrientos (in García, *Dos Antiguas Relaciones de la Florida*, p. 43) describes its site: "A la mano derecha, En entrando la barra [*i. e.*, of the Rio de sant mateo] Ay Vna isleta do Está Vn pueblo grande como saturiba que llaman Alicamani."

[2] See Appendix H, Timuqua.

[3] *Histoire Notable*, Basanier, Paris, 1586, pp. 4–7; *Hak.*, vol. ii., pp. 413–416. Indorvm Floridam provinciam inhabitantium eicones, primum ibidem ad vivum expressæ à Iacobo Le Moyne cui cognomen De Morgves addita ad singulas brevi earum declaratione. Francoforti ad Moenvm. . . . Sumtibus Theodori de Bry, Anno MDXCI., Plates XI., XII., XIV.–XXVII., XXIX., XXX., XXXIII.–XL. This has been translated in *Narrative of Le Moyne*, Boston, 1875, by Fred. B. Perkins, which has been largely used in this description.

customs, and which at the risk of some repetition, we will now consider, because it was in the midst of this Timuquanan population that the most enduring of the Spanish settlements on our Atlantic coast was afterwards planted.

The men and the women were all of fine proportion and went naked. The men were of an olive hue, very corpulent and handsome, and without any apparent deformity. They painted the skin around the mouth blue, and were tattooed on the arms and thighs with a certain herb, which they pricked in with a thorn [1] and which left an indelible colour. The chiefs were probably tattooed over the entire body, as shown in Le Moyne's drawings, where the design is so complex and elaborate as to remove all sense of nakedness. The process was a severe one and sometimes was followed by an illness lasting for seven or eight days. They rubbed their bodies with oil to protect them from the heat of the sun, and also during the observance of one of their religious ceremonies, to which usage they attributed their dark complexion, for at birth they were of a far whiter colour. They trussed up their long black hair upon the top of the head, and wore loin-cloths made from well-tanned deer-skins. Their warriors wore a head-dress of feathers, leaves, and grasses, or covered their heads with the skin of some wild animal, suspended over the breast small disks of gold and silver, which were engraved, and when on the war-path painted their faces to give themselves a fierce appearance.[2] Venereal disease was prevalent, for the men were much addicted to women, and to girls who were called "Daughters of the Sun," and some were given to pederasty.

[1] "The voyage made by M. Iohn Hawkins, Esquire," etc., *Hak.*, vol. iv., p. 241; Ribaut in "The true and last discoverie," etc. (reprint in *Hist. Col. Louisiana and Florida*, 2d series, "Historical Memoirs and Narratives," p. 171), says: "The forepart of their bodies and arms they also paint with pretty devices in azure, red, and black," which may possibly mean that they were tattooed in these colours.

[2] Hawkins, *Hak.*, vol. iv., pp. 241, 247.

Their sense of smell was highly developed, for they were able to follow an enemy by his scent, and to recognise his approach. Their abstemiousness, even at their festivals, produced a marked impression on the French, who attributed to it the great age to which they attained. Laudonnière, to whom their mode of warfare was entirely novel, thought them deceitful and traitorous, but acknowledged their great courage in fighting, while Le Moyne dwells upon their honesty among themselves in the distribution of the communal stores.

The women were tall and painted like the men, but much whiter. Their hair was allowed to grow down to the hips, about which it fell freely. They could climb the trees with agility, and were so robust they could swim across the broad and shallow rivers bearing their children in one arm. They attended to the household, where it was their duty to maintain the fire, which was kindled in the usual savage fashion by rubbing two sticks together.[1] They assisted in the planting of the corn-fields and took part in some of the public ceremonies. They lived apart from their husbands during their pregnancy, and the food which they ate during their courses was not touched by the man. Both men and women allowed the nails of their toes and fingers to grow long, and their finger-nails were sharpened to a point so that they might dig them into the forehead of a prisoner and tear down the skin over his face to wound and blind him. They pierced the lobe of the ear, through which small oblong fish-bladders dyed red were passed, which when inflated shone like light-coloured carbuncles. There were many hermaphrodites[2] among them, upon whom fell the heaviest

[1] *Arte de la Lengua Timvqvana compuesto en 1612 por el Pe Francisco Pareja y publicado conforme al original único*, por Lucien Adam y Julien Vinson, Paris, 1886, p. xvi. ; Hawkins, *Hak.*, vol. iv., p. 240.

[2] This is the term employed by Le Moyne, who gives no further explanation. It is possible that they were identical with the *mujerados* of the Pueblo

work; they carried the provisions when the Indians went on the war-path, transported the sick, cared for those who had contagious diseases, and prepared the dead for burial.

The title of a chief was *paracusi*, and when spoken of in his quality of a war-chief he was called *urriparacusi*, *urri* or *iri* meaning war.[1] The chiefs were united in various confederations, which acknowledged a head chief, such as Outina, who ruled over some forty villages on the west side of the St. John's and who dwelt near the mouth of the Oklawaha, and Saturiba at the mouth of the St. John's, who had thirty chiefs under him.[2] These chieftains

Indians of New Mexico, described by Dr. William A. Hammond in "The Disease of the Scythians," New York, 1882, p. 5 *et seq.*, reprint from *The American Journal of Neurology and Psychiatry*, 1882.

[1] Albert S. Gatschet, "The Timucua Language" in *Proceedings of the American Philosophical Society*, Philadelphia, 1877, vol. xvi., p. 627; xviii., p. 502.

[2] Fontanedo, Memoria de las cosas y costa y Indios de la Florida, *Col. Doc. Inedit. Indias*, tomo v., p. 545; *Hist. Notable*, Basanier, pp. 49, 59; *Hak.*, vol. ii., pp. 458, 468. When, in the summer of 1567, Avilés ascended the St. John's and found himself a few leagues beyond the village of Outina, he observed that the tides were perceptible at a distance of forty leagues from its mouth. (Barrientos, in Genaro García, *Dos Antiguas Relaciones de la Florida*, p. 123; Merás, in Ruidíaz, *La Florida*, tomo i., p. 251.) Fontanedo (*ibid.*, p. 545) mentions two of Outina's villages by name, Saravay and Moloa, and states that on landing in Outina's country, Tocobaga (which was on the west coast) could be reached. Mr. O. H. Tittmann, Superintendent of the Coast and Geodetic Survey, Washington, in a letter to the author, of May 20, 1904, says he is informed by the Fish Department that practically the water of the St. John's is fresh at Palatka. At Beecher Point, at the mouth of the Oklawaha and foot of Little Lake George, a small effect of the tide is noticeable, or rather measurable, the range being about 1.3 feet, but the average rise and fall is only one-quarter foot. These data indicate that Outina was on the west bank of the St. John's near the Oklawaha, which is also the location given by Fairbanks in his *History of Florida*, p. 139; Albert S. Gatschet, in *The Proceedings of the American Philosophical Society*, Philadelphia, 1877, vol. xvi., p. 627, places Outina on Lake George, and adds that "Uitna, or Utinama, simply means 'my country.'" See also *ibid.*, 1878, vol. xvii., p. 492, where Utinama is said to signify "upper chief."

were continually at war with each other, and it was the advent of so powerful an ally as the French to aid him in his raids that had caused Saturiba to receive Laudonnière with so much civility. The tribes were divided into various gentes or kinships, such as those of the upper chiefs, from which were taken the councillors or chief men, and the lower gens of the common people, called the "Dirt or Earth Pedigree." [1]

Next in importance to the chief stood the shamans or *iaruas*, a name which Father Pareja, who dwelt among them about fifty years later, and who wrote several works in their language, translates by "sorcerer," [2] and which referred to their prophetic powers and the convulsions affected by them to obtain oracles of war. These were "great magicians, great soothsayers, and callers upon devils," says Laudonnière, and were held in the highest esteem. Their duties were as manifold as were the occupations of those to whom they ministered. Mr. Gatschet deduces from the questions put by Father Pareja to the catechumen in his "Confessionario," [3] that most of the old men acted as conjurers. They consecrated the arrows before the departure of a hunting party, and, if the game was not killed by the first arrow, prayed over a second, which was sure to accomplish its mission. They caused rain, found lost objects for the owner, recited blessings or incantations over ears of corn, over the newly constructed fish-ways, over a good haul, and over the baskets

[1] A. S. Gatschet, "The Timucua Language," *Proceedings of the American Philosophical Society*, Philadelphia, 1878, vol. xvii., p. 492.

[2] "The Timucua Language," *ibid.*, vol. xviii., p. 500, where Gatschet derives it from *yuru*, to tremble, to be shaken or contorted; *Arte de la Lengua Timvqvana*, Paris, 1886, p. xiii.

[3] "Confessionario En lengua Castellana y Timuquana . . . Ordenado por el Padre Fr. Francisco Pareja . . . Mexico . . . 1613." Passages from it are given by Mr. Gatschet in his "The Timucua Language" in *Proceedings of the American Philosophical Society*, Philadelphia, 1877, vol. xvi., pp. 635–638.

of fruit, taking one-half of the catch of fish, or the first deer killed in payment for their services.[1] They foretold the future and cured the sick by means of incantations and by administering herbs and drugs which they carried about with them in a bag. Their cures were generally but half made in order to secure a greater reward from the sufferer.

Le Moyne gives us some of their methods of procedure in this latter capacity. They fumigated the sick man by turning him upon his face above a bed of hot coals upon which certain seeds were cast. The smoke arising therefrom, passing through his nose and mouth, acted as a vomit, and was supposed to reach all parts of the body. Another form of administering a fumigation was by smoking tobacco in a pipe. They also operated by bleeding, cutting into the skin of the forehead with a sharp shell, and sucking the blood out, which the shaman then spat into an earthenware or gourd receptacle. Women who were suckling boys, or who were with child, drank the blood, particularly if it was that of a strong young man, to strengthen their milk and to make their children bolder and more energetic.

Their villages consisted of a gathering of only a few huts, for they lived a hundred together in great communal houses, built with stanchions and rafters made out of whole trees, and roofed with palmettos, having only one small room divided off for the chief and his wife. In the centre stood a hearth, where a great fire was kept burning all night. Along the sides of the house, which they occupied only during the night-time, were placed their beds, where they slept upon head-rests or pillows made from wooden blocks hollowed out for the shoulders and raised for the head.[2] Their fortified villages were usually situated in the neighbourhood of a stream and

[1] "Confessionario," *ibid.*, vol. xvi., p. 635.

[2] Hawkins, *Hak.*, vol. iv., p. 240.

were each surrounded by a circular palisade having but one entrance. This was formed by the overlapping of the two ends of the palisade after the fashion of a spiral, and was so narrow that not more than two persons at a time could pass through it. Two guardhouses were stationed, the one within, the other without the entrance, and the course of the stream was also diverted to it. The chief's house stood in the centre of the enclosure, somewhat sunken in the ground on account of the summer heats, and was surrounded by those of the principal men. All of the huts were roofed with a light thatch of palm leaves, which rendered them exceedingly inflammable.

Their corn plantings, of which there were two, one in March and the other in June, occurred during the period of nine months which they annually spent in their villages. When seeding time was at hand the chief sent an Indian to gather his subjects together for the work; the field was then cleared by burning off the weeds, and the earth was cultivated with a kind of hoe made from a fishbone fitted to a handle. After the ground was sufficiently broken up and levelled the women did the planting, some of them going first and making a hole in the ground with a stick, into which another group of women, who followed them, dropped the corn or beans. The plantings, however, were small and calculated to produce only enough food for six months. The fields were then left alone until the crop was ripe, when it was gathered and stored in the communal storehouse for the winter's use, none of it being used in trade. These granaries or storehouses, called *barbacoa*, built of stone and earth, roofed over with palm branches, were usually erected near some hill, where they were sheltered from the sun for the better preservation of their contents, or on the bank of a stream where ready access could be had to them by water. Here, also were stored what other provisions they collected, such as game, fish, and alligators, which were dried and smoked over a fire. The storehouse was under the custody of a special guardian, who was killed with a blow from a club on the slightest neglect of his duty.[1] These stores were only resorted to in case of extreme necessity, when full notice was given to all interested, whereupon the distribution took place to each according to his rank, the chief alone being at liberty to take whatever supply he chose.

The food was supplemented by a drink called *casina*, which was drunk upon all ceremonial occasions as well as at other times. It consisted of a decoction of the leaves of a certain root, which was strained and served hot. It was not an intoxicant, but strengthened and nourished the body to such an extent that it was possible to go for twenty-four hours without food or water after drinking it, for which reason it was the principal supply taken along when the warriors went on the war-path. The drink had the property of at once throwing into a sweat whoever partook of it, and of producing vomitings, for which reason he who was unable to retain it upon his stomach was considered unfit for a difficult commission or for any military responsibility. It was so greatly prized that no one was allowed to drink it in council unless he had proved himself a brave warrior.

During the winter months the natives deserted their villages and migrated into the forest, where they constructed shelters of palm branches, and subsisted on acorns, oysters, terrapin, fish, dogs, snakes, and game, which they roasted over the coals; Laudonnière adds that in necessity they ate "a thousand rifraffs, even to the swallowing down of coles, and putting sand into the pottage which they make of [corn] meal." The fish were caught in ponds dug for the purpose and from which the water was afterwards withdrawn.[2] Their method of hunting the deer has been previously described, and con-

[1] *Arte de la Lengua Timvqvana*, Paris, 1886, p. xvii. [2] *Ibid.*, p. xvi.

sisted in disguising themselves in its skin and stealing upon it. The alligators, which were so numerous and dangerous that the natives were compelled to keep a constant watch against them both day and night, were hunted by the Indians in parties. A watch was set, concealed in a little hut near a stream, and when an alligator, driven on to the shore by hunger, gave notice of his presence by his bellowing, which could be heard at a great distance, the watchman summoned his companions, and they attacked him with a long pointed pole, thrusting it down his throat as he advanced against them with open mouth. He was then turned over on his back and his soft belly pierced with arrows and beaten with clubs until he was killed.

The chief and his principal men, whom Le Moyne calls his nobles, were accustomed to meet during certain days of the year for deliberation on important affairs, in a public place set apart for the purpose, where a bench was constructed, having a projecting seat for the chief, to distinguish his rank. After he had taken his appointed place his councillors approached him led by the oldest member, and each in turn saluted him twice, raising both hands to the height of his head, and exclaiming, "Ha, he, ye, ha, ha," to which the others replied, "Ha, ha," and then took his seat beside him. This was followed by the drinking of a potation of casina prepared by the women and served in a large shell. It was drunk by the chief first and the others in succession according to their rank after a blessing had been invoked upon the assembly and the drink by one of the councillors. Their councils were very deliberate and well advised, and where the question was one of importance the chief called upon the shaman and upon the elders, one at a time, to deliver their opinions.

Laudonnière informs us that they had "no knowledge of God, nor of any religion, saving that which they see, as the Sun and the Moon." Le Moyne has left us an account of the annual sun worship in the country of

Outina, which was observed at the end of February. The skin of the largest stag that could be found with the horns still on, was stuffed full of the choicest roots, and its horns, neck, and body were hung with long garlands of the finest fruits. Thus decorated it was carried with music and song to a large level space, where it was set up on a very high tree, with its head and breast towards the sunrise. Then the chief, standing with his shaman near the tree, offered prayers to the sun, beseeching it to cause their lands to grow such good things as those they now offered it, and the common people placed at a distance made the responses. Then the chief and the worshippers, saluting the sun, departed, leaving the deer's hide there until the next year.

Human sacrifice also existed among them, the first-born son being offered to the chief according to Le Moyne, who possibly but half understood the office which he filled in the ceremony. The chief seated himself near the tree stump, which served as the sacrificial altar, before which the mother of the victim squatted on her heels, her face covered with her hands in sorrow. Her principal female friend or relative then offered the child to the chief in worship, after which the women who attended her danced in a circle around the stump with great demonstrations of joy. The woman who held the child danced in the middle, singing the praises of the chief. At one side stood a group of six Indians, surrounding the individual who performed the sacrifice, and who was decorated for the ceremony and carried a club. When the dancing was over this official stepped up to the improvised altar, where, in the presence of the assembly, he sacrificed the child.

The belief in witchcraft was widespread,[1] and super-

[1] Extract from Father Pareja's "Confessionario" in A. S. Gatschet, "The Timucua Language," *Proceedings of the American Philosophical Society*, Philadelphia, 1878, vol. xvii., pp. 500, 501.

stitious practices were attached to almost every act of their daily life. Their character is indicated by the following, selected from among those condemned by Father Pareja[1]: Drinking out of another's cup after eating bear's meat prevented one from falling sick; a tremor passing over the body indicated that some one was coming or that something was about to happen; the hooting of an owl brought luck and should not be interrupted; whistling during a storm caused it to cease; women were in the habit of washing themselves with the infusion of a certain herb in order to recall an absent husband; to dye their palm-leaf hats with a certain vegetable dye to induce men to fall in love with them; to fast for the same reason, and so on. Other practices cited as superstitious partook of the nature of propitiatory sacrifice, such as exposing corn at the door of the house, when ill, the refusal to eat the first fruit, or the first ear of corn, or the first harvest gathered from a newly cultivated field.[2]

The Timuquanans were monogamous, and although the chief was allowed two or three wives, only the children of the first wife inherited from him. In common with most of the tribes of North American Indians, intermarriage was prohibited among the members of certain lineages, as among those of the upper chief and councillors.[3] On the death of the men in war, or from disease, it was the custom for their widows to select some occasion on which they approached the chief with loud demonstrations of sorrow, calling upon him to avenge the death of their husbands, for support during their widowhood, and for permission to remarry after the expiration of the period appointed for mourning. Having received his assent, they proceeded to the burial-place, where they cut off their long hair below the ears, and scattering it over

[1] See the passages from his "Confessionario" in *ibid.*, vol. xvi., pp. 635–638.

[2] *Arte de la Lengua Timvqvana*, Paris, 1886, p. xviii.

[3] A. S. Gatschet, "The Timucua Language," *Proceedings of the American Philosophical Society*, Philadelphia, 1878, vol. xvii., p. 492.

the graves of their husbands, placed upon them the weapons and drinking-shells of the dead. Only when their hair had grown long enough to cover the shoulders were they permitted to remarry.

When the chief wished to marry he directed the tallest and handsomest one of the daughters of the principal men to be selected. She was brought to him with great ceremony on a litter covered with the skin of some rare animal and sheltered under a canopy of boughs which formed part of the litter. Four men carried it on their shoulders, each of them provided with a forked pole on which to rest it when halting. Two more walked at the sides, shielding her from the sun with large screens or fans. She was preceded by trumpeters blowing on horns made of bark hung with oval balls of silver, gold, and brass which tinkled as they marched, and she was followed by a procession of the most beautiful of the Indian girls clad in skirts made of pendant Spanish moss, their necks and arms decorated with necklaces and bracelets of pearls, and each carrying in her hand a basket of fruits. Behind them came the body-guards. The chief received her seated on a platform erected for the purpose, where she was placed at his left. The principal men sat below them on long benches placed on either side of the platform. The chief then congratulated the maiden on her accession and informed her why he had chosen her, to which she replied, holding her fan in her hand. A dance was then performed before them by young girls dressed for the occasion, their hair tied back of their heads and flowing down over their shoulders, and wearing belts from which were suspended ovals of gold and silver. As they danced about in a circle to the tinkle of the trinkets they sang the praises of the chief and his bride, raising and lowering their hands in unison. Le Moyne had described the ceremony attending an evening promenade of Saturiba and his wife. The chief was clad in a deer-skin painted in various colours, the train of which was carried by a young man wearing a belt from which dangled little balls of gold and silver, while two young men walked at his side fanning him. His wife and her handmaidens were clothed in cloaks and skirts of the slender blue-green filaments of the Spanish moss, woven together in links, and of so delicate a texture as to be mistaken for filaments of silk.

On the death of a chief his drinking-shell was placed upon his grave, and arrows were planted in the ground around it; all of his household goods were put into his house, which was then burned down. His subjects mourned for him, fasting, three days and nights, and cut off half of their long tresses. In addition to this certain women were chosen, who for a period of six months mourned him three times a day, at dawn, noon, and twilight, with a great howling. When the priests died their bodies were buried in their own houses, which were then set on fire and consumed, with all of their furniture.

We shall have ample illustration in this history of their method of fighting. It was preceded by a declaration of war, which consisted in sticking up in the public ways arrows having locks of hair fastened at the notches. Le Moyne relates a ceremony at which the French were present, preceding one of the raids of Saturiba, and which resembled in several details that of the Coças in their war against the Napochies described in the previous volume.[1] Having assembled his warriors, the army sat down in a circle with Saturiba in the centre. A fire stood at his left and two great vessels of water at his right. After various demonstrations of rage he suddenly set up a horrible yell in which his warriors joined, striking their hips and rattling their weapons. Then Saturiba, taking a wooden platter of water, turned toward the sun and worshipped it, praying for victory over the enemy and that

[1] *Spanish Settlements*, 1513–1561, p. 365.

their blood might be poured out like the water he was about to scatter from the platter. He then flung the water with a great cast up into the air, and as it fell down upon his warriors he addressed them, saying: "As I have done with this water, so I pray that you may do with the blood of your enemies." Then he poured the water from the other vessel upon the fire and said: "So may you be able to extinguish your enemies, and bring back their scalps."

While proceeding on the war-path each chief appears to have followed his own devices. Le Moyne tells us that Saturiba preserved no order in his ranks, but that the men marched along, one after the other, just as they saw fit. Outina, on the other hand, marched his warriors in regular ranks, himself alone, in the middle, painted red, while the swiftest of his young men, also painted red, acted as advance-guards and scouts, reporting immediately to the army as soon as they came upon any trace of the enemy. The movements were directed by heralds, who shouted the orders. After sunset the army halted and no longer gave battle, and encamped in concentric circles, with the chief and his body-guard in the centre. The commissary consisted of hermaphrodites, who carried the food, which consisted principally of the drink casina, although bread, honey, and roasted corn were also taken along.

Before the attack the shaman was sometimes consulted that he might furnish the necessary information concerning the movements of the enemy. Le Moyne has given us a curious account of such an occasion, in which an ancient sorcerer, more than one hundred and twenty years old according to his own story, having made a place in the centre of the army, borrowed a shield from one of the Frenchmen present, laid it on the ground, and drew around it a circle inscribed with strange characters and signs. Then he knelt on the shield so that no part of his person touched the earth, and began a low recitation accompanied by various gestures. In the course of a quarter of an hour he was seized with convulsions attended with such violent contortions

"that he was hardly like a human being; for he twisted his limbs so that his bones could be heard to snap out of place, and did many other unnatural things. After going through all of this he came back all at once to his ordinary condition, but in a very fatigued state and with an air as if astonished; and then stepping out of his circle he saluted the chief, and told him the number of the enemy and where they were intending to meet him."

An enemy slain in battle was instantly dragged off and scalped by means of slips of reed "sharper than any steel blade," and with which an incision was made around the skull. The scalp was then dried over a fire and suspended from the belt. After the victory the limbs of the slain were amputated in the same manner, the bones broken, the yet bleeding members dried and carried back in triumph, suspended from the ends of the spears, and the bodies were then further mutilated, after the manner of most savage peoples. They spared the women and children, bringing them back with them. On returning to the village the victory was celebrated in a place set apart for the purpose, where the scalps and other trophies were affixed with solemn ceremonies to tall poles set in a row in the ground, around which the men and women sat in a circle. The shaman stood within the circle, holding in his hand a small image and muttering in a low voice a form of imprecation against the enemy. At the side of the circle opposite to him knelt three men, one of whom marked the time to each word of the imprecation by beating on a flat stone in front of him with his club, while his companions on each side shook rattles made from dried seeds, all three chanting an accompaniment.

The youths were trained in running, and a prize was given the one who showed the greatest endurance in the contest. They played a game in which a ball was cast at a square target placed on the summit of a high tree, and they were fond of fishing and hunting.

We gather from the drawings of Le Moyne and from occasional remarks elsewhere that they excelled in many of the savage industries. They could weave fans and hats and baskets from the palm leaves. They had a knowledge of the manufacture of pottery. They fashioned trinkets out of the gold and silver recovered from the vessels wrecked along the coast and from that obtained by barter from the mountains to the north. They were skilful in the preparation of their weapons, making the strings of their bows from the gut and hide of the stag, and the heads of their arrows of stones and fish-bones. Judging from Le Moyne's drawings, their boats were made by hollowing out the trunks of large forest trees. They appear to have woven the long filaments of the Spanish moss into some sort of a loose texture, and were remarkably deft in the preparation of the animals which they killed in the chase, dressing the skins with shells and dying them yellow and red, black and russet,[1] giving them a finish which evoked the ceaseless admiration of the Europeans.

[1] Hawkins, *Hak.*, vol. iv., p. 241.

CHAPTER IV

THE SECOND FRENCH COLONY—*Continued*

THE fort had hardly been completed when Laudonnière, who was not disposed to "lose a minute of an houre, without employing of the same in some vertuous exercise," sent Ottigny up the river with two Indians for guides in search of Thimogoa. The lieutenant shortly returned with the news of having ascended nearly thirty leagues where he had heard of a "King," rich in gold and silver, who dwelt at a distance of three days' journey in the interior of the country. Ottigny, in spite of his previous treaty with Saturiba, "the most ancient and natural enemy of Thimogoa," had also made advances towards establishing friendly relations with the latter. This he accomplished by rescuing some of the villagers from the assault of his two guides, and he left one soldier at each village he visited to seek for additional information. Two weeks later Captain Vasseur ascended the river a second time, and after two days sailing, came upon one of these soldiers in the village of another petty chief, Mollona, where he had secured five or six pounds of silver by trafficking with the natives. Here Vasseur heard of Outina, head chief of a great confederacy, whose allies when at war covered their bodies with plates of gold and silver; of Potauou,[1] "cruel in war, but pitiful in the execution of his furie," who was usually at war with Outina;

[1] This is the form given by Basanier, p. 49; Hakluyt writes "Potanou."

and of the two chieftains, Onatheaqua and Houstaqua, dwelling near the Appalachian Mountains, who painted their faces black. When Vasseur promised the assistance of Laudonnière in conquering them, the delighted Mollona "answered that the least of these Kings which hee had named should present vnto the Generall of these succours the height of two foot of gold and siluer." On his way back with this encouraging news, Vasseur passed a night with a small chief, who, under the impression that the French had subdued the village of Thimogoa, showed the greatest delight. The lieutenant, perceiving it, encouraged his fancy, until the savage ended by praying the Frenchman "that hee would shew him by signs how all things passed." Nothing loath at a bit of gasconade in the presence of so credulous an audience, La Caille, sergeant of the band, "tooke his sword in his hand, saying that with the point thereof he had thrust through two Indians, which ranne into the woods, and that his companions had done no lesse for their partes. And that if fortune had so fauoured them . . . they had had a victorie most glorious and worthie of eternall memorie."[1]

On the 28th of July,[2] the *Isabella* departed on her return voyage to France, bearing with her as a present to the Queen some small pieces of gold and silver, fifty pearls, which Laudonnière had obtained from the natives,[3] and the hide of an alligator which had been killed in the river.[4] There remained behind in the settlement two hundred colonists. One hundred and fifty of these were soldiers who garrisoned the fort; the balance were the

[1] *Hist. Notable*, Basanier, pp. 49, 50; *Hak.*, vol. ii., pp. 458, 459.

[2] Meleneche in his deposition in Noriega to Philip II., March 29, 1565, fol. 4, says July 22nd; Le Moyne in *De Bry*, p. 7.

[3] Rojomonte in *Noticias de la Población*, etc., p. 1.

[4] "Coppie d'une lettre venant de la Floride" in *Recueil de Pièces sur la Floride*, p. 245, where an alligator is described. Also in "Hist. Mémorable" in Gaffarel's *Hist. de la Floride*, p. 462, where Le Challeux expresses his surprise at its having no wings!

artisans and servants already noted, as well as the four women.[1] The arrival of reinforcements from France was not expected before March of the following year,[2] and in the interval Laudonnière was left to derive what profit he could out of the tricks with which he had beguiled the Indians about him. And now Saturiba began to press the Frenchman for the promised assistance against Thimogoa, and was put off with evasive words, that served only to awaken his displeasure. Weary with the prolonged delay the Indian chief at last departed alone on the war-path against his enemy, from which he soon returned triumphant with scalps and prisoners.[3]

Laudonnière, who himself tells us how he "trauailed to purchase friends, and to practice one while with one herc, and another while with another there,"[4] improved the opportunity to exercise his short-sighted policy of making to himself a present enemy in the hope of securing a possible friend in the future. It occurred to him that could he release some of the prisoners brought back by Saturiba, and return them to Thimogoa, he would establish a still firmer claim to his friendship. As Saturiba angrily refused to deliver them up to one who had broken faith with him and left him to do battle alone, Laudonnière sent a band of soldiers to his house and intimidated him into compliance. Saturiba, although deeply offended and brooding vengeance, continued to lull the suspicions of the French with presents, while Laudonnière fatuously counselled him to make peace with his enemy. The month of August was drawing to an end when there arose a severe thunder-storm in which the lightning fell with such force as to consume the

[1] Rojomonte in *Noticias de la Población*, etc., p. 2; Meleneche in Noriega to Philip II., March 29, 1565, fol. 4.

[2] Rojomonte in *Noticias de la Población*, etc., p. 2.

[3] *Hist. Notable*, Basanier, pp. 53–55; *Hak.*, vol. ii., pp. 463, 464; Le Moyne in *De Bry*, p. 10, and in *Eicones*, Plate XV.

[4] *Hist. Notable*, Basanier, p. 60; *Hak.*, vol. ii., p. 469.

harvests of the Indians, burning the green meadows and killing the birds in the fields. Saturiba mistook it for a cannonade directed against his dwelling by the French. In this belief he was again encouraged by the ill-advised Frenchman, and, no longer able to disguise his deep-rooted hatred, withdrew from the neighbourhood. And now war broke out between Outina and Potauou. Under the impression that the only road to the Appalachian Mountains, where gold and silver were found, lay through Outina's dominions,[1] Laudonnière sent Arlac[2] to Outina's assistance, and thus enabled him to secure the victory.

Laudonnière's bearing towards the settlers was as ill-judged as his dealings with the savages. Le Moyne complains that he surrounded himself with two or three favourites and frowned upon the common soldiers. As a result of this and of the dissatisfaction of some of the noblemen with the results so far attained, discontent began to show itself. The more serious element of the community was indignant at the absence of a pastor to minister to its spiritual wants.[3] And yet an effort was made to give some religious instruction to the savages in the neighbourhood. Two or three of the colonists, among whom was probably "Maistre" Robert, learned in Holy Writ, and who conducted the prayers of the fort,[4] took upon themselves the teaching of the chiefs and Indians, collecting some two hundred of the native children for that object,[5] with such signal results, and the binding of such close ties of affection between them, that Menéndez

[1] Le Moyne in *Eicones*, Plate XII.

[2] Charlevoix in *Histoire de la Nouvelle France* (Nyon Fils), Paris, 1744, tome i., p. 37, says in a note that this orthography is merely the result of an incorrect pronunciation of the well-known Swiss family name of Erlach.

[3] Le Moyne in *Brevis Narratio*, pp. 9, 10.

[4] Le Challeux in "Hist. Mémorable" in Gaffarel, *Hist. de la Floride*, p. 466.

[5] Fourquevaux to Charles IX., Feb. 22, 1566, *Dépêches*, p. 61.

himself pays them a tribute for their devotion. "These French have many Indian friends and have showed much sorrow for the perdition" of the Indians, who followed their teachers about "as the Apostles did our Lord; so that it is a wonder to see how these Lutherans have bewitched this poor savage people."[1] This dissatisfaction soon assumed a more serious phase. A conspiracy arose against Laudonnière among some of the colonists, lured by the pretended magical discovery of a mine of gold and silver up the river, by which they hoped to enrich themselves. But their attempts, first to poison him and then to blow him up with a barrel of gunpowder concealed beneath his bed, were happily frustrated, and their leader escaped to the Indians.[2] On the 4th of September Captain Bourdet arrived from France with reinforcements. An expedition sent to discover the interior remained there for six months, and on the 10th Bourdet returned to France, carrying back with him a few of the least trustworthy of the colonists.

On September 20, 1564, occurred the first of the series of incidents which served to confirm the Spaniards in their conviction of the piratical designs of the French colony. Thirteen men stole one of the barks with the intention of preying upon the Spaniards, and having provisioned it put to sea, and coming across a Spanish vessel with a treasure of gold and silver in the neighbourhood of Cuba they captured it. All of them being well armed with sword, shield, and arquebuse, they next proceeded to plunder a small hamlet, the inhabitants of which fled before them. From there they made for the harbour of Matanzas, after they had abandoned the small boat in

[1] Avilés to Philip II., Oct. 15, 1565; Ruidíaz, *La Florida*, tomo ii., p. 87.

[2] *Hist. Notable*, Basanier, pp. 60, 61; *Hak.*, vol. ii., pp. 469–471. It is not improbable that this leader, La Roquette, is the ex-monk, cosmographer, and necromancer, mentioned by Mendoza ("Relación" in Ruidíaz, *La Florida*, tomo ii., p. 460), as having been killed at Fort Caroline.

which they had made their escape from Fort Caroline for the better one they had captured, and had forced its captain to enter into their service. Ill luck caused them to miss Matanzas and land in a small harbour called Arcos, and while they were searching about for water, the man they had impressed escaped to Havana, where he gave the alarm. The adventure ended with the capture of the entire party, some of its members being sent prisoners to Spain and the others remaining in Havana.[1] This affair was followed by the desertion of two Flemish carpenters, who had but recently arrived with Bourdet, and who stole Laudonnière's remaining boats, so that he was compelled to go to work to construct others.

The want of active employment among the colonists, the discontent fed by the dissipation of their golden visions, and the bad example set by the escape of the thirteen sailors now bore fruit in a much more serious mutiny, fraught with far more damage to the good repute of the settlement than the previous revolt. During the month of November[2] a band of sixty-six men, not content to "take the paines so much as to fish in the riuer before their doors, but would haue all things put in their mouthes,"[3] urged on by two Frenchmen and a Genoese, and tempted by the sight of the two barks, which were near completion, entered into a conspiracy to seize them and seek their fortune on the neighbouring Spanish islands. Their number was sufficiently formidable to enable them to proceed with a high hand. They seized Laudonnière, who, as on the occasion of the former mutiny, was sick of an illness that seemed designed to conceal his own want of determination, and carried him a prisoner aboard

[1] Deposition of Meleneche in Noriega to Philip II., March 29, 1565, fol. 5. Meleneche was one of the three prisoners sent to Spain.

[2] This occurred about November, 1564; see *Noticias de la Población*, etc., p. 2.

[3] Hawkins, *Hakluyt*, vol. iv., p. 242.

a boat which was anchored in the harbour, wounding one of his gentlemen in the endeavour. There they held him prisoner until the two boats were in condition to set sail, compelled him to furnish them with arquebuses and cannon, powder and provisions, and finally, having threatened him with death in case of his refusal to accede to their wishes, they obtained his signature to their passport, with the grant of additional sailors and of a pilot.[1]

On December 8th[2] they set out upon their piratical adventures. Scarcely had they left Fort Caroline when the two vessels became separated, owing to internal dissensions or the violence of a tempest.[3] One of the vessels, after cruising two weeks among the Lucayan Islands, made the Cape of St. Nicolas, near which it took a vessel on its way to Cabray, and finally reached Havana. The second bark, in which were one of the chief conspirators and the pilot furnished by Laudonnière, kept along the coast to Cuba in order to double the cape more easily, and captured a brigantine loaded with cassava, losing two of its crew in the affray. Being a vessel of greater size than their own roughly made bark, the mutineers transferred their belongings aboard of her, and taking the bark along with them made for Baracou, a village in Jamaica, where they seized a caravel of some fifty tons burden, in which they all re-embarked, and after a carouse of five or six days in the village returned to the Cape of Tiburon. Off the cape they captured a vessel from Santo Domingo

[1] *Hist. Notable*, Basanier, p. 63 *et seq.*; *Hak.*, vol. ii., pp. 473-475; Le Moyne in *De Bry*, p. 12, 13. Rojomonte, who was one of the mutineers, says in his deposition (*Noticias de la Población*, etc., p. 2), that these alleged mutineers were sent off by Laudonnière in search of provisions; and see also Confesion que se tomó á un hombre que bino de la Ysla de Cuba sobre lo tocante á la Florida, 1551-1565. MS. Arch. Gen. de Indias, Sevilla, Patronato, est. 1, caj. 1, leg. 1/19, ramo 5, p. 5.

[2] Le Moyne in *De Bry*, p. 12.

[3] *Hist. Notable*, Basanier, p. 66; *Hak.*, vol. ii., p. 476; *Noticias de la Población*, etc., p. 2.

bound for Santiago de Cuba, on board of which was a judge[1] commissioned by the Royal Audiencia of Hispaniola for its port of destination, together with a store of slaves, sugar, merchandise, and wine. The judge and his negro servant were slain in the encounter. The pilot and crew they transferred to their own vessel, where they were imprisoned for eight days in the hold. By this time their provisions had become reduced to a supply for two days only, and they enquired of the pilot of the captured vessel how they could reach Jamaica, where they expected to trade the merchandise they had captured for food. The pilot readily consented to help them, in the hope that on reaching a Spanish port the Frenchmen might fall into some trap and himself and his companions escape.

At last the mutineers arrived off Jamaica, and even before making a harbour sent the pilot ashore with two of the prisoners, who bore letters to the Governor, from one of the Spaniards aboard the vessel, asking for food. The answer was not long in coming. At dawn of the third day after they had entered the harbour, a frigate and two vessels bore down upon them. The bark with a small number of the mutineers succeeded in making its escape, but the large vessel, with thirty-three of the Frenchmen, was forced to surrender, and its crew were ultimately all hanged as pirates.[2] The bark with the escaped mutineers took a northerly course, and passing in sight of Havana, the pilot and trumpeter with some of the sailors who had been compelled to join them, being again short of provisions, determined to ascend the Bahama

[1] "Juez de comision."

[2] De Silva to Philip II., Oct. 1, 1565, *Col. Doc. Inedit. España*, tomo lxxxvii., p. 197. English translation in *Spanish State Papers*, 1558–1567, I. Elizabeth, p. 486. Confesión que se tomó á un hombre que bino de la Ysla de Cuba sobre lo tocante á la Florida, 1551–1565. MS. Arch. Gen. de Indias, Patronato, est. 1, caj. 1, leg. 1/19, ramo 5. The deponent was the pilot of the vessel captured by the mutineers. See Appendix I.

Channel by night, while their companions slept, return to Fort Caroline, and make what terms they could with Laudonnière. On the 25th of March, 1565, the neighbourhood of Fort Caroline was reached. After some parleying Laudonnière consented to receive them back, but the four ringleaders were condemned to be hung. Their sentence, however, was commuted to shooting, and their bodies were hung from gibbets about the mouth of the haven.[1]

Laudonnière, who had been confined on board the bark by the mutineers, was released, on their departure, by Ottigny and returned to the fort. Matters now progressed with no especial event for some time. The fort was strengthened against attack from the natives, and two other barks were constructed. One day two Spaniards, who had been wrecked on the Martyr Islands some fifteen years before, and had lived in servitude to Carlos at the south-western end of the peninsula, were brought into the

[1] De Silva to Philip II., Nov. 5, 1565, *Col. Doc. Inedit. España*, tomo lxxxvii., p. 230. English translation in *Spanish State Papers*, 1558–1567, I. Elizabeth, p. 503; *Hist. Notable*, Basanier, pp. 63–70; *Hak.*, vol. ii., pp. 473–479. Le Moyne relates that on the arrival of the mutineers at the mouth of the St. John's they were overpowered by a party sent out by Laudonnière; De Bry, *Brevis Narratio*, pp. 20, 21. Dr. Shea, in *The Catholic Church in Colonial Days* (New York, 1886, p. 136), infers that the mutineers put to death the Spaniards on board of the boat which they captured. Fortunately for the humanity of the Frenchmen the Spanish pilot distinctly negatives Dr. Shea's inference, so far as his own crew is concerned, stating that it was put in the hold of the vessel and evidently escaped when the ship was recaptured. The pilot does not say whether or not there were any Spanish prisoners on board the bark in which part of the mutineers fled. It is only fair to Dr. Shea to say that he did not have before him the testimony which is presented in these papers, as to the fate of "the cruisers from Caroline and Ribaut." But he is unfortunate in charging Ribaut, who was absent in France, with the responsibility of sending out cruisers, whereas Laudonnière, our only source of information as to the origin of these pirates, says they were mutineers. The statement of some of the mutineers, that they had been sent out by Laudonnière in search of food, is open to doubt, as it was probably made with a view to obtaining better treatment at the hands of their captors.

French settlement, after experiencing various vicissitudes under one and another Indian chief. They regaled Laudonnière's ears with the usual tale of treasure, which in this instance was probably founded on fact, the gold and silver having been saved from Spanish vessels wrecked along the coast; they told him of the annual sacrifice at harvest time of a human victim selected from among the Spaniards who had been cast ashore among the Indians; and they tickled the Frenchman's imagination with a romantic story of Indian love and ambush.[1]

Captain Vasseur was sent up the coast to Port Royal and renewed his former friendly relations with Audusta.[2] Another excursion was made up the St. John's, where the Frenchmen discovered the entrance of a lake, probably Lake George,[3] whose opposite shores, according to Indian report, could not be seen even from the tops of the highest trees, and on their return visited the picturesque Drayton Island, called by the Indians Edelano.[4] A gentleman from Fort Caroline, who had remained some time with Outina, brought back an account of the primitive method by which the natives recovered the gold from the sands of the rivers which flowed down from the mountains; how the sand was collected in dry, hollow reeds, in which, on being shaken, the gold and silver grains became separated from the sand owing to their greater weight.[5] Later on a band of soldiers under Ottigny was

[1] *Hist. Notable*, Basanier, p. 71 *et seq.*; *Hak.*, vol. ii., pp. 481–483.

[2] *Ibid.*, p. 74; *Hak.*, vol. ii., p. 484; Le Moyne in *De Bry*, p. 18.

[3] Fairbanks, *Hist. of Florida*, p. 125; Gaffarel, *Hist. de la Floride Française*, p. 177, identifies the lake with Lake Okeechobee. There can be little question as to the correctness of Fairbanks. See Appendix J, Maps of the French Colony.

[4] *Hist. Notable*, Basanier, p. 75; *Hak.*, vol. ii., p. 485; Le Moyne in *De Bry*, pp. 15, 19; Fairbanks, *Hist. of Florida*, p. 105. Velasco also mentions this island as situated at the outlet of "una laguna, que bojara ocho leguas."—*Geografia*, p. 168.

[5] Laudonnière says "gold or copper." *Hist. Notable*, Basanier, p. 76; *Hak.*, vol. ii., p. 486; Le Moyne in *De Bry*, p. 19. This is one of the

sent to assist Outina on one of his expeditions against a neighbouring chief.

So the time passed until the opening of the following year (1565), when the French, like the Spaniards before them, began to reap the first fruits of their improvidence in failing to make sufficient provision against the diminution of their store of food. It was the custom of the Indians of that region to withdraw into the forests during the winter and early spring, where they subsisted by hunting until their crops began to ripen; and the French, who had made no plantings against such a contingency, but had lived off the maize and beans which they obtained by barter from the natives, were suddenly thrown upon their own resources. For a while they made out to live upon the stores which Laudonnière had thoughtfully laid by, but with the approach of the month of May, the first gnawing of famine began to be felt; for the soldiers with characteristic thoughtlessness had lavishly consumed the food in expectation of the arrival of succour from France, which did not come. A little fish was obtained from the natives, who had by this time returned to their homes, but the Indians were now without maize or beans, having used what remained to them in planting for the coming season, and the soldiers, enfeebled by hunger and unable to continue to work, wandered disconsolately to the top of the bluff, where Laudonnière had dreamed his dream of Paradise, and despairingly scanned the surface of the glittering waters for the arrival of the ship from France.

most detailed of the exceedingly rare descriptions of primitive Indian gold-mining. Le Moyne, who says the Indians dug ditches in the river in which the sand was deposited by gravity, has given us a picture of the natives at work collecting gold out of the bed of the river in his *Eicones*, Plate XLI., Auri legendi ratio in rivis á montibus Apalatcy decurrentibus. Shipp in his *Hernando de Soto and Florida*, Philadelphia, 1881, p. 526, note, thinks these mines were in the north of Georgia, where are now the Georgia gold fields, and were probably the same as those of which De Soto was informed.

One day followed the other, and as they watched in vain, the prolonged anxiety bred within them, with the abandonment of hope, its companion despair, and finally the determination to leave the inhospitable shore. With that they went to work to build a boat for the voyage and to enlarge the brigantine, which the mutineers had captured from the Spaniards, by raising it two decks higher. But this required time and "there remained now the principal, which was to recouer victuals with which to sustain vs while our work endured," writes Laudonnière.[1] The commander himself headed an expedition in search of food, living the while on berries gathered in the forest and the roots of the palmettos which grew by the river-bank; but he was constrained to return empty-handed to the fort. The Indians, seeing to what straits the colonists were put, had now lost all fear of them. They demanded even the shirts off the backs of the soldiers in exchange for a single fish, and tauntingly exclaimed, when the soldiers complained of its excessive cost, "If thou make so great account of thy merchandise, eat it, and we will eat our fish." "Then they fell out laughing and mocked vs with open throat."[2] And now began the desperate struggle to wrest from the Indians enough food to keep body and soul together while the brigantine was being completed. Outina, to whom they turned in their necessity, pushed his advantage, sending just sufficient supplies to goad them into acceding to his harsh conditions of aiding him against his enemies.

Considering that as the country was to be abandoned, the colony would derive no further advantage from the continuance of its previous friendly relations with the natives, Laudonnière, who was intent on securing provisions by force when more pacific means had failed, de-

[1] *Hist. Notable*, Basanier, p. 81; *Hak.*, vol. ii., p. 491.

[2] *Ibid.*, p. 82; *Hak.*, vol. ii., p. 492.

termined to seize the person of the Indian chief and hold him as a hostage for the food of which they stood in such imminent need. Taking two boats, he embarked with fifty of his best soldiers, and, descending upon the village, carried Outina off as prisoner; he then signified to the natives that he would do their chief no harm, but would return him to them in exchange for food. But the Indians, accustomed themselves to put their prisoners of war to death, mistrusted his promise, and by every art of Indian deceit sought to recover their chief, bringing the Frenchmen a little fish and cornmeal in order to entice them into ambush. During the month of May the famine became extreme; "for the very riuer had not such plentie of fish as it was wont, and it seemed that the land and water did fight against vs," says Laudonnière. Even the work upon the boat was delayed. Some gathered roots and pounded them to a pulp in mortars; others ground the wood of the sarsaparilla into a meal and ate it boiled in water; others went hunting for fowl.

"Yea, this miserie was so great, that one was found that gathered vp among the filth of my house, all the fish bones that he could finde, which he dried and beate into powder to make bread thereof. The effects of this hidious famine appeared incontinently among vs," continues Laudonnière, "for our bones eftsoones beganne to cleaue so neere vnto the skinne, that the most part of the souldiers had their skinnes pierced thorow with them in many partes of their bodies." [1]

About the beginning of June Laudonnière heard of ripe maize up the river, where he went and obtained a little, but his soldiers fell sick from eating more of it than their weakened stomachs could digest. So the time passed wearily, until one day Outina, who still remained a prisoner, induced Laudonnière to make another attempt

[1] *Hist. Notable*, Basanier, pp. 82–85; *Hak.*, vol. ii., p. 496. See also Hawkins's account of the famine in *Hakluyt*, vol. iv., p. 242.

at exchanging him for maize and beans. When the village was finally reached, the previous tactics were repeated by the natives, who tried by every strategy known to Indian wiles to free their chief and to be avenged of his captors. But the Frenchmen saw through these designs, and after prolonged negotiations Outina was finally surrendered and some maize collected. As Ottigny was leaving the village by an avenue four hundred paces long and planted with great trees on both sides, he was suddenly attacked from ambush by the Indians. Observing how the armour protected the bodies of his soldiers, the Indians shot at their faces and legs, killing two of his men and wounding twenty-two. In the mêlée most of the corn was lost.[1] Another serious calamity which now befell the colonists was the killing by the Indians of two of the carpenters employed on the ship. When the soldiers learned that this would still further protract its completion, they became so mutinous that they were with difficulty appeased, and in order to hasten matters it was determined to work no more upon the ship, but to concentrate all their efforts on the repairing of the brigantine. With the energy of despair the houses without the fort were demolished, and their woodwork was converted into charcoal, and the palisade of the fort on the river was also torn down to furnish timber, leaving it defenceless on that side.

On the 3rd of August, while these final preparations were being pushed forward with feverish haste, Laudonnière went out walking on a little hill, "much tormented in mind" with conflicting emotions, in which the fact that provisions for ten days was all that remained, frustrated ambition, and bitter disappointment at the complete failure of the colony played no little part. Suddenly he descried four sails at sea. "I sent immediately one of

[1] *Hist. Notable*, Basanier, pp. 88 *et seq.; Hak.*, vol. ii., pp. 498–502; Hawkins, *Hak.*, vol. iv., p. 243.

them which were with me to aduertise those of the Fort thereof, which were so glad of those newes, that one would haue thought them to bee out of their wittes to see them laugh and leape for joy."[1] After the ships had cast anchor, a boat was seen making for land, and Laudonnière promptly sent an armed man to meet it, and drew up his soldiers in readiness for an attack, fearing that the strangers might be Spaniards, a fear in which he was largely justified if he considered his proximity to the route of Spanish commerce, and the presence in his midst of the pirates who had sacked and plundered the Spanish merchantmen off the neighbouring islands. The newcomer proved to be Master John Hawkins, the father of the English slave-trade, on his way home from a second prosperous venture undertaken with the sanction of the Council.[2] He had been capturing negroes on the Guinea coast and had sold them to the Spaniards in the West Indies at the point of his sword, forcing them with faulcon and arquebuse to give him "a testimoniall of his good behauiour"[3] while there. His ships were the *Swallow*, the *Tiger*, and *Salomon*, small vessels of from thirty to one hundred and forty tons, and a stately ship of seven hundred tons, the *Jesus of Lubeck*, belonging to Queen Elizabeth, which she herself had lent him for the adventure.[4] He had been sailing along the coast for several days since sighting Havana, in search of fresh water; and now he had sent one of his company ashore with a request to be permitted to refill his empty tanks. This messenger proved to be one Martin Atinas, of

[1] *Hist. Notable*, Basanier, p. 94; *Hak.*, vol. ii., p. 504.

[2] Hawkins, *Hak.*, vol. iv., p. 241. According to Hawkins (*ibid.*, p. 239) he appears to have reached Fort Caroline about the middle of July and left (p. 24) on the 28th. The date of Aug. 3rd is that given by Laudonnière.

[3] *Ibid.* 233. De Silva to Philip II., Nov. 15, 1565, *Col. Doc. Inedit. España*, tomo lxxxvii., pp. 28, 29, English translation in *Spanish State Papers*, 1558–1567, I. Elizabeth, 503.

[4] Hawkins, *Hak.*, vol. iv., p. 205; Froude, *English Seamen*, p. 44.

Dieppe, who had taken part in Ribaut's first colony, and had readily found employment with the adventurous Englishman. Atinas was the bearer of two flagons of wine and some wheaten bread, a present from Hawkins, "which greatly refreshed me, forasmuch as for seuen moneths space I neuer tasted a drop of wine," writes Laudonnière, who generously divided it among his soldiers.[1]

Next day Hawkins himself came up the river and was entertained by Laudonnière in his dismantled fort. With French hospitality he killed for his English guest some sheep and poultry brought from France, and so precious to him that notwithstanding all his "necessities and sicknesse," he "would not suffer so much as one chicken to be killed."[2] And perhaps when the feast was over, and "the gentlemen honourably apparelled yet unarmed," who attended Hawkins, were seated about in the shade listening to his relation, Laudonnière may have solaced them with a Floridian custom to which the French themselves had become addicted. For

"the Floridians haue a kinde of herbe dried, who with a cane and an earthen cup in the end, with fire, and the dried herbs put together, doe sucke thorow the cane the smoke thereof, which smoke satisfieth their hunger . . . and this all the Frenchmen vsed for this purpose: yet do they holde opinion withall, that it causeth water and fleame to void from their stomacks."

Thus gravely and wisely did Master Hawkins describe his first pipeful of tobacco, as he saw the pleasant vapour roll

[1] *Hist. Notable*, Basanier, p. 95; *Hak.*, vol. ii., p. 504. Meleneche in his deposition (Noriega to Philip II., March 29, 1565, fol. 4b) says the colonists "han hecho en este año despues que llegaron diez barricas o quartos de vino, y dicen que salió bueno y de color clarete." Bartram in his *Travels*, p. 87, mentions grape-vines on the St. John's.

[2] *Hist. Notable*, Basanier, p. 95; *Hak.*, vol. ii., p. 505.

in fleecy, fantastic clouds from between the lips of his French hosts.[1]

Hawkins, perceiving the sorry condition of the colony and the anxiety of the French to return home, offered to transport all the company in his ships to France. The complete isolation of the settlers, the extreme difficulties of the situation, and the wariness incumbent upon their leader in those times, in which the scurviest of tricks were played upon each other by nations ostensibly at peace, and above all Laudonnière's estimate of the sincerity of his English friend, are illustrated in his refusal to accept the proffered aid. "For I knewe not how the case stood betweene the French and the English," he writes, "and although hee promised me on his faith to put mee on land in France, before hee would touch England, yet I stood in doubt least he would attempt somewhat in Florida in the name of his mistresse."[2]

When it became known among the soldiers that Hawkins's offer had been refused, there arose such a turmoil among them that a council was called, and the decision reached to purchase a small ship, which Hawkins had offered to give them, after seeing the insufficiency of those which they had for the proposed journey. It was further decided that its price should be paid in artillery and powder, for Laudonnière feared that if the payment were made in the silver which he had collected while in Florida, the sight of it might excite the cupidity of the English Queen. Hawkins, in place of taking offence at the suspicions cast upon him by the flat refusal of the Frenchmen, readily consented to the bargain, selling his vessel to them at the price which the French themselves put upon it. Moved with pity at their distress, he sold them a quantity of his provisions, and fifty pairs of shoes

[1] *Hak.*, vol. iv., pp. 244, 245. Le Moyne in Plate XX. of his *Eicones* shows an Indian smoking a pipe and describes it in the legend to the plate.

[2] *Hist. Notable*, Basanier, p. 96; *Hak.*, vol. ii., p. 505.

for the barefooted soldiers. In payment for these Laudonnière gave him his note of hand, "for which vntil this present I am indebted to him," writes the lieutenant. Over and above this Hawkins gave them oil and vinegar, olives, rice, and biscuits, and made various gifts to the French officers, showing such humanity and generosity that Laudonnière gratefully exclaims, "I may say that we receiued as many courtesies of the Generall as it were possible to receiue of any man liuing. Wherein doubtlesse he hath wonne the reputation of a good and charitable man, deseruing to be esteemed as much of vs all as if he had saued all our lives."[1] It is one of those mysterious paradoxes in the make-up of a human soul, that the doughty slave-trader, who had been stealing negroes with fire and sword, packing them like human cattle in the holds of his ships, and selling them under the muzzles of his guns, dismisses this humane incident in half a dozen lines in his own narrative, and that it is only from the pen of those whose lives he had saved that we learn the striking details.

Menéndez subsequently wrote Philip that at the time of Hawkins's visit there were two vessels loaded with hides and sugar at Fort Caroline which the French had robbed off Yaguana, on the west coast of Hispaniola, and had thrown their crews overboard. As the French had not enough sailors to man the prizes themselves Hawkins, who, after a stay of only a few days, was ready to set sail for home, was commissioned by Laudonnière to sell their cargoes in France or England, leaving two Englishmen at Fort Caroline as hostages for the fulfilment of his agreement.[2] By the 15th of August the supplies

[1] *Hist. Notable*, Basanier, p. 87; *Hak.*, vol. ii., p. 507. For Hawkins's account of this to the Spanish ambassador to England see De Silva to Philip II., Oct. 22, 1565, *Col. Doc. Indit. España*, tomo lxxxvii., pp. 218, 230. English translation in *Spanish State Papers*, 1558–1567, I. Elizabeth, pp. 495, 503.

[2] Avilés to Philip II., Oct. 15, 1565, Ruidíaz, *La Florida*, tomo ii., p. 90.

left by the English and those accumulated by Laudonnière were stored aboard the ship, and only the absence of a favourable wind now stood between the colonists and their departure for their beloved France.[1]

There can be no reasonable doubt that the English vessels referred to in the letter were those of John Hawkins, for there is an agreement as to their number, the great size of the *Jesus* and the date of Hawkins's visit to La Caroline, although no names are mentioned in the letter. The French accounts make no reference to any such vessels as these two found at La Caroline by Menéndez. Dr. Shea in *The Catholic Church in Colonial Days* (New York, 1886, p. 140), and in his "Ancient Florida" (in *Narr. and Crit. Hist. Am.*, New York, 1886, vol. ii., p. 276), infers that they were Spanish vessels, which is not improbable, given the nature of their cargoes.

[1] *Hist. Notable*, Basanier, p. 98 ; *Hak.*, vol. ii., p. 507.

CHAPTER V

THE THIRD FRENCH EXPEDITION

THROUGHOUT these long days of waiting Coligny had not forgotten his plantation, and early in 1565 preparations were made to relieve it. The necessity was all the more pressing, because the very first vessel returning from Florida had brought with it strange rumours. It was said that Laudonnière was disposed to play the king, and to resent in a tyrannous manner any interference with his designs; that his men were treated with undue cruelty, and that he was currying favour and advancement by other means than at the hands of the Admiral, writing to the Lords of the Council with the promise of sending them gifts of the objects which he had found in Florida. And Coligny, himself an austere man, was indignant at his having taken a woman with him to the distant colony. It boded ill for the fortunes of the infant settlement if such a man were left in charge, so Jean Ribaut, who was again back in France, was put in command of a fleet of seven vessels and given the necessary authority to supersede Laudonnière, who, for his part, was directed to return to France.[1]

Again there gathered a miscellaneous company of adventurers at the port of Dieppe, including soldiers who refused to pay for their lodgings, and who set the town in an uproar with their carousings, "preferring to incur the

[1] *Hist. Notable*, Basanier, pp. 99–102; *Hak.*, vol. ii., pp. 509, 512.

wrath of the waters, rather than laying down their arms, to return to their first condition," says Le Challeux[1]; others, attracted by the report of a land of Cocaigne, where the grateful earth yielded up her fruits unscathed by the plough, where the heat of the sun was tempered to a pleasant ardour, and where frost and hail were unknown; and others by a more sordid desire for gold. There were also several gentlemen, among them a relative of Admiral Coligny, and Jacques Ribaut, son of Jean, who went in command of one of the ships; six Portuguese pilots to direct the fleet,[2] and a number of artisans with their families.[3]

The expedition was undertaken with the full knowledge and consent of the Queen, who was even thought to have an interest in it,[4] and the usual perfunctory charges were given Ribaut not to trespass upon Spanish possessions.[5] But he had also received a letter from Coligny informing him of the intended departure of a Spanish armada with probably a like destination and the laconic instructions which accompanied the letter left little doubt as to what action he should take in the event of an encounter with the Spaniards. "Capitaine Iohn Ribault," it ran, "as I was enclosing vp this letter, I receiued a certaine aduice, that Don Pedro Melendes departeth from Spaine to goe to the coast of Newe France: see you that you suffer him not to encroch vpon you, no more than he would

[1] "Hist. Mémorable" in Gaffarel, *Hist. de la Floride*, p. 457.

[2] Avilés to Philip II., Oct. 15, 1565, Ruidíaz, *La Florida*, tomo ii., p. 92.

[3] "Hist. Mémorable" in Gaffarel, *Hist. de la Floride*, p. 458. Merás in his "Jornadas de Pedro Menéndez de Avilés" (Ruidíaz, *La Florida*, tomo i., p. 83) says Ribaut forbade Roman Catholics to embark under pain of death, and allowed only Protestant books to be taken along. Barrientos in his "Vida y Hechos de Pero Menéndez de Avilés," in Genaro García's *Dos Antiguas Relaciones de la Florida*, p. 33, makes substantially the same statement.

[4] Philip II. to Alava, June 2, 1565, MS. Arch. Nat. Paris, K (2), 1504. Alava to Philip II., June 8, 1565, MS. Arch. Nat. Paris, K, 1504 (6).

[5] Le Challeux in "Hist. Mémorable" in Gaffarel, pp. 457, 470.

that you should encroch vpon him."[1] Menéndez, writing to Philip some five months later, told him that Ribaut carried orders to fortify a position on the Martyr Islands, where he could command the Bahama Channel so that no vessel could pass except under his eyes. Six galleys were to be stationed there, with the object of seizing Havana, freeing the negroes, and subsequently those of Hispaniola, Puerto Rico, and Tierra Firme. And it was also proposed to build a fort at the Bay of Ponce de Leon, because of its proximity to New Spain and Honduras.[2]

On the 10th of May the three hundred colonists[3] embarked aboard the ships, the names of five of which are still known to us, the *Trinity*, Jean Ribaut's flag-ship, the *Union*, the *Trout*, the *Shoulder of Mutton*, and the *Pearl*, the last of which went in command of Jacques Ribaut; but they were detained until the 22nd, awaiting supplies. Then came so violent a storm that the sailors cut their cables and ran before the wind. Three days more were spent in Havre pending the arrival of news from Dieppe, and over two weeks at the Isle of Wight, in expectation of a favourable wind. It was a delay fraught with fatal consequence to French enterprise in Florida, for had Ribaut reached there in season, the colonists would have

[1] *Hist. Notable*, Basanier, p. 106; *Hak.*, vol. ii., p. 516. Le Moyne, who also gives this letter (De Bry, *Brevis Narratio*, p. 23) says it was written in Coligny's own hand.

[2] Avilés to Philip II., Oct. 15, 1565, Ruidíaz, *La Florida*, tomo ii., pp. 29 and 107, 108. Menéndez says he was so informed by a Frenchman, whose life he had spared at the capture of Fort Caroline.

[3] "Hist. Mémorable" in Gaffarel, p. 459; Philip II. to Alava, June 2, 1565, MS. Arch. Nat., Paris, K, 1504 (2), says 500 soldiers. Mendoza in his "Relación" (Ruidíaz, *La Florida*, tomo ii., p. 442), says 700 men and 200 women. Gaffarel (*Hist. de la Floride Française*, p. 145), thinks they may have amounted to 1000. Silva in his letter of June 25, 1565, to Philip II., referring to the presence of Ribaut's fleet in Portland harbour, says they were 1200 (*Col. Doc. Inedit. España*, tomo lxxxvii., p. 133, English translation in *Spanish State Papers*, 1558–1567, I. Elizabeth, p. 242.)

been in a far more advantageous position to resist the attack of the Spaniards than afterwards proved to be the case, and the reinforcement which he brought would certainly have greatly retarded if not entirely diverted the nemesis which finally overtook them.

Meanwhile the colonists on the St. John's were impatiently awaiting a favourable opportunity to abandon the country, and on August 28, 1565, the wind and tide being propitious, the two ships were about to set sail for France, when their captains, Vasseur and Verdier, observed some sails at sea, of which they promptly informed their commander. An armed boat was immediately despatched to learn who the strangers might be, and the sentinels, who had climbed the highest trees to follow their movements, reported that the great boat of the ships appeared to be chasing the small boat sent out to meet them, which had already passed beyond the bar at the mouth of the river. Again the soldiers were drawn up in line, lest the newcomers should prove to be enemies, and through all the sweltering day and the long watches of the following night the colonists awaited in painful suspense the report of their messenger; for though the small boat had come up with the ships by two o'clock, it had entirely failed to send back any report. The following morning at about eight or nine o'clock seven boats were seen entering the river, among them that of Laudonnière's messenger of the previous day. The boats were full of soldiers, each carrying an arquebus, and wearing a morion on his head; silently and in battle array they moved past the outposts on the bluff, vouchsafing no kind of reply to the eager enquiry of the sentry as to who they might be. Unable to control his suspense at these mysterious movements, one of the sentinels fired a shot at them, which fell short of the mark, owing to the distance between him and the boats. Still no reply, and Laudonnière, warned of their approach, placed each of his men at his post, and trained two small field-pieces, which still remained to him, in readiness to fire upon the advancing line. Nearer still drew the silent company, making directly for the fort, when to the intense surprise and relief of the colonists Captain Jean Ribaut was recognised by his great beard[1] as the leader of the advancing host. The sight of his well-known face quickly dispelled the fear which his warlike array had excited, and the arquebuses, but a moment before turned against him, now welcomed him "with a gentle volley of shot, whereunto he answered with his."[2]

Ribaut soon came ashore and Laudonnière conducted him to his own house, where he entertained him with the store which Hawkins had left behind. After the demonstrations of joy had subsided, Ribaut drew his lieutenant aside, out of the fort, and informed him of the charges against him, while at the same time he delivered to him the letter of recall from Coligny. This was couched in no ambiguous terms as to the Admiral's personal friendship for him, but required his return to France to clear his credit.[3] Laudonnière readily disposed of the first two charges, observing, with much reason, that in a new country, and with such a company as had come to inhabit it, authority must be strictly enforced in order to retain that ascendency over its various elements that was necessary to the maintenance of order. To the charge of underhanded dealings with the Council, he replied, that he had but written to them in conformity with instructions received from the Admiral himself and with the sole object of securing their influence in dealing with the Queen Mother for the continuance of the enterprise. And finally as for the woman he explained that she was

[1] *Hist. Notable*, Basanier, p. 103; *Hak.*, vol. ii., p. 513.

[2] *Hist. Notable*, Basanier, p. 101; *Hak.*, vol. ii., p. 510.

[3] Coligny's letter is given in full in *Hist. Notable*, Basanier, p. 102; *Hak.* vol. ii., p. 511.

but a poor chambermaid, whom he had taken up in an inn to oversee his household, and to attend to the poultry and sheep which he had brought over with him. He dwelt upon the necessity of her ministrations to the sick and to himself in his own illness, and added, with great naïveté, that "all my men thought so well of her, that at one instant there were sixe or seuen which did demand her of mee in marriage." [1]

Ribaut, after hearing Laudonnière's explanations, urged him to remain in Florida and generously offered to share the command with him, leaving him in charge of Fort Caroline, while he himself would withdraw and build another fort elsewhere. This Laudonnière declined with much dignity, saying that there could be but one Lieutenant of the King, and here the matter rested for awhile. But the blow was a severe one to him, falling as it did out of a clear sky, and at the very moment when he had thought to see an end to all he had endured in the service of his country. The false reports preyed upon his mind, and he fell sick of a fever which continued for eight or nine days.

As four of his vessels proved to be too large to cross the bar, Ribaut anchored them about a mile off shore, where the water was shallow. His three smaller vessels, one of which was the *Pearl*, commanded by his son Jacques, he sent across the bar, the *Pearl* going as high up as the fort, near which she anchored.[2] The colonists were now disembarked and the provisions brought ashore and put away in a storehouse, which had been constructed about two hundred paces from the fort near the bakehouse, which also stood without in order to avoid danger of fire.[3] The neighbouring chiefs came in to visit Ribaut

[1] *Hist. Notable*, Basanier, pp. 102, 103; *Hak.*, vol. ii., p. 522. Laudonnière says that one of his men did marry her after their return to France.

[2] Le Moyne in *Brevis Narratio*, pp. 22, 26.

[3] *Hist. Notable*, Basanier, p. 104; *Hak.*, vol. ii., p. 514; "Hist. Mémorable," Gaffarel, p. 461.

and to welcome him after their fashion; and in their mimicry of the French would stretch out their hands reverently to the sky, when the bell of the fort rang for prayers.[1]

Ribaut had scarcely been a week at Fort Caroline, when on Tuesday, September 4th,[2] at about four o'clock in the afternoon, some soldiers, who had been walking on the beach, brought him word that they had seen six ships steering in the direction of the *Trinity* and her three companions, which lay outside the bar. There were but a few men in charge of these, for most of the crews were ashore, engaged upon the restoration of the fort and the houses to which Ribaut had turned his attention. On hearing the astounding news, Ribaut and a large number of the colonists hurried to the shore which they reached in time to learn that the strange vessels had anchored alongside their own ships, whereupon the French vessels had cut their cables and sailed away, with the others in pursuit. Straining their eyes through the limpid air of the September night, which had just been cleared by a thunder-storm, Ribaut and his companions could see their hulls disappearing below the horizon.[3] The fleet which had so unexpectedly presented itself was that of Pedro Menéndez de Avilés, Admiral of Spain, and one of the most accomplished seamen and commanders of the day, who had been sent by Philip II. to drive the French out of Florida.

[1] "Hist. Mémorable," *ibid.*, p. 463.
[2] Laudonnière (*Hak.*, vol. ii., p. 514), says Sept. 4th.
[3] Le Moyne in *De Bry*, p. 22.

CHAPTER VI

PHILIP'S NOTICE TO FRANCE

WHILE events were thus shaping themselves in distant Florida Philip was not kept in ignorance of the activity of the French by his ambassador, Don Frances de Alava, who had succeeded Chantone at the Court of Charles IX. Every movement of Laudonnière was narrowly watched, and the King was duly informed of his sailing.[1] From Normandy, from Brittany, from Nantes, from Bordeaux, and from Bayonne reports continued to arrive of the arming of vessels whose destination was either for Florida, or to rob the fleets from the Indies.[2] The piracies on the high seas continued with unabated vigour because "the first thing that a pirate did after he had robbed a vessel of 20,000 or 30,000 ducats was to

[1] Alava to Philip II., June 7, 1564, MS. Arch. Nat., Paris, K, 1501 (85).

[2] Alava to Philip II., Jan. 2, 1565, MS. Arch. Nat., Paris, K, 1505 (28); Barchino to Philip II., March 21, 1565, MS. *ibid.*, K, 1503 (58); Alava to Philip II., Apr. 27, 1565, MS. *ibid.*, K, 1503 (79); same to same, July 12, 1565, MS. *ibid.*, K, 1504 (45). The Nantes expedition was under the command of the son of the Mayor of Nantes, and Philip ordered that a copy of the report be laid before the Council of the Indies. Alava to Philip II., Jan. 18, 1565, MS. *ibid.*, K, 1503 (33). The Bayonne expedition was being armed by the eldest son of Montluc. Alava to Philip II., Jan. 18, 1565, MS. *ibid.*, K, 1503 (33). A month later he applied to Alava for a license, and on the refusal of the ambassador to give it, he obtained one from the Queen Mother; same to same, Feb. 20, 1565, MS. *ibid.*, K, 1503 (50). In the ensuing May the father gave his word that the son would not go to Florida; same to same, May 26, 1565, MS. *ibid.*, K, 1503 (101), and the expedition was finally abandoned; same to same, June 4, 1565, MS. *ibid.*, K, 1504 (4).

distribute 10,000 or 15,000 of them among those who were to judge him, or among their children, or to place the money in some matter in which they were interested." [1] Protests on the part of the Spanish ambassador were received with evasive excuses,[2] or contemptuously set aside. Coligny and Catherine continued to cajole him with empty promises that the pirates and robbers would receive condign punishment, the Queen's real object appearing to be that her subjects should arm themselves in whatever way they pleased, provided that they profited by so doing.[3]

In the early spring of 1565, the news began to reach Spain of the depredations committed by the French colonists,[4] who represented to their Spanish captors that they had been sent out by Laudonnière in search of food.[5] By April the King was already aware of the equipment and destination of Ribaut's reinforcements,[6] of whose departure for Florida and visit to Plymouth he was also informed.[7] The situation was already assuming serious

[1] Alava to Philip II., Oct. 31, 1565, MS. Arch. Nat., Paris, K, 1504 (72).

[2] Chantone to Philip II., Jan. 18, 1563, MS. *ibid.*, K, 1500 (81), fol. 5; Alava to Philip II., April 27, 1565, MS. *ibid.*, K, 1503 (79); Alava to Francisco de Erasso, May 7, 1565, MS. *ibid.*, K, 1503 (88).

[3] Alava to Philip II., Feb. 20, 1565, MS. Arch. Nat., Paris, K, 1503 (50).

[4] Rojomonte's deposition, made February 28, 1565, in Noticias de la Población que habian hecho los Franceses en la Florida. MS. Arch. Gen. de Indias, Seville, Patronato, est. 1, caj. 1, leg. 1/19, ro. 14; Noriega to Philip II., March 29, 1565, MS. Direc. de Hidrog., Madrid, *Col. Navarrete*, tomo xiv., Doc. No. 33, fol. 1.

[5] Deposition of Rojomonte in *Noticias de la Población*, etc., fol. 2; Confesión que se tomo a un hombre que bino de la Ysla de Cuba sobre lo tocante a la Florida, 1565. MS. Arch. Gen. de Indias, Seville, Patronato, est. 1, caj. 1, leg. 1/19, ro. 5, p. 5.

[6] Avis du duc d'Albe, April 11, 1565, MS. Arch. Nat., Paris, K, 1503 (69). Barrientos in his "Vida y Hechos de Pedro Menéndez de Avilés" (*Dos Relaciones de la Florida*, por Genaro García, Mexico, 1902, p. 33) says Philip was also advised of the preparations of Ribaut by Don José de Guevara, Viceroy of Navarre.

[7] Avilés to Philip II., May 18, 1565, Ruidíaz, *La Florida*, tomo ii., p. 66; Alava to Philip II., June 8, 1565, MS. Arch. Nat., Paris, K, 1504 (6); De Silva to Philip II., June 25, 1565, *Col. Doc. Inedit. España*, tomo lxxxix.,

proportions; for the "pirates of Normandy and Brittany were so ravenous in their greed for the Indian fleets" that they threatened to create graver complications than those involved in the mere question of the title to Florida, which might even lead to a war between the two nations.[1]

The denial of Philip's abstract right of possession was in itself sufficient to arouse the ire of the Spanish King, but the renewed attempt to invade the country was of even more urgent significance. If the reader will consult the map of Florida, and recall what has been said in a previous chapter of the route pursued by the return treasure galleons, he will at once recognise that if Ribaut's colony at Port Royal was considered so potential a danger to the fleets as to induce Philip to send Manrique to uproot it, the site selected by Laudonnière was fraught with far more immanent peril to their safety. It was at the very mouth of the Bahama Channel, where the ships were compelled to proceed with the greatest caution on account of the current, the inhospitable coast, and the prevalence at certain seasons of tempestuous weather. Not only did it threaten the fleets, but its nearness to Cuba and Hispaniola, to Jamaica and Tierra Firme, enabled the French, in the event of war between the two countries, to attack and plunder this region long before succour could be sent from Spain. And to crown all, while both countries were still at peace, the colony had already become a nest of pirates, and its settlers were beginning to plunder the neighbouring islands, while their sovereign turned a deaf ear to every protest of the Spaniards, and closed her eyes to the actions of her subjects.

p. 128. English translation *Spanish State Papers*, 1558–1567, I. Elizabeth, p. 242.

[1] Alava to Philip II., May 7, 1565, MS. Arch. Nat., Paris, K, 1503 (88). Barchino in his letter to Alava of March 21, 1565, calls them "queste gente piene de vana gloria."

There was no ambiguity in the interpretation which the Spaniards gave to the situation, and from every side Philip was assailed with letters sounding the note of alarm and advising prompt action. Before the French had set foot in Florida, Menéndez had warned Philip of the risks which would be incurred by their presence there.[1] Again, at a later date, he had sought to arouse his religious fanaticism by impressing upon him the ready sympathy which would arise between the Indians and the English or French, "a Lutheran people, because the Indians and they are of almost the same faith." "I am certain," he writes, "that the object of those who went to settle Florida was to possess those islands, and impede the navigation of the Indies, which they could do with the greatest ease, having settled or being about to settle the other Florida"; and he reiterated his fear of their stirring up an insurrection among the negroes.[2]

Chantone had pointed out how Ribaut's first settlement threatened the fleets from its proximity to the Bahamas and the difficulty of expelling the French if once they obtained a foothold.[3] Alava had given a like warning on the departure of Laudonnière.[4] Barchino wrote that the intention of the French was to establish a new kingdom in the Indies.[5] Granvelle, after informing him that the French had constructed two forts in

[1] Pero Menendez (Avilés) sobrel Remedio pa q̄ haya muchos nabios. Brit. Mus. Add. MSS. 28,366, fol. 296.

[2] "Memorial" (undated) in Ruidíaz, *La Florida*, tomo ii., pp. 322, 324. This memorial appears to have been written during the interval between his second and third voyages and before Ribaut's first settlement, for on p. 323, Menéndez speaks of "la Florida" in its largest extension, referring, it would seem, to the French settlements in Canada; and but two lines farther he writes of the possibilities should the French settle "la otra Florida."

[3] Chantone to Philip II., Jan. 24, 1563, MS. Arch. Nat., Paris, K, 1500 (43), fol. 1b.

[4] Alava to Philip II., June 7, 1564, MS. *ibid.*, K, 1501 (85).

[5] Barchino to Philip II., March 21, 1565, MS. *ibid.*, K, 1503 (58).

Florida which it would be no easy matter to take, had added:

"For if there are no Spaniards to drive them out, there are over forty thousand men in France of which it is necessary to rid the country. Every day their proverb becomes but too true, when they say that with two things they can make sure of the Spanish King: He has no money, and we will arrive and provide for everything in season." [1]

Noriega but echoed the prevalent opinion, and tersely defined the situation: "For the sum of all that can be said in the matter, is that they put the Indies in a crucible, for we are compelled to pass in front of their port, and with the greatest ease they can sally out with their armadas to seek us, and easily return home when it suits them." Act promptly, he advised, before the Admiral of France can forestall you, "and seeing that they are Lutherans, as the three French prisoners affirm, it is not needful to leave a man alive, but to inflict an exemplary punishment, that they may remember it forever." [2] Philip waited neither for Noriega's letter nor for the final preparations of Ribaut's fleet. Indeed it appears that his determination had been already reached shortly after the arrival of three of the first mutineers from Fort Caroline, captured in Cuba, who had been sent to Spain in a dispatch-boat, bringing with them the conclusive evidence of the French depredations in the neighbouring Spanish islands.[3] In the latter part of March he had already

[1] Granvelle to Philip II., June 2, 1565, *Lettres et papiers d'État du Cardinal de Granvelle*, tome ix., p. 248.

[2] Noriega to Philip II., March 29, 1565. MS. Direc. de Hidrog. Madrid, *Col. Navarrete*, tomo xiv., Doc. No. 33, fols. 2, 3, 5, "no es menester dexar hombre." On the importance of the danger of a settlement in the Bahama Passage see also "Memoria de las cosas y costa y indios de la Florida" by Hernando de Escalante Fontanedo, *Col. Doc. Inedit. Indias*, tomo v., p. 545; "Ancient Florida" by John Gilmary Shea in *Narr. and Crit. Hist. Am.*, vol. ii., p. 254.

[3] Noriega to Philip II., March 29, 1565, fol. 5.

selected the man best fitted for the carrying out of his intentions and invested him with full power to execute his will upon the intruders.

About the end of March or the beginning of April he had learned from Alava of the preparations which Ribaut was making in France for the relief of Laudonnière's colony, and he turned for advice to one of his councillors, a man destined in the course of the next few years to achieve a fame for cruelty and bloodshed second to but few in history; a man of fearless courage and of fierce determination, and a man of great military talent, although it had as yet scarcely received that recognition to which it was entitled. This was Fernando Alvarez de Toledo, Duke of Alba. Alba's counsel was brief, concise, and energetic. It behooved the King to issue orders that an armament be equipped with the least possible delay to drive the Frenchmen promptly out from where they had settled. At the same time the Council of the Indies should be ordered to put in writing the reasons which justify the King in excluding the French from Florida. Such reasons appearing sufficient, the Queen Mother should be spoken to in a very bold way to induce her not only to cease from sending more reinforcements, but also to recall the settlers who were already there. Alava should then be directed to urge a decision upon the matter, and in the event of none being forthcoming, Philip should send a member of his Council to treat of it.

It had already been arranged that Isabella of Savoy, Philip's wife, should replace her husband in the interview with Catherine de' Medici which was to take place at Bayonne in June, and which Catherine herself had sought in order to confer with him on important matters of state; and Alba craftily advised that the solution of the difficulty should be urged previous to the conference upon which Catherine was so intent.[1] Philip was not

[1] Avis du duc d'Albe, April 11, 1565, MS. Arch. Nat., Paris, K, 1503 (69).

slow to follow the advice thus given. Don Juan de Acuña, Captain-General of Guipuzcoa, was dispatched in person to verify the particulars of the French preparations, and Alava was directed to report further details.[1]

While awaiting the arrival of fuller information the question of Philip's title to Florida was formally laid before the Council of the Indies, which rendered its opinion in writing on the 5th of May, confirming it in every detail. It was founded, said the Council, upon the right and title conveyed to him by

"the bull of Pope Alexander, to whom, as Vicar of Our Saviour, it pertains to procure the conversion of all the heathen to his Holy Catholic Faith, and [who] to this end could appoint a Supreme Christian Prince over all the native Kings and Lords of all the Indies, . . . and thus he selected and chose the Kings of Castile and of Leon. Convinced of their zeal and Christianity, and aware of the great expense to which they had been put in beginning the discoveries with their people and fleets, he granted them the Lordship over all that had been or should be discovered within the limits set forth in the said bull, within which is the said Florida; and for the same reason he prohibited and was able to prohibit, under the penalties therein contained, that any other should enter them or send people to them without license from the said Kings of Castile and of Leon. And possession was taken of the said Province in the name of Your Majesty in many and diverse parts of it by Angel de Villafañe in the same region and Port which the French now occupy. . . ."

[1] "Consulta hecha al Rey por el Consejo Real de las Indias en 5 de Mayo de 1565 sobre el apresto de los 500 soldados, y Navíos, y vituallas que Su Magestad mando hacer para el viage á la Florida á cargo del General Pero Menéndez de Avilés, con motivo de los 16 Navíos que se entendio se armaban en Abra de Gracia, y otros Puertos de aquella costa, con 2 M soldados y mucha provisión de vituallas y municiones para ir á la Florida." MS. Direc. de Hidrog, Madrid, *Col. Navarrete*, tomo xiv., Doc. No. 35.

"It also appears that possession was taken of the said Province of Florida in the name of Your Majesty, in the same region which the French now occupy, by Guido de Labazares in the year 1558. . . . And there is also information of the taking possession of the said Province in the name of Your Majesty on other occasions, although the evidences of such have not yet been found . . . and since the year 1510 onward, Fleets and Vessels of these Kingdoms, have gone to occupy the said Florida in the name of Your Majesty . . . for in the said year two Vessels of the Island of Hispaniola, which discovered it, went there, and in the year 1522 Juan Ponce went to its discovery . . . and afterwards the Licenciate Lucas Vazquez de Aylon [*sic*], and after Aylon, Narvaez, and after Narvaez, Hernando de Soto; all Captains and sent under the instruction and command of Your Majesty, and of your predecessors. And even had the said possessions not been taken, Your Majesty acquired the dominion of the whole of the said Province by the bull and donation of Pope Alexander, because his Holiness is Prince of the Church . . . and for these reasons, which are the chief ones, and for other reasons which could be rehearsed, it appears to the Council that Your Majesty's title is very clear. . . . And we pray, as we have done at other times, that it may please Your Majesty to observe, that if the French remain in Florida, as they [now] are, they can impede the passage of all the ships which come from the Indies, which would be a matter of great inconvenience." [1]

Notwithstanding the report that the French armament was not as extensive as the Council had at first been led to believe, and that no details had as yet been received

[1] "Parecer del Consejo Real de las Indias, dirigido al Rey con fecha 5 de Mayo de 1565, sobre el derecho que tiene S. M. á las Provincias de la Florida." MS. Direc. de Hidrog., Madrid, *Col. Navarrete*, tomo xiv., Doc. No. 34. There is an abridged Spanish version entitled Avis du Conseil des Indes au sujet des droits de la Couronne d'Espagne sur la Floride. Bayonne, 18 juin, 1565. MS. in Arch. Nat., Paris, K, 1504 (19), and there is also a short notice of it in *Recueil de Pièces sur la Floride*, par H. Ternaux-Compans, Paris, 1871, p. 153.

from Acuña and Alava, it rendered a decree on the same day, re-forming the armada that was to sail for Florida, "because as the port of the French is in the Channel of Bahama, which is the passage of the Indies, it is of great importance to the service of Your Majesty to drive that people out from there."[1] A letter received from Alava on the day of the Council had informed the King that the French were already aware of the size and destination of the Spanish armada which was to sail for Florida, and that this knowledge might have a salutary effect upon their activity and induce them to abandon the enterprise. In view of this Philip prudently postponed the increase of the fleet until the arrival of the fuller reports from Acuña and Alava.[2] Alava sent Doctor Gabriel de Enveja to Madrid to report to the Council of the Indies, and himself left for the conference at Bayonne. On his way thither his religious susceptibilities became so confounded at the expected visit of an emissary of the Grand Turk to the French sovereigns, that he seriously informed Philip of his suspicions that Ribaut's fleet was destined to Florida, because France had sold it to the Turk![3]

On the very verge of the conference Philip finally commanded Alava to speak to the Queen Mother on the subject, complaining of Ribaut's armament, that it had been undertaken at her instigation, and expressing Philip's surprise that notwithstanding the friendship existing between the Most Christian King, her son, and himself, and the treaties of peace between them, she should endeavour to conquer a province to which he held the title.

[1] "Consulta hecha al Rey por el Consejo Real de las Indias en 5 de Mayo de 1565," etc. MS. Direc. de Hidrog., Madrid, *Col. Navarrete*, tomo xiv., Doc. No. 35.

[2] Philip II.'s marginal notes on the *Consulta hecha al Rey en 5 de Mayo de 1565*, etc., and see Alava to Philip II., Oct. 31, 1565, MS. Arch. Nat., Paris, K, 1504 (72).

[3] Alava to Philip II., May 28, 1565, MS. *ibid.*, K, 1503 (106).

"And if we have dissimulated until now in urging her, or in pressing matters concerning other vessels which we have heard have gone to Florida, it has been because we believed that they were corsairs, and went to rob without the orders or command of either herself or the King, her son; and that I had given orders that such should be chastised, as it is reasonable that infractors of the public peace should be, who undertake such enterprises without the order and command of their King."

If Ribaut had already set sail, Alava was directed to say nothing on the subject to Catherine, but to await the arrival of the Duke of Alba, who was to leave in two days to accompany the Queen of Spain on the visit to her mother.[1]

Philip in this letter was pursuing his habitual crafty and disingenuous methods. If Ribaut had sailed, the question could be more effectively solved by blows in Florida than by words at Bayonne. Meanwhile it was important that the antagonism of Catherine should not be aroused in view of the scheme for the simultaneous extermination of all heretics in both dominions, which his Queen, Isabella, and Alba had been instructed to bring about through their interview with Catherine.[2] As Ribaut had already set sail, the message was not delivered, and Alava was obliged to resort to his imagination to explain the contents of the letter, the arrival of which had so excited Catherine's curiosity "that she sent me a hundred persons to enquire what Your Majesty's post had brought," writes the ambassador.[3]

While Alba was negotiating at Bayonne, Alava was giving ear to every extraordinary rumour which French wit could devise, and on the 22nd of June wrote Philip

[1] Philip II. to Alava, June 2, 1565, MS. *ibid.*, K, 1504 (2).

[2] *Rise of the Dutch Republic* by J. L. Motley, vol. i., p. 476; *Hist. de France* par Henri Martin, 4[eme] edit., Paris, 1857, tome ix., pp. 189–194.

[3] Alava to Philip II., June 8, 1565, MS. Arch. Nat., Paris, K, 1504 (6).

that he had received a letter from Normandy informing him that the one hundred and fifty Frenchmen who garrisoned the fort in Florida, driven by hunger, had sallied out in search of provisions, and had all, with the exception of six, been eaten up by the Indians. "It were indeed good news," he writes, "and the more so, that these [Frenchmen] are so set upon going on that enterprise, that it may abate their fury."[1]

Philip, meanwhile, had considered the expediency of sending a special envoy to treat of the Florida question, as suggested by Alba, and had come to the conclusion that the presence of a member of his Council on such a mission would betray too great a lack of confidence in the sincerity of the French king to justify the proceeding. He thereupon informed the Duke of his determination to avoid a step which would give the matter so much prominence, but enclosed him a copy of the decision reached by the Council of the Indies as to his title, and directed him to introduce the subject incidentally when the proper occasion arose, presenting the unreasonableness of the steps which the French were taking, and urging them to revoke Ribaut's commission and to disarm his vessels. But the news of the departure of the French reinforcements, followed by Alava's cautious avoidance of the subject in compliance with the royal order, wrought a change in his plan, and he added a postscript in his own hand, leaving any further action entirely within the discretion of the Duke of Alba.[2]

The latter, who, on the receipt of the letter, was already at Bayonne, approved of Philip's policy, and did not broach the subject of Florida to the Queen Mother, because, Ribaut having already sailed, a better opportunity

[1] Alava to Philip II., June 22, 1565, MS. *ibid.*, K, 1504 (23).

[2] Philip to Alba, Madrid, June 15, 1565, *Nuevos Autógrafos de Cristóbal Colón y Relaciones de Ultramar;* La Duquesa de Berwick y de Alba, Madrid, 1902, p. 59.

might arise for treating the question in the interval between the conference and the departure of the succour which France expected to send in September or October. He also feared the effect of its discussion upon certain French counsellors of "infamous views," who, as he wrote his King, learning Philip's sentiments on the subject, "might turn against the Catholics and say to the latter: Since Your Majesty was somewhat offended at this, what confidence could they have that you would assist them in graver matters?" And finally, having announced that the sole subject under discussion at the conference would be that of the Faith, he thought it would be inconsistent to raise another.[1]

It is impossible not to be impressed with this last remark of Alba which he addressed to the King. It meant in substance that if the Florida question were raised it could be used as a means to inspire the French Catholics themselves with distrust in Philip, and indicates without disguise how little the religious faith of the Florida colonists had to do with the motives of the enterprise so far as France was concerned, and how clearly this was recognised by Philip's able counsellor. And it also shows how entirely secondary must have been the interest of both Philip and his adviser in the religion of the intruders to that of the royal title, that the mooting of the Florida question could be considered as foreign to that of the purification of the Faith in France and Spain.[2] The

[1] Alba to Philip II., June 28, 1565, MS. Arch. Nat., Paris, K, 1504 (30). "La otra es que auiendose de hazer con ellos el offs^o q̄ V. m^d manda podrian facilm^te algunos consejeros q̄ aqui ay de Ruynes intenciones boluerse contra los catholicos y dezir'es que pues en esto V. m^d mostraua estar sentido que confiancia podrian tener que los ayudara en cosas mas graues porq̄ como tenemos spto a V. m^d todo su estudio es poner desconfiança entre V. m^d y este Rey, y tambien pareceria repugnar a lo q̄ auemos dicho que es no traer otro negocio q̄ el de la Religion. . . ."

[2] De Silva, Philip's ambassador to England, in his letter of Oct. 8, 1565 (*Col. Doc. Inedit. España*, tomo lxxxix., p. 205. English translation *Span-*

Bayonne Conference therefore proved a failure, not only as to French intrusions in Philip's transatlantic dominions, but also so far as his scheme for purifying both countries of heresy was concerned, and the Massacre of St. Bartholomew was destined to sleep for seven years longer. Catherine successfully met the tactics of Philip's emissaries, and persisted in maintaining her power by holding the balance between Leaguer and Huguenot.

On the 29th of June the Spanish armada destined for Florida set sail from Cadiz. Philip allowed a sufficient time to elapse for it to be well in advance of any fleet that the French could send to overtake it, when he finally concluded that the moment had come to inform Catherine of the steps he had taken. On September 30th he wrote Alava:

> "It is now my wish that you speak to the Queen Mother and say to her, that having understood that some of her subjects had gone to Florida to usurp that province, which we had discovered and possessed for so many years, I have given orders to send and chastise them as thieving pirates and perturbers of the public peace. And having made this provision I had thought to have done with it, but that the brotherly relations which I have had with the Most Christian King, the frankness and sincerity that should be observed with him and with her in all matters, have induced me not to conceal this from them."

He was ordered to repeat the threadbare demand that the French subjects be withdrawn,

ish State Papers, 1558-1567, I. Elizabeth, p. 488) writes: "En lo que toca á la Florida, bien creo que asi franceses como estos [*i. e.*, the English] han deseado meter el pie en ella, mas por estar al paso de los navíos que vienen de la Nueva España y el Peru, que por otro fin." See also Philip II. to De Silva, March 22, 1566, *Col. Doc. Inedit. España*, tomo, lxxxix., p. 276; English translation, *Spanish State Papers*, 1558-1567, 1 Elizabeth, p. 527; and Granvelle to Philip II., June 2, 1565, *Lettres et papiers d'État du Cardinal Granvelle*, tome ix., p. 248, cited in Gaffarel, p. 154.

"for it is not becoming what with the love, conformity, and brotherly relations existing between the Most Christian King and myself, here, that our subjects yonder should go warring the one against the other. And you are to press the Queen strongly in regard to this, not with entreaties, but by showing her that it is a matter which should not and can not be concealed, and you are to inform me what answer she gives you." [1]

Not until the 23rd of November, and probably a month after Philip had received the news of the arrival of the armada in Florida, did Alava at last deliver the long-delayed message. Charles, who had been in Anjou, made his entry into Tours on the 21st, and the following day Alava had an audience with the King and Queen. He found them surrounded by "Cardinal de Chatillon and all the chief heretics who now move about in this Court." Although the subject was not broached at this interview, the Queen was not unprepared to meet it. She had already learned from Fourquevaux, her ambassador in Spain, who stood on the closest terms of intimacy with her daughter, Queen Isabella, what Philip's sentiments were.

"For that matter, Madame," wrote the Ambassador, "I have learned from the Queen, your daughter, that which I wrote you concerning Florida in my other letter, how that this King will not suffer that the French nestle so near his conquests, so that his fleets in going and coming from New Spain are constrained to pass in front of them. For which reason if they go from France to said country, it is well for them to go with sufficient strength and equipped for defence."

He counselled her "neither to acknowledge nor disavow your subjects who are there or who may go thither, for before the conquest be decided time will pass, the which

[1] Philip II. to Alava, Sept. 30, 1565, MS. Arch. Nat., Paris, K, 1504 (66). The substance of this letter first appears in a marginal note on a letter of Alava to Philip II. of August 5, 1565, MS. *ibid.*, K, 1504 (57).

may bring this Majesty and the Germans into such difficulties, that he will abandon the said quarrel, or let it sleep."[1] Catherine had also heard of the arrival of the Spanish fleet in Santo Domingo[2] and of the reinforcements that had been sent to it, and her daughter had again informed her how near to the heart of the Spanish monarch lay the expulsion of the French from Florida.[3]

At noon, the 23rd, Alava was again summoned into the royal presence. The King was in a large hall with all his Court, and began to receive him with still greater demonstrations of friendship than at the previous audience; so much so, that the Court were amazed at it, "especially the heretics." Alava told the King that he had come to see his mother, and not him.

"I assure Your Majesty that he took me by the hand and did not leave me until he had conducted me to his mother's chamber. His mother was also surrounded by heretics and Catholics and many people. She received me with the same demonstrations with which her son had received me, but not wishing to give me a private audience, saw me there, in public, drawing her son very close to her and causing me to draw near also. I began to repeat the subjects of Your Majesty's letter, when I had so severe a chill that I had to take out the paper I carried with me and begin to read it. I was as little able to do that, and finally they called l'Aubespine,[4] but not finding him, Saint Sulpice[5] had to read it. The Queen held her head so that the company could not well see her face and assumed a very melancholy expression until the subject of the Imperial

[1] Fourquevaux to the Queen, Nov. 3, 1565, *Dépêches*, p. 6.

[2] Fourquevaux to Charles IX., Nov. 5, 1565, *ibid.*, p. 8. Same to same, Nov. 21, 1565, *ibid.*, p. 13.

[3] Fourquevaux to the Queen, Nov. 5, 1565, *ibid.*, p. 9.

[4] Probably Claude de l'Aubespine, Secretary of State under Francis I., Henry II., Francis II., and Charles IX.

[5] Jean d'Ébrard de Saint Sulpice, French ambassador to Spain immediately preceding Fourquevaux.

alliances was reached, when she lighted up a little and said that it seemed well to her. We then began upon the matter of Florida, upon which Saint Sulpice attempted to comment before she had answered. I observed that I had come to converse with them, and hoped they would be contented with Saint Sulpice's reading of the paper, and so they dismissed him. The Queen would not allow me to say a word on the subject, at one moment telling me, 'The subjects of my son are going only to a mountainous region called Hercules discovered by the French crown over two hundred years ago.' I turned to the King and began to enlarge upon the matter with the urgency which your Majesty had directed me to use. The Queen's eyes kindled and she poised herself like a lioness to hear what I was saying to her son. I said in substance that it was a business of great consequence and that he should beseech his mother to weigh it well. At this she grew angry with me, and to tell Your Majesty the truth, I did the same with her, for she would not answer to the point and feigned wonder at everything I said. At last, closing her eyes, she exclaimed that for the life of her she understood nothing of this matter. By this Your Majesty can see with what sincerity she deals."

Several days elapsed, during which Charles took the advice of his council upon the subject two or three times. On the 30th Burdin, the King's secretary, handed Alava his master's reply. In substance it set out that it was neither his intention nor his will that his subjects should occupy lands or provinces discovered by Spain; but that Philip was not "to restrict them so and check them with so short a bridle" as to prevent them from going where he had neither discovered nor taken possession, as was the case with the "country where his subjects were going, a country called *la Tierra de los Bretones*," discovered many years before by the French Crown. He promised to do his best to establish the safety of navigation and trade, and that he would chastise his subjects as infractors and perturbers of the public peace if they offended those of Philip.

But Alava was not to be put aside by the royal quibble, and answered Burdin,

> "Why do you want us to talk this nonsense? Whether you call it the Land of the Bretons or the Mountains of Hercules, as the Queen does, the province where the vassals of your King are going is the same which we call Florida, and you New France, to which it is requested that none of the subjects of your master go."

Burdin could only reply, "The French discovered the Land of the Bretons a hundred years ago, as can be seen by the maps of the newly discovered provinces." "Now we have proved that the land you call Land of the Bretons and we Florida is one and the same," replied Alava, "and you mean to say that you first discovered it, so that the issue turns on the right of your King to it, and not that it is a different country from Florida, where the French are going, as may be gathered from your King's answer, and what you yourself are saying." Again Burdin could only answer that the King his master had sent this reply and would transmit it to his ambassador so that he might communicate it to Philip. After a little more fencing as to the title to the country Burdin took his leave, but not before Alava had told him how superficial a consideration the French Council had given so important a matter.

"The fact is," writes Alava in the same letter in which he relates the audience and the conversation, "that in the midst of their ill-luck and misery, and without hope in any one except Your Majesty, they are still determined to show Your Majesty that they are whole, and have no need of Your Majesty and are able to resist you whenever they are fretted." [1] The upshot of the interview shows

[1] Alava to Philip II., Nov. 29, 1565, MS. Arch. Nat., Paris, K, 1504 (80).

that Catherine had recognised the force of Fourquevaux's advice, had followed it to the letter, and in spite of Alava's bluntness had again outwitted him by evading the real issue and turning the question upon a technical matter of geographical boundaries.

The *Terre des Bretons*, upon the title to which Catherine had succeeded in turning the issue, embraced the peninsula which is now called Nova Scotia, with an ill-defined region to the west of it occasionally bearing the same name, but more frequently called *La Nouvelle France* or *Nova Gallia*, and to which France laid claim in virtue of Verrazano's discovery. Its southern boundary was as vague as was the northern boundary of Philip's Florida, and in a certain sense the Portuguese map-makers admitted her claim as early as the first quarter of the century by designating Nova Scotia on their maps as the land discovered by the Bretons.[1] But Catherine had now given Philip a Roland for an Oliver, and if he, in virtue of his discoveries to the south, was disposed to lay his clutch upon the entire continent to the north, she had capped his pretensions with a counter-claim to the south founded upon French discoveries to the north, saving always the title conveyed by the papal bull, to which neither party had made any reference, although Philip still held it in reserve.

And yet so great was the ignorance of the immensity of the territory for which both sovereigns were contending, so little did the French really know of the relative positions of the *Terre des Bretons*, of the Florida peninsula, and of the countless leagues which separated them, that Catherine herself may have been labouring under a genuine misapprehension as to the real conditions. Notwithstanding all her duplicity and wile, the reading of the prejudiced correspondence of the Spanish ambassador with his King frequently raises the doubt as to whether

[1] See Appendix K, La Terre des Bretons.

she may not, after all, have been sincere in her belief that her French subjects were going to colonise the *Terre des Bretons*. The doubt is accentuated by her adherence to this position in the course of subsequent events, her very genuine bitterness at the punishment inflicted upon the Florida colony, and the attitude subsequently taken by herself and her son toward the French avenger. If such indeed be the case, she had been misled by those around her who were more directly interested in the enterprise than herself, and was for once filled with a righteous indignation at the arrogance of Philip's demands. For though the opinion of the Council of the Indies as to the scope of his title had not been shown her, its purport was unquestionably known to her. It is only the dim shadow of a doubt, the vague semblance of a suspicion which the correspondence awakens, one that lurks rather in the atmosphere than in any concrete fact upon which the historian can put his finger; and as such it must pass.

And so Philip had quieted his conscience in view of "the brotherly relations between himself and the Most Christian King, and the frankness and sincerity that should be observed between them" by giving him due notice of his intention to oust the French from his possessions, but he had done so only after the blow had been struck and the footprints of France in the white sands of Florida had been washed out in a sea of blood.

CHAPTER VII

PEDRO MENÉNDEZ DE AVILÉS

THE man to whom Philip had entrusted the task of driving the French out of Florida was no mere adventurer of the common sort, but a nobleman of unusual ability, who had held high and distinguished positions in the service of his country. His name was Don Pedro Menéndez de Avilés,[1] a descendant of Doña Paya, an ancient family of the Asturias, where the "earth and sky," according to his biographer, "bear men who are honest, not tricksters, truthful, not babblers, most faithful to their King, generous, friendly, light-hearted, and merry, daring, and warlike."[2] He was born on the 15th of February, 1519, in the sea-port of Avilés, which had been granted to the founder of the house by King Dom Pelayo, and from which he derived his surname.

His active and adventurous disposition showed itself at a very early age; and on the death of his father, who had

[1] His full name as given in Vignau y Uhagón's Index of the members of the Order of Santiago is: Pedro Menéndez de Avilés y Alonso de la Campa (*Indice de pruebas de los caballeros que han vestido el hábito de Santiago desde el año 1501, hasta la fecha*, formado por D. Vicente Vignau . . . y D. Francisco R. de Uhagón . . . Madrid, 1901, p. 222).

[2] "Vida y hechos de Pero Menendez de Auiles, cauallero de la hordem de santiago, adelantado de la florida: do largamente se tratan las conquistas y poblaciones de la prouincia de la florida, y como fueron libradas de los luteranos que dellas se auian apoderado. Compuesta por el maestro barrientos, Catredatico de salamanca." In *Dos Antiguas Relaciones de la Florida* . . . por . . . Genaro García, México, 1902, p. 1.

served in the conquest of Granada,[1] and the second marriage of his mother, he was affianced when only eight years of age to Doña María de Solís, herself but two years his senior, in the hope of keeping him at home. But the lad would not submit to restraint, for the rugged mountains in which he was cradled were the home of a restless generation, rovers of the ocean and intrepid crusaders, and Avilés, after marshalling the mimic combats of his playfellows, soon felt the spell of the fierce sea which breaks on the Asturian coast. When barely fourteen years of age he ran away one day, and embarking in a tender with a crew of eighteen or twenty men, fell in with a Frenchman in command of a well-armed vessel, who attempted to capture him. In the encounter the boat of Menéndez was so greatly damaged by the guns of the corsair that his crew at first wished to surrender, but the boy urged them on with such valour that he infused them with his own confidence, and the Frenchman, not daring to board it, let them escape in safety to Galicia.[2]

As his father's property had to be divided between him and his nineteen brothers and sisters, it will readily be understood that the share which fell to him was not large, and for two years he followed the profession of a seaman, fighting the French on the water for most of the time, during the war which was then being waged between France and Spain. His sea service ended, he returned home possessed with a love of the rough and adventurous career of a sailor, for which he seems to have been especially endowed by nature. Selling part of his

[1] Barcia, *Ensayo Cronologico*, Año MDLXIV., p. 57.

[2] Barrientos in García, *Dos Antiguas Relaciones de la Florida*, p. 9. "Memorial que hizo el Doctor Gonzalo Solis de Merás de todas las jornadas y sucesos del Adelantado Pedro Menéndez de Avilés, su cuñado, y de la Conquista de la Florida y Justicia que hizo en Juan Ribao y otros franceses." In E. Ruidíaz y Caravia, *La Florida su conquista y colonización por Pedro Menéndez de Avilés*, Madrid, 1893, tomo i., p. 2.

patrimony he purchased a vessel of his own and successfully directed his attention to the corsairs which infested the coast and the neighbouring seas.[1]

In 1549, during the interval of peace with France, the corsair Jean Alfonse, the pilot of Roberval,[2] made a rich haul of some ten or a dozen Biscay vessels off Cape Finisterre, and Avilés was ordered by Maximilian, Regent of Spain during the absence of Charles V. in Flanders, to go against him and capture him. Although the Regent gave him neither money nor men for the enterprise, Menéndez boldly undertook the commission, and in an encounter with Alfonse off La Rochelle so punished him that he died of a wound which he there received; and Avilés rescued five of the vessels which the corsair had seized. Off Teneriffe he also defeated Alfonse's son, who had vowed vengeance against his father's slayer, sent Avilés a challenge, and had gone to the Canaries to encounter him on his way to the Indies.

His energy and success did not escape the attention of Charles V., who, recognising the ability shown by the young seaman, commissioned him to fight the corsairs even in time of peace, and granted him and his descendants all that he succeeded in capturing.[3] Shortly upon this followed his appointment to one of the most responsible offices that could be held by a Spanish seaman of that day.

The sailing of the India fleets, both on their outward-

[1] Both Barrientos in García (*Dos Antiguas Relaciones de la Florida*, p. 9) and Merás in Ruidíaz (*La Florida*, tomo i., p. 2), relate a romantic story of his attempted rescue of a bridal party which had been captured by a French corsair.

[2] Called Juan Alonso the Frenchman by the Spaniards. He was from Saintonge, near Cognac, and had been the pilot of Roberval when in Canada in 1542–1543. J. C. Brevoort in his "Notes on the Verrazano Map" (*Journal of the Am. Geographical Soc. of New York*, 1873, vol. iv., p. 292).

[3] Barrientos in García, *Dos Antiguas Relaciones de la Florida*, pp. 10, 11; Merás in Ruidíaz, *La Florida*, tomo i., pp. 4–7.

bound and return passage, had come to be attended with frequent delays through the carelessness or ignorance of the commanders, and the navigation of the ocean had become so perilous that not only many ships, but even entire fleets had been lost. Discipline had grown lax; the masters and captains of the ships were insubordinate and disobedient, and sometimes, deserting the fleet in the attempt to arrive ahead of it, their vessels fell a frequent prey to the French corsairs and the pirates. These incidents had come to assume such proportions as to arouse the concern of the King, who ascribed them to the incapacities of the Captains-General in charge of the fleets, whose appointment was made by the Judges, Prior, and Consuls of the Casa de Contratación at Seville. The King determined to make a radical change in these methods, by depriving the officers of the Casa of this power of appointment which they had exercised for many years and considered among the most important of their privileges, and in 1554 he named Avilés Captain-General of the fleet for that year, as against Don Juan Tello de Guzman, the nominee of the Casa.[1]

It was a very important and responsible position, and as it was a command which Avilés filled with distinction on many occasions, we will consider some of its varied duties. The Captain-General had the care of the fleet throughout its entire voyage. His charge began on the day of sailing, and continued until he again cast anchor on his return to Cadiz or San Lucar.[2] It was his duty to see that the crews and passengers were duly authorised to sail,[3] for impostors, bankrupts, unlicensed monks, and

[1] Avilés to Philip II., July 27, 1555; Ruidíaz, *ibid.*, tomo ii., p. 1. Jan. 8, 1564; *ibid.*, tomo ii., pp. 51, 52; Merás in *ibid.*, tomo i., p. 7.

[2] *Memorias Históricas sobre la Legislación y Gobierno de los Españoles con sus Colonias en las Indias Occidentales*, recopiladas por el Sr. D. Rafael Antunez y Acevedo, Madrid, 1797, p. 86.

[3] *Recopilación de Leyes de los Reinos de las Indias*, Madrid, 1841, lib. ix., tit. xv., leyes 21, 23, 29.

other prohibited persons took advantage of the fleets to escape to the Indies in the disguise of sailors, and bribed the masters of the vessels to transport them.[1] He saw to it that the necessary licences for merchandise and slaves had been procured, that the passengers went properly armed, that there was sufficient powder, that the weapons were kept in readiness for an attack, that the ships were not overcrowded and were properly ballasted, that the fleet was furnished with priests to perform the necessary offices for the sick and the dying, with physicians, and with notaries for the making of wills[2]; in a word, he attended to an infinite number of details relating to the proper equipment of his fleet.

To this end he was required to inspect his vessels, either in person or through his admiral, at least twice during the outward-bound passage, to call the roll every fifteen days, to punish all infractions of the laws, and to ward off all strange vessels and pirates, compelling the latter to surrender.[3] In the earliest instructions of which we have any notice, those of Jan. 21, 1572, he was ordered to proceed against pirates in the open sea, at once and with the greatest rigour, hanging them as soon as their guilt was established.[4] On the arrival of the fleet at its destination it was his office to notify the proper officials and to see that the soldiers and sailors committed no excesses while in port, to prevent and punish desertions, and to see to the loading and unloading of the cargoes. He was also required to make reports of the condition of

[1] Avilés to Philip II., July 27, 1555; Ruidíaz, *La Florida*, tomo ii., p. 6; *Recopil.*, lib. ix., tit. xv., ley 29.

[2] *Recopil.*, lib. ix., tit. xv., leyes 26, 30, 32, 37, 40, 51.

[3] *Recopil.*, lib. ix., tit. xv., leyes 13, 49, 50, 53, 66.

[4] Antunez, pp. 88, 89. These instructions contain some curious provisions to prevent the smuggling of gold or silver from out of the ships, and forbid the presence aboard ship of any woman with her lover, and if any woman be allowed she can only go in the capacity of "washerwoman for the general service of the armada."

the countries which he visited.[1] In addition to all of these requirements relating to the equipment of his fleet, the ordering of its departure and return, and the interior policing of the vessels, he was required to advise the home Government of his arrival and of the date of his intended return, on reaching the port of San Juan de Ulua.

The position offered many and great opportunities for gain by irregular methods, of which some were not slow to avail themselves. Where, for instance, owing to any particular reason, the return fleet sailed in two sections it lay in the option of the General to indicate which vessels should go in the first division. The advantage accruing to those first to sail was so great that influence was frequently brought to bear, and high bribes were paid for the privilege.[2] On the other hand, it was sometimes to the interest of the merchants to delay the sailing of the fleet, and high bribes were offered to bring it about. In a case of this description we have an interesting anecdote of the integrity of Avilés. Being in the port of San Juan de Luz, about to set sail for Castile, certain merchants offered him a thousand ducats a day to postpone the departure for three days, and double that amount for every additional day of delay. Avilés observed that it was "good money," ordered the chaplain of his fleet to say mass, boarded his flag-ship, and having discharged a cannon as a signal to his vessels, immediately set sail, with the outspoken remark that no one knew what the loss of an hour could bring in the service of God and the King.[3]

[1] *Recopil.*, lib. ix., tit. xv., leyes 50, 51, 53, 54, 55, 60, 69, 71, 72, 83, 84.

[2] See "Relación de los trabajos que la gente de una nao llamada Nra Señora de la Merced padecio" . . . por fray Andres de San Miguel, in García, *Dos Antiguas Relaciones de la Florida*, p. 160, where a vessel is said to have paid 1500 ducats for such a licence in addition to transporting two of the General's horses free of cost.

[3] "Información de algunos servicios prestados por el Adelantado Pedro Menéndez de Avilés," México, 3 de Abril de 1595, Ruidíaz, *La Florida*,

By far the greatest opportunity lay in conniving at the smuggling of gold and silver and of prohibited merchandise, which was so general a practice in those days. Here, again, Avilés appears in the character of a man of honour. In 1563, after his return from his third voyage, the Casa de Contratación, with all its powerful machinery and its violent animus, could find no charge against him except one relating to smuggling alleged to have been committed nine years before, during his first voyage,[1] for which, after a prolonged suit, it succeeded only in condemning him to a fine of two thousand ducats, half of which was remitted by the King, whose confidence he had. The office also offered opportunities of legitimate profit. One of these was the custom of the merchants, whose ships were in convoy, to make gifts to the highest officers, concerning which Menéndez naïvely complained to Philip that although the fleets of the Carrera de las Indias were far more valuable than those of the Levant, the merchants were less liberal in giving.[2] And yet Menéndez died poor.[3]

During the interval which elapsed between his appointment and the date fixed for the sailing of the India fleet Avilés accompanied Philip on the latter's visit to England to be married to Queen Mary, sailing from Corunna in July,[4] and from there he returned to Seville, still in

tomo ii., p. 621; and see the charges against his brother, Bartolomé Menéndez, in Avilés's letter to Philip II. of July 27, 1563, *ibid.*, tomo ii., p. 35.

[1] Barrientos in García, *Dos Antiguas Relaciones de la Florida*, p. 21.

[2] Avilés to Philip II., July 27, 1563, Ruidíaz, *La Florida*, tomo ii., pp. 35, 36.

[3] One of the seven interrogations put to the witnesses in the "Información de algunos servicios prestados por el Adelantado Pedro Menéndez de Avilés," México, 3 de Abril de 1595 (in Ruidíaz, *La Florida*, tomo ii., p. 590 *et seq.*) was: If they know that the said Adelantado, being in his Majesty's service, died and passed away from this present life, and that his children were left very poor and in much need? (p. 592). To this all of the witnesses testified in the affirmative (see pp. 591, 598, 605, 609, 612, 619, 623).

[4] Avilés to Philip II., Jan. 8, 1564, Ruidíaz, *ibid.*, tomo ii., pp. 51, 53;

Philip's service, being attacked on his sea journey by pirates, whom he successfully routed.[1] In September, 1555, Charles V., being in need of money to conduct his war with France, dispatched him to the Indies with a fleet of six men-of-war and seventy merchantmen and orders to winter in Havana, should he be unable to sail by the 7th of September of the following year. Menéndez fully realised the pressing necessities of the Emperor, and, with the devotion of a faithful servant and the self-reliance of a brave man, determined to exceed his instructions. Although aware, as he himself wrote, that "in the event of failure Your Majesty will have my head off," he was back in Spain by the 12th of September of 1556, nine months before he was due, having made the entire trip and collected the huge sum of seven millions of ducats in the unusually short space of one year.[2]

The Casa de Contratación was awaiting its opportunity to be avenged of the man who had been instrumental in depriving it of one of its most important prerogatives; and when Menéndez reached Seville on his return, he and a brother of his, who had been Admiral of the Fleet, were seized, sentenced, and put to great expense on accusations probably relating to the conduct of the fleet; but they were finally freed by the Council of the Indies and their innocence established.[3]

In February, 1557,[4] Avilés was again appointed in command of another fleet for the Indies, but his experience with the Casa de Contratación had taught him that in such

Noticias biogrdfico-genealógicas de Pedro Menéndez de Avilés . . . por D. Ciriaco Miguel Vigil, . . . Avilés, 1892, p. 23; Froude, *Hist. of England*, New York, 1870, vol. vi., p. 223.

[1] Merás in Ruidíaz, *La Florida*, tomo i., p. 7; Vigil, *Noticias*, p. 23.

[2] "Memorial de Pero Menéndez de Avilés," Ruidíaz, *La Florida*, tomo ii., p. 328; Merás in *ibid.*, tomo i., pp. 9, 10; Barrientos in García, *Dos Antiguas Relaciones de la Florida*, p. 12; Vigil, *Noticias*, p. 23.

[3] Avilés to Philip II., Jan. 8, 1564, Ruidíaz, *La Florida*, tomo ii., p. 53.

[4] February 26, 1557, "Memorial," *ibid.*, tomo ii., p. 329.

service the pirates and corsairs were not the only enemies with whom he would have to contend, so he requested Philip for another command. The King acceded to his petition and by royal patent of March 22, 1557, named him Captain-General of a powerful armada to pursue the pirates and protect the fleets and the coasts of Spain and Flanders.[1] This duty, too, he executed with promptness and energy, and in June of the same year, while he was shipping some artillery at Laredo, he was appointed to the command of twenty-four vessels to carry twelve hundred thousand ducats and fifteen hundred men to the relief of the army in Flanders, where Philip was already at war with France, which had finally been induced to break the truce of Vaucelles through the artful machinations of Cardinal Caraffa.[2] On his arrival at Laredo, from which he was to sail, he found that half of his fleet was in Galicia and that he would be compelled to await its return. Impatient at the delay, and knowing Philip's urgent need of money, he again exceeded his instructions, boldly set out with the four ships at his command, and successfully accomplished the undertaking, reaching Dover in fifteen days, landing his troops and money in Calais, and allowing the wool merchantmen whom he had escorted to proceed in safety to Holland. He captured on the way two corsairs, and beat off Pie de Palo, who had attacked him with a fleet of eight ships, and sunk one of his galleons. The timely arrival of the money and men due to the prompt action of Avilés

[1] "Titulo otorgado á Pero Menéndez de Avilés de Capitan General de la Armada dispuesta para proteger las flotas de la carrera de Indias y perseguir á los corsarios," Valladolid, 22 de Marzo de 1557, *ibid.*, tomo ii., p. 379. Barcia, *Ensayo*, p. 59, gives the same date. Barrientos in *Dos Antiguas Relaciones de la Florida*, p. 12, says May 12, 1557; Avilés to Philip II., Jan. 8, 1564, Ruidíaz, *ibid.*, tomo ii., p. 53.

[2] "Memorial," *ibid.*, tomo ii., p. 329; Avilés to the Princess of Portugal, June 2, 1567, *ibid.*, tomo ii., p. 25; *Rise of the Dutch Republic*, vol. i., p. 157 *et seq.*

largely contributed to the victory of St. Quentin, says his biographer, for not until two months after his departure did the balance of his fleet return from Galicia, and in the interval the battle had been fought and won.[1]

He did good service in warding off the attacks of corsairs from the auxiliaries sent by Queen Mary to the assistance of her husband in Flanders. On one particular occasion he showed signal personal bravery in rescuing the fleet in command of Diego de Mendoza, and of which his brother, D. Alvar Sanchez de Avilés, was Admiral. Mendoza was conducting the Prince of Eboli with reinforcements to Philip in Flanders, and lay to outside of a port on the English coast[2] to enable the Prince to disembark and proceed by land to Philip with the news of his arrival. Don Diego's fleet having set sail the following day in company with that of Menéndez, which had joined it shortly before, there arose a fierce storm which compelled them to return to the harbour. This was found to be barricaded with an iron chain which the Mayor had caused to be stretched across the entrance, and refused to remove. Avilés, seeing the peril to which the fleet was exposed, took with him fifty soldiers, and, converting a heavy beam into a battering-ram, he beat down the gate of the tower to which the chain was attached, allowing the ships to enter the harbour. So violent was the storm that six English and two Spanish vessels went down in it and over four hundred persons were drowned. Avilés worked all night long, tying up some of the ships, extricating others, animating the pilots

[1] "Memorial," Ruidíaz, *La Florida*, tomo ii., pp. 329–330; Barrientos in García, *Dos Antiguas Relaciones de la Florida*, pp. 12, 13; Barcia, *Ensayo*, p. 59.

[2] Possibly the haven of Dartmouth in Devonshire. The name of "Artamu" occurs on the map of Domingo Olives of 1568 in Nordenskiold's *Periplus*, Plate XXIX., in a location corresponding to that of Dartmouth on other contemporary maps. The Spanish name appears both as Artamua and Hartamua.

and sailors with directions and advice, and rescuing the drowning, of whom he succeeded in saving over three hundred with his boats.[1]

Ordered by Philip to return to Laredo, he was in that port, when, on the 17th of January, 1558, Calais was finally lost to the English. Philip, who was still in Flanders fighting the French, was again in straits for money, and as a large French armada was arming at San Juan de Luz, he ordered Avilés to add four great galleons to his fleet and to bring a thousand soldiers by way of the sea. Avilés, aware of the necessity of prompt action, went himself to Valladolid, where the Council of War was sitting, and after showing the delay and great expense to which the Government would be put in collecting the ships and men, and by following the course which had been determined upon, suggested an expedient, which he was authorised to try. Hastening to Castro, he secured four small fishing-smacks and daringly made a winter passage to Antwerp, which he reached in fifteen days from the date of his leaving Valladolid. So unprecedented was a voyage in these small vessels at that tempestuous season of the year that he could find none bold enough to sail them except the few men he took with him.[2] Either on this occasion or on a succeeding expedition of the same nature he is said to have carried not only a large sum of money, but also a force of soldiers concealed in what appeared to be cargoes of apples, with which he passed through the midst of the French corsairs without being discovered.[3]

[1] Barrientos in *Dos Antiguas Relaciones de la Florida*, pp. 13, 14; Merás in Ruidíaz, *La Florida*, tomo i., p. 22 *et seq.*; "Información de algunos servicios," *ibid.*, tomo ii., p. 595. Menéndez merely touches upon the incident in his letter of Oct. 6, 1557, to the Princess of Portugal, *ibid.*, tomo ii., p. 27.

[2] Barrientos in García, *Dos Antiguas Relaciones de la Florida*, pp. 14, 15.

[3] Deposition of Grauiel de Rivera in "Información de algunos servicios." Ruidíaz, *La Florida*, tomo ii., p. 601.

On his returning to Laredo for money and men he was ordered to add two other smacks to his fleet. These two boats were at the time in San Sebastian, where they had gone to escort four vessels in search of supplies. Avilés, hearing that he was watched by the French corsairs in San Juan de Luz, who had learned that he would not sail without these two boats, again showed his remarkable energy and decision of character, and setting out in his four fishing smacks eluded the Frenchmen, and reached Antwerp in nine days.[1] On his return voyage with his fishing-smacks, he escorted two vessels having aboard of them the Archbishop of Toledo, the Regent Figueroa, and other gentlemen, besides a large fleet of merchant vessels, which for fear of the corsairs had not dared to leave the port. While on his way he came across a French armada of twelve galleons, in command of the Admiral of Normandy, and conducted himself with so much skill and daring, that the Frenchmen fled, and he eventually convoyed his charge in safety to Laredo.[2] On his arrival in Spain, he was charged by the Regent, the Princess of Portugal, to escort the Queen to Flanders; but her death put an end to the proposed voyage,[3] and on the conclusion of the peace with France he conducted Doctor B. Velasco, a member of the King's Council, and Camara to Flanders.[4]

The close of the war with France at last afforded Philip the opportunity he desired of returning to Spain, and

[1] Barrientos in García, *Dos Antiguas Relaciones de la Florida*, p. 15; "Memorial," Ruidíaz, *La Florida*, tomo ii., pp. 330–333.

[2] "Memorial," *ibid.*, tomo ii., pp. 332–334.

[3] "Real Cédula de la Princesa de Portugal disponiendo que no se proceda contra Pero Menéndez por las reclamaciones de los dueños y maestres de varios naos, y ordenando se remitan al Consejo de Guerra." Valladolid, 30 de Noviembre de 1558, Ruidíaz, *ibid.*, tomo ii., p. 348; Merás in *ibid.*, tomo i., p. 27.

[4] "Real Carta referente á un viaje de Pero Menéndez de Avilés á Flandres." Valladolid, 25 de Enero de 1559, *ibid.*, tomo ii., p. 350; Merás, in *ibid.*, tomo i., p. 27.

having organised the government of the Netherlands to his satisfaction, and appointed Margaret of Parma as his regent, preparations were begun for his departure. At the end of April Avilés, accompanied by his only son, Juan Menéndez, and Sebastian de Estrada, started on another of his expeditious trips to Spain, in order to make ready for the King's departure, travelling by post through France in disguise, and was back again in Flanders by the 10th of July with fifty vessels.[1]

On the 27th of August the fleet of eighty sail set out from Flanders to escort the King to Laredo, with Avilés in command as Captain-General. On the tenth day Avilés perceived the indications of an approaching storm, and, the fleet being free of the English and French coasts, a council was held as to where the King should disembark. The advice of Avilés prevailed, and the fleet made for the coast of the Asturias, where he had selected a landing on the shore of a point of land near Gijon. Three leagues off Laredo Avilés realised that the storm was about to break over them. At his request the King entered a boat, and under shelter of Mount San Tona landed on Lady's Day, September 8th. Dreading the consequences of the storm to the large vessels off the point of Laredo, Avilés worked all through that night and succeeded in landing one hundred and fifty coffers of the King and all of the furniture,[2] and then the storm broke. The fleet was richly ladened, for Philip had determined to fix his future capital in Spain. Some of the ships foundered, and to save others the cargoes had to be lightened, and much of the rich tapestries and treasures accumulated by Charles and Philip was lost.

Shortly afterwards Avilés went to pay his respects to Philip, who asked him to what cause he attributed the

[1] Merás, in *ibid.*, tomo i., p. 28.

[2] Barrientos in García, *Dos Antiguas Relaciones de la Florida*, pp. 17, 18; Merás in Ruidíaz, *La Florida*, tomo i., pp. 30, 37.

storm. "For many months all Spain has prayed for Your Majesty, beseeching our Lord to conduct you in safety to your realm," replied Menéndez, "and during that season the devils could do you no harm; but when Your Majesty landed the prayers ceased, and thereupon they found the opportunity to work what evil they could." [1] From Laredo the King proceeded to Valladolid, where a month later he was enabled to enjoy the auto-da-fé in which thirteen heretics were burned before his eyes, and where he made the memorable reply to the appeal of one of them, the young Carlos de Sessa: "I would carry the wood to burn my own son, were he as wicked as you." [2]

The hardships and anxieties of his frequent journeying between Spain and Flanders had brought on a quartan fever, of which Avilés was hardly recovered when he was summoned to Toledo, and in January, 1560, [3] was put in command of an armada destined for New Spain and Tierra Firme, in which went the Count of Niebla, Viceroy of New Spain. Avilés sought to excuse himself on the grounds of his ill-health and his prolonged separation from his wife; but Philip, who had as small regard for the domestic ties of others as he had for his own when they stood in the path of his sense of duty, merely observed that a quartan fever was not a dangerous malady. [4] Further objections raised by Avilés on account of the ill-will of the Casa de Contratación were also overridden and he was compelled to sail, but the King considerately increased his salary beyond what it was customary to pay the generals of the armada. [5]

His instructions were to remain only fifty days in New

[1] Merás in *ibid.*, tomo i., p. 37.

[2] *The Rise of the Dutch Republic*, vol. i., pp. 220, 222.

[3] "Memorial," Ruidíaz, *La Florida*, tomo ii., p. 335.

[4] Merás in *ibid.*, tomo i., p. 38.

[5] Avilés to Philip II., Jan. 8, 1564, *ibid.*, tomo ii., p. 54.

Spain, and then, without another day's delay, to return with what money he could collect. But subordination played no part in the General's plans, when he thought that his King and country could profit by his disobedience, and again he deliberately set the instructions at naught. He found, on his arrival in Mexico, that the money he had been sent to fetch was already a month on its way to Spain, and in order to avoid the great expense to the Crown of returning with empty holds he remained there ten months, during which he succeeded in securing a large treasure, and was back safely in Seville by the 6th of July of 1561.[1]

Following shortly upon his return, Menéndez was named Captain-General of the Carrera de las Indias by a royal provision of October 18, 1561,[2] and his brother, Bartolomé, Admiral. The departure of Menéndez on this his third voyage to the West Indies was delayed until late in the spring of 1562 by various causes, among which was a renewed contest with the Casa de Contratación, which refused to pay him his increase of salary, and

[1] Menéndez in his "Memorial" (Ruidíaz, *La Florida*, tomo ii., pp. 335, 336), says he was ordered to the Indies in January, 1560. The Admiral of his fleet was ordered back by letter of Feb. 21, 1560, and reached Spain in "Noviembre pasado" (p. 334), *i. e.*, 1560. This is in agreement with the apparent date of the "Memorial," which from internal evidence (see pp. 334–338) was written Oct.–Dec., 1561. Avilés returned July 6th, eight months later than the Admiral, *i. e.*, July 6, 1561. De Merás in his "Jornadas" (*ibid.*, tomo i., p. 39) gives the date of his return as July 11, 1560, in which he is followed by Barcia (*Ensayo*, Año MDLXIV., p. 64). Barrientos in his "Vida y Hechos" (García, *Dos Antiguas Relaciones de la Florida*, p. 20) leaves the year in blank and gives the month only, July 6th, as the date of his return. Avilés in his "Memorial" (Ruidíaz, *La Florida*, tomo ii., p. 334), and Barrientos as well, relate that he remained ten months in port in the Indies. As the passage was usually made in about forty days, and there were at least twelve months consumed in the entire expedition, at the shortest he could not have been back before September, 1560, which date is in conflict with the month of July named by Avilés as that of his return. Vigil in his *Noticias*, p. 24, merely says that he returned in 1560.

[2] Barrientos in García, *Dos Antiguas Relaciones de la Florida*, p. 20.

accused him of exceeding his instructions in many particulars. From this he was relieved only by the direct interposition of the King, who ordered that he should henceforward serve under the instructions of the Council of the Indies, which alone would hold him accountable for their performance.[1] By June of 1563, Menéndez was back again in Spain with a rich cargo.[2]

Scarcely had Avilés returned to Seville from his third voyage, when he fell again into the clutches of his implacable enemies, the officers of the Casa, whose old animosity against him as the original cause of their diminished privileges and loss of prestige now found vent against him and his brother Bartolomé.[3] Nor was

[1] Avilés to Philip II., Jan. 8, 1564, Ruidíaz, *La Florida*, tomo ii., pp. 54, 55. And see his letter to Philip II., April 5, 1562, *ibid.*, p. 32; Barrientos, in García, *Dos Antiguas Relaciones de la Florida*, p. 20.

[2] Barrientos in his "Vida y Hechos" (in García, *Dos Antiguas Relaciones de la Florida*, p. 20), says Avilés made the voyage in 1563. Merás in his "Jornadas" (Ruidíaz, *La Florida*, tomo i., p. 42) omits the voyage altogether, Barcia (*Ensayo*, Año MDLXIV., p. 64) says Avilés was ordered to the Indies in 1561, in which he is followed by Vigil, in his *Noticias*, p. 24. But as there is a warrant addressed to Avilés of Feb. 3, 1562 (Brit. Mus. Add. MSS. *Cotton Vesp.* c. vii., fol. 266, and printed in Ruidíaz, *ibid.*, tomo ii., p. 401), and a letter of Avilés dated from San Lucar, April 5, 1562 (*ibid.*, tomo ii., p. 32), it is highly improbable that he could have made the expedition in the interval of six months between the date of his appointment and that of the letter, given the time necessary to gather and equip the fleet and the minimum of eighty days for the voyage to and fro. There is, however, an interval of fifteen months between this letter and the following one of July 27, 1563, dated at Seville (*ibid.*, tomo ii., p. 34), which is more than sufficient time for the accomplishment of the journey. Subsequent to that date he was continually present in Seville, as his successive letters from there show. See letters of Aug. 21, Sept. 15 and 24, 1563, and Jan. 8, 1564, all dated at Seville (*ibid.*, tomo ii., pp. 38, 43, 51, 60). That the period consumed by this voyage extended from the spring of 1562 to June of 1563, is confirmed by the "Reg. del C. de I." fol. 68 and 68 vto, given by Don Césareo Fernández Duro in his *Armada Española* (Madrid, 1896, tomo ii., pp. 464, 465), showing that Avilés passed the winter of 1562–1563 in New Spain, while his brother Bartolomé returned without waiting for him.

[3] Barrientos in García, *Dos Antiguas Relaciones de La Florida*, p. 30; Avilés to Philip II., April 5, 1562, Ruidíaz, *La Florida*, tomo ii., p. 32;

this his only offence, for he had also grossly insulted them in a public and outrageous manner. One day, when some of the officials of the Casa were inspecting the vessels of a fleet of which he was Captain-General, Menéndez observed that their boat flew a banner of crimson damask, emblazoned with the royal arms, such as the King himself displayed when on a campaign, and which the Captain-General alone, by special authority was entitled to fly. Menéndez wasted no words with them, but simply hauled it down and kept it. "And such is their anger against me," he writes, "that since they have seized me, they publicly proclaim, that forasmuch as I have deprived them of the power of appointing the Generals, and have taken their royal standard from them, it matters little to them if they deprive me of my honour, and even of my life." [1]

Anticipating trouble, Avilés had on his arrival escaped post-haste to Madrid, but the officials had gotten the ear of Philip and he was compelled to return to Seville to answer the charges against him. About the 21st of August, 1563, while in an enfeebled condition from having been bled and purged, he was pounced upon by the constables of the Casa. At the moment of his arrest he was surrounded by a hundred of his soldiers who had seen continued service with him, and there were some fifteen hundred more of them in Seville at the time, but he submitted quietly to the arrest and was imprisoned in the Arsenal with two guards. From there he was subsequently transferred to the "Golden Tower," the graceful treasure-house of the Almohades, which still guards the banks of the Guadalquivir at Seville.[2] It was a very

July 27, 1563, *ibid.*, tomo ii., p. 34; Aug. 21, 1563, *ibid.*, tomo ii., pp. 38 and 39; Sept. 15, 1563, *ibid.*, tomo ii., pp. 43, 44; Sept. 24, 1563, *ibid.*, tomo ii., p. 49; Jan. 8, 1564, *ibid.*, tomo ii., pp. 51, 52.

[1] Avilés to Philip II., Sept. 15, 1563, *ibid.*, tomo ii., p. 44.

[2] Avilés to Philip II., July 27, 1563, *ibid.*, tomo ii., p. 40; Aug. 21, 1563, *ibid.*, tomo ii., p. 38; Sept. 15, 1563, *ibid.*, tomo ii., pp. 43, 46; Sept. 24, 1563, *ibid.*, tomo ii., p. 48; Jan. 8, 1564, *ibid.*, tomo ii., p. 56.

serious inconvenience to him, for he was under heavy bonds to equip three galleons by the 20th of September to transport to Peru the Licentiate Castro, who had been appointed its President and Governor. He was released for eight days on bail, and succeeded in fitting out the ships, but his imprisonment prevented their sailing in time to join the departing fleet for that year.[1]

It is difficult to ascertain what was the precise misconduct with which he was charged. According to his biographer, Barrientos, the Casa de Contratación, unable to find any cause of complaint against him in relation to the voyage just completed, accused him of having greatly exceeded his authority in his first voyage to the West Indies, of having connived at the smuggling of a large quantity of money, and of having in many ways infringed upon its regulations. From his own letters we gather that its enquiries extended over all the twelve years he had passed in the royal service, although during the entire term he had acted under the instructions of the Casa, which had laid no charge against him until its jealousy had been aroused by his removal from under its jurisdiction.[2] He informs us that he was accused of accepting a bribe of five hundred ducats to delay the sailing of the fleet during his second voyage of 1560–1561, and of giving insufficient rations to the soldiers; both of which accusations, together with others made against him, he sums up as old charges, the most of them of four and five years' standing.[3]

In successive letters Avilés besought the King, saying:

"If I deserve punishment, let it be justly done, not a single one of my acts being forgiven; and if the judges deserve it for

[1] Avilés to Philip II., Sept. 15, 1563, *ibid.*, tomo ii., p. 45. Same to same, Jan. 8, 1564, *ibid.*, tomo ii., pp. 56, 58.

[2] Avilés to Philip II., Sept. 15, 1563, *ibid.*, tomo ii., pp. 43, 44.

[3] Avilés to Philip II., July 27, 1563, *ibid.*, tomo ii., p. 36; same to same, Aug. 21, 1563, *ibid.*, tomo ii., p. 38.

doing what they have no right to do, let not their punishment be a secret reprimand, but in accordance with what they deserve; for I do not care to retain my honour, unless it follows a just discharge of their accusations, and clears me, so that Your Majesty and the Council may understand the passion and daring of these men." [1]

The judges, finding nothing against him, protracted the suit and delayed sentence, until compelled to pass judgment by the receipt of two successive cédulas from the King himself. After spending twenty months in prison, the suit was ended by condemning Menéndez to pay a thousand ducats, of which sum the King remitted one-half, and took him again into his favour, "for," says Barrientos, "it was well understood throughout the Kingdom that he had been falsely accused." [2]

Nearly eighteen years had now elapsed, during which his constant occupation in the King's service had allowed him but few opportunities to visit his home, which stood within two leagues of the town of Avilés. It was one of the most ancient dwellings in that country, and its name of Monte de Rey arose from its former occupation as a royal habitation.[3] He longed to see his wife again, and his three little girls, who had grown to womanhood since his last visit.[4] But before so doing he had a painful and urgent duty to perform. While at Havana in 1563, and about to return to Spain, Menéndez had sent his only

[1] Avilés to Philip II., Sept. 15, 1563, *ibid.*, tomo ii., p. 47, and see also same letter, p. 45; same to same, Jan. 8, 1564, *ibid.*, tomo ii., p. 58.

[2] Barrientos in García, *Dos Antiguas Relaciones de la Florida*, p. 21; Merás in Ruidíaz, tomo i., p. 43. His brother Bartolomé was involved in the same trouble with him and was imprisoned for twenty-five months (*ibid.*). A question of jurisdiction appears also to have arisen and possibly some jealousy between the Casa de Contratación and the Council of the Indies. At any rate Avilés tried to raise such an issue in his letters.

[3] Barrientos in García, *Dos Antiguas Relaciones de la Florida*, p, 8; Merás in Ruidíaz, *La Florida*, tomo i., p. 1.

[4] Avilés to Philip II., Jan. 8, 1564, *ibid.*, tomo ii., 59.

son, Don Juan Menéndez, a gentleman of the Royal Household, to Mexico to command the fleet from New Spain. Don Juan had been wrecked on his way home off the Bermudas and nothing more had been heard of him. A number of Menéndez's relatives, as well as some of his old friends and soldiers who had served under him for many years, had been lost at the same time. It was a severe trial to his affections, and before taking the repose to which he was so justly entitled, he asked permission of the King to seek for his son and his companions at the Bermudas and along the neighbouring coast.[1] Philip himself was anxious to carry out the suggestion of the Council of New Spain, and explore farther up the Florida coast in search of suitable harbours, and Avilés readily consented to lend himself to this enterprise, while he at the same time prosecuted the search for his lost son.[2] It was under these circumstances that the quarrel with France reached its crisis and Philip selected him to command the fleet which was to sweep aside the tergiversations of the French Court.

Avilés was now in his forty-seventh year, a trained soldier, a skilful seaman, and with perhaps a larger experience in the special requirements of the undertaking than any other man in Spain, perhaps in Europe. He was decisive and prompt in an emergency, yet cool and resourceful. He was of indomitable energy, with a courage beyond reproach. In one of his memorials to

[1] Merás in *ibid.*, tomo i., p. 46, says he was his only son. Extract from "Reg. C. de I.," fol. 68 vto, printed in Duro's *Armada Española*, tomo ii., p. 465. "Información de algunos servicios prestados por el Adelantado Pero Menéndez de Avilés," México, 3 de Abril de 1595, Ruidíaz, *La Florida*, tomo ii., pp. 598, 608. There is a note appended to Rojomonte's deposition in *Noticias de la Población*, etc., 1564, pp. 3 and 4, which refers to the loss of three ships of Don Juan Menéndez on the Florida coast. Fontanedo in his "Memoria," XIII., *Doc. Inedit. Indias*, p. 541, appears to say that Juan Menéndez was wrecked upon the coast of Ays, Indian River, Florida.

[2] Barrientos in García, *Dos Antiguas Relaciones de la Florida*, p. 22.

Philip he writes that "there were neither French nor English nor any other nation on the Florida coast that could terrify him."[1] His loyalty was above suspicion. In a letter written from his prison in Seville, he exclaims with all of the pride of a faithful subject and of a brave soldier, "I possess but my sword, and my cloak, and my honour, which are great riches to me, because I have been fortunate in my service to Your Majesty."[2]

His prolonged service in countless naval engagements with the French had given him a thorough knowledge of their ways and methods, and had infused him with a deep hatred of these relentless enemies of his country, while it had also bred in him a due respect for their courage and ability, of which his tribute to Jean Ribaut is a remarkable testimony. On occasion he knew how to exercise that courtesy which befitted his rank, and Merás tells us that he was much liked by Queen Mary, Philip's English wife, on account of his liberality and hospitable treatment of the Englishmen in her service.[3] He was no theologian. His parallel of the religions of the Protestants and the Indians shows us that. His faith was that of a soldier, imbued with all that hatred of heresy peculiar to his age and race; and he showed as little compunction in executing upon heretics what was taught to be the will of the Church as he was relentless in performing the commands of his sovereign. And yet his letters show that in carrying through the appalling massacre of the French Huguenots in Florida, he was neither impelled by rage, nor violence, nor acting under the impulse of a blind fanaticism, but was deliberately and conscientiously performing what he believed to be his duty towards his King and his faith. And in this light we cannot with-

[1] "Memorial," Ruidíaz, *La Florida*, tomo ii., p. 324.

[2] Avilés to Philip II., Sept. 24, 1563, *ibid.*, tomo ii., p. 50.

[3] "Jornadas," in *ibid.*, tomo i., pp. 15, 16. See also his treatment of the French prisoners at Ays, p. 215, in this volume and of Osorio, p. 221, *ibid.*

hold from him the respect due a courageous and faithful soldier, while we shudder at the distorted logic which could calmly justify his crime.

We have a portrait of him, at about the age of fifty, subsequent to his return from the conquest of Florida. In it he bears a curious resemblance in the contour of the face to the monarch whom he served, but there the resemblance ceases. In place of the bulging eyes and sensuous lips which we see in Titian's famous portrait of his master, painted at Philip's command for a gift for his English bride, we have shrewd, sharp eyes, under the heavy brows of a seaman, and lips pressed firmly together with a determination that bodes ill for those who run counter to it; he is "bearded like the pard," and bears on his left breast the cross of Santiago.[1]

[1] See Appendix L, Portraits of Avilés.

CHAPTER VIII

THE DEPARTURE OF AVILÉS FOR FLORIDA

THE asiento under which Avilés was to undertake the conquest of Florida was executed March 20, 1565. It first disposed of the rights of prior adventurers, and especially of those in the last asiento made with Ayllon, because of their failure to settle the country. It then directed Avilés to equip six sloops of fifty tons each, and four smaller vessels, taking with him the *San Pelayo*, a large ship of six hundred tons, in which to transport the colonists across the ocean, because the sloops, being small and uncovered, were not fitted for that purpose, but were apparently intended for the shallow Florida waters.

The colonists were to number five hundred, of which one hundred should be soldiers, one hundred sailors, and the balance officials, and artisans, such as stone-cutters, carpenters, locksmiths, sawyers, smiths, and barbers, all fully armed. Two hundred of the settlers were to be married, and at least one hundred were to be labourers and farmers. Avilés was authorised to divide out the land in repartimientos among the settlers, and to construct at least two towns, each of them to have not less than one hundred inhabitants, and to be provided with a fort for its protection. The company was to include four members of the Society of Jesus with ten or twelve monks of any order he saw fit; and he was granted the privilege of transporting to Florida five hundred negro slaves,[1] taken from Spain, Portugal, the Cape de Verde Islands, or Guinea, of whom one-third were to be women, to assist in the construction of the towns, the cultivation of the land, the planting of sugar-cane, and the manufacture of sugar. He was especially enjoined to see that none of his colonists were contaminated by heresy, and that there were no Jews, Moors, or Marranos among them.[2] He was ordered to take with him a hundred horses and mares, two hundred sheep, four hundred swine, four hundred lambs, and some goats, with what other stock he saw fit.

He was ordered to reconnoitre the Gulf coast of the peninsula and from the Florida Keys as far north as Newfoundland, and to make a full report upon the ports, currents, rocks, shoals, and bays of the same. And finally came the main purpose of the asiento, the expulsion of the French. As the two countries were not only at peace, but ostensibly entertaining the most amicable relations with each other, Frenchmen could not openly be named as having invaded Spanish territory, which might be construed as a formal threat against the French Government in the face of its solemn protestations that it harboured no designs upon Florida. It was, therefore, necessary to disguise the instructions under a comprehensive term which should include the case of the French colonists without attributing their irregular action to the connivance of the French Crown, and Avilés was directed to ascertain "if in the said coast or land there were settlers or corsairs or other nations whatsoever not subject to Us," and to seek "to drive them out by what means you see fit."

In return for these vast services, which Avilés agreed

[1] Avilés did not immediately avail himself of this provision.

[2] "Y que sea gente limpia y no de los prohividos." "Capitulación y asiento con Pero Menéndez de Avilés para la población y conquista de la Florida, Madrid, 20 de Marzo de 1565," Ruidíaz, *La Florida*, tomo ii., p. 418.

to undertake entirely at his own expense and without recourse either to the King or his successors, Philip graciously awarded him an aid of fifteen thousand ducats, which Menéndez bound himself to repay; a salary of two thousand ducats to be derived from the rents and products of the land, without recourse to the King in the event of any failure to collect; a grant of land twenty-five leagues square, with the title of Marquis attached to it, and two fisheries, the one of pearls and the other of fish, to be selected by himself. He was allowed to have a few vessels of his own and to trade with certain of the West India Islands which were carefully specified, and he was released from various export and import duties for a stated period. He was also allowed to retain all that he found aboard the pirates he captured, during a term of five years.

He and his successors were granted in perpetuity the title of Adelantado of Florida, and he was appointed captain-general of the fleet under his command. He was invested with authority to appoint a lieutenant-governor for the country to hold office during his absence; he was given the exclusive control of his fleet for six years, so that none of his vessels could be detached from his service under any pretence, and finally he was empowered to appoint an executor to carry out the intentions of the asiento in the event of his own death within the term of three years set for the fulfilment of its conditions.[1]

The asiento, which in most respects observes the customary formulæ employed in such documents, deserves our attention for a moment in view of the influence it exerted upon subsequent events. Its most remarkable provision was that the colonists were to be transferred,

[1] "Capitulación y asiento con Pero Menéndez de Avilés para la población y conquista de la Florida, Madrid, 20 de Marzo de 1565," *ibid.*, tomo ii., pp. 415-427.

bound hand and foot in absolute dependence, to Avilés. The trade with Florida from the nearer West India ports was exclusively subject to his control, and this power came to be exerted to the great detriment of the colony, and to the repression of all individual initiative. His salary was dependent upon the productions of the soil, and as the latter at no period during the sixteenth and seventeenth centuries ever became a source of revenue either to the colony or to the Crown, but as the colony, on the contrary, proved a constant source of expense, so that even flour and provisions had to be supplied from abroad, a great and irresistible temptation was presented to eke out by illegitimate means a salary which otherwise could never be collected.

Finally, the importation into Florida of the five hundred negro slaves was a perquisite of Menéndez, and on his failure to bring them the severe labour which they were intended to perform would fall upon the few white colonists, or, in their default, upon those of their Indian neighbours whom the Spaniards might be able to impress. The result would be a small zone of the weaker natives, its extent limited by the ability of the colonists to hold them in subjection, surrounded by the countless braver and hostile tribes which would not submit to slavery. It is true that the written law was tender of the treatment of the Indians and hedged them in every conceivable way from the ill-usage of the colonists. But the country was greatly isolated, and the colonists, like many before and after them, became in this particular a law unto themselves, with what result we shall see in due time. Two days after the execution of the asiento the various titles and privileges which the King had bestowed upon Menéndez in pursuance of the contract were duly confirmed.[1]

[1] "Real Cédula donando al Adelantado Pero Menéndez de Avilés 25 leguas en cuadro de territorio en la Florida, Madrid, 22 de Marzo de 1565," *ibid.*, tomo ii., p. 351. "Real Cédula eximiendo á Pero Menéndez

**.—10.

No one perhaps realised better than Avilés himself the importance of anticipating the arrival of the French reinforcements and of striking promptly. So he went in person to Madrid and asked to be given four vessels already equipped with which to carry out at once the reconnaissance, in place of submitting to the delays and annoyance of fitting out a great fleet. But the Turk was moving on Malta and there were but few vessels to meet him, and the request of Menéndez was denied. As some compensation he was authorised to collect four additional vessels and five hundred men in the West India Islands.[1] Menéndez, therefore, was thrown back upon the original plan and began upon the equipment of his fleet. Money for the enterprise was collected from his friends. One of these, Pedro del Castillo, an alderman of Cadiz, embarked his entire fortune in the adventure and also raised the sum of twenty thousand ducats for it.[2] Diego Flores de Valdes, who had seen fifteen years' service under Menéndez in most of his daring ventures in the Indies as well as in the Flanders fleets, sold and pawned the greater part of his patrimony to further the undertaking of his chief, whom he accompanied to Florida.[3] Menéndez himself em-

del pago de derechos de fundición de metales." Same date, *ibid.*, p. 354. "Real Cédula concediendo al Adelantado Pero Menéndez de Avilés participación en las rentas, minas y frutos de la Florida." Same date, *ibid.*, p. 356. "Real Cédula concediendo á Pero Menéndez dos pesquerías en la Florida, una de perlas y la otra de pescado." Same date, *ibid.*, p. 358. "Título de Capitán General, expedido al Adelantado Pero Menéndez de Avilés, de la armada que llevó para el descubrimiento de la Florida." Same date, *ibid.*, p. 383. "Título de Gobernador y Capitán General de la Florida, otorgado á Pero Menéndez de Avilés." Same date, *ibid.*, p. 385.

[1] Merás, "Jornadas," in *ibid.*, tomo i., pp. 56, 57.

[2] Merás in *ibid.*, tomo i., p. 53; Avilés to Philip II., Oct. 15, 1565, *ibid.*, tomo ii., p. 100.

[3] Avilés to Philip II., Aug. 21, 1563, *ibid.*, tomo ii., p. 41; Oct. 15, 1565, *ibid.*, p. 101.

barked all of his fortune[1] in the enterprise; and as the entire expense of it was borne by him, excepting that of one ship and two hundred and ninety-nine soldiers furnished by the King, he is said by Barcia to have expended upon it nearly a million ducats in less than fourteen months.[2]

With his customary energy and promptness Menéndez had assembled a fleet of ten vessels at Cadiz by the end of June. Most of them ranged from sixty to seventy-five tons, except the caravel *San Antonio*, which was of one hundred and fifty, and the *San Pelayo*, his flag-ship, of over nine hundred tons, a very large vessel for that day. One was a galley called the *Victoria*, propelled by oars. These were all well supplied with artillery and ammunition. The company consisted of fifteen hundred souls, eight hundred and twenty of whom were soldiers. Many of the latter united in their person the arts of peace with their warlike occupation. There were twenty-one tailors who sailed in this double capacity, fifteen carpenters, and ten shoemakers; indeed nearly all of the trades were represented: millers, masons, silversmiths, gardeners, and barbers, a hat-maker, and even a weaver of silk and a brewer, in all, one hundred and thirty-seven soldiers, representing among them thirty-eight trades, besides one hundred and seventeen tillers of the soil. There were one hundred and seventy seamen including eighteen artillery men, and in the *San Pelayo* sailed twenty-seven families. Seven priests accompanied the colonists.[3] Avilés took with him the three mutineers

[1] "All of my fortune," Avilés to Philip II., May 18, 1565, *ibid.*, tomo ii., p. 64.

[2] Barcia, *Ensayo Cronologico*, Año MDLXV., p. 69. This probably includes the money borrowed from his friends as well as his own fortune.

[3] Barrientos, ("Vida y Hechos," in García, *Dos Antiguas Relaciones de la Florida*, p. 35), says there were twelve priests. Mendoza, in his "Relación" (in Ruidíaz, *La Florida*, tomo ii., p. 437), says there were seven priests. "Inventario y relación de los navíos . . . que lleva el Adelantado Pero

from Fort Caroline, whom the Cuban authorities had sent prisoners to Spain, as related in a previous chapter.[1]

So great was the demand for experienced mariners among the various fleets sailing for the Indies that only by paying much higher wages than they did was Avilés enabled to obtain his crews; and even then so inadequate was the supply of native sailors that he wrote Philip it would be necessary for him to be authorised to embark foreigners in his service.[2] Diego de Amaya, an experienced sailor, accompanied the fleet as "piloto mayor."[3]

A number of the relatives of Avilés joined the armada: among these were his brother, Bartolomé, who had already seen fifteen years' service in the royal navy[4]; Gonzalo de Solís de Merás, his brother-in-law, to whom we are indebted for the history of the Adelantado, to which reference has so frequently been made; Hernando de Miranda, who was married to Avilés's daughter, Doña Catalina[5]; and Pedro Menéndez de Valdez, a young man of twenty-five, relative of the Archbishop of Seville, and who was engaged to another of his daughters. So eager had

Menéndez de Avilés en su armada para la conquista y población de la Florida" . . . June 28, 1565, *ibid.*, tomo ii., p. 558. On p. 561 it says there were four priests. Merás says he was given four additional vessels and 500 additional men at the King's cost (*ibid.*, tomo i., p. 57), and (p. 52) that there were 2150 men in all, probably including Las Alas's fleet. Barcia, (*Ensayo*, Año MDLXV, p. 67), says the 500 additional men were not furnished him, although the King had ordered them to be sent. On p. 68 he says there were nineteen vessels and he gives the names of thirteen of them. This probably includes the fleet of Las Alas. Mendoza, in his "Relación" (in Ruidíaz, *ibid.*, tomo ii., p. 442), says there were ten vessels in the fleet with which Menéndez sailed from Cadiz.

[1] Avilés to Philip II., Sept. 11, 1565, Ruidíaz, *La Florida*, tomo ii., p. 75.

[2] Avilés to Philip II., May 18, 1565, *ibid.*, tomo ii., p. 64. He says that some were deterred because he was leaving for Florida so late, and in the hurricane season.

[3] Avilés to Philip II., May 18, 1565, *ibid.*, tomo ii., p. 65; Sept. 11, 1565 *ibid.*, p. 83.

[4] Avilés to Philip II., July 27, 1563, *ibid.*, tomo ii., p. 37.

[5] *Ibid.*, tomo i., p. ccxxvi.

Valdez been to accompany the expedition, that, against the desire of his prospective father-in-law, he hid himself aboard the fleet until after it had sailed.[1] Francisco López de Mendoza Grajalas, the author of another account of the voyage, went as chaplain of the fleet, and other gentlemen, drawn from the south, as well as from Galicia, Biscay, and his native Asturias, sailed with it.[2]

Some of his soldiers as well as his officers were men of experience, who had fought in the Italian wars, such, for example, as Pedro Menéndez Valdez, just mentioned, who had seen five or six years of service and had been raised in the galleys.[3] The asiento had authorised him to equip a second fleet in the Asturias. The man whom Menéndez had appointed to this command was Esteban de las Alas, from his native town of Avilés, and before setting sail Menéndez ordered him to join the armada at the Canaries with the ships at his disposition without touching at Cadiz.[4]

He set sail from Cadiz, June 29, 1565, but was compelled to put back into port by a violent tempest. While awaiting the return of fair weather, his fleet received several accessions, and finally he again set out on the 28th of July, reaching the Canaries without further adventure on the 5th of the ensuing month. He remained there three days awaiting the arrival of Esteban de las Alas from Gijon. On his failure to appear, Avilés left the islands on the 8th,[5] with the intention of going directly to Dominica;

[1] Avilés to Philip II., Sept. 11, 1565, *ibid.*, tomo ii., p. 82. Mendoza, "Relación" in *ibid.*, p. 462.

[2] Barrientos in García, *Dos Antiguas Relaciones de la Florida*, pp. 34, 35. Barcia, Año MDLXV., p. 69.

[3] Avilés to Philip II., Sept. 11, 1565, Ruidíaz, *La Florida*, tomo ii., p. 82.

[4] "Asiento," *ibid.*, tomo ii., pp. 416, 419; Barrientos in García, *Dos Antiguas Relaciones de la Florida*, pp. 34, 35; Vigil, *Noticias*, p. 120.

[5] Mendoza, "Relación," in Ruidíaz, *La Florida*, tomo ii., p. 431. Avilés to Philip II., Aug. 13, 1565, *ibid.*, p. 70; Barcia, *Ensayo*, Año MDLXV., p. 68; Barrientos, in García, *Dos Antiguas Relaciones de la Florida*, p. 34.

for the winter was now approaching, and although he had first planned to stop at Puerto Rico and Cuba for horses and more vessels, he feared that he could not draw from the islands sufficient supplies for so prolonged a campaign.[1] The night of his leaving the Canaries his flag-ship, the *San Pelayo*, and another vessel became separated from the remainder of the fleet, and Menéndez determined to continue his journey alone. Within three hundred and fifty leagues of Florida he was assailed by a violent storm, which carried away all of his masts and sails excepting the mainmast; and some of the artillery had to be thrown overboard to lighten the vessel. Being a seaworthy boat the *San Pelayo* weathered the gale, which lasted two nights and one day, but was compelled to put into Puerto Rico for repairs,[2] where Avilés arrived on the 8th of August.

The balance of the fleet had a no less trying experience. Thursday the 28th, arose a violent storm, accompanied by thunder and lightnings that "sought to eat us up alive" writes the chaplain. The seas swept entirely over the vessels, which had to be lightened, and Mendoza was all night long confessing and consoling his companions. The storm continued for three days. On Monday the 6th of August, the fleet anchored at Dominica, where the crew of the chaplain's ship captured an immense turtle, which it took five men to cut up.

With naïve and graphic egotism Mendoza wrote the King an account of his experiences during his stay at Dominica:

"I called an Italian lad of mine and ordered him to take half a dozen shirts that were soiled and other clothes, and I gave him a little piece of soap to wash them out on shore, which he did very well. While my boy remained behind with

[1] Barrientos in *ibid.*, pp. 35, 36.

[2] Avilés to Philip II., Aug. 13, 1565, Ruidíaz, *La Florida*, tomo ii., pp. 70, 71; Mendoza, "Relación" in *ibid.*, p. 436.

four other men washing their clothes, I took a walk in the direction of some rocks on the seashore, and amused myself gathering shellfish of which there was an abundance; raising my eyes, I saw three naked men coming down the side of a hill, and as I was in a land of enemies, I felt certain that they were Caribs; I took to my heels as fast as I could, and ran to my party, and made them all come out and take each half a dozen knives and we went to meet them. Drawing near to each other until we could talk, they called out that they were of our people, which was no small satisfaction to me by reason of the risk myself and the others might have run."

They proved to be the survivors of a party of five sailors who had swum ashore from the ships to see the land, two of whom had been drowned on the way. Having taken in wood and water, Mendoza and his company again set sail, and on Friday, July 10th, reached Puerto Rico, where they found the flag-ship and the other small vessel already in port.[1]

Avilés, fearful that reinforcements would arrive before him and strengthen the position of the French in Florida, bent all his energies to outsail them. His purpose was, if possible, to seize the island which the three French prisoners had told him lay at the mouth of the St. John's, possibly Fort George Island, and to fortify it so that Fort Caroline would be cut off from reinforcements by sea.[2] With this object in view he pressed his preparations forward as rapidly as possible. Hernando de Miranda was dispatched to Santo Domingo, where he was to collect the horses and the men, which the King had agreed to furnish, and take them to Havana, there to be joined by Esteban de las Alas, with his fleet, for whom he left the necessary directions in Puerto Rico.[3]

[1] Mendoza, " Relación" in Ruidíaz, *La Florida*, tomo ii., pp. 432–436.

[2] Avilés to Philip II., Aug. 13, 1565, *ibid.*, tomo ii., p. 72; Sept. 11, 1565, *ibid.*, tomo ii., p. 75.

[3] Barrientos in García, *Dos Antiguas Relaciones de la Florida*, p. 37.

He appointed Juan Ponce de Leon, the royal accountant, and governor of the fort at Puerto Rico, to be his lieutenant, as it was the place of rendezvous of all of the fleets and forces destined for Florida. He added another ship to his squadron, with fifty men and twenty horses, and the Governor gave him two barks, one of which he took with him to unload the larger vessels, and to replace the ship from Puerto Rico which was to be sent back. He used the other as a dispatch boat for Santo Domingo and Havana.[1]

"Over thirty men deserted and hid themselves in this town," writes Mendoza, "among which were three priests, for there were seven of us, and could not be found dead or alive, which my lord the General felt very greatly, and I no less, for it makes hard work for us. The fact is that they offered me in this port a chaplaincy with a dollar of alms for every mass said, which would not fail me the whole year round; I did not do it because I did not wish that to be said of me, which I hear said of others, and because it is a town where one cannot prosper very much, and in order to see if by continuing the journey Our Lord will not give me some advantage in exchange for my labour."[2]

So anxious was Menéndez to reach Florida in advance of the French, that he determined to start without awaiting the arrival of the balance of his Cadiz fleet which had not yet reached Puerto Rico, and on the 15th, he sailed with only five vessels, on the final stage of his journey, with eight hundred souls, five hundred of which were

[1] Avilés to Philip II., Aug. 13, 1565, Ruidíaz, *La Florida*, tomo ii., p. 73; Mendoza, "Relación" in *ibid.*, p. 438.

[2] Mendoza in *ibid.*, tomo ii., p. 437. Mendoza relates that a dispatch boat sent to Santo Domingo was captured while on the way by a French vessel, which, after taking its papers, dismissed it with the charge to inform the Spaniards that the French would be advised of their arrival before the Spaniards could get there; *ibid.*, p. 439. Mendoza thought it was a vessel of Ribaut's fleet, *ibid.*, p. 442, and Barcia also, *Ensayo*, Año MDLXV., p. 69.

soldiers, two hundred mariners and "the other hundred being of useless people," as he called them, "married men, women, children and officials."[1] Arrived off Santo Domingo August 17th, he called a council of his captains, informed them of his intention to proceed, and urged their acceptance of it in view of the favourable weather.[2] The council having agreed to it, the bows of the ships were turned to the north notwithstanding the timidity of the pilots in the dangerous passages amidst the reefs and shoals, and the seasickness of the crews in the rough waters of the Gulf Stream.[3]

During the passage the various officers were named, the weapons were put in order and distributed, the soldiers practised daily in shooting at a mark for a prize, and the Christian doctrine and litanies were recited with prayers and supplications to the Lord for victory.[4] While in the Bahama Channel a happy omen was seen in the shape of a brilliant meteor.[5] Just before making land a general rejoicing was held aboard the fleet, flags were unfurled, drums were beaten, guns were fired, and a double ration was served out.[6] On Sunday, August 25th,[7]

[1] Mendoza, "Relación" in Ruidíaz, *La Florida*, tomo ii., p. 447; Avilés to Philip II., Sept. 11, 1565, *ibid.*, tomo ii., p. 75. Deposition of Grauiel de Riuera in "Información de algunos seruicios," etc., in *ibid.*, tomo ii., p. 306; Barrientos in García, *Dos Antiguas Relaciones de la Florida*, pp. 36, 37.

[2] Mendoza ("Relación" in Ruidíaz, *La Florida*, tomo ii., pp. 442, 443) thought that Ribaut was perhaps lying in wait for Menéndez on the way to Havana and that this change of course to Florida was taken in order to avoid him.

[3] Mendoza, "Relación," in *ibid.*, tomo ii., pp. 439–446.

[4] Merás in *ibid.*, tomo i., p. 69.

[5] Mendoza, "Relación" in *ibid.*, tomo ii., p. 445.

[6] Barrientos in García, *Dos Antiguas Relaciones de la Florida*, pp. 37–39.

[7] Avilés to Philip II., Sept. 11, 1565, Ruidíaz, *La Florida*, tomo ii., p. 75. Mendoza, "Relación" in *ibid.*, tomo ii., pp. 445–447, says Aug. 28th, and that the landfall was near the mouth of the St. John's. Merás in *ibid.*, tomo i., p. 69, also says Aug. 28th, and that the landfall was near St. Augustine.

the peninsula was made off Cape Canaveral, and four days were spent sailing along the coast in search of the French port. Failing to discover it, Menéndez at last sent ashore to learn of the Indians where it lay, and was informed by signs that it was twenty leagues to the north. Coasting along eight leagues farther Menéndez came upon the harbour of the River of Dolphins, previously visited by Laudonnière, into which he entered and gave it the name of St. Augustine, having discovered it on the festival of that saint, the 28th of August, and here the fleet remained for several days.[1]

[1] Barrientos in García, *Dos Antiguas Relaciones de la Florida*, pp. 39, 40; Avilés to Philip II., Sept. 11, 1565, Ruidíaz, *La Florida* tomo ii., pp. 75–77; Merás in *ibid.*, tomo i., pp. 69–72.

CHAPTER IX

THE CAPTURE OF FORT CAROLINE

ON Tuesday, September 4th,[1] Menéndez set sail from the harbour of St. Augustine and, coasting north, at two o'clock in the afternoon came upon four vessels lying at anchor off the mouth of a river. These were the *Trinity* and three other of Ribaut's ships, which he had left at the mouth of the St. John's because they were too large to pass the bars in safety. One of them was flying the Admiral's flag, another the flag of the Captain.[2] Menéndez recognised at once that the French reinforcements had arrived before him, and called a council of his captains to consider what action should be taken. In the opinion of the council it was deemed advisable to return to Santo Domingo, there to await the balance of the fleet, which had been dispersed by the tempest, and the arrival of the reinforcements under Esteban de las Alas, to winter in Havana, and to return to Florida in March of the following year. But Menéndez was of another way of

[1] Both Avilés (letter to Philip II., Sept. 11, 1565, Ruidíaz, *La Florida*, tomo ii., p. 76) and Laudonnière (*Hist. Notable*, Basanier, p. 104; *Hak.*, vol. ii., p. 514), give the date September 4th. Mendoza ("Relación" in Ruidíaz, *ibid.*, tomo ii., p. 447) says Wednesday, September 5th, and Le Challeux ("Hist. Mémorable" in *Recueil de Pièces sur la Floride*, p. 265) says Monday, September 3rd. Le Moyne, Merás, and Barrientos do not mention any date.

[2] Avilés to Philip II., September 11, 1565, Ruidíaz, *La Florida*, tomo ii., p. 76; Mendoza, "Relación" in *ibid.*, p. 447.

thinking. His presence was already known to the enemy, four of his ships were so crippled by the gale that they could not make good time, and he feared that if the French should undertake to chase his fleet, they could outsail it. He concluded that it was better to attack at once, and, having beaten them, to return to St. Augustine and await reinforcements. His advice prevailed, so the Spaniards proceeded on their way. When within half a league of the French a thunder-storm passed over them, followed by a calm, and they were compelled to lie still until ten o'clock in the evening, when a land breeze sprang up, and they again got under way. Menéndez had given orders to approach the French ships bow to bow, and then to wait and board them at daybreak, for he feared they would fire their own vessels and thus endanger his, and would then escape to land in their row-boats.[1]

The Frenchmen soon perceived their approach and began firing at them, but their aim was directed too high, and the shot passed harmlessly between the masts without doing any damage.[2] Regardless of the firing and without vouchsafing any reply Menéndez kept on his course until, passing right in their midst, he drew up the bow of the *San Pelayo* between that of the *Trinity* and another of the enemy's ships. Then he sounded a salute on his trumpets and the French replied. When this was over Menéndez asked, "very courteously," "Gentlemen, from where does this fleet come?" "From France," answered a voice from the *Trinity*. "What are you doing here?" "Bringing infantry, artillery, and supplies

[1] Barrientos in García, *Dos Antiguas Relaciones de la Florida*, pp. 41–44; Merás in Ruidíaz, *La Florida*, tomo i., pp. 72–74; Avilés to Philip II., Sept. 11, 1565, *ibid.*, tomo ii., p. 76.

[2] Barrientos in García, *Dos Antiguas Relaciones de la Florida*, p. 45; Merás in Ruidíaz, *La Florida*, tomo i., p. 75. Mr. Parkman in his *Pioneers of France in the New World*, Boston, 1893, p. 112, note, discredits the statement that the French opened fire on the Spaniards as they approached.

for a fort which the King of France has in this country, and for others which he is going to make." "Are you Catholics or Lutherans?" he asked next. "Lutherans, and our General is Jean Ribaut," came the response. Then the French in turn addressed the same questions to the Spaniards, to which Menéndez himself replied: "I am the General; my name is Pedro Menéndez de Avilés. This is the armada of the King of Spain, who has sent me to this coast and country to burn and hang the Lutheran French who should be found there, and in the morning I will board your ships; and if I find any Catholics they will be well treated."[1] In the dead silence which prevailed while the parley was in progress, "a stillness such as I never heard since I came to the world," writes the Spanish chaplain, those aboard his ship heard a boat put out from one of the Frenchmen, carrying a message to their flag-ship and the reply of the French commander, "I am the Admiral, I will die first," from which they inferred that it was a proposition to surrender. When the conversation was ended there followed an exchange of abuse and foul words, until Avilés, exasperated and unable to restrain his impatience, ordered his crew to draw their swords and to pay out the cable so as to board at once. The sailors showed some hesitation, and Menéndez sprang down from the bridge to urge them on and found that the cable was caught in the capstan, which caused some delay. But the Frenchmen had also heard the signal and, taking advantage of the momentary pause, cut their cables, passed right through the Spanish fleet, and fled, three vessels turning to the north and the other to the south, with the Spaniards in hot pursuit. Menéndez with two of his ships took the northerly course, but the three

[1] Avilés to Philip II., Sept. 11, 1565, Ruidíaz, *La Florida*, tomo ii., p. 67; Mendoza, "Relación" in *ibid.*, p. 448; Merás in *ibid.*, tomo i., pp. 76, 77; Barrientos in García, *Dos Antiguas Relaciones de la Florida*, pp. 44, 45.

French galleons outsailed him, and at dawn he gave up the chase, and, returning to the mouth of the St. John's with the intention of pursuing his original plan of seizing and fortifying it, reached it at ten o'clock in the morning. On attempting its entrance he discovered three ships up the river and at the point of the land two companies of infantry, who brought their artillery to bear upon him. So he abandoned the attempt to capture the entrance and made for St. Augustine.[1]

The three Spanish vessels which took the southerly course in pursuit of the remaining French ship continued all night. Menéndez had ordered them to rejoin him at the mouth of the St. John's in the morning, and, if unable to do so, to return to St. Augustine. But a storm arose and they were obliged to cast anchor off the coast, the vessels being so small they did not dare to take to the sea. One of the three broke away, and while in this peril a French ship was sighted and they were in terror of being boarded; but she did not attack them, although she hove to within a league. The following day, Thursday, September 6th, after sighting a second French vessel they made for a harbour near at hand, which proved to be that of St. Augustine, and on landing found that the other two vessels had preceded them, having also arrived the same day (September 6th). The harbour was near the village of an Indian chief named Seloy, who received them with much kindness. The Spaniards at once went to work to fortify a large Indian dwelling, probably a communal house of the natives, which lay near the water's edge. They dug a ditch around it and threw up a breastwork of earth and fagots, "these two good captains of ours,"

[1] *Histoire Notable*, Basanier, pp. 104, 105; *Hak.*, vol. ii., p. 514; Le Challeux, reprint in Gaffarel, *Hist. de la Floride Française*, p. 463; Barrientos in García, *Dos Antiguas Relaciones de la Florida*, pp. 45, 46; Merás in Ruidíaz, *La Florida*, tomo i., pp. 78, 79; Aviles to Philip II., Sept. 11, 1565, *ibid.*, tomo ii., p. 77.

Patiño and San Vincente, "working with such industry, that with only the nails of their soldiers, and without other tools, they made a fort for their defence," says Mendoza.[1] And this was the birth of St. Augustine, the oldest city in the United States. Its ancient site can no longer be determined, but it is known to have been such that it did not command the entrance to the harbour, could not be discovered from the sea, and was much exposed to the attacks of the Indians. When, in May of the following year, the settlement was moved to a more advantageous position, the first location received the name of Old St. Augustine from the Spaniards.[2]

Avilés at once began disembarking his troops, landing two hundred of them. On Friday, the 7th, he sent his three smaller ships into the harbour, and three hundred more colonists were landed, along with the married men, their wives, and children, and most of the artillery and

[1] Mendoza, "Relación" in *ibid.*, tomo ii., pp. 449–451; Avilés to Philip II., Sept. 11, 1565, *ibid.*, p. 81; "Información de algunos servicios prestados por el Adelantado Pedro Menéndez de Avilés, México, 3 de Abril de 1595," in *ibid.*, p. 615.

[2] Barrientos in García, *Dos Antiguas Relaciones de la Florida*, pp. 114, 141; Juan López de Velasco in his *Geografía de las Indias, 1571–1574*, Madrid, 1894, p. 160, says of St. Augustine, "fundóle primero en el cabo de una isla de media legua de ancho y cinco de largo; y pasóse el año de 72 á la parte de Tierrafirme," etc. This corresponds substantially to Anastasia Island or perhaps the second site of the fort on the promontory formed by the sea and North River to the north of the island, for "isla" does not necessarily mean an island. In the anonymous "Discurso sobre la población de la costa de la Florida é inconvenientes que se ofrecieren para su fortificación é defensa" (MS. Direc. de Hidrog., Madrid, *Col. Navarrete*, tomo xiv., Doc. No. 47, 1577–1580), it is said "Sancto Agustin donde primero estubo el Fuerte y gente, es una Islilla pequeña, y Sancto Agustin donde agora está el Fuerte y gente es otra que está junto á la primera, donde solia estar primero el Fuerte, y esta dende agora está es casi Isla," etc. (see note p. 252, in this volume). Fairbanks, who was not aware of these changes of the site of the settlement, says, in his *History of Florida* (Philadelphia, 1871, p. 133,) "The old town of St. Augustine is built upon the precise point that was occupied by Menéndez."

ammunition.[1] On Saturday, Lady's day, September 8th, the balance of the colonists, one hundred in number, and supplies were put ashore. Then the General himself landed amidst the waving of flags, the sounding of trumpets and of other instruments of war, and the salutes of the artillery. The chaplain, Mendoza, who had gone ashore the previous day, advanced to meet him, chanting the *Te Deum Laudamus* and carrying a cross which Avilés and those with him reverently kissed, falling upon their knees. Then Menéndez took possession in the King's name.[2] The mass of Our Lady was solemnly chanted, and the oath was administered to the various officials in the presence of a large concourse of friendly Indians who imitated all of the postures of the Spaniards. Gonzalo de Villarroel was appointed adjutant, and ten captains were also named. With an eye to the growth of the colony the offices of Royal Accountant, Factor, and Treasurer were assigned to Esteban de las Alas, Pedro Menéndez Marqués, nephew of the Adelantado, and Hernando de Miranda. "For many years they have served under me," wrote Avilés to the King, "and since all three are married to women of rank it may be that on account of their offices and through love for me they may bring their wives and households, which may draw other married people. For it is a good plan to begin to settle these Florida provinces with people of rank."[3] The ceremony was concluded by the serving out of food to colonists and Indians alike. The negro slaves were quartered in the huts of the Indian village and the work on the defences was proceeded with. While this was in progress, two of Ribaut's ships, which the Spaniards had

[1] Avilés to Philip II., Sept. 11, 1565, Ruidíaz, *La Florida*, tomo ii., pp. 71, 81.

[2] Mendoza, "Relacion" in *ibid.*, tomo ii., p. 451.

[3] Avilés to Philip II., Sept. 11, 1565, *ibid.*, tomo ii., p. 82; Dec. 5, 1565, *ibid.*, tomo ii., p. 124.

chased on the night of September 4th, made a demonstration at the mouth of the harbour, offering combat to the *San Pelayo* and the *San Salvador*, which were unable to cross the bar on account of their size, and lay outside in a very exposed situation. But the challenge was not accepted, and after watching from a distance the landing of the troops, the Frenchmen sailed away the same afternoon, and returned to the mouth of the St. John's.[1]

Menéndez was in great fear lest Ribaut should return, attack his fleet while he was unloading, and perhaps capture the *San Pelayo*, which carried the major part of his supplies and ammunition; and he was also most anxious to send two of his sloops back to Havana for reinforcements. For these reasons the unloading was pushed rapidly forward. In the meantime he strengthened his position, and sought what information he could obtain of the situation of the French fort from the Indians. They told him that it could be reached from the head of the harbour of St. Augustine, without going by sea, indicating probably a way by North River and Pablo Creek.

On September 11th Avilés wrote from St. Augustine his report to the King of the progress of the expedition. In this first letter from the soil of Florida, Menéndez exhibited the sound judgment which characterised him, the result of a wide observation and experience, by seeking to provide against those difficulties which had proved the chief obstacle in the path of both the French and Spanish colonies before him.

"It will be desirable that Your Majesty give orders, that I be provided with a year's supply of corn for each horse which I shall bring to these provinces. . . . And for the future, in the course of a year I will give orders to sow and plant corn

[1] Aviles to Philip II., Sept. 11, 1565, *ibid.*, tomo ii., pp. 77, 78; Merás in *ibid.*, tomo ii., pp. 79, 80; *Histoire Notable*, Basanier, pp. 105, 106; *Hak.*, vol. ii., pp. 514, 515.

so that they shall have provender here; for by no means would it do to take it from the Indians, in order not to make enemies of them; on the contrary, it will be advisable for us to feed those who have none, in order to win their love and friendship. Let Your Majesty rest assured," he continues, "that if I had a million more or less, I would spend it all upon this undertaking, because it is of such great service to God Our Lord, and for the increase of our Holy Catholic Faith and the service of Your Majesty. And therefore I have offered to Our Lord, that all that I shall find, win, and acquire, in this world shall be for the planting of the Gospel in this land, and the enlightenment of its natives, and thus I pledge myself to Your Majesty."[1]

Every age and every nation has had its euphemism for conquest and aggrandisement, whether it be the service of God and the spiritual welfare of the conquered, or the interests of civilisation and the material advancement of the race. It becomes the Court jargon, the caption of bulls and encyclicals, the stock-in-trade of edicts and proclamations, until by force of repetition it rings true even to those who coin it. How far Menéndez was amenable to this fashionable insincerity it is difficult to judge. But it is worthy to remark that when in the course of subsequent events his mercy was appealed to for the rescue of the French prisoners who fell into his hands, it was extended to drummers, fifers, and trumpeters, and that it was only at the intercession of the priest that it embraced his co-religionists.[2]

[1] Avilés to Philip II., Sept. 11, 1565, Ruidíaz, *La Florida*, tomo ii., pp. 80, 83.

[2] Avilés to Philip II., Sept. 11, 1565, *ibid.*, tomo ii., pp. 89, 103; Mendoza, "Relación" in *ibid.*, tomo ii., pp. 464, 465; Merás in *ibid.*, tomo i., pp. 116, 126; Barrientos in García, *Dos Antiguas Relaciones de la Florida*, pp. 66, 69; Relation of the Dieppe sailor in De Bry, *Brevis Narratio*, p. 29, quoted p. 203, in this volume; Fourquevaux to Charles IX., Feb. 23, 1566, *Dépêches*, p. 62.

In two days the ships were for the most part unloaded, yet so convinced was Menéndez that Ribaut would return as promptly as possible that the *San Pelayo* did not wait to discharge her entire cargo, but set sail for Hispaniola at midnight, September 10th, with the *San Salvador*, which was carrying the General's dispatches.[1] The *San Pelayo* took with her some interesting passengers. On leaving Cadiz Avilés had been informed by the Seville Inquisition that there were "Lutherans" in his fleet, and, having made a perquisition, he discovered and seized twenty-five of them, whom he dispatched in the two vessels to Santo Domingo or Puerto Rico, to be returned to Spain. Through one of those singular coincidences by which earthly events sometimes compensate each other, it so happened that at the very time Avilés was killing "Lutherans" in Florida, the "Lutherans" aboard the *San Pelayo*, convinced of the fate which awaited them in Seville, rose against their captors. With an equanimity equal to that of Menéndez himself, they killed the captain, master, and all the Catholics aboard, and made their way past Spain, France, and Flanders, to the coast of Denmark, where the *San Pelayo* was wrecked and the heretics appear finally to have escaped.[2] Menéndez also sent two sloops to Havana for the reinforcements expected to arrive with Esteban de las Alas, and for horses. Upon the latter he especially counted in his campaign

[1] Barrientos in García, *Dos Antiguas Relaciones de la Florida*, pp. 46, 47; Merás in Ruidíaz, *La Florida*, tomo i., p. 80; Avilés to Philip II., Oct. 15, 1565, *ibid.*, tomo ii., p. 84; Vasalenque in "Información de algunos servicios," etc., in *ibid.*, tomo ii., p. 615, says the *San Pelayo* was sent to Havana.

[2] Barrientos in García, *Dos Antiguas Relaciones de la Florida*, p. 47; Barcia (*Ensayo*, Año MDCLXV., pp. 77, 84, 85), says (p. 77) that there were only 15 of them. Seville was not only the rendezvous of many "Lutherans" from abroad, but a Protestant community had existed there for some time. See *Beitrage zur Geschichte des Spanischen Protestantismus und der Inquisition im sechzehnten Jahrhundert* von Dr. Ernst Schäfer, Gütersloh, 1902, vol. i., p. 345, "Die Gemeinde zu Sevilla."

against the French, as he had lost all but one of those he had shipped in Puerto Rico.

Meanwhile the French at Fort Caroline had remained without news of the outcome of the attack. But on the reappearance of two of his vessels at the mouth of the St. John's, Ribaut went down the river to learn what had happened. He met on his way out a boat-load of men returning from one of the ships, who told him of their encounter with the Spaniards, and informed him that they had seen three of the enemy's ships in the River of Dolphins and two more in the roads, where the Spaniards had disembarked and were fortifying their position.[1] Ribaut returned at once to the fort and, entering the chamber of Laudonnière, who lay there sick with the anxiety brought on by the news of his disgrace, proposed in his presence and that of the assembled captains and other gentlemen, to embark at once with all of his forces in the four ships which lay in the harbour, for the *Trinity* had not yet returned, and to seek the Spanish fleet. Laudonnière, who was familiar with the sudden storms to which the region was subject during September, disapproved of his plan, pointing out the danger to which the French ships would be exposed of being driven out to sea, and the defenceless condition in which Fort Caroline would be left. The captains, who had received from a neighbouring chief the confirmation of the landing of the Spaniards and of the defences which they were erecting, also advised against Ribaut's plan, and counselled him at least to await the return of the *Trinity* before putting it into execution. But Ribaut obstinately persisted in his design, showed the unwilling Laudonnière

[1] *Histoire Notable*, Basanier, pp. 105, 106; *Hak.*, vol. ii., pp. 514, 515; Le Moyne says all four French ships returned the following morning, and a sailor swam ashore with a letter from Captain Cossette informing Laudonnière that it was a Spanish fleet, and giving a brief account of the escape of the French, and of the Spanish landing at St. Augustine (De Bry, *Brevis Narratio*, pp. 22, 23).

Coligny's instructions, and proceeded to carry it into effect. Not only did he take all of his own men with him, but carried off thirty-eight of the garrison and Laudonnière's ensign, leaving behind him M. du Lys with the sick and disheartened lieutenant in charge of the depleted garrison.[1] September 8th, the very day that Menéndez was taking solemn possession of Florida in the name of Philip, he embarked aboard his fleet, but waited two days in the harbour until he had prevailed upon Captain La Grange to accompany him, although La Grange was so distrustful of the enterprise that he wished to remain with Laudonnière. September 10th, Ribaut sailed away.

It was said that on the departure of the fleet a carousal was held on board the vessels, in which Ribaut and his captains drank two whole pipes of wine in mock healths to the Spaniards. "I drink to the head of Pedro Menéndez and those with him," cried one. "Cursed Spaniards! we will hang them from the yard arms of their own ships as well as from ours, so that they will not come again to smell out this country of ours!" cried another in a way most displeasing to those of the nobler sort among the Frenchmen.[2]

If we are to trust to the muster-roll of the dispirited Laudonnière, the garrison which Ribaut left behind him to defend Fort Caroline was ill-fitted to resist an attack of the well-fed and well-disciplined Spanish soldiery. Here it is in Laudonnière's own words:

[Of Captain Ribaut's company] "I found nine or tenne whereof not past two or three had euer drawen sword out of

[1] *Histoire Notable*, Basanier, pp. 106, 107; *Hak.*, vol. ii., pp. 515, 516; De Bry, *Brevis Narratio*, pp. 23, 24.

[2] Barrientos in García, *Dos Antiguas Relaciones de la Florida*, p. 72; Merás in Ruidíaz, *La Florida*, tomo i., p. 128. Merás says the incident was learned from the French women and children captured at Fort Caroline. The toast began with "Marranos Españoles," literally, "Spaniards of Jewish blood but professing Christianity."

the scabbard; as I thinke. . . . Of the nine there were foure but yong striplings, which serued Captain Ribault and kept his dogs, the fift was [his] cooke; among those that were without the fort . . . there was a Carpenter of threescore yeeres olde, one a Beere-brewer, one olde Crosse-bowe maker, two Shoomakers, and foure or fiue men that had their wiues, a player on the [spinet], two seruants of Monsieur de Lys, one of Monsieur de Beauhaire, one of Monsieur de la Grange, and about fourescore and fiue or sixe in all, counting aswel Lackeys as women and children. . . . Those that were left me of mine owne company were about sixteene or seuenteene that coulde beare armes, and all of them poore and leane; the rest were sicke and maymed in the conflict which my Lieutenant had against Vtina." [1]

The total number of colonists remaining in the fort was about two hundred and forty.[2]

Three days passed without any news of Ribaut, and with each departing day the anxiety of the sick Laudonnière grew upon him. Knowing the proximity of the Spaniards, and dreading lest they should make a sudden descent upon him, he resolved to make what shift he could for his own defence. Although food was again at a low ebb, for Ribaut had carried off two of his boats with the meal which had been left over after making the biscuit for the return to France, and although Laudonnière himself was reduced to the rations of a common soldier, he yet commanded the allowance to be increased in order to inspirit his men. He also set to work to re-

[1] *Histoire Notable*, Basanier. p. 108; *Hak.*, vol. ii., p. 518. Parkman in his *Pioneers of France in the New World*, Boston, 1893, p. 117, note 1, states that Hakluyt's translation is incorrect. The bracketed words are those which occur in the original French text, incorrectly translated by Hakluyt.

[2] Le Challeux in "Histoire Mémorable," reprint in Gaffarel, *Histoire de la Floride Française*, p. 465; Le Moyne in De Bry, *Brevis Narratio*, p. 24, says that about 150 persons remained in the fort, of whom scarcely 20 were in a serviceable condition.

pair the palisade which had been torn down to supply material for the ships, but continued storms hindered the work, which was never completed. Two watches were set to relieve each other, and two officers, Monsieur Saint Cler and Monsieur de la Vigne, were named to go the rounds at night and inspect them, for which purpose they were each provided with a lantern on account of the stormy and foggy weather, and a sand-glass to measure the time for the sentinels. And so in weary watching and waiting, in rain and discomfort, in uncertainty and anxiety,—for no news had yet come from Ribaut,—ten days sped by.[1]

Ribaut made at once for St. Augustine[2] with two hundred sailors and four hundred soldiers, which included the flower of the garrison at Fort Caroline. At dawn the next day he came upon Menéndez in the very act of attempting to pass the bar and to land a sloop and two boats filled with men and artillery from the *San Salvador* which had sailed at midnight with the *San Pelayo*. The tide was out and his boats so loaded that only by a miracle was he enabled to cross it with his sloop, and escape; for the French, who had at once attempted to prevent his landing and thus to capture his cannon and the supplies he had on board, got so close to him, that they hailed him, and summoned him to surrender, promising that no harm should befall him. As soon as Ribaut perceived that the boats had gotten out of his reach, he gave up the attempt and started in pursuit of the *San Salvador*, which was already six or eight leagues away.[3]

Two days later, in confirmation of Laudonnière's forebodings, so violent a "norther" arose that the Indians

[1] *Histoire Notable*, Basanier, pp. 107–109; *Hak.*, vol. ii., pp. 517, 518.

[2] Avilés to Philip II., Oct. 15, 1565, Ruidíaz, *La Florida*, tomo ii., p. 88.

[3] Mendoza, "Relación" in *ibid.*, tomo ii., pp. 452, 453; Avilés to Philip II., Oct. 15, 1565, *ibid.*, p. 85; Merás in *ibid.*, tomo i., pp. 80, 81.

themselves declared it to be the worst they had ever seen on the coast.[1] Menéndez at once realised that the proper moment had presented itself for an attack upon the fort. Calling his captains together, the mass of the Holy Ghost was said to bring him enlightenment in forming his plans, and then he addressed them:

"We bear upon our shoulders a very heavy charge, full of labour and danger, and were it only in the service of our lord the King, I should not wonder at some cowardly weakness and faint-heartedness on our part in meeting the hardships that come upon us; but the charge which we bear is of the Lord Our God and of our King, and miserable must he be counted who in such a case would show weakness and fail to encourage those under him, . . . for in this we serve God and our King, and the guerdon of heaven cannot fail us."

He then set before them the advantage which the moment presented for an attack upon Fort Caroline, with its defences weakened by the absence of Ribaut who might have taken the best part of its garrison with him, and Ribaut's inability to return against the contrary wind, which in his judgment would continue for some days. His plan was to reach the fort through the forest and to attack it. If his approach was discovered, he proposed, on reaching the margin of the woods which surrounded the open meadow where it stood, to display the banners in such wise as to lead the French into the

[1] Avilés, in his letter of Oct. 15, 1565 (*ibid.*, tomo ii., p. 85), says the storm came on two days after the French fleet had left. Barrientos (in *Dos Antiguas Relaciones de la Florida*, p. 48) and Merás (in Ruidíaz, tomo i., p. 81), both call it a norther, and they as well as Mendoza (*ibid.*, tomo ii., p. 453) observe that it followed the French attack. Laudonnière (*Histoire Notable*, Basanier, p. 107; *Hak.*, vol. ii., p. 517) says the storm began on the same day that Ribaut set sail. It is highly improbable that Ribaut would have attempted this attack on the shallow and dangerous Florida coast in the midst of a storm. There was probably a succession of storms.

belief that he was two thousand strong. A trumpeter should then be sent to summon them to surrender, in which case the garrison should be sent back to France, and, if they did not, put to the knife. In the event of failure the Spaniards would have become acquainted with the way, and could await at St. Augustine the arrival of reinforcements in March.[1]

Although his plan failed to meet with general approval at first, it was finally agreed upon[2]; but on the following day, finding that the soldiers and the women had gotten wind of it, and that some dissatisfaction was beginning to show itself, Avilés quietly summoned to dine with him certain of the captains who had informed him of the discontent and had urged him to change his plan. After chiding them for their indiscretion, he advised silence on such matters in the future, "as he would punish a venal sin in such a case as if it were mortal," and he added that, although he gave them leave to express their opinions in council, he would "chastise the captain who murmured after a decision was reached by depriving him of his command and excluding him from the council." And so it came about that Avilés, who in the words of his chaplain, "was a great friend of his own opinion," was able to write to the King in his letter of October 15th, that his captains had approved his plan.[3]

Menéndez's preparations were made promptly; he placed his brother Bartolomé in charge of the fort at St. Augustine, in case of the return of the French fleet. He then selected a company of five hundred men, three hundred of whom were arquebusmen and the remainder

[1] Barrientos in García, *Dos Antiguas Relaciones de la Florida*, pp. 48–51; Merás in Ruidíaz, *La Florida*, tomo i., pp. 82–85.

[2] Merás in *ibid.*, tomo i., p. 85; Mendoza, "Relación" in *ibid.*, tomo ii., p. 454. Avilés says briefly in his letter to Philip that all agreed to it (letter, Oct. 15, 1565, *ibid.*, p. 85).

[3] Ruidíaz, *La Florida*, tomo ii., p. 85; Merás in *ibid.*, tomo i., pp. 85–88; Barrientos in García, *Dos Antiguas Relaciones de la Florida*, pp. 51, 52.

pikesmen and targeteers. On September 16th[1] the force assembled at the call of trumpets, drums, fifes, and the ringing of the bells. After hearing mass, it set out, each man carrying on his back his arms, a bottle of wine, and six pounds of biscuit, in which Menéndez himself set the example, for the servants were left at St. Augustine.[2] Two Indian chiefs, whose hostility the French had incurred, and who had visited Fort Caroline six days before, accompanied the party to show the way, "angels sent by God," observes Merás,[3] and Jean François, one of the three French prisoners.[4] A picked company of twenty Asturians and Basques under their captain, Martin de Ochoa, led the way armed with axes with which they blazed a path through the forest and swamps for the men behind them, and Menéndez carried a compass with which to assist in finding the direction, for it was completely unknown to him.[5]

The point of land on which Fort Caroline was situated is separated from the seacoast by an extensive swamp through which flows the Pablo Creek, which rises but a short distance from the head of North River. Around this it was necessary for the Spaniards to go, for owing

[1] Mendoza ("Relación" in Ruidíaz, *La Florida*, tomo ii., pp. 454, 458), says September 16th, and Merás (in *ibid.*, tomo i., p. 89), says they were four days on the way, which would also bring the start on the 16th. Avilés does not give the date of departure, but speaks of a storm on the 18th (letter to Philip II., Oct. 15, 1565, *ibid.*, tomo ii., p. 86). It is, however, to be noted that the punctuation of this paragraph in the letter is in all probability that of the editor.

[2] Avilés to Philip II., Oct. 15, 1565, *ibid.*, tomo ii., p. 85.

[3] Merás in *ibid.*, tomo i., p. 89; Mendoza, "Relación" in *ibid.*, tomo ii., p. 454; Barrientos in García, *Dos Antiguas Relaciones de la Florida*, p. 52.

[4] *Histoire Notable*, Basanier, p. 110; *Hak.*, vol. ii., p. 519; Merás in Ruidíaz, *La Florida*, tomo i., p. 84.

[5] Noriega had enquired of Meleneche, one of the three Frenchmen sent to Seville, how Fort Caroline could be reached by land, and the Frenchman had described an approach from the St. John's River (Noriega to Philip II., March 29, 1565, MS. Direc. de Hidrog., Madrid, *Col. Navarrete*, tomo xiv., doc. 33, fol. 6).

to the continued rains all of the creeks and rivers were full and the lowlands flooded. At no time was the water lower than up to their knees. No boats were taken along, so the soldiers swam the various creeks and streams, Avilés taking the lead with a pike in his hand at the very first one they encountered. Those who could not swim were carried across on the pikes. It was extremely fatiguing work, "for the rains continued as constant and heavy as if the world was again to be overwhelmed with a flood."[1] Their clothes became soaked and heavy with water, their food as well, the powder wet, and the cords of the arquebuses worthless, and some of the men began to grumble, but Menéndez pretended not to hear. The vanguard selected the place for the night encampment, but it was difficult to find high ground on account of the flood. During the halts a fire was built, but when within a day's march of Fort Caroline, even this was forbidden, lest it betray their approach to the enemy.[2]

Thus the Spaniards pushed on for two days through wood and thicket, river and marsh, with not even a trail to follow. On the evening of the third day, September 19th, Menéndez reached the neighbourhood of the fort. The night was so stormy and the rain fell so heavily, that he thought he could approach it without being discovered, and he encamped for the night in the pine grove on the edge of the meadow within less than a quarter of a league from it. The spot he had chosen was marshy and comfortless; in places the water stood up to the belts of the soldiers, and no fire could be lighted for fear of revealing their presence to the French.[3]

[1] De Bry, *Brevis Narratio*, p. 24.

[2] Barrientos in García, *Dos Antiguas Relaciones de la Florida*. pp. 52, 53; Merás in Ruidíaz, *La Florida*, tomo i., pp. 89, 90; Mendoza, "Relación" in *ibid.*, tomo ii., pp. 454, 458, 459.

[3] Barrientos in García, *Dos Antiguas Relaciones de la Florida*, pp. 53, 54; Merás in Ruidíaz, *La Florida*, tomo i., pp. 89, 90; "Información de algunos servicios," etc., in *ibid.*, tomo ii., p. 615.

Inside Fort Caroline La Vigne was keeping watch with his company, but his sentinels, wet and worn with the heavy rain, so moved his heart to pity, that with the approach of day he let them depart, and finally went himself to his own lodging.[1]

With the break of day, September 20th, the feast of St. Matthew, Menéndez was already alert. Before dawn he held a consultation with his captains, after which the entire party knelt down and prayed for a victory over their enemies. Then he set out for the fort over the narrow path which led to it from the woods. The French prisoner, Jean François, led the way, his hands bound behind him, and the end of the rope held by Menéndez himself. So intense was the darkness that the Spaniards soon lost the path in crossing a marsh with water up to their knees, and were compelled to wait until daybreak in order to find the way again. When morning came, Menéndez set out in the direction of the fort, and on reaching a slight elevation Jean announced that Fort Caroline lay just beyond, down on the river's edge. Then the camp master, Pedro Menéndez Valdez and the Asturian, Ochoa, went forward to reconnoitre. They were hailed by a man they took to be a sentinel. "Who goes there?" he cried. "Frenchmen," they answered, and, closing with him, Ochoa struck him in the face with his knife, which he had not even unsheathed. The Frenchman warded off the blow with his sword, but in stepping back to avoid a thrust from Valdez he tripped, fell backwards, and began shouting. Then Ochoa stabbed him and killed him. Menéndez, hearing the shouting, thought that Valdez and Ochoa were being slain, and cried out "Santiago, at them! God help us! Victory! the French are killed! The camp master is inside the fort and has taken it," and the entire force rushed down the

[1] *Histoire Notable*, Basanier, p. 109; *Hak.*, vol. ii., p. 519.

path. On the way two Frenchmen whom they met were killed.[1]

Some of the Frenchmen living in the outhouses set up a shout on seeing two of their number killed, at which a man within the fort opened the wicket of the main entrance to admit the fugitives. The camp master closed with him and killed him, and the Spaniards poured into the enclosure.[2] Laudonnière's trumpeter had just mounted the rampart, and seeing the Spaniards coming towards him sounded the alarm. The French,—most of whom were still asleep in their beds,—taken entirely by surprise, came running out of their quarters into the driving rain, some half-dressed, others quite naked, or clad only in their night-shirts. Among the first was Laudonnière, who rushed out of his house in his shirt,[3] his sword and target in his hands, and began to call his soldiers together. But the enemy had been too quick for them, and the wet and muddy court was soon reeking with the blood of the French, cut down by the Spanish soldiers, who now filled it. At Laudonnière's call, some of his men had hastened to the breach on the south side, where lay the ammunition and the artillery. But they were met by a party of Spaniards who repulsed and killed them, and who finally raised their standards in triumph upon the walls. Another party of Spaniards entered by a similar breach on the west, overwhelming the soldiers who attempted to resist them there, and also planted their ensigns on the rampart.[4]

Le Challeux, the old carpenter, had just left his cabin on his way to his work with his chisel in his hand, when

[1] Barrientos in García, *Dos Antiguas Relaciones de la Florida*, pp. 53–55; Merás in Ruidíaz, *La Florida*, tomo ii., pp. 93–96.

[2] Barrientos in García, *Dos Antiguas Relaciones de la Florida*, pp. 55, 56.

[3] Avilés to Philip II., Jan. 30, 1566, Ruidíaz, *La Florida*, tomo ii., p. 145.

[4] *Histoire Notable*, Basanier, p. 109; *Hak.*, vol. ii., p. 519; Le Moyne also says that the fort was attacked in three places at once (De Bry, *Brevis Narratio*, p. 24).

he was surprised by the Spaniards. Two of them immediately set upon him with a pike and partizan. Although an old, grey-headed man of sixty, he jumped the rampart, which was eight or nine feet high, and fled to the forest, still gripping his chisel in the excitement of the escape. As he crossed the meadow and neared the edge of the wood, he reached an elevation, and finding that he was no longer pursued, he turned to look back.

"And as from that point, all of the fort and even the court was visible, I saw there a horrible killing which was being made of our people and three ensigns of our adversaries planted upon the ramparts. Losing all hope of seeing our people rally, I resigned all of my senses to the Lord, recommended myself to his mercy, grace, and favour, and plunged into the forest, for it seemed to me I could find no greater cruelty among the wild beasts than that of the enemy, which I had seen overflow upon our people."[1]

Le Moyne, the artist, still lame in one leg from a wound he had received in the campaign against Outina, was of the watch which had just turned into its quarters. Wet through as he was, he laid down his arquebus and threw himself into a hammock to get a little sleep. But the outcries and the sound of blows proceeding from the court aroused him, and as he rushed to the door to see what was the matter, two Spaniards with drawn swords brushed by him into the house. He quickly saw that the court had been turned into a slaughter pen by the Spaniards who now held it, so he fled back at once, and made for one of the embrasures. Passing over the dead bodies of five or six of his fellow-soldiers, he pushed through it, leaped down into the ditch, and escaped into the neighbouring wood.[2]

[1] "Histoire Mémorable," reprint in Gaffarel, *Histoire de la Floride*, pp. 465, 466.

[2] De Bry, *Brevis Narratio*, pp. 24, 25.

Menéndez had remained outside urging his troops on to the attack, but when he saw a sufficient number of them advance, he ran to the front, shouting out that under pain of death no women were to be killed, nor any boys of less than fifteen years of age.[1] Avilés had headed the attack on the south-west breach, and after repulsing its defenders, he came upon Laudonnière, who was running to their assistance. Jean François, the renegade Frenchman, pointed him out to the Spaniards, and their pikemen drove him back into the court. Seeing that the place was lost, and unable to stand up alone against his aggressors, Laudonnière turned to escape through his house. The Spaniards pursued him, but a tent standing in the way distracted their attention, and while they were busy cutting its cords, he escaped by the western breach. As he was making for the woods, one of the pikemen nearly overtook him and gave him a thrust with his spear.[2] His maid-servant, who also made her escape, received a dagger-thrust in the breast.[3]

Meanwhile the trumpeters were announcing a victory from their stations on the ramparts beside the flags. At this what French remained alive entirely lost heart, and while the main body of the Spaniards were going through the quarters, killing without mercy the old, the sick, and the infirm, quite a number of the Frenchmen succeeded in getting over the palisade and escaping.[4] Some of the fugitives made their way into the forest. Jacques Ribaut with his ship the *Pearl*, and another vessel with a cargo of wine and supplies, were anchored in the

[1] Barrientos in García, *Dos Antiguas Relaciones de la Florida*, p. 56; Merás in Ruidíaz, *La Florida*, tomo i., p. 98.

[2] Avilés to Philip II., Oct. 15, 1565, *ibid.*, tomo ii., p. 86; *Histoire Notable*, Basanier, p. 110; *Hak.*, vol. ii., p. 520.

[3] De Bry, *Brevis Narratio*, p. 26; Le Challeux, reprint in Gaffarel's *Histoire de la Floride*, p. 465.

[4] Barrientos in García, *Dos Antiguas Relaciones de la Florida*, p. 56; Merás in Ruidíaz, *La Florida*, tomo i., pp. 97, 98.

river but a very short distance from the fort[1] and rescued others who rowed out in a couple of boats; and some even swam the distance to the ships.

By this time the fort was virtually won, and Menéndez turned his attention to the vessels anchored in the neighbourhood. A number of women and children had been spared owing to his exertions, and his very first thoughts turned on how he could rid himself of them. His decision was promptly reached. A trumpeter with a flag of peace was sent to summon some one to come ashore from the ships to treat of conditions of surrender. Receiving no response, he sent Jean François to the *Pearl* with the proposal that the French should have a safe-conduct to return to France with the women and children in any one vessel they should select, provided they would surrender their remaining ships and all of their armament.[2] But Jacques Ribaut would listen to no such terms, and on his indignant refusal, Le Challeux tells us that the enraged Spaniards, who had gathered down by the river-bank, where the corpses of the slain had been heaped together, tore out the eyes of the dead with the points of their daggers and hurled them at the French ships amidst howls and insults.[3] Menéndez then turned the guns of the captured fort against Ribaut and suc-

[1] Avilés to Philip II., Oct. 15, 1565 (Ruidíaz, *La Florida*, tomo ii., p. 86), says there were three ships, but he afterwards speaks of them as only two. Le Moyne says the *Pearl* of Jacques Ribaut was the only one of Jean Ribaut's three vessels within the bar at the time which was taken up to the fort (De Bry, *Brevis Narratio*, p. 26); and this is confirmed by Avilés in the letter just cited (p. 86), where he says that two of the seven ships from France were down the river.

[2] Barrientos in García, *Dos Antiguas Relaciones de la Florida*, p. 57; Merás in Ruidíaz, *La Florida*, tomo i., pp. 98–101. He says that the man sent to the ship was the sentinel first captured. This is improbable, as he is said to have been killed in the first attack. Avilés, in his letter of Oct. 15, 1565 (*ibid.*, tomo ii., p. 86), mentions no such conditions; Le Challeux, reprint in Gaffarel, p. 468.

[3] "Histoire Mémorable," reprint in Gaffarel, *Hist. de la Floride*, p. 468.

ceeded in sinking one of the vessels in shallow water, where she could be recovered without damage to her cargo.[1]

Jacques Ribaut received the crew of the sinking ship into the *Pearl*, and then dropped a league down the river to where stood two more of the ships which had arrived from France, and which had not even been unloaded. Hearing from the carpenter, Jean de Hais, who had escaped in a small boat, of the taking of the fort, Jacques Ribaut concluded to remain a little longer in the river to see if he might save any of his unfortunate compatriots.[2]

So successful had been the attack, that the victory was complete within an hour[3] without loss to the Spaniards of a single man, and only one was wounded. Of the two hundred and forty French in the fort, one hundred and thirty-two were killed outright, including the two English hostages left by Hawkins.[4] About half a dozen drummers and trumpeters were held as prisoners, of which number was Jean Memyn, who has left us a short account of his experiences[5]; fifty women and children were captured, and the balance of the garrison got away

[1] Avilés to Philip II., Oct. 15, 1565, Ruidíaz, *La Florida*, tomo ii., p. 86. There can be hardly any doubt but that the incomplete sentence in Mendoza's "Relación" (*ibid.*, tomo ii., p. 460): "Tiraronla un tiro de los que ellos [*i. e.*, the French] tenian en su fuerte y hecháronla á fondo, pero está en parte donde . . . ni lo que en él está se perderá," has the significance given it in the text. This may account for Le Challeux's saying that no harm was done the ship by the Spanish shot, the rain having affected the cannon; "Histoire Mémorable," reprint in Gaffarel, *Hist. de la Floride*, p. 468.

[2] Avilés to Philip II., Oct. 15, 1565, Ruidíaz, *La Florida*, tomo ii., p. 86; Barrientos, in García, *Dos Antiguas Relaciones de la Florida*, p. 57; *Histoire Notable*, Basanier, p. 111; *Hak.*, vol. ii., pp. 520, 521.

[3] Mendoza, "Relación" in Ruidíaz, *La Florida*, tomo ii., p. 459. Vasalenque says two hours. "Información de algunos servicios," etc., in *ibid.*, tomo ii., p. 615.

[4] Avilés to Philip II., Oct. 15, 1565, *ibid.*, tomo ii., p. 90.

[5] See Appendix M, The Deposition of Jean Memyn.

as has been related.[1] In a work written in France some seven years later, and first published in 1586,[2] it is related that Avilés hanged some of his prisoners on trees and placed above them the Spanish inscription, "I do this not to Frenchmen, but to Lutherans."[3] The story found ready acceptance among the French of that period, and was eagerly believed and repeated subsequently by historians, both native and foreign,[4] but it is unsupported by the testimony of a single witness, and bears all the earmarks of an apocryphal origin.

[1] Avilés to Philip II., Oct. 15, 1565, Ruidíaz, *La Florida*, tomo ii., pp. 86, 87. Le Challeux (reprint in Gaffarel's *Histoire de la Floride*, p. 465) says all of the women and children were killed. Mendoza in his "Relación" (Ruidíaz, *ibid.*, tomo ii., p. 459), says that 142 were killed. Vasalenque, who was in the attack on the Spanish side, testifies thirty years later that 600 French were killed! ("Información de algunos servicios," etc., in *ibid.*, tomo ii., p. 615). Avilés in the letter just cited (*ibid.*, p. 80) says 132 men were killed in the attack and 10 more on the next day, and 50 or 60 escaped. Fourquevaux, in his letter to Charles IX., of Feb. 22, 1566 (*Dépêches*, p. 61), says 30 women and 18 children were saved.

[2] *La Reprise de la Floride*, Larroque, p. 23, note 1.

[3] Larroque, *ibid.*, p. 61.

[4] Lescarbot, *Histoire de la Nouvelle France*, Paris, MDCXI., liv. i., p. 127; Charlevoix, *Histoire et Description generale de la Nouvelle France*, Nyon Fils, Paris, 1744, vol. i., p. 81; Bancroft, *History of the United States*, 15th ed., Boston, 1855, vol. i., p. 71; Gaffarel, *Histoire de la Floride*, p. 229; Parkman (*Pioneers of France in the New World*, 1895, p. 127) very candidly gives his own opinion on the subject: "Though no eyewitness attests it, there is reason to think it true." Shea omits the incident entirely in his *The Catholic Church in Colonial Days*, and discredits it in his "Ancient Florida" (*Narr. and Crit. Hist. Am.*, vol. ii., p. 272), as does Barcia (*Ensayo*, Año MDLXVIII., p. 136). To an impartial judgment the doubt as to the credibility of the story of the alleged inscription amounts almost to a certainty, although based entirely upon negative evidence. One asks, Why was it not mentioned by Jean Memyn, who remained for some time after the event at Fort Caroline? Why does not Avilés refer to it in his letters to Philip? Why is it not spoken of in the "Información de algunos servicios," or by Mendoza, who would heartily have approved of it? What interest or object had the contemporary Spanish accounts in suppressing an incident, which, in their estimation, could only redound to the credit of the Adelantado? And why did Avilés hang the Huguenots at Fort Caroline and not at Matanzas?

Throughout the attack the storm had continued and the rain had poured down, so that it was no small comfort to the bedraggled soldiers, weary with the difficult march and the excitement of the fight, when Jean François pointed out to them the storehouse, where they all obtained dry clothes, and where a ration of bread and wine with lard and pork was served out to each of them. Most of the food stores were looted by the soldiers. Menéndez found five or six thousand ducats' worth of silver, largely ore, part of it brought by the Indians from the Appalachian Mountains,[1] and part collected by Laudonnière from Outina, from whom he had also obtained some gold and pearls.[2] Most of the artillery and ammunition brought over by Ribaut had not been landed, and as Laudonnière had traded his with Hawkins for the ship but little was captured.[3] To the horror of the Spaniards not a cross nor an image could be discovered about the fort, but they found six good strong-boxes "filled with books well bound and gilded, all pertaining to their evil sect." Packs of playing-cards were also discovered with pictures of the Host and Chalice on their backs, and saints carrying crosses in mockery of holy things.[4] The books were at once ordered to be burned, a fate which was probably shared by the playing-cards. Menéndez further captured eight ships, one of which was a galley in the dockyard; of the remaining seven, five were French, including the vessel sunk in the attack, the other two were those captured off Yaguana, already mentioned, whose cargoes of hides and sugar Hawkins had taken with him.[5]

[1] Avilés to Philip II., Oct. 15, 1565, Ruidíaz, *La Florida*, tomo ii., p. 90.

[2] De Bry, *Brevis Narratio*, pp. 9, 12.

[3] Avilés to Philip II., Oct. 15, 1665, Ruidíaz, *La Florida*, tomo ii., p. 90.

[4] Barrientos in García, *Dos Antiguas Relaciones de la Florida*, p. 57; Merás in Ruidíaz, *La Florida*, tomo i., p. 111; Mendoza, "Relación" in *ibid.*, tomo ii., p. 460.

[5] Avilés to Philip II., Oct. 15, 1565, *ibid.*, tomo ii., p. 91. See Appendix N, The Captured French Vessels.

In the afternoon Menéndez assembled his captains, and after pointing out how grateful they should be to God for the victory, called the roll of his men, and found only four hundred present, many having already started on their way back to St. Augustine. Menéndez was himself anxious to return at once, for he was in constant dread of a descent of the French fleet upon his settlement there. He also wished to attempt the capture of Jacques Ribaut's ships before they had left the St. John's, and to get ready a vessel to transport the women and children of the French to Santo Domingo, and from there to Seville, for the fate of the latter weighed heavily upon his mind. "It is with the greatest sorrow that I see them in company with my people, on account of their evil sect," he wrote the King, "and yet I feared that Our Lord would punish me, if I acted towards them with cruelty."[1]

He appointed Gonzalo de Villarroel harbour master and governor of the district and gave the fort, which he had named San Mateo, into his charge, having captured it on the feast of St. Matthew. The camp master, Valdez, who had proved very daring in the attack and a garrison of three hundred men were left to defend the fort, and the arms of France were torn down from over the main entrance and replaced by the royal arms surmounted by a cross supported above the crown by two angels. The device was painted by two Flemish soldiers in his little army. Then two crosses were erected inside the fort, and a location was selected for a church to be dedicated to St. Matthew.

When Menéndez came to look about him for an escort he found his soldiers so utterly exhausted with the march, the wet, the mire, the sleepless nights, and the battle, that not a man was to be found willing to accompany him.

[1] Merás in *ibid.*, tomo i., pp. 105, 106; Avilés to Philip II., Oct. 15, 1565, *ibid.*, tomo ii., p. 87.

He therefore determined to remain over night and then to proceed to St. Augustine in advance of the main body of his men with a picked company of thirty-five of those who were least fatigued.[1]

The fate of the fugitives from Fort Caroline was various and eventful. When Laudonnière reached the forest, he found there a party of men who had escaped like himself, and three or four of whom were badly wounded. A consultation was held as to what steps should be taken, for it was impossible to remain where they were for any length of time, without food, and exposed at every moment to an attack from the Spaniards. Some of the party determined to take refuge among the natives, and set out for a neighbouring Indian village.[2] These were subsequently ransomed by Menéndez and returned by him to France.[3] Laudonnière then pushed on through the woods, where his party was increased the following day by that of the artist, Jacques Le Moyne.

Wandering along one of the forest paths with which he was familiar, Le Moyne had come upon four other fugitives like himself. After consultation together the party broke up, Le Moyne going in the direction of the sea to find Ribaut's boats, and the others making for an Indian settlement. Setting out alone, Le Moyne soon encountered a soldier, a tailor by trade, who had been at work on a suit of clothes for Ottigny. The two joined company, and were all day pushing through the woods. Then came the swamps with their heavy growth of reeds, the laborious struggle all night long to get through them, the continuing rain, and the rising of the tide until the water reached to the waists of the fugitives. When morning broke and the sea was not yet sighted, the poor

[1] Merás in *ibid.*, tomo i., pp. 102–104; Barrientos in García, *Dos Antiguas Relaciones de la Florida*, p. 58.

[2] *Histoire Notable*, Basanier, p. 110; *Hak.*, vol. ii., p. 520.

[3] Barrientos in García, *Dos Antiguas Relaciones de la Florida*, p. 59; Merás in Ruidíaz, *La Florida*, tomo i., p. 105.

tailor gave up in despair, and determined to return to the Spaniards, hoping that his gentle trade would arouse their compassion, and Le Moyne, after vainly trying to dissuade him, finally agreed to go with him. Back through the forest they plodded painfully until in sight of Fort Caroline, when the noise of the uproar and rejoicings which arose from the victorious Spaniards impressed Le Moyne so deeply that he again pleaded with his companion to remain with him. But the tailor was determined to make the attempt and, writes Le Moyne,

"he embraced me, saying, 'I will go; so farewell.' In order to see what should happen to him, I got up to a height near by and watched. As he came down from the high ground, the Spaniards saw him, and sent out a party. As they came upon him, he fell on his knees to beg for his life. They, however, in a fury, cut him to pieces, and carried off the dismembered fragments of his body on the points of their spears and pikes."[1]

What little hope Le Moyne himself may have entertained of receiving mercy from the victors, was now utterly abandoned, and again hiding himself in the forest, he retraced his steps, encountering on the way other fugitives like himself, and the poor maid-servant; and finally, while still in the forest, came upon the party of Laudonnière.[2]

Laudonnière had taken the direction of the sea in the evident hope of finding the vessels Ribaut had sent inside the bar. After a while the marshes were reached,

"where," he writes, "being able to go no farther by reason of my sicknesse which I had, I sent two of my men which were with me, which could swim well, vnto the ships to aduertise them of that which had happened, and to send them word to come and helpe me. They were not able that day to get

[1] De Bry, *Brevis Narratio*, p. 26; English translation by Fred. B. Perkins in *Narrative of Le Moyne*, Boston, 1875, p. 19.

[2] De Bry, *Brevis Narratio*, pp. 24–26.

vnto the ships to certifie them thereof: so I was constrained to stand in the water vp to the shoulders all of that night long, with one of my men which would neuer forsake me." [1]

And now through the water and the tall reeds came the old carpenter, Le Challeux, with another party of refugees. After his escape from the fort he wandered for half an hour through the forest until he heard a sound of weeping and groaning, and drawing near to it discovered a party of men, among whom was M. Robert; and farther along he came upon another company. Deliberating as to what should be done, some of the fugitives decided to surrender themselves to the mercy of the Spaniards, and on leaving the forest for that purpose they were seized and killed, and their bodies thrown onto the heap of the dead, on the river-bank. Le Challeux and six others of the company decided to make their way to the coast in the hope of being rescued by the ships which had remained below in the river. On reaching the summit of a high mound they finally discovered the sea, which still lay a great distance off, and on descending from the hill they entirely lost sight of it. Pursuing the direction in which they had seen the ocean, they plunged onwards through bushes and thickets, which tore and cut their hands, waded marshes where the sharp leaves of the grasses and reeds pricked their feet and cut their legs until the blood ran, and where the water reached to their waists, until they came to a stream so swift that none dared swim it. Le Challeux cut a pole with the chisel which he still carried in his hand. Floating it upon the water the end next the bank was held steady while a comrade clung to it as he made his way to the centre of the stream, and when he had reached the end and his head disappeared under the swift current, a vigorous push sent him across into the shallow water,

[1] "A Notable Historie," in *Hak.*, ii., p. 520; Basanier, p. 110.

where he scrambled to his feet with the aid of the reeds and grasses. They passed the night in a grove of trees in view of the sea, and the following morning, as they were painfully struggling through a large morass, they observed some men half hidden by the reeds, whom they took to be a party of Spaniards come down to cut them off. But closer observation showed that they were naked, and terrified like themselves, and when they recognised their leader, Laudonnière, and others of their companions, they joined them. The entire company now consisted of twenty-six.

Two men were now sent to the top of the highest trees from which they discovered one of the smaller of the French ships, that of Captain Maillard, which presently sent a boat to their rescue. The boat next went to the relief of Laudonnière, who was so sick and weak that he had to be carried to it. Before returning to the ship, the remainder of the company were gathered up from among the reeds and rushes, the men, exhausted with hunger, anxiety, and fatigue, having to be assisted into the boat by the sailors.[1]

A consultation was now held between Jacques Ribaut and Captain Maillard, and the decision was reached to return to France. But in their weakened state, with their arms and supplies gone and the better part of their crews absent with Jean Ribaut,[2] the escaped Frenchmen were unable to navigate all three of the vessels; they therefore selected the two best and sank the other. The armament of the vessel bought from Hawkins was divided between the two captains and she was abandoned. Thursday, September 25th, the prows of the two ships were turned for France, but they parted company the following day. Jacques Ribaut with Le Challeux and his party, after an

[1] *Histoire Notable*, Basanier, pp. 110, 111; *Hak.*, vol. ii., pp. 520, 521; Le Challeux, reprint in Gaffarel, pp. 467–471.

[2] De Bry, *Brevis Narratio*, p. 27.

adventure on the way with a Spanish vessel, ultimately reached La Rochelle.[1] The other vessel, with Laudonnière aboard, was driven by foul weather into Swansea Bay in South Wales, where he again fell very ill. Part of his men he sent to France with the boat. With the remainder he went to London, where he saw M. de Foix, the French ambassador, and from there he proceeded to Paris. Finding that the King had gone to Moulins, he finally set out for it with part of his company to make his report, and reached there about the middle of March of the following year.[2]

[1] "Histoire Mémorable," Le Challeux, reprint in Gaffarel, *Hist. de la Floride*, p. 472. Alava to Philip II., Dec. 21, 1565, MS. Arch. Nat., Paris, K, 1504 (88), mentions the arrival of Jacques Ribaut in Normandy.

[2] *Histoire Notable*, Basanier, pp. 112–114; *Hak.*, vol. ii., pp. 521–523.

CHAPTER X

THE FATE OF RIBAUT'S FLEET

THE morning following the capture of Fort Caroline Menéndez set out on his return to St. Augustine. But he first sent the camp master with a party of fifty men to look for those who had escaped over the palisade, and to reconnoitre the French vessels which were still lying in the river, and whom he suspected of remaining there in order to rescue their compatriots. Twenty fugitives were found in the woods, where they were all shot down, and towards evening the camp master returned to Fort Caroline, having found no more Frenchmen.

The return to St. Augustine proved still more arduous and dangerous than the journey out. After marching through the forest for some time Menéndez reached a hummock by which he had passed before, but on attempting to proceed beyond it he found the country overflowed. Nothing daunted by this, he continued the advance, the water continually increasing in depth, until he was at last forced to retrace his steps. But the direction had been lost: in vain he searched for a little dry ground where he could camp for the night; everywhere under the tall palmettos stretched the waste of waters. Then Menéndez sent the most agile of his companions up one of the highest trees to look for dry land. The soldier's answer brought no comfort; even from the summit of the tall trees no dry land was visible. Then Menéndez ordered him to find the direction of the setting sun, but the cloud-banks were so heavy that it was impossible to determine even that. Wearily the party waited for the weather to clear, and towards the afternoon the clouds parted sufficiently for Menéndez to recover his direction and push forward. On went the Spaniards, crossing the deeper and larger streams on the trunks of trees, which they felled in such wise as to afford them a bridge. Again a tall palmetto was climbed, and at last the trail found by which they had come. They encamped that night on a bit of dry ground, where a roaring fire was built to dry their soaking garments, but all in vain, as the heavy rain began again.[1]

Three days after Menéndez's departure from St. Augustine, September 19th, a force of twenty men was sent to his relief with supplies of bread and wine and cheese, but the settlement remained without further news of him. On Saturday "we clergy, wishing to eat a little fish," writes Mendoza, the fishermen went down to the beach to cast their nets, where they discovered a man whom they seized and conducted to the fort. He proved to be a member of the crew of one of Jean Ribaut's four ships and was in great terror of being hung. But the chaplain examined him, and finding that he was "a Christian," of which he gave evidence by reciting the prayers, he was promised his life if he told the truth. His story was that in the storm that arose after the French demonstration in front of St. Augustine their frigate had been cast away at the mouth of a river four leagues to the south of St. Augustine and five of the crew were drowned. The next morning the survivors had been set upon by the natives and three more had been killed with clubs. Then he and a companion had fled along the shore, walking in the sea

[1] Barrientos in García, *Dos Antiguas Relaciones de la Florida*, pp. 58–61; Merás in Ruidíaz, *La Florida*, tomo i., pp. 104–108.

with only their heads above the water in order to escape the observation of the Indians.

Bartolomé Menéndez sent at once a party to float the frigate off and bring it up to St. Augustine, for on that low and sandy beach, shelvy and devoid of rocks, vessels are frequently driven high up on the land.[1] But when the Spaniards approached the scene of the wreck, the Indians, who had already slaughtered the balance of the crew, drove them away. A second attempt proved more successful and the vessel was brought up to St. Augustine, to the great delight of the Spaniards.[2]

The continued absence of news from the expedition against Fort Caroline had begun to cast a gloom over the Spaniards at St. Augustine. San Vincente, one of the captains who had remained behind, prophesied that Avilés would never come back, and that the entire party would be killed.[3] This impression was confirmed by the return of a hundred men, made desperate by the hardships of the march, and who brought with them their version of the difficulty of the attempt. On the afternoon of Monday, the 24th, just after the successful rescue of the French frigate, the settlers saw a man coming towards them, shouting at the top of his lungs. The chaplain went out to meet him, and the man threw his arms around him, crying, "Victory, victory! the harbour of the French is ours!"[4] He proved to be the soldier who had guided Menéndez by climbing the trees. When within a league of St. Augustine he had obtained permission to run forward and announce the victory. "I promised him his reward for the good news and gave him the best I could," writes Mendoza, "and having learned the news I ran to my house as fast as I could and

[1] Fairbanks, *History of Florida*, Philadelphia, 1871, p. 121.

[2] Mendoza, "Relación" in Ruidíaz, *La Florida*, tomo ii., pp. 455–457.

[3] Merás in *ibid.*, tomo i., p. 91.

[4] Mendoza, "Relación" in *ibid.*, tomo ii., pp. 457, 458.

took a new cassock, the very best I had, and a surplice, and I took a crucifix in my hands, and went forward to receive Menéndez before he reached the door." The chaplain was accompanied by the clergy, each carrying a cross, and by the women and children, laughing and weeping with joy, all chanting the *Te Deum Laudamus.*[1]

The General was well deserving their homage, for he had shown a determination, an intrepidity, and an endurance that had successfully encountered and overcome the very forces of nature. In the face of every difficulty, the incipient discontent of the soldiers, and an undercurrent of disapproval on the part of his captains, he had triumphed in the execution of those plans of his own, to which he was so wedded. The chaplain in an exuberance of pious joy exclaims:

"So great is his zeal and Christianity, that all these labours are but repose for his mind, for it veritably seems to me that no earthly man could have the strength to endure what he has; but the fire and longing which possess him to serve our Lord in humbling and destroying that Lutheran sect, enemy of our old Catholic faith, cause him not to feel the fatigue so greatly."[2]

On reaching St. Augustine Menéndez at once armed two boats to send to the mouth of the St. John's after Jacques Ribaut, to prevent his uniting with his father or returning to France with the news of the Spanish attack; but, learning that Jacques had sailed, he abandoned his plan and dispatched a single vessel with supplies to Fort San Mateo.[3]

September 28th some Indians brought to the settle-

[1] *Ibid.*, tomo ii., p. 460; Merás in *ibid.*, tomo i., p. 109; Barrientos in García, *Dos Antiguas Relaciones de la Florida*, pp. 61, 62.

[2] Mendoza, "Relación" in Ruidíaz, *La Florida*, tomo ii., p. 461.

[3] Barrientos in García, *Dos Antiguas Relaciones de la Florida*, p. 62; Merás in Ruidíaz, *La Florida*, tomo i., p. 109; Avilés to Philip II., Oct. 15, 1565, *ibid.*, tomo ii., p. 87.

ment the information that a number of Frenchmen had been cast ashore on an island six leagues from St. Augustine,[1] where they were imprisoned by the river, which they could not cross. They proved to be the crews of two more of the French fleet which had left Fort Caroline September 10th. Failing to find the Spaniards at sea, Ribaut had not dared to land and attack St. Augustine, and so had resolved to return to Fort Caroline, when his vessels were caught in the storm before mentioned, the ships dispersed, and two of them wrecked along the shore between Matanzas and Mosquito Inlet.[2] Part of the crews had been drowned in attempting to land, the Indians had captured fifty of them alive and had killed others, so that out of four hundred there remained only one hundred and forty. Following along the shore in the direction of Fort Caroline, the easiest and most natural course to pursue, the survivors had soon found their further advance barred by the inlet, and by the lagoon or "river" to the west of them.

On receipt of the news Menéndez sent Diego Flores in advance with forty soldiers to reconnoitre the French position; he himself with the chaplain, some officers, and twenty soldiers rejoined Flores at about midnight, and pushed forward to the side of the inlet opposite to their encampment. The following morning, having concealed his men in the thicket, Menéndez dressed himself in a French costume with a cape over his shoulder, and, carry-

[1] Avilés to Philip II., Oct. 15, 1565, *ibid.*, tomo ii., p. 87. Merás (in *ibid.*, tomo i., p. 110), and Barrientos (in García, *Dos Antiguas Relaciones de la Florida*, p. 62), say four leagues.

[2] Avilés to Philip II., Oct. 15, 1565, Ruidíaz, *La Florida*, tomo ii., p. 88; Le Challeux, "Histoire Mémorable," reprint in Gaffarel, *Hist. de la Floride*, p. 473. Vasalenque ("Información de algunos servicios" in Ruidíaz, *ibid.*, tomo ii., p. 616) says: "En un rio que se llama Matanças." Gaffarel (p. 222), "sans doute la lagune de Matanzas." Fairbanks (*Hist. of Florida*, p. 121) says: "They were driven ashore between Matanzas and Mosquito Inlet."

ing a short lance in his hand,[1] went out and showed himself on the river-bank, accompanied by one of his French prisoners, in order to convince the castaways by his boldness that he was well supported. The Frenchmen soon observed him, and one of their number swam over to where he was standing. Throwing himself at his feet the Frenchman explained who they were and besought the General to grant him and his comrades a safe-conduct to Fort Caroline, as they were not at war with Spaniards.

"I answered him that we had taken their fort and killed all the people in it," writes Menéndez to the King, "because they had built it there without Your Majesty's permission, and were disseminating the Lutheran religion in these, Your Majesty's provinces. And that I, as Captain-General of these provinces, was waging a war of fire and blood against all who came to settle these parts and plant in them their evil Lutheran sect; for I was come at Your Majesty's command to plant the Gospel in these parts to enlighten the natives in those things which the Holy Mother Church of Rome teaches and believes, for the salvation of their souls. For this reason I would not grant them a safe passage, but would sooner follow them by sea and land until I had taken their lives."[2]

The Frenchman returned to his companions and related his interview. A party of five, consisting of four gentlemen and a captain, was next sent over to find what terms they could get from Menéndez, who received them as before, with his soldiers still in ambush, and himself attended by only ten persons. After he had convinced them of the capture of Fort Caroline by showing them

[1] Mendoza ("Relación" in Ruidíaz, *La Florida*, tomo ii., p. 464) says he wore a naval dress. Parkman (*Pioneers of France in the New World*, Boston, 1893, p. 134) says in the dress of a French sailor.

[2] Avilés to Philip II., Oct. 15, 1565, Ruidíaz, *La Florida*, tomo ii., p. 89.

some of the spoil he had taken, and some prisoners he had spared, the spokesman of the company asked for a ship and sailors with which to return to France. Menéndez replied that he would willingly have given them one had they been Catholics, and had he any vessels left; but that his own ships had sailed with artillery for Fort San Mateo and with the captured women and children for Santo Domingo, and a third was retained to carry dispatches to Spain. Neither would he yield to a request that their lives be spared until the arrival of a ship, which would carry them back to their country. To all of their demands he had but one reply to give: "Surrender your arms and place yourselves at my mercy, that I may do with you as Our Lord may command me." "And from this I did not depart, nor will I, unless God Our Lord inspire me otherwise," he adds in his letter.[1] The gentlemen carried back to their comrades the terms he had proposed, and two hours later Ribaut's lieutenant, "a very cunning man in these matters," writes Menéndez, returned and offered to surrender their arms and to give him five thousand ducats if he would spare their lives. Menéndez indignantly replied that the sum was large enough for a poor soldier such as he, if in his heart he were capable of such weakness and cupidity, but when generosity and mercy were to be shown they should be actuated by no interest whatever. Again the envoy returned to his companions, and in half an hour came the acceptance of the ambiguous conditions.

The story of the attempted bribery, if true, and there is little reason to doubt it, but too plainly indicates how little room there was for question among those unfortunate Frenchmen as to the nature of the divine inspiration in such a foe of France and of heresy as was the cool and determined soldier before them. "They came and surrendered their arms to me, and I had their hands tied

[1] See Appendix O, The Oath of Avilés.

behind them, and put them all excepting ten to the knife," laconically writes this servant of God and the King.

Both of his biographers give a much more detailed account of the occurrence, evidently taken from a common source. The Frenchmen first sent over in a boat their banners, their arquebuses and pistols, swords and targets, and some helmets and breast-pieces. Then twenty Spaniards crossed in the boat and brought the now unarmed Frenchmen over the lagoon in parties of ten. They were subjected to no ill-treatment as they were ferried over, the Spaniards not wishing to arouse any suspicions among those who had not yet crossed. Menéndez himself withdrew some distance from the shore to the rear of a sand hill, where he was concealed from the view of the prisoners who were crossing in the boat. In companies of ten the Frenchmen were conducted to him behind the sand hill and out of sight of their companions, and to each party he addressed the same ominous request: "Gentlemen, I have but a few soldiers with me, and you are many, and it would be an easy matter for you to overpower us and avenge yourselves upon us for your people which we killed in the fort; for this reason it is necessary that you should march to my camp four leagues from here with your hands tied behind your backs." The Frenchmen consented, for they were unarmed and could offer no further resistance, and their hands were bound behind them with cords of the arquebuses and with the matches of the soldiers, probably taken from the very arms they had surrendered.[1] Then Mendoza, the chaplain, "being a priest and having the bowels of a man," asked Menéndez to grant him the lives of those who should prove to be "Christians." Ten Roman Catholics were found, who, but for the compassion of this poor egotistical and bigoted priest, would have suffered the

[1] Both Barrientos and Merás say 208 Frenchmen were thus tied.

last penalty along with the heretics.[1] These were sent by boat to St Augustine. The remainder confessed that they were Lutherans. They were given something to eat and drink, and then ordered to set out on the march. At the distance of a gun-shot from the hill behind which these preparations were in progress, Menéndez himself had drawn with his spear a line in the sand, across the path they were to follow. Then he ordered the captain of the vanguard which escorted the prisoners that on reaching the place indicated by the line he was to cut off the heads of all of them; he also commanded the captain of the rearguard to do the same. It was Saturday, the 29th of September, the feast of St. Michael, patron and prince of the Church militant, conqueror of the hosts of hell, out of whose nethermost depths was reckoned to have sprung the heresy these French pirates had brought with them. The sun had already set, and the night was falling when, near the banks of the placid lagoon, the Frenchmen came abreast of the mark drawn in the sand, and the orders of the Spanish General were executed.[2] That same night Avilés returned to St. Augustine, which he reached at dawn.

On the 10th of October the distressing news reached the garrison at St. Augustine that eight days after its capture Fort San Mateo had burned down, with the loss of all the provisions which were stored there. It was accidentally set on fire by the candle of a mulatto servant of one of the captains; but for all that, suspicions arose that it might be the result of certain jealousies between the master of the mulatto and another officer stationed

[1] Mendoza, "Relación" in Ruidíaz, *La Florida*, tomo ii., p. 465. Elsewhere on the same page he says that 14 or 15 were saved. Avilés in the letter already cited (*ibid.*, tomo ii., p. 89), says 10.

[2] Barrientos in García, *Dos Antiguas Relaciones de la Florida*, pp. 62–66; Merás in Ruidíaz, *La Florida*, tomo i., pp. 110–117; Mendoza, "Relación" in *ibid.*, tomo ii., p. 465; Avilés to Philip II., Oct. 15, 1565, *ibid.*, tomo ii., pp. 87–89.

there. Menéndez promptly sent food from his own store to San Mateo.[1]

Within an hour of receiving this alarming report some Indians brought word that Jean Ribaut with two hundred men was in the neighbourhood of the place where the two French ships had been wrecked. They were in much suffering, for the *Trinity* had gone to pieces farther down the shore, and their provisions had all been lost. They had been reduced to living on roots and grasses and to drinking the impure water collected in the holes and pools along their route. Like the first party, whose fate has just been related, their only hope lay in a return to Fort Caroline. Le Challeux tells us that they had saved a small boat from the wreck; this they caulked with their shirts, and thirteen of the company had set out in her for Fort Caroline in search of assistance, and had not returned.[2] As Ribaut and his companions made their way northward in the direction of the fort, they eventually found themselves in the same predicament as the previous party, cut off by Matanzas Inlet and river from the mainland, and unable to cross.

On receipt of the news Avilés repeated the tactics of his previous exploit, and sent a party of soldiers by land, following himself the same day in two boats with additional troops, one hundred and fifty in all. He reached his destination on the shore of the Matanzas River at night,[3] and the following morning, October 11th, he

[1] Merás in *ibid.*, tomo i., p. 127; Avilés to Philip II., Oct. 15, 1565, *ibid.*, tomo ii., pp. 101, 102; Vasalenque, "Información de algunos servicios," etc., in *ibid.*, tomo ii., p. 616.

[2] Le Challeux, "Histoire Mémorable," reprint in Gaffarel, *Hist. de la Floride*, p. 474.

[3] Vasalenque ("Información de algunos servicios," etc., in Ruidíaz, *La Florida*, tomo ii., p. 616) says: "llegados al proprio rio de Matanças." Ribaut must have been wrecked north of Mosquito Inlet in order to reach Matanzas. Fairbanks, *History of St. Augustine*, New York, 1858, p. 64, note. On Mexia's map of 1605 (MS. Arch. Gen. de Indias, Sevilla,

discovered the French across the water where they had constructed a raft with which to attempt a crossing. At the sight of the Spaniards, the French displayed their banners, sounded their fifes and drums, and offered them battle, but Menéndez took no notice of the demonstration.[1] Commanding his own men, whom he had again disposed to produce an impression of numbers, to sit down and breakfast, he turned to walk up and down the shore with two of his captains in full sight of the French. Then Ribaut called a halt, sounded a trumpet-call, and displayed a white flag, to which Menéndez replied in the same fashion. The Spaniards having refused to cross at the invitation of Ribaut, a French sailor swam over to them, and came back immediately in an Indian canoe, bringing the request that Ribaut send over some one authorised to state what he wanted. The sailor returned again with a French gentleman, who announced that he was Sergeant Major of Ribaut, Viceroy and Captain-General of Florida for the King of France. His commander had been wrecked on the coast with three hundred and fifty of his people, and had sent to ask for boats with which to reach his fort, and to enquire if they were Spaniards, and who was their captain.

"We are Spaniards," answered Avilés. "I to whom

Patronato, est. 1, caj. 1, leg. 1/19, ramo 29), the name of Barreta de Ribao is given to an inlet into the Matanzas River south of Matanzas Inlet, which appears at that time to have connected it with the sea. Velasco (in his *Geograffía, 1571–1574*, p. 167), says the river was called Matanzas "porque junto á él, á la parte del norte, en la mesma costa, murieron los franceses luteranos que estaban con Juan Ribau." The "Relación escrita por el Tesorero Joan Menéndez Marqués," June 6, 1606 (in Ruidíaz, *ibid.*, tomo ii., 501), mentions "la barra y barrera de Juan Ribao y Matanças, cinco leguas deste puerto [of St. Augustine], en la buelta del Sur . . . y allí mataron al dicho Juan Ribao y á la mayor parte de los franceses, de que resultó quedar á la barra el nombre de Matanças."

[1] Vasalenque says the Spaniards made a similar demonstration. "Información de algunos servicios," etc., in Ruidíaz, *La Florida*, tomo ii., p. 616.

you are speaking am the Captain, and my name is Pedro Menéndez. Tell your General that I have captured your fort, and killed your French there, as well as those who had escaped from the wreck of your fleet." And thereupon he offered Ribaut the identical terms which he had extended to the first party and grimly led the French officer to where, a few rods beyond, lay the dead bodies of the shipwrecked and defenceless men he had so wantonly massacred but twelve days before. When the Frenchman viewed the heaped-up corpses of his familiars and friends, not a muscle quivered in his face, and he quietly asked Menéndez to send a gentleman to Ribaut to inform him of what had occurred; and he even requested Menéndez to go in person to treat about securities, as his General was greatly fatigued. "Go yourself, brother, in God's name, to convey my answer; and if your General wishes to talk with me, I give him my word that he can come in safety with five or six of his companions," replied Menéndez.

In the afternoon Ribaut crossed over with eight gentlemen and was entertained by Avilés. The French accepted some wine and preserves; more they would not take, for their hearts were heavy at learning the fate of their companions. Then Ribaut, pointing to where lay the bodies of his comrades, which were visible from where he stood, said that they might have been tricked into the belief that Fort Caroline was taken, referring to a story he had learned from a barber who had survived the first massacre by feigning death when he was struck down, and had then escaped to him. But Ribaut was soon convinced of his mistake, for he was allowed to converse privately with two Frenchmen captured at Fort Caroline. Then he turned to Menéndez and said: "What has happened to me may happen to you. Since our Kings are brothers and friends, do you also play the part of a friend and give me ships with which to return to France." But the Spaniard was inexorable, and Ribaut returned to his companions to acquaint them with the results of the interview. Within three hours he was back again. Some of his people were willing to trust to the mercy of Menéndez, he said, but others were not, and he offered one hundred thousand ducats on the part of his companions to secure their lives[1]; but Avilés stood firm in his determination. As the evening was falling Ribaut again withdrew across the lagoon, saying he would bring the final decision in the morning.

Between the terrible alternatives of death by starvation or at the hands of the Spaniards, the night brought no better counsel to the castaways than that of trusting to the mercy of their fellow-men. When morning came Ribaut returned with six of his captains, and surrendered his own person and arms, the royal standard which he bore, and his seal of office. His captains did the same, and Ribaut declared that about seventy of his people were willing to submit, among whom were many noblemen, gentlemen of high connections, and four Germans. The remainder of the company had withdrawn and had even attempted to kill their leader. Then the same gruesome ceremony was rehearsed as on the previous occasion. Diego Flores de Valdes ferried the Frenchmen over in parties of ten, which were successively conducted behind the same sand hill, where their hands were tied behind them. The same lying excuse was made that they could not be trusted to march unbound to the camp. When the hands of all had been bound except those of Ribaut, who was for a time left free, the ominous question was put: "Are you Catholics or Lutherans, and are there any who wish to confess?" Ribaut answered that they were all of the new Lutheran religion. Then he repeated the passage from Genesis, "From earth we

[1] See also the deposition of Grauiel de Riuera in "Información de algunos servicios," etc., in *ibid.*, tomo ii., p. 603, to the same effect.

come, and unto earth must we return"[1]; and observed that twenty years more or less were of little account; that Menéndez could do with them as he chose, and he sang the psalm *Domine, memento mei.*[2] Avilés pardoned the drummers, fifers, trumpeters, and four others who said they were Catholics, some seventeen in all.[3] Then he ordered that the remainder should be marched in the same order to the same line in the sand, where they were in turn deliberately massacred.

Avilés had confided Ribaut to his brother-in-law, and biographer, Solís de Merás, and to San Vincente, with directions to kill him. Ribaut was wearing a felt hat and on Vincente's asking for it Ribaut gave it to him. Then the Spaniard said: "You know how captains must obey their generals and execute their commands. We must bind your hands." When this had been done and the three had proceeded a little distance along the way, Vincente gave him a blow in the stomach with his dagger, and Merás thrust him through the breast with a pike which he carried, and then they cut off his head.[4]

[1] Probably Genesis iii., 19.

[2] Merás, who relates the incident (Ruidíaz, *La Florida*, tomo i., p. 126), says: "empezó á decir el salmo *Domine, memento mei.*" As Merás was one of his murderers the statement must be accepted. But there is no psalm beginning with these words. Parkman (*Pioneers of France in the New World*, Boston, 1893, p. 143) quotes from *Histoire Générale des Voyages*, xiv., p. 446, where it is suggested that Merás probably intended to say *Domine, memento David*, which is Psalm 131 of the Vulgate and 132 of the King James Version, and the quotation further suggests that Ribaut repeated it in French. But it is difficult to see what particular bearing the 132nd Psalm could have on the circumstances attending his assassination, except, perhaps, a very obscure reference to his planting of the Reformed religion in the New World.

[3] This is the number given by Barrientos ("Hechos," in García, *Dos Antiguas Relaciones de la Florida*, p. 69); Merás (Ruidíaz, *La Florida*, tomo i., p. 126) says the pipers, drummers, and trumpeters, with four Catholics, sixteen in all. Avilés himself (letter Oct. 15, 1565, *ibid.*, tomo ii., p. 103) says five only, two lads of eighteen years of age, a piper, drummer, and trumpeter.

[4] Barrientos in García, *Dos Antiguas Relaciones de la Florida*, pp. 66–70; Merás in Ruidíaz, *La Florida*, tomo i., pp. 119–126; Avilés to Philip II.,

"I put Jean Ribaut and all the rest of them to the knife," Avilés wrote Philip four days later, "judging it to be necessary to the service of the Lord Our God, and of Your Majesty. And I think it a very great fortune that this man be dead; for the King of France could accomplish more with him and fifty thousand ducats, than with other men and five hundred thousand ducats; and he could do more in one year, than another in ten; for he was the most experienced sailor and corsair known, very skilful in this navigation of the Indies and of the Florida Coast." [1]

There was one remarkable escape from this massacre, that of a sailor from Dieppe, whose name has been omitted from the records. According to his own account, as related by Le Moyne,

"he was among those who were pinioned for slaughter, and was knocked in the head with the rest, but, instead of being killed, was only stunned; and the three others with whom he was tied falling above him, he was left for dead along with them. The Spaniards got together a great pile of wood to burn the corpses; but, as it grew late, they put it off until the next day. The sailor, coming to his senses among the dead bodies in the night, bethought himself of a knife which he wore in a wooden sheath, and contrived to work himself about until little by little he got the knife out and cut the ropes that bound him. He then rose up and silently departed, journeying all the rest of the night. After travelling three days without stopping, he came to a certain Indian chief, . . . with

Oct. 15, 1565, *ibid.*, tomo ii., pp. 102, 103. Le Challeux in "Histoire Mémorable" (reprint in Gaffarel, *Hist. de la Floride*, p. 476) says he was first stabbed from behind, as does also the "Requeste au Roy" (*ibid.*, p. 478). There is a curious confirmation of the conversation between Ribaut and one of his murderers in the story of the Dieppe sailor reported by Le Moyne (De Bry, *Brevis Narratio*, p. 29). See p. 203 in this volume. Fourquevaux, in his letter to Charles IX., of Aug. 11, 1566 (*Dépêches*, p. 104), says: "Tout le demeurant fut incontinent mis en pièces jusques au nombre de 873"!

[1] Avilés to Philip II., Oct. 15, 1565, Ruidíaz, *La Florida* tomo ii., p. 103.

whom he remained hidden eight months before he was betrayed to the Spaniards." [1]

After serving as a slave for a year in the fort at St. Augustine, and then being sent to Cuba, where he was chained to another Frenchman, the two unfortunates were finally sold together and put on board a ship bound for Portugal. On her way she was captured by a French vessel, and the two Frenchmen, still in chains, finally obtained their liberty.

The Dieppe sailor gave his own account of the final massacre of the French to Le Moyne, and as it is a type of the version which was generally accepted and believed in by the French it deserves our consideration. Following his shipwreck Ribaut determined to make for Fort Caroline, and after enduring many hardships he finally reached a point in its neighbourhood, as the sailor supposed, but really at Matanzas Inlet. Here he encamped, and sending one Vasseur with six men in an Indian canoe to reconnoitre, they presently returned with the distressing information that the Spanish flag was floating above Fort Caroline.[2] Ribaut at once recognised how desperate was his situation, with his men in danger of perishing by starvation and exposure, and sent two of his officers to sound the Spaniards, who the narrator supposed were at Fort Caroline, across the river.

[1] De Bry, *Brevis Narratio*, p. 29; English translation of Fred. B. Perkins in *Narrative of Le Moyne*, Boston, 1875, p. 22. Barcia (*Ensayo*, Año MDLXVII., pp. 129, 130, 135) relates a similar story of an escaped Frenchman named Pedro Breu, subsequently taken by Avilés, and not recounted by Merás or Barrientos.

[2] See Le Challeux's similiar statement that Ribaut sent a reconnoissance to Fort Caroline, "Histoire Mémorable," reprint in Gaffarel, *Hist. de la Floride*, p. 474 and p. 195, in this volume. Barcia (*Ensayo*, Año MDLXV., p. 84) says the party did not return to Ribaut, but escaped to Orista or Santa Elena on finding that Fort Caroline had fallen. He appears to identify the party with the Frenchmen heard of by Avilés on his first visit to Guale. See p. 245 in this volume.

" They went in a canoe with five or six soldiers, and, according to orders, showed themselves a good distance off. The Spaniards on seeing them, came in a boat to the other bank of the river, and held a parley with our men. The French asked what had become of the men left in the Fort? The Spaniards replied that their commander, who was a humane and clement person, had sent them all to France in a large ship abundantly supplied, and that they might say to Ribaut that he and his men should be used equally well."

The French returned with this message, to which Ribaut too hastily gave credence. Urged on by the majority of his men to secure terms of surrender, although there were some who questioned its wisdom, he sent La Caille to the Spanish commander, with the orders that

" if the latter should seem inclined to clemency, to ask in the name of the Lieutenant of the King of France, for a safe-conduct, and to announce, that, if the Spanish leader would make oath to spare all their lives, they would come in and throw themselves at his feet. . . . Coming to the fort he [La Caille] was taken before the Commander, and, throwing himself at his feet, delivered his message. Having heard La Caille through, he not only pledged his faith to La Caille in the terms suggested, and confirmed the pledge with many signs of the cross, and by kissing the Evangelists, but made oath in the presence of all his men, and drew up a writing sealed with his seal, repeating the oath, and promising that he would without fraud, faithfully, and like a gentleman and a man of honesty, preserve the lives of Ribaud and his men. All of this was handsomely written out, and given to La Caille."

The assurance thus solemnly given

" was joyfully received by some, while others did not entertain any great expectations from it. Ribaud, however, having made an excellent speech to his people, and all having joined in offering prayer to God, gave orders to proceed, and with all his company came down to the bank of the river near the fort. Upon being seen by the Spanish sentinels, they were taken over in boats. Ribaud himself, and D'Ottigny, Laudonnière's Lieutenant, were first led into the fort by themselves; the rest were halted about a bowshot from the fort, and all were tied up in fours back to back; from which, and other indications, they quickly perceived that their lives were lost. Ribaud asked to see the Governor, to remind him of his promise; but he spoke to deaf ears. D'Ottigny, hearing the despairing cries of his men, appealed to the oath which had been taken, but they laughed at him. As Ribaud insisted on his application, a Spanish soldier finally came in, and asked in French if he were the commander, Ribaud. The answer was 'Yes.' The man asked again if Ribaud did not expect, when he gave an order to his soldiers, that they would obey; to which he again said 'Yes.' 'I propose to obey the orders of my commander also,' replied the Spaniard; 'I am ordered to kill you,' and with that he thrust a dagger into his breast; and he killed D'Ottigny in the same way. When this was done, men were detailed to kill all the rest who had been tied up, by knocking them in the head with clubs and axes; which they proceeded to do without delay, calling them meanwhile Lutherans, and enemies to God and the Virgin Mary. In this manner they were all most cruelly murdered in violation of an oath, except a drummer from Dieppe named Dronet, a fifer, [the narrator], and a fiddler named Masselin, who was kept alive to play for dancing."[1]

That same night Avilés returned to St. Augustine; and when the event became known, there were some, even in that isolated garrison, living in constant dread of a descent by the French, who accounted him cruel, an opinion which his brother-in-law, Merás, the very man who helped to kill Ribaut, does not hesitate to record. And when the news eventually reached Spain, even there a vague rumour was afloat that there were those who

[1] Le Moyne in *Brevis Narratio*, pp. 27–29; English translation of Fred. B. Perkins in *Narrative of Le Moyne*, pp. 20–22.

condemned Avilés for perpetrating the massacre against his given word.[1] Others among the settlers thought that he had acted as a good captain, because, with their small store of provisions, they considered that there would have been an imminent danger of their perishing by hunger had their numbers been increased by the Frenchmen, even had they been Catholics.[2] Don Bartolomé Barrientos, Professor at the University of Salamanca, whose history was completed two years after the event, expresses still another phase of Spanish contemporary opinion:

"He acted as an excellent inquisitor; for when asked if they were Catholics or Lutherans, they dared to proclaim themselves publicly as Lutherans, without fear of God or shame before men; and thus he gave them that death which their insolence deserved. And even in that he was very merciful in granting them a noble and honourable death, by cutting off their heads, when he could legally have burnt them alive. . . . He killed them, I think, rather by divine inspiration, than through any counsel of the human understanding, for he had no wish that his own people by touching pitch, should be defiled by it."[3]

Another curious side light upon the aspect in which these massacres presented themselves to those who were in frequent and long continued intercourse with Menéndez, is furnished by an enquiry into his service to the King, accompanying a request for relief made in 1595, and addressed to the Crown by one of his sons-in-law. Five out of seven of the deponents in the enquiry mention Avilés's conquest of Florida and add in the most matter-of-fact way that he killed all of the French there. The striking feature in the statements is the entire ab-

[1] Fourquevaux to Charles IX., July 5, 1566, *Dépêches*, p. 94.

[2] Merás in Ruidíaz, *La Florida*, tomo i., p. 127; Barrientos in García, *Dos Antiguas Relaciones de la Florida*, p. 70.

[3] "Hechos" in García, *Dos Antiguas Relaciones de la Florida*, p. 72.

sence of all sectarian bitterness, and the evident inference that the killing was an action to be recorded to his credit along with the conquest of the country.[1]

The motives which prompted Avilés in these deeds of blood must not be too rashly attributed exclusively to religious fanaticism, or to race hatred. The position subsequently taken by the Spanish Government in its relations with France to justify the crime turned on the large number of the French and the fewness of the Spaniards; the scarcity of provisions, and the absence of ships with which to transport them as prisoners. These reasons do not appear in the brief accounts contained in Menéndez's letter of October 15, 1565, but some of them are explicitly stated by Barrientos, and even Mr. Parkman[2] feels constrained to admit the danger to which the Spaniards would have been exposed by the preponderance in numbers of the French had they been spared. It is quite probable that Menéndez clearly perceived the great risk he would run in granting the Frenchmen their lives and in retaining so large a body of prisoners in the midst of his colonists; that it would be a severe strain upon his supply of provisions and seriously hamper the dividing up of his troops into small garrisons for the forts which he contemplated erecting at different points along the coast. In arriving at his sanguinary solution of the difficulty, he probably thanked God that they were "Lutherans," and that in fulfilling the counsels of prudence he could also execute the divine will upon heretics.[3]

[1] See "Información de algunos servicios prestados por el Adelantado Pedro Menéndez de Avilés, México, 3 de Abril de 1595," in Ruidíaz, *La Florida*, tomo ii., p. 590. Testimony of Sebastian de Arguelles, pp. 594, 598; of Grauiel de Riuera, pp. 601, 603; of Augustin Espinola, pp. 607, 608; of Gonzalo Menéndez de Valdés, pp. 611, 612; of Antonio García Vasalenque, pp. 614–617.

[2] *Pioneers of France in the New World*, Boston, 1893, p. 150.

[3] See Appendix Q, The Situation of Avilés at the Time of the Massacre. In connection with these massacres by Menéndez Professor E. G. Bourne

Philip's comment on the event was characteristic. On the back of a dispatch from Avilés in Havana, of October 12, 1565, there appears in his well-known handwriting: "As to those he has killed he has done well, and as to those he has saved, they shall be sent to the galleys." In the letter of May 12, 1566, written in accordance with these instructions, and conveying Philip's approval, he said:

"And as for the judgment you have executed upon the Lutheran corsairs, who have sought to occupy and fortify that country, to sow in it their evil sect, and to continue from there the robberies and injuries which they have committed and are still committing, wholly contrary to the service of God and of me, we believe that you have acted with entire justification and prudence, and we hold that we have been well served."[1]

In his official utterances in justification of the massacre Philip laid perhaps a greater stress upon the contamination which heresy might have wrought among the natives than upon the invasion of his dominions. But in considering the various motives which may have prompted his approval of the ghastly massacre, one should not forget that when, seventeen years later, measures were under way in England for the sending of a Roman Catholic colony to Florida, Philip's ambassador, Mendoza, informed the leaders that in the event of such an undertaking

in his "Spain in America" (*The American Nation, A History*, vol. iii., p. 186), very appositely calls attention to the massacre of the English at Amboyna by the Dutch in 1623, and to Cromwell's massacre of the Irish at Drogheda in 1649. Cromwell, who in his own words believed himself to be executing the "righteous judgement of God," relates in his dispatch that "when they submitted, their officers were knocked on the head [and], every tenth man of the soldiers killed."

[1] Parkman, *Pioneers of France in the New World*, Boston, 1893, p. 150; Philip II. to Avilés, May 12, 1566, Ruidíaz, *La Florida*, tomo ii., p. 362. The letter is also given in Barcia, *Ensayo*, Año MDLXVI., p. 116.

"they would at once have their heads cut off, as was done to the French, who went with Jean Ribaut." [1]

On his return to St. Augustine Avilés wrote to the King a somewhat cursory account of the preceding events and summarised the results in the following language:

"The other people with Ribaut, some seventy or eighty in all, took to the forest, refusing to surrender unless I grant them their lives. These and twenty others who escaped from the fort, and fifty who were captured by the Indians, from the ships which were wrecked, in all one hundred and fifty persons, rather less than more, are [all] the French alive to-day in Florida, dispersed and flying through the forest, and captive with the Indians. And since they are Lutherans and in order that so evil a sect shall not remain alive in these parts, I will conduct myself in such wise, and will so incite my friends, the Indians, on their part, that in five or six weeks very few if any will remain alive. And of a thousand French with an armada of twelve sail who had landed when I reached these provinces, only two vessels have escaped, and those very miserable ones, with some forty or fifty persons in them." [2]

And so it was that Avilés purged Florida of the French and of heresy.

[1] "Copia de carta descifrada de Don Bernardino de Mendoza, Lóndres á 11 de Julio de 1582," *Correspondencia de Felipe II.*, etc., tomo v., p. 397. English translation in *Spanish State Papers*, 1580–1586, III., Elizabeth, p. 349.

[2] Avilés to Philip II., Oct. 15, 1565, Ruidíaz, *La Florida*, tomo ii., p. 103.

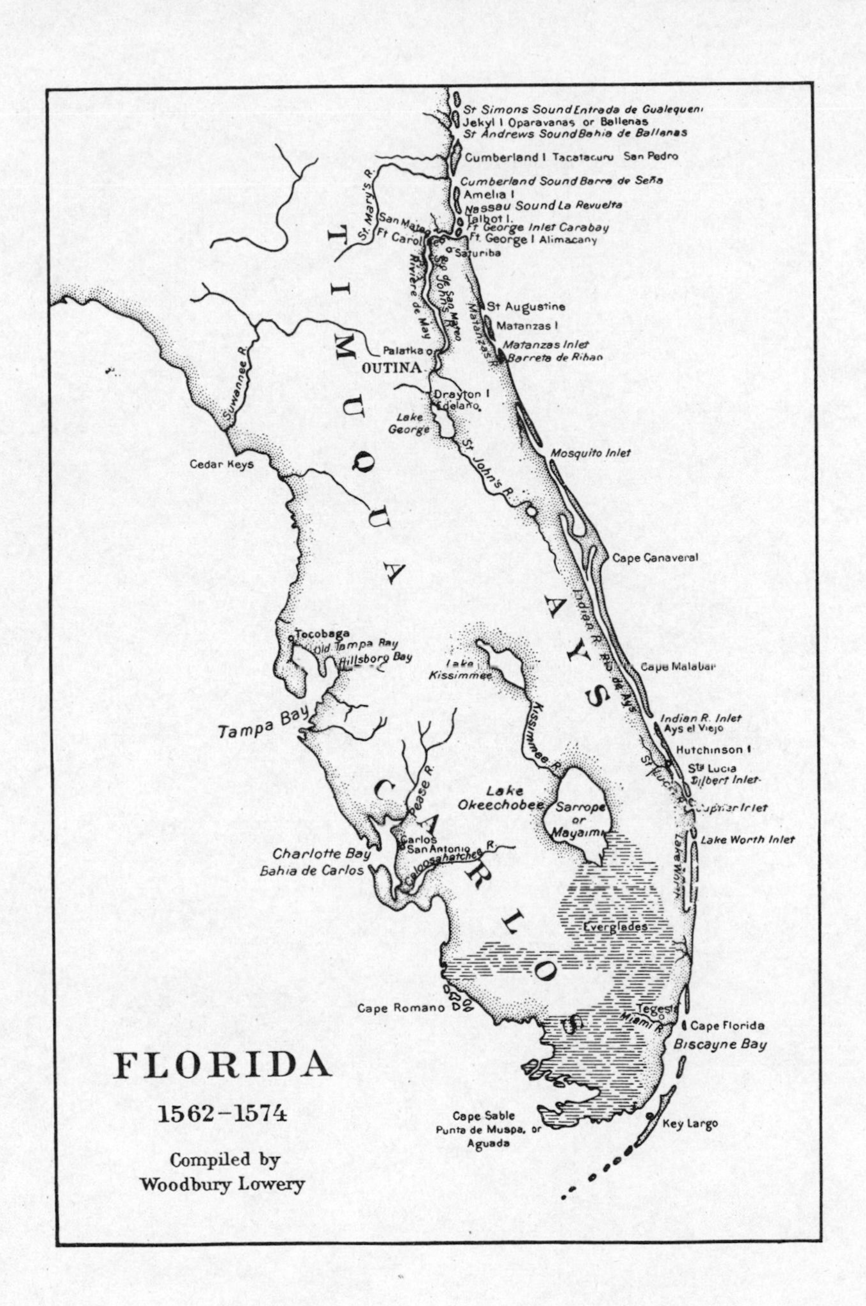
FLORIDA
1562–1574
Compiled by
Woodbury Lowery
St Simons Sound Entrada de Gualequeni
Jekyl I Oparavanas or Ballenas
St Andrews Sound Bahia de Ballanas
Cumberland I Tacatacuru San Pedro
Cumberland Sound Barra de Seña
Amelia I
Nassau Sound La Revuelta
Talbot I.
Ft George Inlet Carabay
Ft. George I Alimacany
St. Mary's R.
San Mateo
Ft Caroline
Saturiba
Riviere de May
Rio de San Mateo
St John's R.
Matanzas R.
St Augustine
Matanzas I
Matanzas Inlet
Barreta de Ribao
Palatka
OUTINA
Drayton I
Edelano
Lake George
Suwannee R.
Cedar Keys
TIMUQUA
Mosquito Inlet
St John's R.
Cape Canaveral
Indian R. Rio de Ays
AYS
Cape Malabar
Indian R. Inlet
Ays el Viejo
Hutchinson I
Sta Lucia
St Lucie R.
Jupiter Inlet
Lake Worth Inlet
Lake Worth
Tocobaga
Old Tampa Bay
Hillsboro Bay
Lake Kissimmee
Kissimmee R.
Tampa Bay
Pease R.
Lake Okeechobee
Sarrope or Mayaimi
Carlos
San Antonio
Caloosahatchee R.
Charlotte Bay
Bahia de Carlos
CARLOS
Everglades
Cape Romano
Tegesta
Miami R.
Cape Florida
Biscayne Bay
Cape Sable
Punta de Muspa, or Aguada
Key Largo

BOOK II

THE SPANISH COLONY

CHAPTER I

THE AYS EXPEDITION. AVILÉS AT HAVANA

FOR the moment the cool judgment of Avilés seemed almost carried away by his success, and he dreamed dreams of extending the empire of his master over the entire northern continent. In the same letter which conveyed the announcement of the two massacres, he wrote Philip II.:

"Considering these lands to be of so great an extent and the climate so good, and the injury and disturbance which enemies and corsairs can cause them every day, and how they can possess themselves of the countries to the North of here, near Newfoundland, where they are masters by violence, and can easily maintain themselves, the following is what should be done in every particular."[1]

First of all, he proposed to run down the coast of the peninsula and visit the Florida Keys in search of a suitable harbour where he could construct a fort to protect the seaboard from enterprises such as he had attributed to

[1] Avilés to Philip II., Oct. 15, 1565, Ruidíaz, *La Florida*, tomo ii., p. 93.

Ribaut in conjunction with the English.[1] Having garrisoned it with reinforcements from Havana, he expected to be back at St. Augustine and San Mateo by the beginning of April. He then proposed to ascend the coast as far as Chesapeake Bay, which he called the Bay of Santa Maria in 37°, constructing a fort there and another at Santa Elena.

He had formed a notion that an arm of the sea extended in a south-westerly direction from Newfoundland and terminated at the foot of a range of mountains eighty leagues inland to the north of the Chesapeake, and that one of the north-western branches of the bay, possibly the Potomac, was the much-sought-for passage to the Pacific. For this reason he dwelt upon the great importance of controlling the bay, which in his mind not only defended the approach to Mexico, but also commanded the pathway of commerce with China and the Moluccas.[2] Prudential reasons also entered into this part of his plan, and he was in haste to put it into effect for fear of the return of Jacques Ribaut the following year.[3] He also proposed to establish a fort and garrison in the Bay of Juan Ponce which he vaguely confounded with Appalachee Bay, and to found a settlement at Coça in 38° or 39° "at the foot of the mountains which come

[1] See p. 96 in this volume.

[2] It is difficult to understand from Menéndez's letter what was the particular conformation he attributed to North America. Possibly he entertained the idea that it tapered to a narrow neck in the vicinity of Chesapeake Bay, connecting the more northerly portion with a somewhat similar extension of the continent to the south, such as we see in the Vesconte Maiollo map of 1527, and in the *Novæ Insulæ* of Ptolemy's *Geographia Universalis* of 1540. "It seems clear," writes Mr. Parkman, "that Menéndez believed that Chesapeake Bay communicated with the St. Lawrence, and thence with Newfoundland on the one hand, and the South Sea on the other" (*Pioneers of France in the New World*, p. 149, note).

[3] Avilés to Philip II., Oct. 15, 1565, Ruidíaz, *La Florida*, tomo ii., pp. 93–95, 100, 101; Dec. 5, 1565, *ibid.*, tomo ii., p. 121; Dec. 25, 1565, *ibid.*, tomo ii., pp. 131, 132.

from the mines of Zacatecas and San Martin," on account of its advantageous situation on the way to these mines.[1]

He pictured to the King the many and great profits that would accrue to Spain from the abundant wine of the country, the sugar plantations, the herds of cattle, the pitch and tar and ship timber, the salt and wheat, the fruits and waters, the quantities of rice and pearls, and even the silk from the interior, until, carried away by the vision he had himself conjured into existence, he exclaimed:

"And I assure Your Majesty that in the future Florida will be of little expense, and will pay Your Majesty much money, and will be of more value to Spain than New Spain or even Peru, and it may be said that this country is but a suburb of Spain, for it does not take more than forty days' sailing to come here, and usually as many more to return." [2]

It was an alluring picture which Avilés had drawn for his master's eye, and intended perhaps rather to arouse the cupidity of his sovereign and induce him to assist the enterprise in a more liberal spirit than he had as yet shown than due to any illusions lurking in the hard head of the Adelantado. This rhapsody was interrupted by the two massacres and the burning of San Mateo, only to be resumed again, and it was sent to Spain by the hand of Diego Flores de Valdes, who probably arrived there in December.[3]

But more immediate considerations were pressing hard

[1] Avilés to Philip II., Oct. 15, 1565, *ibid.*, tomo ii., pp. 98, 99; Dec. 25, 1565, *ibid.*, tomo ii., p. 133.

[2] Avilés to Philip II., Oct. 15, 1565, *ibid.*, tomo ii., pp. 99, 104. In his letter of Dec. 5, 1565, *ibid.*, tomo ii., p. 121, he says 40 or 50 days from Spain to Florida.

[3] Avilés to Philip II., Oct. 15, 1565, *ibid.*, tomo ii., p. 101. Diego Flores de Valdes was expected to arrive in Spain by the end of November (same to same, Dec. 5, 1565, *ibid.*, p. 105). He was certainly there by February, 1566, see Philip II. to Alava, Feb. 23, 1566, MS. Arch. Nat., Paris, K, 1505 (75), fol. 2.

upon Avilés. Shortly after his arrival he had informed the King that his supply of biscuit could be made to last him through January,[1] and the capture of Fort Caroline had greatly increased his store of meal; but a month later he found that the biscuit he had brought with him was already spoiling. Although many of the soldiers voluntarily decreased the amount of their rations,[2] the deterioration of the bread, coupled with the burning of the fort, was rapidly reducing his colony to such straits, that he informed Philip "unless we are succoured very shortly we shall be in actual need, and many will depart this world from starvation." [3]

Three weeks had barely passed since the final massacre when word was brought by the Indians that the seventy or eighty Frenchmen belonging to Ribaut's company, who had refused to surrender, were constructing a fort thirty leagues distant from St. Augustine in the neighbourhood of Cape Canaveral, where the *Trinity* had been wrecked, and were also building a vessel which they intended to send to France for succour. Again Menéndez determined to act promptly. He sent to San Mateo for reinforcements, and while awaiting their arrival he appointed his brother Bartolomé Governor of St. Augustine, directed the number of hours that should be spent each day upon the fortifications which he had marked out, the proper distribution of the work among the troops, and provided for the criminal jurisdiction among his colonists.

On the 23rd of August his reinforcements arrived from San Mateo, and November 2nd [4] he set out for the fort of the French. He embarked a force of one hundred men

[1] Avilés to Philip II., Sept. 11, 1565, Ruidíaz, *La Florida*, tomo ii., p. 79.

[2] Merás in *ibid.*, tomo i., p. 178.

[3] Avilés to Philip II., Oct. 15, 1565, *ibid.*, tomo ii., p. 104. Barrientos in García, *Dos Antiguas Relaciones de la Florida*, p. 74.

[4] Avilés to Philip II., Dec. 5, 1565, Ruidíaz, *La Florida*, tomo ii., p. 106; Barrientos (in García, *Dos Antiguas Relaciones de la Florida*, p. 75) and Merás (Ruidíaz, *ibid.*, tomo i., p. 129) say he started August 26th.

aboard of three light boats which he furnished with provisions for forty days, while he himself marched by land at the head of one hundred and fifty more, guided by the Indians. At night the men in the boats landed and the entire force encamped together. On November 4th,[1] All Saints' Day, at dawn, the Spaniards came upon the fort, approaching it by water as well as by land, but the French discovered them in time to abandon it and escape into the forest. The Spaniards secured six guns, which had been saved from the wreck of the *Trinity*, some powder, and, best of all, some provisions, for the soldiers had been put upon half rations on setting out from St. Augustine. Avilés caused the boat to be burnt, as well as the fort, which was constructed of wood, buried the guns, which were too heavy to transport in his boats, and sent a French trumpeter, whose life he had spared, to summon the fugitives to surrender, promising to grant them their lives.

The poor shipwrecked Frenchmen, pushed to the last extremity, with no other alternative before them but captivity and death at the hands of the savages, notwithstanding the fate which had befallen their comrades, trusted themselves to the promises of the General, and came in, laying down their arms. Their captain alone, with three or four others, refused to yield, sending word that they preferred to be devoured by the Indians rather than to surrender to Spaniards. Then followed a curious illustration of the character of the man with whom they had to deal. Avilés received the prisoners, who proved to be from Navarre, servants of the Prince of Condé, with great kindness. He seated the noblemen at his own table and gave them clothing, while the sailors messed with his sailors and the soldiers with his soldiers.[2] The

[1] Barrientos in García, *Dos Antiguas Relaciones de la Florida*, p. 76.

[2] Aviles to Philip II., Dec. 5, 1565, Ruidíaz, *La Florida*, tomo ii., pp. 105, 106; Merás in *ibid.*, tomo i., pp. 128–131; Barrientos in García, *Dos Antiguas Relaciones de la Florida*, pp. 73–75.

same afternoon he continued fifteen leagues along the coast to the south of the village of the Ays Indians, situated on Indian River between the St. Sebastian River and Indian Inlet, possibly at that time on the northern end of Hutchinson's Island south of the inlet.[1]

It was an arduous march, but "the Spanish Nation," says Barrientos, "is like sorrel horses, who though lean and famished show mettle until they fall in their tracks."[2] The rations were now reduced to half a pound of bread daily, one-third of the usual allowance, which the seventy Frenchmen shared equally with the Spaniards. This scanty fare was eked out with the hearts of the palmettos, prickly pears, and cocoa-plums. The start was made at two o'clock in the morning and the march continued until daybreak, when a halt was called, and the meagre breakfast was eaten. Two hours later the march began again and continued until sunset, with another interval of rest from half-past eleven or twelve until two. The sand was frequent and heavy and the sun hot. Avilés led the vanguard with eight of the strongest of his company. But the men, weary and hungry, lagged behind, and one of the soldiers who had been among the first to enter Fort Caroline when the assault was given, died from sheer exhaustion. The boats went around to seek the mouth of the inlet.

The Ays chief received the Spaniards with much kindness, kissing them on the mouth, which says Barrientos, was their greatest sign of friendship. His face was decorated with various colours, and he as well as all of his chief men wore frontlets of gold, probably obtained from the vessels wrecked along the coast. Menéndez ordered his men to respect the property of the natives, and presented them with little gifts of knives and mirrors and

[1] See Appendix R, Ays.

[2] "Vida y Hechos," in García, *Dos Antiguas Relaciones de la Florida*, p. 76.

scissors. The Spaniards remained four days at Ays, and Avilés went down the lagoon to look for a suitable place to settle, but failed to find one. The provisions of the explorers had now become so reduced that starvation was pressing upon them, and the General determined to go in person to Havana to seek succour for his various settlements. Before his departure he encamped two hundred of his party under Juan Velez de Medrano at a place on the lagoon three leagues distant from Ays, where there was abundance of fish, in order to remove his men from the neighbourhood of the Indian village and thus avoid the possibility of any conflict between them and the natives during his absence, and he left them supplies for fifteen days.[1]

In the latter part of the month he set sail for Havana in his two open boats with fifty men and twenty of the French prisoners.[2] It was a bold and dangerous undertaking. Impelled only by the wind and by oars in the hands of weary and famishing men, he had to stem the swift-flowing currents of the Gulf Stream, which reaches its greatest velocity in this neighbourhood. He had observed in his previous journeys the existence of back currents along the Florida shore,[3] and availing himself of these he followed down the coast, discovering on his way the two inlets at Gilbert's Bar and Jupiter, and in three days reached Cuba. During the crossing a storm arose, and Avilés shared the tiller with one of the Frenchmen. On leaving Ays his compass had been broken, and,

[1] Avilés to Philip II., Dec. 5, 1565, Ruidíaz, *La Florida*, tomo ii., pp. 106, 107; Merás in *ibid.*, tomo i., pp. 132–136; Barrientos in García, *Dos Antiguas Relaciones de la Florida*, pp. 76, 78.

[2] Both Barrientos (in *ibid.*, p. 78) and Merás (Ruidíaz, *La Florida*, tomo i., p. 130) say 20 Frenchmen. Avilés does not refer to them in his letter of Dec. 5, 1565, but in his letter to Philip II., of Jan. 30, 1566 (*ibid.*, tomo ii., p. 143) he also says 70 men in all.

[3] Avilés to Philip II., Dec. 5, 1565, Ruidíaz, *La Florida*, tomo ii., p. 107.

missing Havana during the night, he made the harbour of Bayahonda, fifteen leagues beyond.

On landing, the entire company kneeled down to render thanks for their deliverance, and then Avilés

"called the Frenchmen and charged them to behold the power and the goodness of God, and if they were Lutherans to repent and turn Catholics; and [he observed] that whatever their religion might be, he was bound to treat them well because they had surrendered on his word: and that he would give them liberty to return to France in the first ships leaving for Spain: that he told them this because of his desire that they should save themselves. There were some of them," continues Barrientos, "who weeping, beat their breasts beseeching Our Lord for mercy; and said that they had been bad Christians and Lutherans, and that they had repented, and from then on would abandon their evil sect, would confess themselves and commune, for they wished to keep that [faith] which the Holy Mother Church of Rome held and believed. The Adelantado gave them all presents and bade them not to trouble about their work, and that he would care for them as if they were his brothers."[1]

Re-embarking, Avilés shortly reached Havana, where he was joyfully received by Diego de Amaya, the commander of the second boat, who had arrived two days before him, and had given him up for lost. He found there Pedro Menéndez Marqués, with two hundred men and three vessels of the Asturian fleet, from which Marqués had become separated in a storm.[2]

The squadron which had been fitted out in Biscay and the Asturias to join Avilés at the Canaries consisted of

[1] Barrientos in García, *Dos Antiguas Relaciones de la Florida*, p. 80; Merás (Ruidíaz, *La Florida*, tomo i., p. 138) tells the same story in identically the same language.

[2] Avilés to Philip II., Dec. 5, 1565, Ruidíaz, *ibid.*, tomo ii., p. 108; Merás in *ibid.*, tomo i., p. 137; Barrientos in García, *Dos Antiguas Relaciones de la Florida*, p. 80.

three vessels from the seaport of Avilés with two hundred and fifty-seven soldiers and sailors, and two additional ships from Gijon with seventy-eight persons, among which were eleven Franciscan friars and one lay brother, a friar of the Order of Mercy, a priest, and eight Jesuits.[1] Esteban de las Alas, who three years before had commanded the fleet arriving from New Spain,[2] went as General, and Pedro Menéndez Marqués, nephew of the Adelantado, was Admiral. So eager was the adventurous population in that country of seamen to embark in the enterprise, its zeal fired by the report that the heretics were to be driven out of the King's dominions, that a number of vessels from Santander and other ports along the coast had joined it, and it was not found necessary to take out the licence for the five hundred negro slaves.[3]

The fleet set sail about the end of May and, on reaching the Canaries, found that Avilés had already left. During the passage many of the accompanying vessels appear to have put back, or to have been lost on account of stormy weather.[4] But Las Alas continued the journey with the five ships and appears to have touched at Puerto Rico. On his way to Santo Domingo, in pursuance of the orders he had found awaiting him at the Canaries, he captured off the northern end of Hispaniola two Portuguese prizes,[5] of which Las Alas secured the one of least

[1] Merás in Ruidíaz, *La Florida*, tomo i., p. 63; Barcia (*Ensayo*, Año MDLXV., p. 69) merely copies from Merás.

[2] Duro, *Armada Española*, tomo i., p. 465.

[3] Merás in Ruidíaz, *La Florida*, tomo i., p. 63; Barrientos in García, *Dos Antiguas Relaciones de la Florida*, p. 35; Barcia (*Ensayo*, Año MDLXV., p. 69) merely copies from Merás.

[4] Merás in Ruidíaz, *La Florida*, tomo i., p. 63.

[5] As typical of the atrocities to which seafaring men were exposed in those days Avilés writes the King that he had set these Portuguese to row the boats, although all of the Spaniards whom the Portuguese captured in the Moluccas were sewed up in the sails and thrown alive into the sea. Letter of Dec. 5, 1565, Ruidíaz, *La Florida*, tomo i., p. 112.

value and Marqués the other. Before reaching Santo Domingo a storm separated them, and Marqués proceeded to Havana with his prize, where, as already related, Menéndez found him.[1]

When Avilés entered the harbour of Havana, his arrival had been announced to the governor, García Osorio. His own vessels had hailed him with salvos of artillery and the blowing of trumpets. Osorio also came down to the quay to receive him, with a drummer and piper and an escort flying a flag and bearing torches, but he did not remain. His treasurer, Juan de Hinestrosa, however, welcomed the General and conducted him and his people to his own house, where they were entertained with great hospitality. It was an unpropitious star for the Florida colony which had brought the Adelantado to Havana at this moment, for the Governor had just committed a very arbitrary and high-handed offence against Juan de la Parra, a captain of the fleet of New Spain, subject to the orders of Avilés. Some three months before, La Parra, while on his way to Havana, had captured a Portuguese prize. Within an hour of his arrival the Governor had forcibly seized it, mutilating the pilot in charge, to which La Parra had quietly submitted; but as the latter had been unable to withhold some expressions of anger at the unwarrantable proceeding, Osorio had also seized him and confined him in a dark prison, where he had been languishing for three months, chained to the walls of his dungeon. All of this Avilés learned from Hinestrosa, who had also warned him that the Governor had forbidden the subject to be broached.

The day following his arrival Avilés met the Governor on leaving church after mass, and later in the day called on him, informed him of the straits to which his Florida colony was reduced, and exhibited his two royal cédulas[2]

[1] Avilés to Philip II., Dec. 5, 1565, *ibid.*, tomo ii., p. 111.

[2] Avilés to Philip II., Jan. 30, 1566, *ibid.*, tomo ii., p. 150.

which ordered Osorio to furnish him with a vessel, five hundred soldiers, and twenty horses for the conquest of the country. The General modestly stated that he did not require the ship and soldiers called for by the royal cédulas and would be content with one-fifth of the amount which the armament would cost. As an alternative, in case Osorio was unwilling to lend this sum, he asked for the proceeds of the sale of the Portuguese prize, amounting to some ten or eleven thousand ducats; added that even four thousand ducats would be sufficient, which he also offered to secure, and ended by asking Osorio to surrender La Parra to his jurisdiction. At this the Governor became enraged, and flatly refused to give up the man or loan the money.[1]

It was a serious situation for the anxious Adelantado, for Cuba was the centre to which his ships were constantly plying in search of supplies for his Florida colony; and he feared the treatment to which his captains and officials would be exposed at the hands of one who could be so arbitrary with their commander. But his tact was equal to his courage. Clearly appreciating the importance of retaining at least the semblance of good terms with the Governor, and the necessity of committing no act of violence which could expose him to contempt of Osorio's legitimate authority, he controlled his temper, courteously doffed his hat,[2] and left his presence. "I assure Your Majesty," wrote Avilés, "that I secured a greater victory in submitting patiently and quietly to his bad treatment than that which I gained over the French in Florida."[3] Avilés was now thrown upon his own

[1] Avilés to Philip II., Dec. 5, 1565, *ibid.*, tomo ii., pp. 113–118. Merás in *ibid.*, tomo i., pp. 141–143. Barrientos in García, *Dos Antiguas Relaciones de la Florida*, pp. 81, 82.

[2] Barrientos, *ibid.*, p. 82. Merás in Ruidíaz, *La Florida*, tomo i., p. 143.

[3] "Real Carta de complacencia otorgada á Pero Menéndez por los servicios prestados en la conquista de la Florida, Madrid, May 12, 1566." Ruidíaz, *La Florida*, tomo ii., p. 364, sets out the action of the King on

resources, and as the necessity of revictualling his starving colonies was pressing, he sold the prize captured by Marqués, and with the proceeds loaded two vessels with sufficient provisions to last until January, one of which, in command of Diego de Amaya, was sent to the relief of the colonists at St. Augustine.[1]

The air at Havana was full of rumours of English, French, and Portuguese pirates infesting the neighbouring islands, and while awaiting the month of March to return to Florida, and possibly also in order to keep his men out of mischief in view of the attitude of the Governor of Cuba, Avilés determined to go and fight them. In the latter part of November he set sail with the three vessels of his nephew and the ship of the unfortunate Juan de la Parra. The very day of his departure he overtook a ship which, mistaking him and his fleet for corsairs, put into the harbour of Matanzas, where her crew abandoned her and made for the land. On searching her she proved to be a royal dispatch boat, and having recalled the crew, he learned that they were bringing him advices from Spain to prepare nine months' supplies of meat and fish for a reinforcement of eighteen hundred men who were to sail for Florida[2] in command of Sancho de Arciniega.[3] Convinced that these reinforcements were

the case of La Parra. Avilés to Philip II., Dec. 5, 1565, *ibid.*, tomo ii., p. 118.

[1] Avilés to Philip II., Dec. 5, 1565, *ibid.*, tomo ii., p. 111.

[2] Aviléz to Philip II., Dec. 5, 1565, *ibid.*, tomo ii., p. 109; Merás in *ibid.*, tomo i., pp. 146, 147; Barrientos in García, *Dos Antiguas Relaciones de la Florida*, pp. 82–84.

[3] "Nombramiento de Capitan General de la Armada destinada para yr á la Provincia de la Florida al socorro del General Pero Menéndez de Avilés, hecho por Su Magestad al Capitan Sancho de Arciniega. Año 1565." MS. Direc. de Hidrog., Madrid, *Col. Navarrete*, tomo xiv., No. 38. See also "Relación de la entrada y de la conquista que por mandado de Pero Menéndez de Avilés hizo en 1565 [*sic*] en el interior de la Florida el Capitan Juan Pardo, escrita por él mismo." Ruidíaz, *La Florida*, tomo ii., p. 465.

sent in view of a threatened attack of a French fleet, Avilés immediately abandoned his designs against the pirates and returned to Havana to forward the necessary material to Florida in anticipation of Arciniega's arrival.[1] He had already dispatched his brother-in-law, Merás, with a ship to Campeche to procure corn, chickens, shoes, and other necessary articles for Florida, with directions to proceed from there to New Spain, where he was to borrow money, enlist soldiers, and obtain some Dominican friars to convert the natives; and he now sent an additional vessel to Campeche for more provisions.[2] On December 19th his nephew, Pedro Menéndez Marqués, had sailed for Spain bearing dispatches.[3]

Osorio continued to subject him to a variety of petty annoyances. Avilés had wished to impress into his own service the dispatch boat which had brought the announcement of the prospective sailing of Arciniega's fleet: this the Governor had refused to allow. Then Avilés fell ill, and during the ten days he lay in bed forty of his men deserted, and Osorio lent him no assistance to recover them. The Governor impeded the departure of vessels going for provisions, and, according to the letter which Avilés wrote the King giving an account of the incident, he even sought to induce Hinestrosa to turn him out of his house, while he was still ill, with the object of driving him out of the town and compassing his death.[4]

Esteban de las Alas arrived early in January of 1566. After separating from Marqués he had encountered Gonzalo de Peñalosa, who had left Santo Domingo on the 28th of September with the armament furnished by the

[1] Avilés to Philip II., Dec. 5, 1565, Ruidíaz, *La Florida*, tomo ii., pp. 110, 119.

[2] Barrientos in García, *Dos Antiguas Relaciones de la Florida*, pp. 83, 84.

[3] Avilés to Philip II., Jan. 30, 1566, Ruidíaz, *La Florida*, tomo ii., p. 142.

[4] Avilés to Philip II., Dec. 25, 1565, *ibid.*, tomo ii., pp. 135–140. Same to same, *ibid.*, Jan. 30, 1566, tomo ii., pp. 150, 151.

Audiencia of Santo Domingo, and had captured a prize on his way. Together they had put into Yaguana for water and provisions, where they spent two weeks, capturing another prize during their detention. Proceeding to Havana by the Old Bahama Channel, they encountered a series of misfortunes. Delayed by the weather at various points along their route, they lost one ship in a storm, and at a harbour on the Cuban coast one hundred and ten men by desertion. Finally, at Sauana, Peñalosa received the news of the capture of Fort Caroline and, summoned to Havana with the remainder of his force, he delivered his dispatches to Avilés and found there his two vessels, which had preceded him in company with Las Alas. His presence being no longer required, Peñalosa attempted to return to Santo Domingo in his own vessels; but Avilés impressed both of them for the Florida service and also took possession of one of his guns and Osorio of the other, and he was compelled to wait two months in Havana, before he secured a ship in which to depart.[1]

The two vessels which had gone to Florida had now returned. That in command of Gonzalo Gallego had been absent but fifteen days. It found the Ays colony in a deplorable condition. Driven by starvation the settlers had divided up into small parties in search of food. The cacique of Ays had risen against them in company with the neighbouring Indians. In their extremity they had moved twenty leagues farther down the lagoon to the neighbourhood of Gilbert's Bar and St. Lucie River, where they had found more abundant food, fish and mulberries, and friendly Indians. During the four days

[1] "Relación del viaje que hizó á la Florida en 1566 [*sic*] el Capitan Gonzalo de Peñalosa en socorro del General Pero Menéndez de Avilés." Ruidíaz, *La Florida*, tomo ii., pp. 473–476. The date is incorrect; it should be 1565. Avilés to Philip II., Dec. 25, 1565, *ibid.*, tomo ii., p. 128. Same to same, Jan. 30, 1566, *ibid.*, tomo ii., p. 152. Merás in *ibid.*, tomo i., p. 149. Barrientos in García, *Dos Antiguas Relaciones de la Florida*, p. 85.

previous to Gallego's arrival they had subsisted solely upon palmettos, grasses, and water, and they had named the place Santa Lucia.[1]

Amaya[2] had also reached St. Augustine in safety, unloaded his supplies including some eighty sows, and then proceeded to San Mateo. Arriving there at the end of December, and overtaken by a storm, he lost his vessel on the bar, but by good fortune saved a small part of the provisions. He returned to Cuba in one of the two brigantines in which Avilés had planned to make his summer reconnaissance along the coast to the north, reaching Havana on the 28th of January.[3] The story which he brought with him was not encouraging. Over one hundred of the colonists at St. Augustine and San Mateo had died, for they were almost naked and had suffered greatly from the cold. The officers in charge reported that discontent was stirring, and that many of the settlers were speaking ill of the country and were anxious to abandon it. Indeed scarcely five days had elapsed after the departure of Avilés before the spirit of insubordination began to assert itself, and with the opening of November its promoters were secretly hatching plans and exchanging letters between the two forts, which were to bear fruit in broil and tumult.[4] It would be a serious matter for Avilés should their evil report get abroad, for it would discourage immigration and make a speedy end of the fortune which he had embarked in the enterprise. With his fear of the consequences the harsh

[1] Barrientos in *ibid.*, pp. 96, 97; Avilés to Philip II., Dec. 5, 1565; Ruidíaz, *La Florida*, tomo ii., p. 111; same to same, Jan. 30, 1566, *ibid.*, tomo ii., p. 144, where Avilés uses the term "aca" for the direction in which Santa Lucia lay. See Appendix S, Santa Lucia.

[2] Avilés calls him indifferently Diego de Maya and Amaya; Merás and Barrientos call him Maya.

[3] Avilés to Philip II., Jan. 30, 1566, Ruidíaz, tomo ii., p. 144; Barrientos in García, *Dos Antiguas Relaciones de la Florida*, p. 98.

[4] Merás in Ruidíaz, *La Florida*, tomo i., p. 176.

nature of the soldier reappeared, and he wrote the King requesting that the justices of the Indies be authorised to seize all persons going to or coming from Florida without his licence, sending them prisoners to him in Florida, where they were to serve perpetually at the oars, like galley slaves.[1]

The report had also reached him that the French had fortified Guale in the neighbourhood of Port Royal, where the Indians were numerous and friendly to them[2]; and Avilés concluded that the garrison must consist of the crews of the two ships which had escaped with Laudonnière and Jacques Ribaut, for he was still unaware of their return to France. In these gloomy tidings there was but one ray of light. It was said that over one thousand ducats' worth of gold and silver had already been collected from the natives. Menéndez, however, concluded not to return immediately to Florida on account of the tempestuous season.[3] He had already formed the plan of exploring the southern end of the peninsula and ascending its western shore as far as the Bay of San Jusepe in search of a good harbour, and his mind was set upon constructing a fort at the Bay of Ponce de Leon, which he believed to be but fifteen or twenty leagues distant from a south-western mouth of the St. John's River, by which a convenient water communication with San Mateo and St. Augustine would be secured. He had also learned that somewhere about the southern end of the peninsula there were Christian men and women reduced to a state of savagery, captives for twenty years in the hands of a chief named Carlos, who yearly sacrificed a number of them to his idols. Before setting out in search of them he caused masses to be said

[1] Avilés to Philip II., Jan. 30, 1566, *ibid.*, tomo ii., p. 153.

[2] Avilés, in his letter of Jan. 30, 1566 (*ibid.*, tomo ii., p. 145), says there were forty villages within a distance of three or four leagues of Guale.

[3] Avilés to Philip II., Jan. 30, 1566, *ibid.*, tomo ii., pp. 145, 146, 153.

before St. Anthony, whose peculiar attribute it is to bring about the recovery of lost objects, that through the saint's intercession he might discover the harbour where they dwelt.[1] Perhaps there still lurked in his mind a secret hope that his son Juan might be alive among them, or that the natives might give him some information by which his son might be found. With this end in view, and in order to reach Guale by the end of March or the beginning of April, after relieving his garrison on the River of Ays, he advanced the date of his departure by a month or two.[2]

[1] Merás in *ibid.*, tomo i., p. 150; Barrientos in García, *Dos Antiguas Relaciones de la Florida*, p. 85.

[2] Avilés to Philip II., Jan. 30, 1566, Ruidíaz, *La Florida*, tomo ii., pp. 145–148.

CHAPTER II

THE CARLOS EXPEDITION—MUTINY AT THE SETTLEMENTS

FEBRUARY 10, 1566,[1] Avilés left Havana on his expedition for the southern point of Florida with seven vessels and five hundred men. One of the objects which he had chiefly in view was the discovery of a safe passage for the fleets of New Spain between the Tortugas and the Florida Keys. Having assured himself of its existence, he took the direction of Florida in search of the captive Christians. Putting Las Alas in command of the fleet, he embarked with Diego de Amaya and thirty men in two small vessels drawing but little water, and proceeded along the coast, while the large ships accompanied him outside.

On the third day a squall separated him from the fleet; and on the following day, about the 18th of the month, as Avilés and his captain was continuing their reconnaissance of the coast, a canoe put out from the shore and, drawing near to the boat in command of Amaya, a man called out to him in Spanish: "Welcome, Spaniards and Christian brothers! God and St. Mary have told us that you were coming. And the Christian men and women who are still alive here have directed me to wait for you here with this canoe, to give you a letter, which I have." The surprise and joy of the Spaniards can be readily pic-

[1] Barrientos in García, *Dos Antiguas Relaciones de la Florida*, p. 85; Merás in Ruidíaz (*La Florida*, tomo i., p. 176) says Oct. 26, 1565, an evident error.

tured, as they received the speaker into their boat. He was naked except for a small deer-skin loin-cloth, and was painted like an Indian. Amaya embraced him and asked for his letter, whereupon the poor fellow drew from beneath his meagre garment a cross, saying: "That is the letter which the captive Christians yonder send you, beseeching you, by the death suffered by Our Lord for our salvation, not to pass by but to enter the harbour and rescue us from the cacique, and carry us to a Christian land." When Avilés himself came up the Spaniard informed him that they were in all twelve men and women in the hands of the Indians, the sole survivors of two hundred persons who, in the course of the past twenty years had been cast ashore on that inhospitable coast. All but these the cacique and his father had sacrificed to their idols. Then they knelt down, and adored the cross, thanking God for His mercy. Directing his boats to land, Avilés entered the harbour and they all sprang ashore.

The country was that of the Caloosas on the southern extremity of the peninsula, extending westward from Point Sable and up the western coast, probably as far north as the southern shores of Tampa Bay. It is for the most part a comparatively narrow strip of land closed in between the Everglades to the north and east, and the Gulf of Mexico, a country of low hills and drowned mangrove swamps, with streams of fresh water which take their rise in the Everglades. The coast is deeply indented with numerous bays and fringed with countless islands. At the time of Avilés's visit, the settlements of the Caloosas and of the Indians subject to them occupied the islands of the northern extremity of the Florida Keys, as well as those along the western coast, and on the mainland their many villages extended into the interior as far as the shores of Lake Miami.[1]

[1] See Appendix T, Caloosa.

Very little is known of the habits of this tribe. The shamans stood next in dignity to the chiefs of the tribe, and, in addition to their religious functions, worked cures among the sick, like others of their kind throughout the continent. They played a very influential part in the public council, and no action of any consequence was undertaken without their advice. The geographer Velasco has left us an account of some of the tribal customs. On the death of the child of a chief, his subjects sacrificed some of their sons and daughters to accompany it on its journey after death. On the death of the chief, his servants were killed. The Christian captives were annually offered up as food to the idols, who were said to feed upon their eyes, and a dance was performed with the head of the victim. A festival was also observed during the summer season, which continued for the space of three months, during which the shamans assembled near the village and ran wildly about at night, wearing horns upon their heads and imitating the cries of wolves and other wild beasts. The idols were certain grotesque masks, probably emblematic of the tribal deities, and which were preserved in a temple; in one of the ceremonies a procession of shamans wearing these masks, preceded by a group of women singing ritual songs, passed through the village, while the Indians would come out of their houses to pay their homage to the idols and accompany them with dancing back to the temple.[1]

Half a league distant from the landing-place was the village called Carlos, where dwelt the chief of the same name.[2] Fontanedo tells us that the name signifies "cruel

[1] Dos breves memorias sobre las costumbres de los yndios de la Florida, MS. Arch. Gen. de Indias, Seville, est. 135, caj. 7, leg. 8. *Javva* is the name given them by Alegre in his *Historia de la Compañía de Jesus en la Nueva España*, Mexico, 1842, tomo i., p. 15. In the *Histoire Notable*, Basanier, Paris, 1566, p. 78, Laudonnière gives *iarua* as the Timuquanan name for the shamans.

[2] Barrientos in García, *Dos Antiguas Relaciones de la Florida*, p. 87,

village,"[1] but the Spaniards, who had corrupted its pronunciation, believed that the Indian chief had assumed it in imitation of Charles V. on learning from some of his white captives that he was the greatest monarch on the earth.[2]

The Christian slave whom the Spaniards had just rescued was sent to inform Carlos of the arrival of an embassy sent by the King of Spain to secure his friendship, and bearing gifts for himself and his wives. Shortly thereafter the cacique came down to receive the newcomers, accompanied by a train of three hundred naked bowmen, each wearing a small deer-skin loin-cloth. Avilés, suspecting treachery, withdrew his boats a short distance from the land. After he had so placed them that the artillery would command the shore, he caused a carpet to be spread out on the ground, on which the cacique and his principal men seated themselves in a group facing the Adelantado, who was attended by thirty of his arquebusmen carrying lighted matches. Then the cacique knelt down and extended his arms with the palms of his hands

says: "Está la tierra de Este Cacique Entre la tierra de los martires digo la caueza de los martires, y baya de Ju° ponce. Al poniente de la Caueca de los martires." From this it would appear that he indicates Chatham Bay as the Bay of Ponce de Leon, and that he locates the village of Carlos about in the position given it in Le Moyne's map, at the southern extremity of the peninsula. But it must be remembered that his geographical information was of the vaguest description, and the village was probably in the same location as when it was visited by Ponce de Leon, *i. e.*, on Charlotte Harbour. See *Spanish Settlements*, vol. i., p. 441, The Bay of Juan Ponce. Merás (*Ruidíaz*, tomo i., p. 164) says it contained over 4000 inhabitants.

[1] "Memoria de las cosas y costa y indios de la Florida," *Col. Doc. Inedit. Indias*, tomo v., p. 534.

[2] Merás in Ruidíaz, *La Florida*, tomo i., p. 167; Barrientos in García, *Dos Antiguas Relaciones de la Florida*, p. 87. On the Spanish corruption of Indian names, see: Herrera, *Historia General*, Madrid, 1726, vol. ii., dec. 3, lib. viii., cap. viii. p. 241; Coxe's "Carolina," reprint in *Hist. Col. of Louisiana*, by B. F. French, Philadelphia, 1850, Pt. II., p. 233; Daniel G. Brinton, *Notes on the Floridian Peninsula*, Philadelphia, 1859, p. 112.

turned upward, upon which the Adelantado in turn placed his two hands. This was the mark of the highest reverence that the Caloosas could pay to a superior. Avilés followed with a distribution of presents. To the chief he gave a shirt, a pair of silk breeches, and a hat. He was a young man of twenty-five, tall and well formed, "and in his dress looked much the gentleman," says Barrientos. Other small gifts were given him for his wives. Bread, wine, and honey were served to the natives, with which they were greatly pleased, and the chief presented Avilés with a bar of silver and some other small objects in gold and jewels, and asked for more food and wine. To this Avilés replied that he had not sufficient for so many people, and invited Carlos and his principal men into his boat, where he promised to serve them a still more savoury repast.

Yielding to his curiosity and cupidity Carlos entered the ship with twenty of his companions, whereupon Avilés drew up the anchors and ran for the open. The Indians sprang to their feet in terror; but a soldier had previously been stationed by each of the natives to prevent his escape, should he make the attempt, and the General informed them through the interpreter, that, as his boats were small, he had only withdrawn from land to prevent the entrance of more Indians. He then regaled them with more food and gifts, and when Carlos finally wished to depart, informed him that the King of Spain wished to make friends with him and requested the return of the Christian captives, threatening him with death if he failed to comply, and making him the usual promises of friendship and assistance against his enemies in case he obeyed. Carlos readily agreed to his demand, and within an hour five women and three men were delivered up. Avilés directed them to be clothed, and the unfortunate creatures wept tears of joy at their deliverance, although their hearts were racked because of the children they left behind. After this, more gifts were distributed among the Indians and Carlos at last returned to his village, inviting the Adelantado to visit him and his wives, and promising to send two more Christian men and a woman, who were living in the interior.

The next morning the cacique, who had planned to slaughter the Spaniards in a grove on the way to his village, sent a number of canoes to bring the General ashore, and soon followed them in person with a large company of unarmed natives, bearing branches of palms, singing, and making great demonstrations of joy. They had come, said Carlos, to bear the Spaniards to their village on their backs as a mark of honour, and he himself would carry the Adelantado, a custom they had observed for other Christians who had visited his country, and his people would accompany them with rejoicings, "for we are all God's creatures," added the wily chief. But Avilés had been warned of the treachery by one of the Christian slaves and answered with equal guile. He thanked the Indians for their courtesy; observed that those who had accepted such treatment were but false Christians; that for his part he would never consent to be so honoured; and that he would visit their village with a few of his Spaniards. But the savages were too shrewd to be thus deceived, and, perceiving that they had been betrayed, at once took flight, whereupon Menéndez, anxious to retain their confidence, and to convince them that he knew nothing of their designs, brought his boats around to the neighbourhood of the village, blew his trumpet, and unfurled his flags as a signal for their canoes to come out and take him ashore. But this the Indians refused to do.

Anxious to rejoin the five ships from which he had become separated, Avilés now determined to set out in search of them, and, hearing of three captive Christians in a neighbouring harbour, went there in the hope of finding his vessels, and recovering the slaves[1]; but the search proved vain. Returning to the port of Carlos, he found that Las Alas had arrived in the meantime and had even visited the Indian town, where he had been well received by the natives, who were cowed at the sight of so strong a force, and where his soldiers had obtained by barter gold and silver to the value of over two thousand ducats.

Menéndez was eager to return to the settlements he had planted, but he was also unwilling to leave the Caloosas without having first secured the friendship of their chief; he therefore dispatched the Christian slave who had met him on his arrival to inform Carlos that the Spaniards were still in ignorance of the treachery which the Indians had planned. Carlos, blinded by his desire to obtain more gifts from these guileless visitors, readily believed the messenger, came to visit the Adelantado with but five or six companions, offered him his sister in marriage, asked him to take her to a Christian land, and then to send her back that he and all his people might become of the same faith, and again renewed the invitation to visit his village and his wives, to all of which Avilés again consented.

While the Adelantado and the Indian chief were each struggling to outwit the other, the one to retain his country and the other to win it for his King, another and less worthy object had stirred the cupidity of the soldiers. The sight of the gold collected by the followers of Las Alas and the report of the great wealth of Carlos had awakened the same emotions in the breasts of the Spaniards as those which had arisen in the heart of the Indian chief on seeing their paltry beads and hatchets; and the former, hoping to work upon the financial necessity in

[1] Merás in Ruidíaz, *La Florida*, tomo i., p. 150, says this harbour was 50 leagues beyond, possibly Old Tampa, at the head of which stood the village of Tocobaga, which he subsequently visited.

which they all knew that Avilés was placed, urged him to hold Carlos for a ransom. Carlos himself was reported to have over one hundred thousand ducats; and even were his treasures not so large, no one could tell how much gold and silver there might be in the possession of his friends and relatives, accumulated from the vessels wrecked along the coast. With this they would readily part, for the natives were in blissful ignorance of its value, bartering a piece of gold worth seventy ducats for an ace of diamonds, and a hundred ducats of silver for a pair of scissors. But the Adelantado was above temptation and simply replied that the Indian had come to him trusting in his word, and would not think the Spaniards were good Christians if he caught them in a lie; and although his soldiers succeeded in collecting from the Indians precious metal to the value of thirty-five hundred ducats, with which the Spaniards at once began to gamble, he persisted in his refusal to take anything for himself. So Carlos returned in safety to his village.

The next day Avilés returned his visit with what pomp and circumstance he could muster, in order to impress the natives with his importance. He must have presented a curious sight to the gaping savages as he threaded his way through the groves of palmettos to the great house of the chief, which stood but a little distance from the shore near which the ships were drawn up. Attended by twenty gentlemen and a very small dwarf, who was an excellent dancer and singer, he marched at the head of his two hundred arquebusiers, each man fully armed, clad in cuirass and morion, with unfurled banner, to the accompanying music of two pipers and drummers, three trumpeters, a harp, a violin, and a psaltery. On reaching the spacious dwelling[1] of the cacique, he stationed his men on the outside, their matches lighted in case of

[1] Barrientos in García, *Dos Antiguas Relaciones de la Florida*, p. 92, says it would accommodate 2000 men, an evident exaggeration.

an emergency, and entered it with the music and his twenty attendant gentlemen.

Carlos, likewise desiring to be duly impressive, had prepared an elaborate reception for his visitors. The cacique sat alone, enthroned on a raised seat, surrounded by a company of one hundred chief men and other personages, who crouched below him. At a little distance from him sat his sister, plain, tall, and sedate, and about thirty-five years of age, around whom squatted the native women. As Avilés entered Carlos courteously offered him his throne and withdrew to some distance, but this the Adelantado would not permit and he placed his host beside him, after which the ceremonious salutation previously described was repeated by the Indian's sister and the chief men. Meanwhile over five hundred youths from ten to fifteen years of age had assembled in front of the open windows and began to sing, while others danced and pirouetted, and the men and women within joined in the singing. Then the brothers and relatives of the chief, some of whom were nearly one hundred years old, performed a dance. During all of the entertainment the Indian women without the house sang alternately in two groups of fifty each.

The dance over, the repast was about to be served when Menéndez, who had noted down some of the native words, asked for a little delay, and addressed Carlos and his sister in their own language, to the amazement of the assembly, who thought that the paper itself spoke. At his request the chieftain's wife was brought in. She proved to be a handsome young woman of twenty, of good address, with fine eyes and eyebrows, shapely hands, and graceful figure, naked as Eve before the fall except for a covering which she wore in front, a rich necklace of pearls and precious stones, and some golden trinkets about her throat.

The Adelantado, who was a courtly man, took her by

the hand and seated her between her husband and his sister "and as he had been told that she was very handsome, he had written down the words in which to tell her so, at which," writes his brother-in-law,

"she showed herself not to be displeased, and blushed very prettily, looking frankly at her husband. The cacique showed that he regretted having brought his wife, and ordered her to depart, fearing she would be taken from him, but the Adelantado told him through the interpreter not to send her away, asking that she dine with them."[1]

This was followed by a succulent repast served by the natives and consisting of cooked fish and oysters roasted, boiled, and raw, to which the Adelantado contributed biscuit, honey, sugar, and wine, with comfits and quince preserve. Throughout the feast his own music played and the dwarf danced, at which the cacique bade his Indians to cease their singing, for he said, "The Christians know many things." Then some of the Spanish gentlemen sang in concert, for the Adelantado was fond of music. The repast was concluded with a distribution of gifts among the natives.

As the Adelantado prepared to depart, Carlos reminded him of the alliance which he had proposed, saying that his Indians would not submit to having his sister rejected, but would rise against him. The unexpected request at once placed Avilés in a difficult if not a dangerous position, for it demanded an immediate answer, and although his bodyguard stood without prepared for every emergency, he was himself surrounded by the savages and for the moment completely in their power. But he met it with tact and discretion, observing that Christian men could only marry Christian women: Carlos answered that they were such already, having taken him as a brother.

[1] Merás in Ruidíaz, *La Florida*, tomo i., p. 162.

To this Avilés replied that in order to become Christians they would have to learn and believe many things,

"and he told them who God was, His wisdom, power, and goodness, and that all creatures born upon earth must worship and obey Him alone, and that we Christians who do so, go to heaven when we die, and that there we live forever without dying, and see our wives, and children, and brothers, and friends, and are ever joyful, singing and laughing; and that they in their ignorance do not serve or worship God, but serve a very warlike and lying chief called the Devil, and when they die, they go to him, and are forever weeping, because they are often very cold, and again very hot, and there is nothing to satisfy them."[1]

Notwithstanding his sound doctrine, Avilés consulted with his captains as to what course he should take. They all agreed that it was desirable to conciliate the Indians in order to bring them to a knowledge of the true faith, and the Adelantado finally accepted the situation, although he did so most unwillingly. So the chief's sister was baptised and named Doña Antonia, and the nuptials were performed that night in some tents which the Spaniards had erected near by amidst the great rejoicing of the natives, who celebrated the occasion with singing and dancing, and to the furtherance among them of the Christian religion.[2] Avilés, having now achieved his object, and secured the friendship of Carlos, determined to continue his journey. His Indian wife and seven of her companions were sent with Las Alas and five of the ships to Havana to be instructed in the Catholic faith. He also caused a great cross to be erected close to the chief's dwelling, which he bade the Indians to reverence as their principal idol and to abandon their other gods. But the

[1] Merás in *ibid.*, tomo i., p. 164.

[2] Merás in *ibid.*, tomo i., pp. 164–166. Barrientos omits the incident in his account.

still distrustful Carlos refused his consent to the new worship until the return of his sister from Havana. Avilés promised to send her back in the lapse of three or four months, and then sailed away in the two remaining vessels, having named the harbour San Antonio, after St. Anthony, to whose intercession he attributed the happy discovery and deliverance of the Christian captives.[1]

While the Adelantado was turning compliments to Indian beauties and marrying a native wife, affairs had reached a desperate pass in the three colonies he had founded along the east coast of the peninsula. The vessel sent to Yucatan in command of his brother-in-law had returned to Havana with a load of provisions, where Merás left it and continued his journey to New Spain to fulfil the mission with which he had been entrusted. Hinestrosa, Avilés's agent in Havana, sent it immediately to the relief of the colony at Santa Lucia, the harbour whither Medrano had gone after leaving Ays. When the ship arrived at the settlement it was found that the Indians had risen and killed fifteen of the colonists, for the soldiers were exhausted with their journey thither, and the natives were so dexterous with their bows that they could discharge twenty arrows while the soldiers were firing a single shot. At first the colonists had driven them away, but when the fort was completed a thousand Indians came down upon them, fought them for four hours, wounded the captain and the sub-lieutenant, killed eight soldiers, and shot six thousand arrows into the fort.

As the attacks were renewed daily, it soon became impossible to search for provisions, and the small garrison,

[1] Merás in Ruidíaz, *La Florida*, tomo i., pp. 150–168; Barrientos, in García, *Dos Antiguas Relaciones de la Florida*, pp. 84–95. The Spanish Relations and geographers usually call the village Carlos after the name of its chief. Since the identity of the Carlos village of Ponce de Leon and of other explorers with the village mentioned by Avilés cannot be positively established, the name of San Antonio is retained in this narrative to indicate the locality visited by the latter.

with their rations reduced to a pound of corn distributed among ten soldiers, began to suffer the pangs of hunger. A dwarf palmetto sold for a ducat, a snake for four, a rat for eight reales. The bones of animals and of fishes which had been dead for years, and even shoes and leather belts were eaten, and the soldiers gradually succumbed to starvation until only thirty men were left capable of bearing arms. At this pass the sub-lieutenant and the vicar, Mendoza, endeavoured to reach Havana in a boat in search of succour, without a soul among the crew who understood navigation; but foul weather drove them back again and forced them to return to Santa Lucia. Eight days later the caravel arrived. Then the soldiers rose, seized its master, wounded Medrano and the sub-lieutenant, captured the boat, and set sail in her for Havana. Fifteen leagues from Santa Lucia they encountered Avilés, who had been reconnoitring a harbour in the Bahama Channel, and was now on his way up the coast with his two vessels. But the unfortunate deserters were doomed to return to Florida, for Avilés took possession of their caravel, embarked in it with a number of his gentlemen, and continued his journey in the direction of St. Augustine, which he reached on the 20th of March (1566).

Similar disturbances had occurred both at St. Augustine and at San Mateo. Early in February, before setting out for Carlos, Menéndez had dispatched a second shipload of corn and other necessities to the former of the two ports. On the arrival of the relief party it found Bartolomé Menéndez absent with a party of soldiers to collect corn from the hostile Indians, and the settlement in a most distressing condition. Hunger and discontent had brought about the usual results. Before the ship could be unloaded the settlers, headed by a captain named Francisco de Recalde, who had previously been suspected of setting fire to Fort San Mateo, and a priest from Seville, named Rueda,[1] rose in mutiny, seized the camp master and other officials, spiked the guns of the fort, appointed a leader and a sergeant major, and captured the vessel with the intention of abandoning the country. As the ship proved to be too small to accommodate all of the mutineers, the sergeant major went about the settlement with a bodyguard, selecting those who were to depart. While he was thus employed in choosing his companions the camp master succeeded in freeing himself and eight of the royal officers and officials. Securing arms they attacked and captured the leader of the mutineers and his sergeant major, and destroyed the boat in which they were about to put out to the ship. Perceiving the turn which affairs had taken, those aboard the vessel spread their sails and escaped with one hundred and thirty men. The leaders were executed on the spot and order was again restored; but the commander of the garrison fell ill of the anxiety caused by the mutiny, as did also Bartolomé Menéndez on his return.[2]

Simultaneously and in connivance with the mutineers at St. Augustine, an uprising had occurred at San Mateo, due to general discontent at the poverty of the country in gold and silver. The ship which Laudonnière had been building to transport his people to France was still unfinished and the mutineers pressed for its completion. They had secretly advised the leaders at St. Augustine to secure the vessel there, and with the arrival of the first succour at San Mateo it was their intention to seize the ship in which it came, and with these three vessels to abandon the country. Villarroel, who was in command at San Mateo, suspected their designs, but could do little to control them, and the camp master at St. Augustine sent him word in a letter concealed in the coat of a

[1] Merás in Ruidíaz, *La Florida*, tomo i., p. 190.

[2] Merás in *ibid.*, tomo i., pp. 171–173; Barrientos in García, ***Dos Antiguas*** *Relaciones de la Florida*, pp. 98, 99.

messenger to delay the completion of the French ship and to temporise as best he could until the arrival of reinforcements. But his efforts were unsuccessful, and the mutineers had not only secured the vessel in which they embarked to the number of one hundred and twenty,[1] leaving Villarroel with only twenty-five men in charge of San Mateo, but had also succeeded in stirring up war with Saturiba.

The friendship which Avilés had established with the Indians, by his judicious treatment of them, had so far continued without interruption. But the mutineers, says Merás,[2] on deserting the fort, hoping that the Indians would quickly attack it and murder the garrison as soon as they became aware of the small number of its defenders, determined to hasten the event. With this object in view the two leaders maltreated the natives, and killed a number of them, including two of the chief men. The revenge came quickly. Villarroel, in ignorance of the Indian outbreak, had sent to St. Augustine for reinforcements as soon as he found himself abandoned. Saturiba, who had doubtless observed with grim contentment the same disintegrating forces at work which had wrought such havoc among the French, seized his two messengers by surprise, split open their breasts, and cut out their hearts. On the same day that the General reached St. Augustine, Las Alas entered the harbour, bringing supplies from Havana, where he had left Doña Antonia and her companions. As the San Mateo mutineers had not yet sailed Avilés at once informed them of the arrival of succour and offered them a general pardon. But their hearts were set upon abandoning the country. They had en-

[1] Merás in Ruidíaz, *La Florida*, tomo i., p. 176, says this mutiny occurred after Avilés's departure for Guale. On p. 180 he speaks of it as prior thereto. As Merás was not present on the occasion, the order of the events followed in the text is that given by Barrientos.

[2] Merás in *ibid.*, tomo i., p. 181.

listed in the hope of conquering another El Dorado; they had encountered but hardship and privation, and they were determined to seek their fortunes elsewhere, in Peru or New Spain, where more substantial returns awaited their endeavours than slow starvation on palmetto roots and grasses. Out of the entire company some thirty-five noblemen, who had joined their ranks, accepted the pardon and returned to the fort. The balance sent word that they had not come over to plough and plant, and that they wished to go to the Indies to live like Christians and not to live like beasts in Florida.[1]

[1] Merás in *ibid.*, tomo i., pp. 169–181; Barrientos in García, *Dos Antiguas Relaciones de la Florida*, pp. 96–100.

CHAPTER III

EXPEDITIONS TO GUALE, ST. JOHN'S RIVER, AND CHESAPEAKE BAY

AVILÉS at once determined to anticipate the departure of the San Mateo mutineers and punish them, when he was delayed by a further defection among the force at St. Augustine. The leader was the same Captain San Vincente who had prophesied a failure of the expedition against Fort Caroline, a grumbler and a coward according to Merás, who may have had some secret grudge against him.[1] At the head of a hundred soldiers he asked leave to set sail in a caravel that was on the point of departure for Hispaniola. In vain Avilés urged upon him his pressing need of men in view of the outbreak among the Indians, and his own immediate departure for Guale. Embarking in the caravel, which was under orders to convey them to Puerto Rico, the deserters compelled the pilot to take the direction of Havana, from which they could best make their way to Honduras, Yucatan, and New Spain. But a contrary wind arose and carried them in thirty days to Puerto de Plata in the island of Santo Domingo, where other fugitives from St. Augustine had already preceded them. They arrived wasted and ill with the long journey, their provisions having spoiled with the heat, and were well received by the governor, Francisco de Cevallos, although the royal cédulas had already reached him direct-

[1] Merás in Ruidíaz, *La Florida*, tomo i., pp. 86, 90, 178.

ing the arrest of all such deserters and their return to Florida. Avilés soon learned of their arrival and urged the enforcement of the orders, but his demands were disregarded, and the mutineers spread abroad such discouraging reports of the country that the result soon followed which the General had anticipated. Intending immigrants abandoned the enterprise, and it was even said that some of the royal ministers condemned the Adelantado for his precipitate action in seeking to colonise so unpromising a region.[1]

Avilés was now at liberty to pursue his expedition to Guale. Leaving one hundred and fifty men distributed between St. Augustine and San Mateo, he set sail the 1st of April (1566)[2] with one hundred and fifty men in two small boats and a ship under the command of Las Alas. He took with him as interpreter the Frenchman Rufin,[3] whom Manrique de Rojas had rescued from Ribaut's colony at Charlesfort. Three days out he entered a harbour, and landed within a quarter of a league of an Indian village, where he was met by a party of forty Indians, from the midst of whom a Frenchman addressed him in Spanish, telling him that the name of the village was Guale, and that he had been sent to prevent their landing if they proved to be Spaniards. The Frenchman explained that he had belonged to the scouting party sent to Fort Caroline by Ribaut after the wreck of the fleet. On arriving there and learning of the capture of the fort by the Spaniards, the scouts had not returned to Ribaut, but had escaped to the neighbourhood of Santa Elena.[4] Avilés

[1] Barrientos in García, *Dos Antiguas Relaciones de la Florida*, p. 101; Merás in Ruidíaz, *La Florida*, tomo i., pp. 184–187; Barcia, *Ensayo*, Año MDLXVI., pp. 102–104.

[2] Barrientos in García, *Dos Antiguas Relaciones de la Florida*, p. 102.

[3] Barrientos in *ibid.*, p. 103, calls him by his Christian name, Guillermo.

[4] Merás in Ruidíaz, *La Florida*, tomo i., p. 193, and see Barcia, *Ensayo*, Año MDLXV., p. 84.

replied that his people did not harm the natives, and would not land against their will. After further parley, the Indians invited the Spaniards to visit their village, and Avilés set out in their company with a small band of soldiers. On the way he learned that two weeks before his arrival a party of fifteen Lutherans, who had escaped from Ribaut's fleet, had set sail for Newfoundland in search of French fishing vessels, after a sojourn of five months in that locality. The Frenchman also informed him that the cacique of Guale was at war with the cacique of Orista,[1] two of whose relatives he had taken prisoners with the assistance of the French fugitives.

The Spaniards were peacefully received at the village, where they were quartered in the house of the French fugitives, and Avilés, as was his custom, began to give the natives some religious instruction. As the local interpreter was Lutheran he ordered him, under pain of death, to tell the Indians that he and his soldiers had come to Christianise them. A cross was set up and three youths of his company chanted the Christian doctrine before it, while the trembling interpreter informed the natives that the Spaniards, who were true Christians, had come to kill the Lutherans, who were false Christians. Other religious instruction was given of a less militant description, and the Indians expressed their willingness to embrace the faith.

Next day the Adelantado assembled the principal men, expressed his desire to re-establish peace between the contending caciques, and asked that the two relatives of Orista be surrendered to him, promising to return them in case Orista would not come to terms. The Guale chief replied that for eight months no rain had fallen, their corn-fields and plantations had dried up, they were sorrowful because of the scarcity of food, and that they wished to sacrifice these two Indians to their gods to in-

[1] Possibly the Audusta of Laudonnière.

duce them to send them rain. "Not so," replied Avilés. "God is angry with you, and denies you the rain, because you are at war with Orista and wish to slay these two Indians and because you kill his people when you capture them"; and then he offered to leave two of his own soldiers as hostages for their return, in case the peace could not be brought about. The following day the Guale chief surrendered his two captives, and Avilés set out for Orista with two small boats, leaving his nephew, Alonzo Menéndez Marqués, and Vasco Zaval with the Indians after he had informed the chief that he would cut off their heads should evil befall the hostages during his absence, and would, moreover, ally himself with their enemy, Orista. "The cacique and the other Indians were terrified at this," says Barrientos, "for they knew already what he had done to the Lutherans, and how victorious he had been in all of his undertakings, for news travels over the country from chief to chief very rapidly."[1] Six Spaniards also remained with the natives to Christianise them.

Avilés had spent four days in Guale, and on leaving he encountered Las Alas, who had gone in search of him in his ship. The next day he entered the harbour of Santa Elena, which was but eighteen or twenty leagues distant from Guale,[2] and visited the neighbouring Indian village, but two leagues distant, in company with Las Alas and a hundred soldiers. The inhabitants were at work rebuilding their huts which had been burned to the ground by the Guale Indians, and, anticipating another attack, at first assumed a hostile attitude, but, on recognising their two comrades, they gave the Spaniards a friendly reception, and sent word of the arrival of the strangers, to the neighbouring subject chiefs. Orista was in another village near at hand, where Avilés visited him, returned his

[1] Barrientos in García, *Dos Antiguas Relaciones de la Florida*, p. 105.
[2] Barrientos in *ibid.*, p. 104.

relatives to him, and invited him through Rufin, who was married to a daughter of one of the subject chiefs, to turn Christian, to which he promptly consented. A public rejoicing was celebrated, attended by the usual ceremonies.

On the following day Orista, with his wife and a party of natives, embarked in the boats and, descending the river, accompanied the Adelantado to his village, where the night was passed. Then a site was selected for the Fort of San Felipe on a small island within a league of the bar, where it would be visible from the sea. The island was covered at the time with a dense forest of oak and pine, liquidambar, nut trees, and laurel. A plan for the fort was traced out on the only elevation which the island contained, at the side of a small haven, and with the assistance of the natives it was completed in fifteen days, mounted with six pieces of artillery, and garrisoned with one hundred and six men under the command of Las Alas. Despite its attractive appearance and advantageous position on the river flowing into the harbour, the situation was a poor one. The island was isolated from the mainland by extensive swamps and marshes, was subject to frequent overflow with the high tides, which rendered cultivation very difficult, and was too small to accommodate the population which ultimately settled there.[1] When the construction of the fort was finished Avilés sent word to the settlers at St. Augustine of the success of his expedition and of his intention to return to them at an early day. Before his departure from San Felipe he left a soldier with each of the subject chiefs, who had asked for some one to instruct them in the faith. He then set out for Guale with a small party,

[1] "Discurso sobre la población de la costa de la Florida, é inconvinientes que se ofrecieren para su fortificación y defensa." 1577–1580. MS. Direc. de Hidrog., Madrid, *Col. Navarrete*, tomo xiv., Doc. No. 47. See Appendix U, San Felipe.

taking two of the principal men with him, and sent Rufin in advance to inform the cacique of the peaceful outcome of the negotiations.

During his absence the drought had continued throughout the region subject to the Guale chief, and when Avilés reached the village the afflicted savage besought him to ask God to send rain. But the Adelantado answered evasively, "God will not hearken to my prayer, because He is angry with you for your failure to comply with our desires," and the chief departed, much depressed at the refusal. The youths who had been left there to instruct the natives, observing his disappointment, determined to play upon his superstition, and informed him, through the interpreter, that they would pray God for rain. At this, full of gratitude for their assistance, he loaded them down with presents of deer-skins, corn, and fish, with which the lads departed, well pleased at their successful deception. But the news of it soon reached the ears of the General, and, indignant at the trick the boys had practised, he ordered their spoils to be taken from them, and had them stripped to receive a whipping. When this in turn became known to the Guale chief, he came in great sorrow to the Adelantado and addressed him, saying, with Indian stoicism: "You have deceived me, for you will not ask God for rain, and now you wish to punish the children because they are willing to pray for it. Do not whip them, for I no longer wish them to pray for water, and am content that it rain when God wills it." Avilés answered that God would bestow it the more readily if he turned Christian himself. Then the poor Indian, in desperation, went directly to the cross, which Avilés had caused to be erected on his previous visit; kneeling down before it, he embraced it, and turning to the Spaniard exclaimed: "Behold, I am a Christian." "This occurred at two o'clock in the afternoon," continues Barrientos. "Half an hour later it began to thunder and lighten and to rain with such violence that it did not cease for twenty-four hours, and extended in a circuit of five leagues."[1] Then the Indians, astounded at the prodigy, came to the house where Avilés was lodged, and casting themselves at his feet, begged him to leave some Christians with them. The General responded by ordering his nephew, Alonzo Menéndez Marqués, with four other Spaniards, to remain among them.

If remorse had played its part in the kindly treatment which Avilés had extended to the Frenchmen captured near Cape Canaveral after the Matanzas massacre, either the Adelantado felt that his misdeeds had been expiated when he released them on his arrival in Cuba, or again the force of circumstances proved stronger than his sense of mercy. His nephew Alonzo and his companions, who had remained as hostages at Guale during his absence at Santa Elena, informed him on his return that the unfortunate Lutheran interpreter was endeavouring to arouse the Indians, telling them that these Spanish Christians were of no account, and spitting upon the cross whenever they assembled to adore it, whereupon Avilés determined to be rid of him without arousing the suspicions of the natives. He caused the Frenchman Rufin to induce his countryman to accompany some Guale Indians who were going to Santa Elena in their canoe, by praising the liberality of Las Alas, who would reward him with many presents. The poor fellow, who had escaped the untutored wiles of the savages, readily fell into the trap set for him by the Christians and left with the Indians. Avilés then wrote Las Alas to murder him secretly, but to show much regret at his disappearance and to inform the Indians, that, being a false Christian, he had escaped to the forest in the hope of finding a French ship in which to return to his own

[1] Barrientos in García, *Dos Antiguas Relaciones de la Florida*, p. 111.

country. His orders were obeyed and the Frenchman was garroted.[1]

Avilés, who had now carried out his plan at Santa Elena, returned to San Mateo by the channel between the islands and the coast, meeting many Indians on his way, who came down to the shore and besought him to give them crosses, as they were all much astounded at the report of the rain which had fallen in Guale. He reached the settlement on the 15th of May, and although he found it in good condition the war with the natives was still in progress. The Indians in the neighbourhood of the two forts were

"an ill set and traitorous," says Barrientos, "for they make friends with the Christians for their own interest on account of the advantage they can derive from them. They go to the forts, and if they are not given food and clothing, and iron hatchets and gifts they depart in great anger, begin a war and kill all the Christians they can find."[2]

Those about St. Augustine had waited for a favourable wind, and, attacking the fort at night, had set fire to the thatched roof of the magazine with their fire arrows.[3] The flames communicating with the powder had destroyed all of its valuable contents including the flags and banners captured from the French as well as those belonging to the Spaniards. Many soldiers had been killed, and the sentinels shot down at night.

The soldiers found the Timuquanans a difficult foe to contend with, and more than a match for their cumbrous arms, owing to their great agility and the rapidity of their

[1] Merás in Ruidíaz, *La Florida*, tomo i., pp. 189-215; Barrientos in García, *Dos Antiguas Relaciones de la Florida*, pp. 102-111. Merás states that the Frenchman was addicted to a crime against nature very prevalent among the Indians. Barrientos merely hints at it.

[2] Barrientos in *ibid.*, p. 113.

[3] Le Moyne in Plate XXXI. of his *Eicones* shows this mode of attack.

movements. While the soldier was loading his arquebus, they ran into the grasses and thickets, and dropped on the ground when they saw the flash. Crawling swiftly through the underbrush and grasses, they rose at another spot than that at which the Spaniard had aimed, and closing upon him delivered another volley of four or five arrows in the time which he took to load. They went about in small skirmishing parties, and fought in ambuscade, shooting the men who went to gather sea-food and dwarf palmettos, piercing their clothes and coats of mail. When the Spaniards pursued them they ran to the streams and marshes, threw themselves into the water, and, being naked and swimming like fish, crossed to the opposite shore, bearing their bows and arrows aloft in one hand to keep them dry; there they would stand shouting and mocking at the Spaniards, and when the latter withdrew, they swam back, dogging their steps and shooting at them from the underbrush. The Spaniards found that to hold them in check it was necessary to burn their villages, seize their canoes, cut down their plantations, and destroy their fishways.

Avilés, seriously disturbed at the loss of the storehouse, went directly to the relief of his brother at St. Augustine, taking with him a small party, what supplies the scant store at San Mateo could afford, and Villarroel, who had fallen ill in consequence of the mental strain to which he had been subjected, and whom he wished to send to Havana. Vasco Zaval was left in charge. May 18th he arrived at the fort, and after advising with his captains, he decided to build a new one at the entrance of the bar, where it could protect the harbour from the attack of hostile vessels and afford a better defence against the Indians.[1] The site was marked out the fol-

[1] The second site of St. Augustine. Barrientos in García, *Dos Antiguas Relaciones de la Florida*, p. 114, says: "Entrando En consejo Con los capitanes salio acordado que se mudase El fuerte de allí y se fundase A la

lowing day, and for the second time the long-suffering colonists set to work with a will upon its construction. From three o'clock in the morning until nine, and again from two in the afternoon until seven in the evening, one hundred and sixty persons toiled at its completion, in constant fear of an Indian attack, and in ten days they had it finished, with the guns in position. As no supplies had reached the settlers for a long season, and the chronic condition of hunger and want was again rife, the General determined to return to Havana for succour, taking with him a hundred soldiers, whom he had enlisted in Cuba from the fleet of New Spain under agreement to remain with him until May. He left but seventy rations at St. Augustine to maintain the garrison until help should arrive.

Early in June he set out for Havana, and the very day of his departure he met one of his own supply ships, with Diego de Amaya aboard, caught in a perilous situation on

entrada de la barra, porq̃ allí los indios no les podian hacer tanto malo y desde allí podian defender q̃ no entrasen nauios de Enemigos." Subsequent to the arrival of Arciniega at St. Augustine another change was made: "Fuese el Adelantado, con todos los capitanes . . . é con acuerdo é parecer de todos . . . señalaron el sitio, lugar é compás donde se habían de fortificar, que era en el mesmo lugar que el Adelantado estaba fortificado; mas porque la mar le iba comiendo el fuerte, retiráronse más á tierra, tomando él un caballero del fuerte que estaba hecho, para él que se habia de hacer." Merás in Ruidíaz, *La Florida*, tomo i., p. 245. The "Discurso sobre la población de la costa de la Florida é inconvinientes que se ofrecieron para su fortificación y defensa" (MS. Direc. de Hidrog., Madrid, *Col. Navarrete*, tomo xiv., Doc. No. 47, fol. 4, 1577–1580) says: "Sancto Agustin, donde primero estubo el Fuerte y gente, es una Islilla pequeña, y Sancto Agustin, donde agora está el Fuerte y gente, es otra que está junto á la primera, donde solia estar primero el Fuerte, y esta donde agora está es casi Ysla, por que está rodeada de agua, aunque tiene por una parte descubierto por donde pueden pasar a la Tierra Firme, está en 29 grados y medio: tiene de largo 3 ó 4 leguas y de ancho muy poco, que es angosta hasta media legua, y por algunas partes menos. Cubre la Mar cada año mucha parte de esta tierra," etc. It should be borne in mind that "isla" does not necessarily mean an island, but may also indicate a promontory, as is the case in this instance.

the bar. He delayed his sailing long enough to rescue it and wrote the camp master at St. Augustine to distribute the provisions between the forts, sending a boat-load to Las Alas at San Felipe; and with that decision of character which he was wont to exert when the emergency called for it, he ordered that the vessel which had brought the succour be sunk in order that the garrison suffer no temptation to desert. The camp master at St. Augustine was then directed to go to San Mateo and take charge there.

The question of provisions being thus happily solved for the time being, Avilés re-embarked and reached Havana in eight days with two of his vessels, the third being carried to Santo Domingo by stress of weather. In Havana he found his brother-in-law, Solís de Merás, who had returned with the fleet from New Spain, bringing with him four Dominican friars, a captain, and eight soldiers, and only three thousand ducats borrowed from the Audiencia of Mexico. Attempts to obtain further assistance from the Governor were renewed, but Osorio was still obdurate, and Avilés was compelled to fall back upon his lieutenant, the treasurer Hinestrosa, who having already exhausted his personal means, promised to secure from his friends the money needed to assist the Florida forts. Doña Antonia, his Indian bride, had quickly acquired some Christian instruction, but the death of all but two of her companions, and the prolonged absence of her Spanish lover, for whom she had acquired a strong attachment, had greatly depressed her spirits. Merás tells us a touching story of her affection and of the harmless subterfuge by which the Adelantado contrived to avoid the renewal of his relations with her.[1] The death of Doña Antonia's companions had placed Avilés under the necessity of returning her to her people,

[1] Merás in Ruidíaz, *La Florida*, tomo i., pp. 215, 232; Barrientos in García, *Dos Antiguas Relaciones de la Florida*, pp. 111–116.

as he feared that in the event of her death the Caloosas would attribute it to the ill-treatment of the Spaniards. So he made a rapid expedition to San Antonio, returned Doña Antonia and her two companions to Carlos, and in ten days was back again in Havana, bringing with him the heir and cousin of the chieftain, who was subsequently baptised under the name of Don Pedro, and some additional white slaves whom he had rescued.

While purchasing supplies with five hundred ducats which he had obtained by pledging some of his wardrobe, a vessel arrived from Spain with the encouraging news that Sancho de Arciniega, who had left early in May, had reached Florida at the end of June[1] with a large squadron sent to the assistance of the colony. Avilés made but a brief stay at Havana, and by the 8th of July was back again at San Mateo, sailing part of the way in company with the return fleet which carried Merás with dispatches to Spain.[2] During his absence the Indians had slain two of his captains: the Asturian, Martín Ochoa, who had led in the attack on Fort Caroline, and Diego de Hevia, a relative of the Adelantado, besides others of his soldiers who had shared in the attack. But Arciniega was anchored at St. Augustine, where he had arrived on the anniversary of Avilés's departure from Cadiz,[3] with a fleet of seventeen ships, fifteen hundred men, and five hundred

[1] "Diligencias hechas en Sevilla con motivo de la venida de Esteban de las Alas, de la Florida" (Ruidíaz, *La Florida*, tomo ii., pp. 581, 585) gives the dates of April and April 2nd; but Fourquevaux, who makes various references to Arciniega in his correspondence (see letter of Jan. 22, 1566, *Dépêches*, p. 48; Feb. 4, p. 50; Feb. 11, p. 52; Feb. 22, p. 61, and March 29, p. 64), says in his letter to Catherine of April 30, 1566 (*ibid.*, p. 82), that the fleet was still lying at anchor at San Lucar. Barcia, *Ensayo*, (Año MDLXVI., p. 114), says it reached St. Augustine at the end of June.

[2] Merás (in Ruidíaz, *La Florida*, tomo i., pp. 223–235), who has every reason to be correct, says he left Havana July 1st. Barrientos (in García, *Dos Antiguas Relaciones de la Florida*, pp. 115–118) says June 1st.

[3] Avilés to a Jesuit friend, Oct. 15, 1566, Ruidíaz, *La Florida*, tomo ii., p. 155.

sailors, and bountiful supplies for the starving colonists. Arciniega had sent Captain Juan Pardo in three vessels with three hundred men to the relief of San Felipe, and Captain Aguirre with two hundred and fifty men to that of San Mateo. Avilés found Aguirre encamped without the fort, there having been some friction between him and Zaval, who was in command. Having restored peace between them, Menéndez departed for St. Augustine.

The meeting with Arciniega was a joyful one for the sorely tried Adelantado, and Arciniega handed over to him the royal dispatches, including Philip's letter of May 12, 1566, in which that monarch expressed his approval of the punishment meted out to the "Lutheran corsairs."[1] Avilés then visited a company of fourteen women, who had come over with the fleet, and five priests to whom he assigned as vicar his chaplain Mendoza. Three days later, in council with his captains,[2] he decided that seven hundred and fifty soldiers should be distributed between the three forts of St. Augustine, San Mateo, and San Felipe, that the remainder should depart in eight of the vessels to search for pirates and corsairs in the neighbourhood of Puerto Rico and Santo Domingo, and that the balance of the fleet should return with Arciniega to Spain. He himself prepared to visit San Mateo, where he proposed to ascend the St. John's, and to proceed from there to Guale and the fort at Santa Elena, to ascertain what had become of Juan Pardo, of whose arrival he had as yet received no notification.[3]

Before his departure the fort at St. Augustine was removed a little inland, for the sea was beginning to eat it

[1] Barcia, *Ensayo*, Año MDLXVI., p. 115.

[2] Avilés had been directed by royal cédula of September, 1565, to advise with Arciniega in all matters relating to land and sea. Ruidíaz, *La Florida*, tomo ii., p. 360.

[3] Merás in Ruidíaz, *La Florida*, tomo i., pp. 235–248; Barrientos in García, *Dos Antiguas Relaciones de la Florida*, pp. 118–122.

away,[1] and finally he took his departure for San Mateo. On his arrival he again placed Villarroel in command, with Captain Aguirre and most of the older soldiers in charge, then he started on an exploring expedition up the St. John's with a company of one hundred soldiers in three vessels. Twenty leagues up the river he landed, and marching five leagues through a fertile country paid a visit to the village of Outina. Within a league of the village he sent forward six of his soldiers, bearing a present to the chief, to inform him of his visit. Outina sent him back word, begging him to bring but twenty men in his company and to pray God to send rain upon his harvests, as none had fallen for a long time. Much amused at his request, Avilés entered the village with only six men, and on his arrival the rain began to fall. The house of the chief was found to be deserted, for a superstitious terror had driven the savage in hiding to the forest, from which he sent word that he was in great fear of a man who was so powerful with God, and begged Avilés to depart in peace, as he was already a friend of the Spaniards. The Adelantado, who was anxious to meet him, as he was reputed to be intelligent and powerful, sent a messenger to urge him to return; but the chief replied that Avilés with his twenty soldiers and the assistance of God as his cacique was more powerful than himself with a thousand warriors, and again besought him to depart, and the General reluctantly complied with his request, after informing Outina that he was ascending the river, and that unless the cacique ordered his subject villages to receive him without fear, he would burn down their towns and destroy their canoes and fishways.

Returning to his boats, Avilés on the following day sent the largest of them back to San Mateo with fifty men, and continued his expedition up the river. He

[1] Méras in Ruidíaz, *La Florida*, tomo i., p. 245, and see note, p. 252, in this volume.

observed that at a distance of forty leagues the tide was still perceptible. At a distance of fifty leagues he came upon the village of Macoya, an ally of Saturiba, two leagues beyond the highest point reached by the French.[1] He found the village deserted by the inhabitants, and Macoya sent him a message similar to that he had received from Outina, asking him to abandon the expedition, as his subjects farther up the river were angry at the approach of the Spaniards. But Avilés disregarded his request, and, failing to obtain any Indian guides, continued his advance. A league farther on, where the river began to narrow, he found it barred with stakes and the natives assembling in a threatening attitude along the banks. Breaking through the obstacles in the river he proceeded.

The river had now become so narrow that its width did not exceed the length of two pikes. The soldiers were exposed to attack from the banks, their powder and arquebuses were damp owing to the rain, and the General determined to return. The Indian guide who accompanied him informed Avilés that twenty leagues farther up dwelt a chief of the Ays named Perucho, where the river narrowed for a distance of thirty leagues and then opened into a great lake called Maymi, which emptied into the sea to the west in the country of Carlos, and to the east at Tegesta at the head of the Florida Keys, and that many streams flowed into it. Seven or eight leagues down the river and but twelve leagues from St. Augustine by land he visited Carabay,[2] a subject chief of Outina. Farther down Outina himself came out to meet him, with whom Avilés left six of his soldiers, and he finally reached San Mateo, having spent twelve days in his voyage. The war with Saturiba was still in progress, owing in part to the want of discipline among the soldiers, who persisted

[1] In the neighbourhood of Lake George.

[2] In the neighbourhood of Picolata (?).

in pillaging his villages, but otherwise the place was in a satisfactory condition.[1]

Avilés, who, during his winter in Havana had been assured by Father Andres de Urdaneta[2] of the existence of a passage through Florida opening into the Pacific, had not forgotten his design to establish a post at the Bay of Santa Maria (Chesapeake Bay) with its promise of a way to China and to Newfoundland, and during his two-days' stay at San Mateo he sent a captain with thirty soldiers and two Dominican friars to form a settlement there. With them went an Indian named Don Luis de Velasco, brother of a chief of that region. Spanish navigators, in company, perhaps, with some Dominican monks, had visited the country in 1559 or 1560 and carried him to Mexico, where the viceroy, Don Luis de Velasco, caused him to be baptised and gave him his name. But the expedition was doomed to failure. The two monks were from Peru and New Spain, possibly of those Merás had brought with him to Havana from the latter country. They had gone through some of the hardships and privations of the Florida colony, and were not of the stuff of which martyrs are made. In conspiracy with the soldiers they won over the pilot to their plan, drew up a statement that they had been deterred from reaching the Bay of Santa Maria owing to bad weather, and sailed for Spain. Reaching Seville they added their voice to the evil reports concerning Florida which San Vincente and his companions had already spread abroad by letters and other channels, and defamed both the King and Avilés because they wished to conquer and settle it.[3]

[1] Méras in Ruidíaz, *La Florida*, tomo i., pp. 248–257; Barrientos in García, *Dos Antiguas Relaciones de la Florida*, pp. 122–126.

[2] Avilés to Philip II., Jan. 30, 1566, Ruidíaz, *La Florida*, tomo ii., p. 151.

[3] Merás in Ruidíaz, *La Florida*, tomo i., p. 258; Barrientos in García, *Dos Antiguas Relaciones de la Florida*, p. 126. Barcia, *Ensayo*, (Año

The little garrison of San Felipe at Santa Elena had not escaped the blight which had fallen upon the other settlements. The arrival of the ship which Avilés had sent to its assistance early in June, before his last visit to Havana, had been attended with the usual disturbances. Before her cargo could be discharged, sixty of the soldiers had risen, and set sail in her for Havana. In the Bahama passage a storm had driven her into a harbour at the head of the Florida Keys, in the vicinity of an Indian settlement called Tegesta[1] by the Spaniards, and ruled by a chief of the same name. The village, which was situated on a stream of sweet water, probably the Miami River, flowing into Biscayne Bay, was at that time governed by a chief closely related to Carlos and his sister, Doña Antonia.

The people of Tegesta were fishermen, and, like all the natives along the coast, passed the winter season chasing the whale, says Velasco. An Indian fully painted approached the whale in his canoe, and throwing a rope around it, passed through its nostrils one of three pointed stakes which he carried in his belt, and thus prevented it from diving; then it was attacked and killed and drawn upon the beach. There its head was opened by the first man to attack it and two special bones were extracted, which were placed in the case in which the bones of the dead were kept, and they were worshipped. On the death of a chief, his large bones were removed and placed in a great box in his hut, where the natives

MDLXVI., p. 119), says that the Dominicans had taken the Indian from the province of Axacan [Chesapeake Bay] to Mexico, and adds the details given in the text. Both Merás (*ibid.*) and Barrientos (*ibid.*) say Don Luis had been six years with Avilés. Sacchini (*Historiæ Societatis Jesu*, *Pars tertia*, Romæ, MDCIL., p. 323), writing of the Jesuit expedition of 1570 to these parts, says that Don Luis had been carried away eleven years before by Spanish navigators. This would make the date of the expedition 1559 to 1560. It will be remembered that Villafañe was in that neighbourhood in 1561. Sacchini calls the Indian chief of the region Regulus.

[1] See Appendix V, Tegesta.

came to worship them, and the smaller bones were buried with the body.[1] Like his relative, Carlos, it had been the custom of the chief of Tegesta to kill all the Christians cast away on his coast. But when the friendly relations which the Spaniards had established with the Caloosas were reported to him, he followed the example of his relative. He received the fugitives with good will, sent them a deputation, and informed them of a neighbouring village where twenty Christians were living, deserters from San Mateo at the time of the mutiny. But, a fair wind having arisen, the ship set sail without them, as they were dwelling in peace with the Indians.

When Juan Pardo arrived at San Felipe with his reinforcements, he found that twenty soldiers had deserted to the interior, and that only twenty-five remained in the fort, that their supplies were entirely exhausted, and that they were dependent for their existence upon the food which the natives brought them. Avilés, after two days spent in San Mateo, left for San Felipe, where he arrived about the 20th of August. Having ordered matters at the fort, he appointed Las Alas his lieutenant in Orista and Guale. The island on which stood Fort San Felipe was in many ways unsuitable for cultivation, at least by the Spanish farmers who had settled it and who were still inexperienced in the climatic and other conditions of the region. Aside from the scanty supplies obtained from the Indians they as well as the garrison were dependent for their subsistence upon the chance arrival of an occasional ship from St. Augustine and from San Mateo, and Avilés must have found them in a very miserable condition, for he determined to reduce their number, and directed Pardo to make an excursion into the interior with a company of one hundred and fifty soldiers, who were to be quartered upon the natives at intervals

[1] Dos breves memorias sobre las costumbres de los yndios de la Florida, MS. Arch. Gen. de Indias, Seville, est. 135, caj. 7, leg. 8.

along the route.[1] Leaving Santa Elena by the end of August,[2] he next paid a visit to Guale, where he learned of the death of his nephew, Alonzo Marqués; and found that the Indians had made rapid progress in learning the faith, were reverently adoring the cross, and could already repeat the Christian doctrine in chorus. He remained at Guale eight days and, leaving a captain and thirty soldiers stationed there, was back again at San Mateo by the 20th of September.[3]

During his first visit to Cuba he had been deterred from proceeding against the corsairs and freebooters which infested the neighbouring seas, by the rumour of French fleets which might jeopardise all of the work which he had so laboriously accomplished. Hastening his return to Florida, he had now completed the inspection of the various posts which he had established, and felt that it was high time to fulfil the commission with which he had been entrusted by the King of purging the sea of pirates. Part of Arciniega's fleet had already returned to Spain, but the vessels with which he was to undertake the expedition against the sea robbers in defence of Puerto Rico and the neighbouring islands were awaiting him in the harbour of St. Augustine. After a stay of only two days at San Mateo, he now bent his steps in that direction, intent upon fulfilling the commands of his King, taking Villarroel along with him. During his absence another mutiny had broken out among the new levies headed by a captain who had come over in the fleet with Arciniega, which the camp master quelled with drastic measures, hanging three of the soldiers, and throwing the ringleader and other of his companions into prison. Avilés, with

[1] Relación de las cosas que han pasado en la Florida tocantes al servicio de Dios y del Rey. Vino con carta de Juan Mendez, 6 de Abril, 1584, MS. Arch. Gen. de Indias, Sevilla, est. 54, caj. 5, leg. 16, p. 2.

[2] Merás in Ruidíaz, *La Florida*, tomo i., p. 262.

[3] Merás in *ibid.*, tomo i., pp. 258–263, 281, 282; Barrientos in García, *Dos Antiguas Relaciones de la Florida*, pp. 126–128.

tactful leniency, released the prisoners, admonished the captain, and pointed out to the camp master that, owing to the unaccustomed conditions to which the soldiers were subjected, there were times when it was necessary to wink at certain infractions of discipline in order not to arouse the entire colony.

Before his departure Avilés directed Francisco de Reynoso to visit Carlos with a company of thirty soldiers, at whose village he was to erect a fort and to discover a waterway to Lake Maymi, through which communication could be established with San Mateo and St. Augustine. He left his brother Bartolomé in charge of the settlement at St. Augustine, which consisted of only twenty-five soldiers under Captains Miguel Henriquez and Pedro de Andrada, with fifty married men and their families, and set sail on the 20th of October in pursuit of the corsairs.[1] It is not our intention to follow the Adelantado in this part of his career, except in so far as it bears upon the history of his Florida enterprise. At Puerto Rico his camp master, who had accompanied him on the expedition, learned of the sailing, September 25, 1566, of the French squadron, one division of which, under Montluc, had already sacked the island of Madeira, while the balance of it had left for an unknown destination. In view of this report it was determined, on consultation with the royal Audiencia of Santo Domingo, that Avilés should at once proceed to put the neighbouring islands in a state of defence and return shortly to Florida.[2]

[1] Barrientos in García, *ibid.*, p. 132; Merás in Ruidíaz, *La Florida*, tomo i., p. 277; Avilés to Philip II., Nov. 29, 1566, *ibid.*, tomo ii., p. 160. Merás (in *ibid.*, tomo i., p. 264) says that Avilés was ready to sail by the end of September, started on the 20th of October, was detained by contrary winds, and finally left Nov. 5th.

[2] Merás in Ruidíaz, *La Florida*, tomo i., pp. 264–269; Barrientos in García, *Dos Antiguas Relaciones de la Florida*, pp. 128, 129. Both Merás and Barrientos give Oct. 6, 1566, as the date of the sacking of Madeira. October 18th the news of it reached Philip II. Fourquevaux to the King, Nov. 2, 1566, *Dépêches*, p. 136.

CHAPTER IV

FATHER MARTINEZ AND HIS COMPANIONS

AVILÉS had been deeply moved at the great need there was for Christian instruction among the savage races with which he had come in contact, and he had observed with some particularity, for a soldier, the various phases of their religion. Writing to a Jesuit friend upon whom he was urging the importance of their conversion he said:

"Their ceremonies consist for the most part in the worship of the sun and moon, and idols of dead game, and other animals. And every year they celebrate three or four festivals in their honour, in which they worship the sun and go three days without food, drink or sleep, which are their fasts. And he who is weak and cannot endure it, they consider a bad Indian and the noble sort become enraged. And he who can best endure these trials, is held most worthy and is treated with more courtesy."[1]

Among the Caloosas and at Guale he had found the practice of human sacrifice in existence, and his heart was sore within him at their idolatries.

He had done all that lay in his power to turn the natives to the faith. "I have already given them crosses, which they worship, and I have given them some lads and sol-

[1] Avilés to a Jesuit friend, Oct. 15, 1566, Ruidíaz, *La Florida*, tomo ii., p. 156.

diers to instruct them in the Christian doctrine," he continues, "but it is only a loss of time to attempt to plant the Holy Gospel in this country by the means of soldiers." This instruction was brief and conveyed through an interpreter, and it is highly probable that the Guale Indians, who had so glibly chanted the prayers and creed, recited them in Latin and in as complete ignorance of their significance as were the birds and the wild beasts of their forests. His attempt at securing the services of competent instructors had proved a failure. Chaplain Mendoza has told us how he had been deserted by his companions on his arrival at Puerto Rico.[1] It seems probable that some, at least, of the priests who accompanied Las Alas had been lured from their duty by the temptations which the chaplain had so bravely overcome, and the temper of the Dominican monks whom Merás had brought with him had not been that of Fray Luis Cancer. The ministrations of Mendoza and of the priests who had accompanied Arciniega were needed among his own people, dispersed as they were along the coast of the great continent, and there was much need of men whose training was such that they could devote themselves exclusively to the care of the natives, and acquire their language.

The Reformation had called into existence an organisation having the special mission of combating its heresies and re-establishing the supremacy of the Holy See. Although pre-eminently designed for intellectual contests with the element which had worked such turmoil in the Church, not a few of the foremost men in its ranks had embraced with pious ardour the vocation of missionaries, and it would appear that its military organisation and discipline had especially appealed to Avilés, himself a Spaniard and a soldier like its great founder. He had promised the Indians that teachers should be sent them,

[1] "Relación" in *ibid.*, tomo ii., p. 437. See p. 152, in this volume.

and was much disappointed that no member of the Society of Jesus nor of any other religious order had accompanied Arciniega's fleet.[1]

The mission of Fray Luis Cancer and the zealous preparations of Fray Domingo de la Anunciacion for the expedition of De Luna, both of them missions inspired by Las Casas and undertaken without the advice of the Provincial Chapter of the Order in Mexico, had awakened some symptoms of jealousy in the mind of its Provincial, Fray Domingo de Santa Maria, who had written Philip, pointing out the importance of an appeal to the judgment and experience of the Chapter in such enterprises.[2] But the King had sufficient confidence in his general to override the advice of the Dominican Provincial, and he had anticipated the wishes of the Adelantado in respect to Jesuit missionaries. May 3, 1566, scarcely five months after the successful termination of the campaign against the French heretics in Florida, he addressed a letter to Francisco Borgia, Duke of Gandia, at that time third General of the Society of Jesus, directing him to appoint twenty-four members of the Company as missionaries in such parts of the Indies as the Royal Council should designate.[3] In compliance with the royal orders, Borgia selected two Fathers, named Pedro Martinez and Juan Rogel, and a lay brother, Francisco de Villareal, who were appointed to go to Florida. As this was the first Jesuit mission to the West Indies,[4] its members command our interest.

[1] Avilés to a Jesuit friend, Oct. 15, 1566, *ibid.*, tomo ii., p. 157.

[2] Fray Domingo de Santa Maria to Philip II., June 25, 1585, *Cartas de Indias*, Madrid, 1877, p. 134.

[3] *Vida del P. Francisco de Borja* . . . por el P. Pedro de Ribadeneyra, Madrid, 1592, lib. iii., cap. 6, p. 140b, gives the letter in full.

[4] *Historia de los Trivmphos de nvestra santa fee entre Gentes las mas barbaras y fieras del nuevo Orbe* . . . por el Padre Andres Perez de Ribas. Madrid, 1645, p. 744. Epist. P. Nadal in *Monumenta Historica Societatis Jesu*, vol. iii., p. 411.

Father Martinez was an Aragonese, born in 1533,[1] in Celda, a suburb of Teruel, famous for the legend of its two lovers. His family was evidently in easy circumstances, for he was sent to the University of the City of Valencia to study the humanities and theology; but being of a turbulent disposition he spent more of his time in the fencing school than with Aristotle and St. Thomas on the benches of the lecture hall. With his boon companions he wandered about, seeking for opportunities to display his skill with the rapier, the sword, and the target, and there was hardly a duel in the town in which he did not take part, either as principal or second. This did not tend to develop his respect for the Jesuits, whom it was his habit to mock and ridicule.

Going to the college one day, in company with three or four of his companions in order to amuse himself for a while at the expense of the Fathers, he observed to his friends, "One of us is going to become a Teatin," referring to an Order affiliated to the Augustinians and given to the strictest observance of the rules of the mendicant friars. At this each of them, with a laugh, answered in turn, "Not I at least." On reaching the college he sat down at the entrance, and the porter courteously enquired of him what he wished, to which he replied, "Only to sit here a little while." Meanwhile he watched attentively the passing of the black-coated Fathers and of the lay brethren on their daily rounds that he might discover something at which to raise a laugh.

"But he was laid hold of by God by that very means," says

[1] *Mortes illustres et gesta eorum de Societate Jesu qui in odium fidei . . . ab ethnicis hæreticis vel aliis . . . necati sunt* . autore Philippo Alegambe. Romæ, 1657, p. 44. P. Francisco Javier Alegre in his *Historia de la Compañía de Jesus en Nueva España* (México, 1842, tomo i., p. 7) says Father Martinez was born October 15, 1523.

Father Nieremberg, who relates the incident.[1] "For he beheld so much modesty, so much devotion and sedateness in their speech and actions, that he began to think upon renouncing the world and joining the Order of which he was before accustomed to make sport, and God having truly called him, he resolved to seek the Company. Whereupon he called the Superior, Father Geronimo Nadel, and asked to be received at once."

But he had to deal with a man versed in the intricate mysteries of the human heart, and the Superior, seeing how emotional was the nature of the lad, answered that he would gladly admit him after he had considered the matter for eight days.

On receiving this answer Martinez departed. Casting aside for the while the memory of the vocation he had so lightly wished to assume, he returned to his former mode of life, and within the week attended a duel where he was obliged to wait an hour and a half for the arrival of his adversaries. But under this semblance of trifling lay the strong sense of honour, peculiar to his race; and the failure of his antagonists to keep their appointment, says one of his Jesuit biographers, recalled to him the engagement upon which he had himself entered with the Superior. At the end of eight days, in order not to prove false to his word, he returned to the college and in 1553 was finally admitted into the Society.

The same ardour which he had previously expended in his amusements was now addressed to penance and mortification. Clothed in a hair shirt he worked for hours in the garden, like a common labourer, and he scourged himself with such severity "that it was found necessary to stay his hand and give him a clock in order that he

[1] *Vidas exemplares y venerables memorias de algunos claros varones de la Compañía de Jesus* . . . por Padre Eusebio Nieremberg, Madrid, 1643–1647, tomo iv., p. 607.

might not exceed half an hour of discipline."[1] From Valencia he was sent to pursue his studies at the college of Gandia, and going to the town of Oliva one day with a brother to stop a bull fight, the Duke, learning of his purpose, forbade the fight.

In 1558 Martin de Cordova, Count of Alcaudete, and commander of the army recruited in Andalusia[2] to fight against the African Moors, asked Francisco Borgia for Jesuits to accompan him, and Fathers Martinez, Pedro Domenec, and a lay brother, Juan Gutierrez, were detailed for the purpose. On their arrival at Carthagena, from which they were to sail for Oran, the Jesuits embarked on a transport in company with eight hundred soldiers, and with no other food than putrid bread and water so corrupt that the smell of it could hardly be borne. On reaching Oran they were ordered to attend in the hospital, although their hearts burned to go to the front with the army that was to attack Montagan. After the disastrous defeat suffered by Alcaudete, in which he was slain, and his son with a great part of the army taken prisoner, the Fathers returned to Spain, where masses had already been said for them as if they were dead men.

Father Martinez went to reside in the profess house at Toledo, where he was actively employed in preaching and hearing confessions, and where he still continued to discipline himself every night for half an hour. From Toledo he went to Cuenca, where he preached his last Lenten sermons in Spain, and from there to Alcala, where he asked permission to cook for the community and "served in the kitchen with the greatest edification for three or four months."[3] It was from there that he

[1] Nieremberg, tomo iv., p. 608.

[2] Mariana, *Historia General de España.* Continuación de la Historia General de España . . . por D. Vicente Romero, Madrid, 1794, tomo ii., p. 196.

[3] Nieremberg, tomo iv., p. 609.

received his call to go to Florida. Nieremberg tells us that while waiting in Seville to embark on the long journey Father Martinez had a premonition of his impending fate, and exclaimed one day to Fray Lobo, a distinguished Franciscan, "Oh! Father Lobo, how I long to pour out my blood at the hands of the savages, and wash those Florida shores in defence of the faith!"[1]

Father Juan Rogel, who was a native of Pamplona, a Licentiate of Arts, and Bachelor of Medicine, had been received into the Order at the College of Valencia in April, 1554, and like Father Martinez, had pursued his subsequent studies at Gandia, where he applied himself to theology. Nothing is known of the previous history of lay-brother Francisco de Villareal, but his subsequent service in Florida shows him to have been no unworthy companion of the two Fathers. Such, then, were the men who were to begin the ministrations of the Jesuits in the New World, labours destined to culminate in the famous missions of Paraguay, of Canada, and of California, with its stirring and tragic history.

July 28, 1566, the three Jesuits, provided by the King with all that was needed for their voyage, embarked at San Lucar de Barrameda aboard a Flemish hooker, and sailed in company with the squadron destined for New Spain, with the intention of proceeding to St. Augustine in response to the call of Avilés. The pilot, inexperienced in West Indian navigation, missed his way, but finally sighted the shores of the continent and coasted along it in search of the port. September 14th, he passed within two leagues of the harbour of St. Augustine without discovering it. The ship was observed from the fort and a rowboat was sent out to meet her; but a high sea was running at the time and the tide was contrary, so that the attempt had to be abandoned. Two days later Father Martinez determined to go ashore and en-

[1] Nieremberg, tomo iv., p. 609.

quire of the natives the direction of St. Augustine. Accompanied by nine Flemings and a Spaniard by the name of Flores, they landed in the pinnace; but it was the season of storms which had proved so fateful to the fleet of Jean Ribaut the previous year, and the boat had scarcely touched the shore when a violent tempest arose and drove the ship to sea. The castaways, who had landed on the Florida coast somewhere above the mouth of the St. John's River, determined to await the arrival of a vessel or the return of their own ship to rescue them. They remained there ten days, not daring to penetrate the interior for fear of the natives; but finally, impelled by hunger, they took to the boat and followed the coast-line in a southerly direction. During the journey they met with many Indians, who treated them with kindness, saying they were friends and brothers of the Spaniards.[1]

At one of the places where they landed the Jesuits came upon a group of huts in a grove of pine trees, from which the owners were absent for the day. Pressed by hunger they searched the village and found in one of the huts a large fish, of which they took half, and Father Martinez left his cassock and a few beads and flowers with the remainder of the fish in payment. Elsewhere, in exchange for some fish, Father Martinez cut figures with his scissors out of a leaf of parchment, taken from a book he carried with him. At last they met with an old Indian and learned from him that the Spanish settlement lay to the south beyond three villages, each of which was situated at the mouth of a river.

On the 28th of September, after having passed the mouths of two of the rivers, the Jesuits were proceeding in search of the third, when they came upon a small island

[1] Avilés to a Jesuit friend, Oct. 15, 1566, Ruidíaz, *La Florida*, tomo ii., p. 157; Alegambe, p. 44 *et seq.*

called Tacatacuru,[1] near the mouth of the St. John's, where they saw four Indians fishing. The Flemings sprang ashore, although Father Martinez was unwilling to land, whereupon one of the fishermen ran off and soon reappeared followed by a party of forty Indians armed with bows and arrows, subjects of Tacatacuru, one of the chiefs under Saturiba who was, as we know, at war with the Spaniards. Father Martinez, although alarmed at their approach, remained near the shore, unwilling to abandon his companions, whereupon twelve of the natives attacked the boat with great fury, seized him, the Spaniard, and three of the Flemings, and dragged them ashore. The Indian who had seized Flores attempted to drown him, but the Spaniard struck the savage a violent blow, and succeeded in freeing himself. With three of the Flemings, two of whom were severely wounded, he made for the boat, which all four managed to regain.

Father Martinez now knew that he was about to attain the martyrdom for which he had so earnestly expressed his desire while still in Seville. He knelt down as best he could and raised his hands to heaven. At the same moment an Indian struck him on the head with his club with such force that he immediately fell dead.[2] Three others of his companions were also killed. The Flemings and Flores were found by the Spaniards the following day anchored at the mouth of the St. John's, half dead with hunger. When Avilés learned from the

[1] Barcia (*Ensayo*, Año MDLXVI., p. 121) and Tanner (*Societas Militans*, p. 446) both say it was the island of Tacatacuru [probably Cumberland Island].

[2] Avilés says his death occurred within a league of the fort of San Mateo (letter to a Jesuit friend, Oct. 15, 1566, Ruidíaz, *La Florida*, tomo ii., p. 158). Tanner (p. 447) gives Oct. 8, 1566, as the date of his death. Others September 24th and 28th, see Alegre, tomo i., p. 9; Barcia, *Ensayo*, Año MDLXVI., p. 121. Gerard van Berghe Montanus gives a Latin epigram on Father Martinez in his *Centuria Epigrammatum in Martires Societatis Jesu.*

survivors of the death of Father Martinez he was deeply moved.

"Blessed be Our Lord for all things," he wrote, "and since the Divine Majesty allows and thus wills it, let us give him infinite thanks for all things; insomuch that it has pleased Our Lord, to visit us here with this affliction, who have deserved so little, by removing from our company so great and good a man as Father Martinez, of whom we Spaniards as well as the natives of the country in which we live stand in such great need."

The bulls and faculties from the Pope which the Jesuit had brought with him were lost.

It had been the intention of the Adelantado to send Father Rogel to Carlos with Reynoso after he acquired some experience in the language of the natives and had prepared vocabularies of their speech. Anxious for the fate of the hooker, aboard of which the Father and lay-brother Villareal had remained, and thinking it might have run for one of the neighbouring islands, he dispatched a servant of his with a vessel to call at Puerto Rico, Santo Domingo, and Havana in search of it. The hooker was probably found at the last-named port, where it arrived in safety on the 15th of December, having touched at Hispaniola on the way. After the Flemish vessel had been driven off the coast, the captain wished to return and rescue the party which the storm had compelled him to abandon. But his Flemish crew obliged him to take the direction of Havana,[1] where the Jesuits employed their time in preaching to and confessing the citizens, while awaiting the arrival of Avilés, who had sailed from St. Augustine on the 20th of October, going to the relief of the neighbouring islands.

Shortly after the incident just related Avilés wrote his Jesuit correspondent begging that the Company send

[1] Alegre, tomo i., pp. 9, 10.

him more of its members "whom I will treat and serve and regale, as if they were the King himself,"[1] he adds, and he also urged Francisco de Toral, Bishop of Yucatan, to provide him with monks of his Order, but the Bishop had none he could send. Many of those in New Spain best fitted for the work had died, and Don Francisco advised Avilés to bring them from Spain.[2]

[1] Avilés to a Jesuit friend, Oct. 15, 1566, Ruidíaz, *La Florida*, tomo ii., pp. 158, 159.

[2] Francisco de Toral to Avilés, April 5, 1567, *ibid.*, tomo ii., p. 296.

CHAPTER V

EXPEDITIONS OF PARDO AND BOYANO—RETURN OF AVILÉS TO SPAIN

IN compliance with the orders of Avilés, Juan Pardo left Santa Elena November 1, 1566, with a party of twenty-five soldiers "to discover and conquer the interior country from there to Mexico!"[1] The expedition was quite devoid of incident. He appears to have traversed the cypress lands in a north-easterly direction, and to have struck the Cambahee at a village called Guiomae, forty leagues distant from Santa Elena, where he ordered the construction of a log house for a Spanish outpost. From thence he turned west until he reached the Savannah River at Cufitatchiqui, which De Soto had visited twenty-five years before him. A few days later he was at another village called Ysa on a large river, possibly one of the northern branches of the Broad, and two days beyond he visited Juada, a village situated on a stream at the foot of the Alleghanies.

The season was far advanced, and there was so much snow on the mountains that he could not proceed. He remained fifteen days at Juada, where he built a block-

[1] "Relación del viaje y reconocimiento que hizo del interior de la Florida en 1566 el Capitan Juan Pardo, por orden del Adelantado Pedro Menéndez de Avilés, escrita por el soldado Francisco Martinez." Ruidíaz, *La Florida*, tomo ii., p. 477. And see Appendix W, The Date of Pardo's First Expedition.

house which he named Fort San Juan,[1] and left his sergeant Boyano in command with a small garrison. He then attempted to ascend the river to the north, but after a day's march retraced his steps down the river for a short distance, and going east reached Guatari, where he again rested for fifteen days. A letter from Las Alas met him at this point, ordering him back to Santa Elena. Leaving there a priest and four soldiers, he struck across the country to the Cambahee and returned to Santa Elena over the same route by which he had gone out. He had thus traversed the extensive region lying between the Savannah and the Wateree, as far north as the Alleghanies. The country was at that time inhabited by the Creeks, if we may judge from the etymology of the names given in the Spanish Relations. At all of these villages through which he passed he had assembled the natives and their chiefs and made them a short address, calling upon them to submit to the Pope and the King, to which the Indians had readily assented, in the evident expectation of thus getting rid of him.[2]

Shortly after the General's departure Reynoso arrived at San Antonio with his company of thirty soldiers and Don Pedro, heir of the chieftain. A house was set apart for him in the town, and a cross erected near by, where morning and evening the Spaniards performed their devotions in the presence of the natives who gathered to worship it. Doña Antonia returned to Havana in the vessel which had brought Reynoso, and with her went five or six of the chief men of the tribe as hostages for the safety of the Spaniards, for, notwithstanding the civil

[1] "Relación del viaje . . . escrita por el soldado Francisco Martinez," Ruidíaz, *La Florida*, tomo ii., pp. 477, 478.

[2] "Relación de la entrada y de la conquista que por mandado de Pero Menéndez de Avilés hizo en 1565 [*sic*] en el interior de la Florida el Capitan Juan Pardo, escrita por él mismo." Ruidíaz, *ibid.*, tomo ii., pp. 465–469. See Appendix X, Pardo's First Expedition.

treatment which they received, but little confidence was reposed in the sincerity of Carlos's protestations. The ship reached Havana in six days, and after delivering Doña Antonia into the care of Alonso de Rojas, alderman of the city, returned to Carlos with additional supplies.

In the meanwhile the situation of Reynoso had grown more and more precarious. Carlos had made several attempts to kill him by treachery, which Reynoso had frustrated through the secret information conveyed to him by the native women. There still remained a large number of Spaniards in the power of the chief, for all of the people wrecked along the coast for a hundred leagues, as well as those cast away on the Florida Keys, were delivered up to him, and the rescue of these unfortunates had been one of the principal objects which Avilés held in view in seeking to establish himself among the Caloosas. But the savage chieftain was unable longer to curb his appetite for their blood, and he began to press the Spanish Captain for the return of his sister, in order to destroy them all as soon as he had her safely back with him.

Avilés had soon completed his disposition of the various forces in the islands, and by January, 1567, was back in Havana, where he received the alarming reports of Reynoso. Before proceeding to his relief he dispatched a vessel to San Mateo with orders to ascend the St. John's as far as Macoya, where it was to await his arrival from San Antonio by the inland waterway, and on the 1st of March set sail himself with seven vessels and one hundred and fifty men for San Antonio,[1] taking with him his nephew, Pedro Menéndez Marqués, who had returned from Spain,[2] Doña Antonia and her companions, Father Rogel and lay-brother Francisco, both of whom had suffered an attack of illness during their stay in

[1] Barcia, *Ensayo*, Año MDLXVII., p. 125.

[2] Alegre, tomo i., p. 10.

Havana.[1] He reached San Antonio in two days, and on landing he ordered a chapel to be built for the convenience of Father Rogel, and gathered from his lieutenant the much-desired information concerning the waterway through the peninsula to San Mateo and St. Augustine. It lay, he was told, in the country of Tocobaga, an Indian chief dwelling near the head of Old Tampa Bay,[2] fifty leagues distant from San Antonio up the west coast. Carlos was at war with Tocobaga and anxious that the Adelantado and Reynoso should accompany him against his enemy. To this the Adelantado replied that his mission was to establish peace among the natives, and to bring them to the faith; to which the unwilling Carlos was obliged to submit and to renew friendly relations with the chief of Tegesta, with whom he had also been at war.[3] The gratifying report of the existence of the waterway induced the Adelantado to proceed at once to Tocobaga to verify the discovery, but so great was the distrust inspired by Carlos's treacherous proceedings, that, unwilling to leave him behind, to work mischief during his absence, he compelled him, with other of his chief men, to accompany the expedition. One vessel was left at San Antonio, and with the remaining six the Adelantado reached Tampa Bay, sailing up the coast by night under the guidance of a Caloosa Indian. He ascended the Bay of Old Tampa and reached the vicinity of Tocobaga's village an hour before the dawn without being discovered. Again the Indian instincts of Carlos were aroused, who begged to be allowed to burn the village and was pacified only by the promise of an honourable peace and the release of some Caloosa Indians, captives at Tocobaga, among whom was a sister of his and of Doña

[1] Alegre, tomo i., p. 11; Barcia, *Ensayo*, Año MDLXVII., p. 125.

[2] See Appendix Y, Tocobaga.

[3] Merás in Ruidíaz, *La Florida*, tomo i., pp. 277–284; Barrientos in García, *Dos Antiguas Relaciones de la Florida*, pp. 132–135.

Antonia. An Indian was sent ashore to proclaim in a loud voice the peaceful mission of the visitors, but the frightened savages, awakened in so unexpected a way at the early hour, fled in terror with their wives and children when they beheld the ship drawn up near their village. Tocobaga alone remained with five or six companions and a woman, and, the day having broken, sent a Christian slave to Avilés to thank him for not having burned his village and slain his people. The man proved to be a Portuguese trader[1] from Avila, in the Province of Algarve, who had been wrecked upon the coast, where all his shipmates had been killed, and himself ultimately reduced to hewing wood and drawing water for Tocobaga, whom he also served in the capacity of a cook.

Still unwilling that Carlos should come in contact with Tocobaga, Avilés went ashore to see the Indian chief, from whom he soon learned that the native fear of the Christians was not ill-founded, for white men had already visited the locality, and on the refusal of the chiefs to supply them with corn had killed them, and had themselves in turn suffered a like fate at the hands of other Christians, who had proved very friendly to the Indians. Avilés then delivered his customary dissertation upon true and false Christians, recapitulated his own pacific intentions, delivered up to Tocobaga those of his subjects whom Carlos had held as prisoners, and ended by receiving the humble submission of the chief.

The following day an interview took place between Carlos and Tocobaga in the presence of two interpreters to hold the tricky chiefs in check. Three days later over fifteen hundred warriors gathered near the village, to receive the Adelantado. It was too threatening an assembly for the still distrustful Avilés, although the disposition of the Indians was friendly and he asked Tocobaga to dismiss them, retaining only the

[1] He traded in corn, chickens, mantas, and honey.

chief men, with whom he wished to treat in regard to a peace, observing at the same time that his own soldiers were overjoyed at the sight of the warriors, thinking that the Indians had come to fight them. The ruse proved successful, and the peace with Carlos and the Spaniards was established. But all efforts to discover the water communication with San Mateo proved abortive. It is true that a neighbouring river was said to pass through the territory of Macoya, but he was the enemy of Tocobaga and the master of many warriors; and Avilés abandoned the voyage because his own forces were insufficient to attempt it,[1] and finally departed, leaving Captain Martinez de Coz with thirty soldiers at Tocobaga[2] to instruct the Indians in the faith.[3] There remains a curious account of the mortuary customs of the natives. On the death of a chief his body was divided up into small pieces and cooked for two days until the skin could be removed from the bones, when the skeleton was reconstructed. During the four days which this required a fast was observed, and on the fourth day the entire village accompanied the bones in procession to a temple in which the reconstructed skeleton was deposited amidst the reverences of the assembly. All who attended the procession were said to gain indulgences.[4]

Avilés now returned to San Antonio, where he left Carlos who was still chafing under the peace which had been forced upon him, and threatening vengeance upon the Christians. The blockhouse was strengthened and the garrison was increased by a force of fifty additional

[1] Merás in Ruidíaz, *La Florida*, tomo ii., p. 298.

[2] Velasco (*Geografía de las Indias, 1571–1574*, p. 161) says the Spanish settlement consisted of 24 houses.

[3] Merás in Ruidíaz, *La Florida*, tomo i., pp. 285–291; Barrientos in García, *Dos Antiguas Relaciones de la Florida*, pp. 135–137.

[4] Dos breves memorias sobre las costumbres de los yndios de la Florida. MS. Arch. Gen. de Indias, Seville, est. 135, caj. 7, leg. 8.

soldiers. Father Rogel, who on his arrival had immediately turned his attention to the study of the language,[1] remained to prosecute his work among the soldiers as well as among the natives, for the former had begged that he might be left to instruct them by his good example "lest otherwise they shortly become as savage as the Indians," writes Barrientos.[2]

It had been the intention of the Adelantado to return the Tegesta Indians, whom Carlos still held prisoners, to their own people, to settle among them Brother Francisco de Villareal, who had begun the study of their language, and then to proceed to St. Augustine and San Mateo; but on leaving the harbour he met a tender which had been sent from St. Augustine to Havana; it brought him from the latter place a request for succour from the islands and letters from the Havana magistrates asking his presence in the city to quiet a conflict which had arisen between the Governor and the Adelantado's aid, Captain Barreda, who had been left under instructions from the King to protect the harbour.[3] It further appeared that Pedro de Rodabán, sent by Philip to reinforce Avilés, had reached Havana during his absence, and, seized with the gold-fever, had mutinied with the intention of going to New Spain, in which he was countenanced by the Governor, who wished to give him the command of the vessel he had brought with him. Avilés sent the Indians to Tegesta, and sailed immediately for Havana. In the course of a month he gained possession of the rebellious Rodabán, and sentenced him to death, but he finally allowed him to make an appeal. Ships were

[1] Merás in *ibid.*, tomo i., p. 284.

[2] Velasco (in his *Geografía de la Indias*, *1571–1574*, p. 161) says that in 1566 Avilés built a Spanish settlement of 36 houses on the island in the Bay of Carlos.

[3] Merás (in Ruidíaz, *La Florida*, tomo i., pp. 294–296) gives a graphic account of the quarrel.

sent to Campeche for supplies and Avilés was at last at liberty to carry out his previous intentions.

His first destination was Tegesta, where he entered into a friendly compact with the chief, who gave him his brother and two other Indians to take to Spain. During his stay of four days Brother Francisco was settled there, a cross erected, a blockhouse built, and a company of soldiers was left in charge.[1] In three days' sail from Tegesta Avilés reached San Mateo. During his absence the war with Saturiba had continued, in which the chief had greatly suffered. Many of his subjects and several chiefs had been killed by the Spaniards, and Villarroel had cast into chains sixteen of the principal men. The camp master had ascended the St. John's fifty leagues to the village of Macoya, but after awaiting in vain the arrival of the Adelantado, returned to San Mateo, on account of the narrowing of the river beyond and the great number of natives which he encountered.

The continuance of the Indian war was little to the liking of Avilés, whose untiring efforts had been directed to the establishment of friendly relations with the natives. His own forces were distributed along the extended coast in small companies, largely dependent upon such relations for their subsistence, and so isolated that despite their courage and endurance they would inevitably succumb to a concerted and sustained attack of the Indians, whose warlike qualities the General was too intelligent to despise. If the war with Saturiba should spread; if the Indians, finally perceiving the importance of burying their mutual jealousies, should combine and rise simultaneously against the Spaniards, it would put an end to his dream of conquest, overwhelm his colony, and sacrifice the fortunes of himself and his friends. He was now upon the point of returning to Spain in order to plead the

[1] Velasco (in his *Geografía de la Indias*, *1571–1574*, p. 162) says that the Spanish settlement consisted of 28 houses.

cause of his colony. He further realised, should these dissensions continue, how dangerous the enmity of the Indians would prove in the case of a descent of the French upon the coast, who would turn to their own advantage the fierce hatred which the Spaniards had aroused among the natives. And Avilés wished to depart with the conviction that peace was established, at least during his absence.

Determined to bring Saturiba to terms, he caused one of the prisoners to be released and sent him to invite the chief to a parley at the end of the bar, two leagues distant from San Mateo. His curiosity was also aroused, for he had never seen Saturiba, by whom he was reported to be held in high esteem and at the same time to be greatly feared. Saturiba replied that he was ready to meet the Adelantado at the appointed place, and asked him to bring his prisoners along with him. The following day, after a final leave-taking in which Avilés cheered and encouraged his half-naked soldiers with the promise of clothing, succour, and pay, which he would send them on his arrival in Spain, he dropped down the river to the appointed place, taking the seven Indian prisoners with him in chains.

Saturiba had preceded him and was stationed on the land at a short distance from the sea with a large party of Indians. All efforts to prevail upon him to come down to the shore proved fruitless, and at his request the Adelantado landed his prisoners, still in chains, but under the guns of his ship, so that no rescue could be attempted. Saturiba, however, would not approach them, and an ineffectual conversation lasting for two hours was carried on between them and the chief by means of messengers. Finally it appeared that he wished Avilés to land in person, and a soldier, who understood the language, informed the Adelantado that Saturiba was plotting to kill him by means of an ambuscade and to free the prisoners. Avilés's patience was now exhausted, and abandoning all hope of coming to an understanding with the indomitable savage, he recalled his prisoners, and sent him word that henceforth he would treat him as an enemy, and would either cut off his head or drive him from his country, on account of the Christians he had killed. Saturiba replied in the same spirit, and Avilés sailed for St. Augustine.

On his arrival he found great discontent prevailing at the settlement owing to the insolent behaviour of Captain Miguel Henriquez, who had insulted the governor, Bartolomé, and had proceeded with a high hand in his treatment of the soldiers. Henriquez was tried, condemned, and carried off to be turned over to the Council of the Indies. Las Alas was appointed Lieutenant of the province, and measures were taken to prosecute an active Indian campaign, following an unsuccessful expedition against Saturiba led by Avilés in person. It was now the latter part of April or the beginning of May, and Avilés took leave of his soldiers and set sail for San Felipe. He took with him three Timuquanan natives, the three Tegesta Indians, Rodabán and Henriquez, all of whom he intended to carry to Spain, and with a fair wind reached San Felipe in the course of three days,[1] where he learned from Pardo the results of the expedition to Juada, and of Boyano's discoveries to the south.

In January, 1567, thirty days after Pardo's return from his first expedition, a letter had reached him from his sergeant Boyano, at Juada, at the foot of the mountains, informing him that he had waged war against the cacique of Chisca in the Georgia mountains, probably the same region where De Soto had sent a scouting party of two Spaniards with some Indians.[2] With a force of only

[1] Merás in Ruidíaz, *La Florida*, tomo i., pp. 291–305; Barrientos in García, *Dos Antiguas Relaciones de la Florida*, pp. 137–140.

[2] See *Spanish Settlements*, vol. i., p. 232, note 1. "Myths of the Cherokee," 19 *Ann. Rep. Bu. Ethn.*, Pt. I., p. 201.

fifteen soldiers he had killed over a thousand natives and burned fifty huts, only two of his soldiers being slightly wounded, and he enquired whether he should not prosecute the advantage. To this Las Alas, who was in command at San Felipe, consented, directing him to leave ten soldiers to garrison the fort. While Boyano was awaiting the reply to his letter, one of the mountain chiefs sent him word that he was coming down to eat him and a dog which the Spaniards had taken with them. Thinking it best to be the first to attack, the sergeant started out with a party of twenty soldiers, and after four days' march through the mountains came upon the Indian stronghold. It was defended by a high palisade of wood, with only one small entrance. Under cover of their shields the Spaniards entered, the sergeant being wounded in the mouth, and nine of his soldiers injured. The Indians, seeing their village captured, took to their underground dwellings, from which they issued to skirmish with the Spaniards; but the latter killed some, drove others back into their huts, and, setting fire to them, killed and burned fifteen hundred natives, according to Boyano's report.[1]

It was there that the letter of Las Alas found him. Having reduced the mountain chieftain, Boyano garrisoned the little fort of San Juan, and began his expedition. Striking south in the direction of Chiaha, in four days' march he reached a great village surrounded by a strong stockade with towers, and situated between two large rivers. It was probably one of the *red* or war towns of the Creeks,[2] for it was inhabited solely by three thousand warriors, and was entirely destitute of women and children. The warriors gave him a friendly reception and entertained his party with food. Twelve days' march from there, and pursuing in all likelihood the same trail

[1] A Spanish proverb says: "Distant countries, big lies."

[2] *Spanish Settlements*, vol. i., p. 59, and note 3.

that De Soto had traversed before them, the Spaniards reached the chief town of the country, Chiaha,[1] in the neighbourhood of where Columbus, Georgia, now is, and distant one hundred and forty leagues from San Juan. Boyano determined to await here the arrival of Pardo, who was to leave San Felipe in August, and so he built himself a fort, with the consent and assistance of the natives, for the cacique wished to be on good terms with the Spaniards. He named it Santa Elena and, with unusual prudence for a soldier, began planting wheat and barley. In the mean time he was treated with the greatest respect. On approaching a town the natives would paint themselves in brilliant colours as if for a festival and come four or five leagues to receive him; then they would conduct him quickly to their village, bearing him along in a litter, and dancing before him, and as he sat enthroned in his chair they would vie with each other in attempts to reach his presence and to bring him gifts of deer-skins and meat, fish and fowl, corn and game in abundance for his soldiers.[2]

A year and eight months had now elapsed since Avilés had first landed in Florida, and he had realised in that short space of time, in almost every detail, the plans with

[1] *Spanish Settlements*, vol. i., p. 231, note 2. Pardo calls it "Chihaque, y por otro nombre se llama Lameco." ("Relación" in Ruidíaz, *La Florida*, tomo ii., p. 471), and "Lameco, que tiene por otro nombre Chiaha." (*Ibid.*, p. 472.) Vandera ("Relación," *ibid.*, p. 484) says: "Solameco y por otro nombre Chiaha." Shea, in his "Pardo's Exploration of South Carolina and Georgia" (*Historical Magazine*, 1860, p. 232), incorrectly translates this sentence in Vandera, as if it contained the names of two different towns, instead of giving two different names for one and the same town. He adds that Talimeco near Cufitatchiqui is interpreted by Buckingham Smith to signify *taliminko*, "rock chief." Shea identifies Chiaha with that of De Soto. Gatschet, in his *Migration Legend of the Creek Indians* (vol. i., pp. 62, 63), derives Solameco from a Creek word *súli mikó*—"buzzard chief," and incorrectly places it on the Savannah River.

[2] "Relación del viaje . . . escrita por el soldado Francisco Martinez," in Ruidíaz, *La Florida*, tomo ii., pp. 478–480.

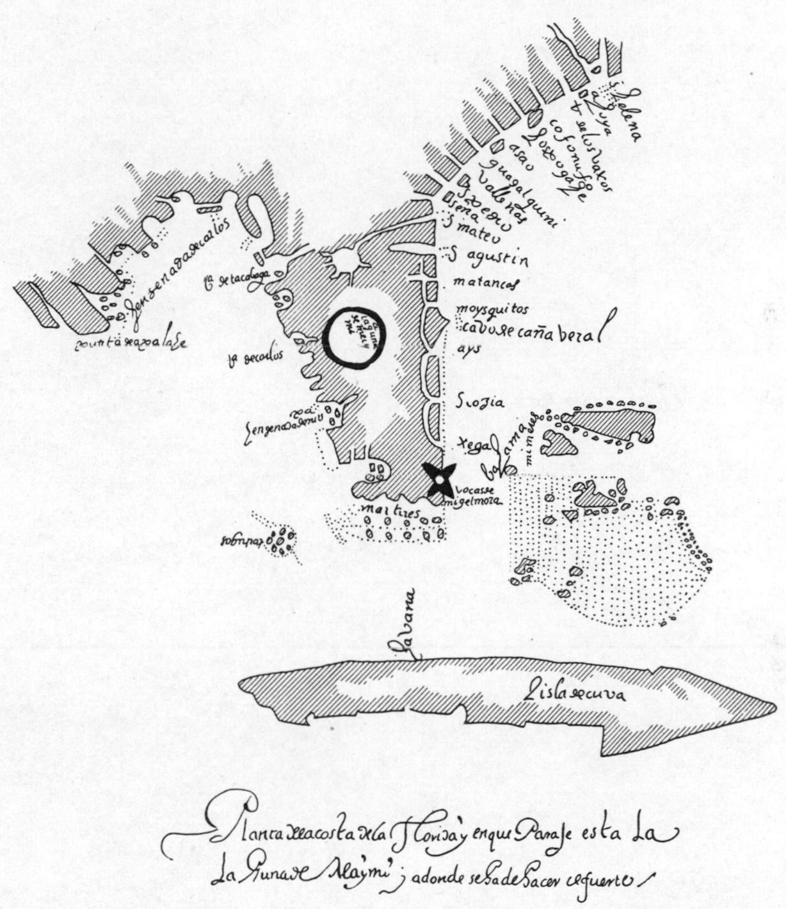

"MAPA DE LA FLORIDA Y LAGUNA DE MAIMI," 1595-1600 (?), IN THE ARCHIVES OF THE INDIES, SEVILLE.

which he had set out. He had successfully expelled the French from the extensive territory under his command. He had in person explored the coast as far north as Santa Elena in South Carolina and circumnavigated the Peninsula from the St. John's on the east to Tampa Bay on the west, discovering three hundred leagues of coast, four deep harbours and twenty shallower ones, which he had marked out and sounded[1]; he had penetrated the country to the interior as far as central Alabama. He had twice explored the St. John's River, in part, and his failure to verify the existence of its supposed communication with the Gulf of Mexico, upon which he laid so much stress, was solely due to his set purpose not to arouse the hostility of the natives.

He had founded three permanent settlements, those of St. Augustine, San Mateo, and San Felipe, in situations along the shore of the Atlantic especially selected to serve as harbours of refuge for the treasure fleets. He had established a line of forts at Ays (St. Lucie), Tegesta (Biscayne Bay), Carlos (Charlotte Harbour), and Tocobaga (Tampa), on each side of the Peninsula, along the course where the treasure fleets in their passage to Spain were most exposed to the violence of storms, where wrecks were of most frequent occurrence, and where those who were cast ashore were subject to the inhuman treatment of the natives. He had carried out his previous intention of forming a settlement on the Chesapeake, the failure of which was due solely to circumstances beyond his control, and he had established a fort at the foot of the Appalachian Mountains, the source from which the Indians in their intercourse with the French had derived a large part of their gold and silver. Finally, he had taken all of the precautions within his power to garrison the colony and had distributed fifteen hundred

[1] Merás in *ibid.*, tomo i., p. 317.

men in the various forts and settlements which he had founded.[1]

He had used his utmost endeavours to establish friendly relations with the natives, in which he had succeeded in every instance, with the exception of that of Saturiba, whose hostile attitude was due in no part to his own want of tact, but to the insubordination and ill-will of his mutinous soldiers; and he had placed in the midst of those who were given to the greatest cruelty the two or three missionaries who had reached him from the mother country. In pursuance of this policy he had been so considerate in respecting the feelings of the natives that he does not appear to have exercised the right of distributing the repartimientos granted him by the Asiento,[2] except, perhaps, at Santa Elena. He had appointed agents in the most accessible centres of the West India trade, Puerto Rico, Santo Domingo, and Cuba, from which assistance could be readily sent to his nursling colonies; and he had been so successful in organising this important department of his government that one hundred and fifty sailors in twelve vessels were engaged in supplying the colonies and in prosecuting the discoveries.[3] The obstacles which he had encountered, the partial failures which had attended his plans, were due rather to the jealousy of officials, the absence of discipline among his soldiers, and the inhospitality of a new country than to any lack of foresight on his part, and these he had partly overcome by means of that prudence with which he was so amply endowed.

Osorio, the Governor of Cuba, from whom Avilés should have received all of the consideration to which his

[1] Barrientos in García, *Dos Antiguas Relaciones de la Florida*, p. 148.

[2] Capitulación y asiento con Pero Menéndez de Avilés para la población y conquista de la Florida," Madrid, March 20, 1565, Ruidíaz, *La Florida*, tomo ii., p. 42.

[3] Barrientos in García, *Dos Antiguas Relaciones de la Florida*, p. 148.

rank and the royal interest which he represented entitled him, had thrown every obstacle in his way which a powerful official with large authority and out of reach of the royal arm could raise. He had refused him money for his starving colonies, he had impressed his men, he had countenanced mutineers and deserters, he had refused him ships, he had driven him from the city of Havana, and had even indirectly threatened his life. To all of this Avilés had submitted with a self-control very remarkable in a man of such decisive and energetic disposition. But Havana was the storehouse nearest at hand to his new government, and in the interest of his enterprise and that of his friends whose fortunes were involved in it, he had put up with Osorio's arbitrary conduct, and, equal to an emergency in which the success of his conquest was at stake, he had revictualled his colonies with the prize money of his captains and what more he could obtain by pledging his own wardrobe. His prudence had finally been crowned with success, and he was now able to return to Spain with the conviction that he had performed his duty in every particular. He had left behind him two sources of weakness, one of which was the Indian war in the region of San Mateo, and the second was the wide distribution of his soldiers. One reason for the latter may have been the reduction of the drain on the store of provisions at San Mateo and St. Augustine, and the lessening of the spread of the ever-present spirit of revolt.

On the verge of his departure Avilés directed that a number of blockhouses be erected in the neighbourhood of St. Augustine and San Mateo, each with a small garrison to keep the Indians in check,[1] to protect the trail

[1] These were at Palican, an island near the Matanzas River, five leagues south of Augustine; at Soloy; at Saturiba, three leagues from and probably to the south of San Mateo; at Alimacany; at Old St. Augustine, Tacatacuru, and at Guale. Barrientos in *ibid.*, pp. 140–142.

between the forts; and stringent orders were given that no Indian should be admitted into them. The station at Palican, an island near the Matanzas River, five leagues south of St. Augustine, was to be built on an elevation where the sea could be watched and the passage of vessels reported to St. Augustine; dogs trained to attack the Indians were to be set loose every night in order to protect the cattle and keep the island clear of natives. He left orders that the chief of Tacatacuru should be killed as a punishment for the murder of Father Martinez and that of Captain Pedro de la Rando, who, with ten soldiers, had been treacherously set upon while asleep in the house of the chief.[1]

May 18, 1567, Avilés set sail from San Felipe in an extremely small vessel of only twenty tons burden. His company consisted of thirty-eight men, including six Indians and a priest; the two captains, Henriquez and Rodabán, went as prisoners.[2] June 15th he was at Tercera, one of the Azores, where he heard that Philip was to sail from Corunna for Flanders. Making for that port he was chased by one English and two French vessels into Vivero, twenty leagues to the east of Corunna. He arrived at Vivero about the 17th or 18th of the month, and learned that the King was still in Madrid. Avilés wrote announcing his arrival, sent forward his prisoners to the Council of the Indies, and then went on to his native town of Avilés.

Merás tells an amusing story of the fright caused by his appearance among some shipping at Artedo, a little bay not far from Avilés, where he passed the night and was at first taken for a Turkish corsair.[3] The day following

[1] Merás in Ruidíaz, *La Florida*, tomo i., pp. 305–308; Barrientos in García, *Dos Antiguas Relaciones de la Florida*, pp. 140–144.

[2] Merás (in Ruidíaz, *La Florida*, tomo i., pp. 308, 309) says he was only 17 days in crossing! Barrientos (in García, *Dos Antiguas Relaciones de la Florida*, p. 144), says Avilés arrived July 17th, an evident mistake.

[3] Merás in Ruidíaz, *La Florida*, tomo i., pp. 311–313.

his arrival at Artedo he visited his home and saw his wife, with whom he remained for eighteen days, and July 25th reached Madrid. He presented himself before the King with his six Indians in their scant Florida dress armed with their bows and arrows. Garcilaso relates that as the Indians were passing through a village, on their way to Madrid, one of the Spaniards who had visited Florida in company with De Soto went out to see them. In order to show his acquaintance with their country he inquired of them if they were from the province of Vetachuco, or Apalache, or Mauvilia, or Chicaça, or from other regions where some great battles had been fought. The Indians immediately perceived his object, and looking at him askance, replied, "Do you want to have news of those provinces, which you left in such a bad condition?" Then, having consulted together a little, saying they would prefer to give him a volley of arrows rather than the news he asked for, two of the Indians shot some arrows in the air. They did this with such skill that the arrows mounted out of sight, and the Spaniard, who himself narrated the incident to Garcilaso, expressed his surprise that they had not shot at him, so great was their proverbial recklessness and daring.[1]

On his arrival at Court Avilés found that the false reports concerning his conduct spread abroad by the Florida deserters and mutineers, among which was the accusation that he had sold the provisions sent to Florida to his own advantage, had produced a bad impression on Philip and his Council. This he successfully dispelled. He told of his plans to impede the passage of the French to Newfoundland, referring probably to his Chesapeake Bay enterprise, and was treated as a veritable Neptune of the

[1] *La Florida del Inca*, Madrid, 1723, lib. vi., cap. 22, p. 268. Garcilaso says the village was near Cordova. This detail casts some doubt on the anecdote, for the Indians could hardly have passed by Cordova on their way from the Asturias to Madrid.

Florida seas, says Fourquevaux, who wrote Charles IX. that Avilés had been summoned to Spain to command the fleet which was on its way to Flanders to plant the Inquisition there.[1] If such had been Philip's original intention, it was subsequently abandoned. November 3, 1567, the King rewarded him with the title of Captain-General of the West, appointed him to command a fleet of twelve galleons, with two thousand soldiers to secure the navigation of the West Indies, and granted him an aid of two hundred thousand ducats.[2] In the early part of January of the following year the King conferred upon him the commandery of the Holy Cross of Zarza of the Knights of Santiago with an income of eight hundred crowns in recognition of his services. If we are to trust Fourquevaux the appointment did not quite come up to the expectations of the haughty Adelantado, who had entertained higher aspirations, and who did not hesitate to show his disappointment in his demeanour.[3]

[1] Fourquevaux to Charles IX., Aug. 2, 1567, *Dépêches*, pp. 241, 242.

[2] "Titulo de Capitán General de una Armada de 12 galeones dispuesta en Vizcaia, destinada a la guarda y seguridad de las costas, islas y puertos de Indias," Escorial, Nov. 3, 1567, Ruidíaz, *La Florida*, tomo ii., p. 390; Merás in *ibid.*, tomo i., pp. 309–320; Barrientos (in García, *Dos Antiguas Relaciones de la Florida*, pp. 144–149) gives the date of September 15th of the same year (p. 148). Fourquevaux to Charles IX., Nov. 13, 1567, *Dépêches*, p. 289.

[3] Fourquevaux to Charles IX., Jan. 19, 1568, *Dépêches*, p. 316. "Pierre Menendes a eu le commanderie de Sainte Croix de la Sarce, vaillant huict cens escuz de rente ; et faict encore le dedaigneux ; car il s'en estoit promis une meilleur." The date appended to the entry in the *Indice de pruebas de los caballeros que han vestido el hábito de Santiago desde el ano 1501 hasta la fecha* (formado por D. Vicente Vignau . . . y D. Francisco R. de Uhagón, . . . Madrid, 1901, p. 222) is 1558. This is evidently a misprint, for the reason that the entry describes him as "Adelantado de la Florida, Gobernador general de la Isla de Cuba," whereas he did not visit Florida until 1565, and his appointment as governor of Cuba was of still later date. It is also apparent, from the context of the paragraph in Fourquevaux's letter above given, that the appointment was of recent date. Indeed, from the character of the misprint and the date of Fourquevaux's letter the appointment would seem to have been made during the first half of January, 1568.

CHAPTER VI

MUTINY AT ST. AUGUSTINE—PARDO'S SECOND EXPEDITION

AVILÉS had scarcely set sail when the authorities at St. Augustine learned of a mutiny which had been fomenting for some time prior to his departure. It had assumed extensive and threatening proportions, for it involved one hundred and fifty of the garrison. Their plan was to spike the guns, gain possession of the higher officials, and to carry off all of the property and the women. The suspicions of the authorities having been aroused shortly before the intended outbreak, an investigation was ordered and five of the conspirators were seized, who, being put to the torture, disclosed the extent of the plot, but were nevertheless executed. This was followed by the seizure of some thirty more, all worthy of death; but the chaplain Mendoza cast himself at the feet of the judges and begged for their lives, on the condition that the mutineers should repent and bind themselves to keep the peace in the future. "And when I preached them a sermon in the presence of the judges, at the sight of their repentance and tears those gentlemen ordered their release from the prison into which they had been cast," writes the chaplain, "and suspended their sentence until they become guilty of another crime."

Notwithstanding the efforts of Bartolomé to smooth the pathway of the little colony, "he was still a man," says the moralising chaplain, and friction arose between him and Arguelles, perhaps Martin Arguelles, father of the first white man born at St. Augustine. The quarrel led to a passage of words between them, and Las Alas at once put the Governor under guard and cast Arguelles into prison, until the arrival of Pedro Menéndez Marqués, who with the assistance of the chaplain patched up a peace between them. Pedro de Andrada, with a force of eighty soldiers, was sent to assist Outina against Saturiba and some other chiefs who had combined to attack him. They appear to have been successful, and Andrada succeeded in burning one of the native villages; but on his return he was attacked by the allied Indians and slain with a large part of his company.[1] About the middle of August, Marqués and Las Alas departed for San Felipe. A curious side-light is cast upon the scant resources of the little colony when we read in a letter of Mendoza in relation to one of his priests, who had been found guilty of a very grave offence,—that he did not write with more detail owing to the lack of writing paper, that which he possessed having been given him "for the love of God."[2]

Towards the end of the month Marqués and Las Alas reached San Felipe, and Pardo was directed to join Boyano at Chiaha, where the latter was awaiting him. September 1st he set out, and ascending the Savannah as far as Cufitatchiqui, he struck across the country and reached Juada over part of the route by which he had returned on his previous expedition. He found that the Indians had surrounded the small garrison in Fort San Juan, but they laid aside their hostile attitude on his appearance and renewed their submission. Crossing the spur of the mountains, probably by the trail which

[1] Fourquevaux to Charles IX., Nov. 19, 1567, *Dépêches*, p. 295.

[2] Mendoza to Philip II., Aug. 6, 1567, MS. Arch. Gen. de Indias, Seville, est. 54, caj. 5, leg. 9.

Boyano had followed before him, he reached Tocalques, perhaps Toxaway, at the foot of the mountains in north-western South Carolina.[1] A beautiful and fertile country now lay before him, which Vandera, who accompanied him, at a loss to describe it, could only compare to Andalusia. At Tanasqui Pardo thought that he discerned the smoke arising from the reduction of silver ore[2]: the trail to Chiaha passed through a region filled with wild grape-vines laden with ripe fruit, and medlar trees, probably the persimmon; it is a land of benediction, a country of angels, writes the delighted Vandera.[3]

At Chiaha, where he rested a while, Pardo found Boyano with his soldiers. Although informed by the friendly natives that hostile Creeks were awaiting him he determined to continue his journey, and struck directly south "in the direction of Zacatecas and the Mines of San Martin,"[4] fascinated by the well-built villages, the pleasant streams, the corn-fields and the groves of wild fruit-trees through which he passed. Four days south of Chiaha at Satapo the report that the Indians had assembled farther on to attack him assumed such proportions that after consultation with his officers he concluded to retrace his steps and return to Chiaha. It had been his intention to proceed by way of Tasquiqui, near the junction of the Coosa and Tallapoosa Rivers,[5] and by way of

[1] "Myths of the Cherokee," James Mooney, *19 Ann. Rep. Bu. Ethn.*, Pt. I., p. 29. Shea in "Pardo's Exploration of South Carolina and Georgia," (*Historical Magazine*, 1860, p. 232) suggests Toccoa.

[2] Shea, *ibid.*, *Historical Magazine*, 1860, p. 232. The silver mines of the Cherokees, "the existence of which, long doubtful, has now been recognised."

[3] "Relación escrita por Juan de la Vandera," in Ruidíaz, *La Florida*, tomo ii., p. 485.

[4] *Ibid.*, tomo ii., p. 485.

[5] Gatschet, *Migration Legend of the Creek Indians*, vol. i., p. 191. "Myths of the Cherokee," James Mooney, *19 Ann. Rep. Bu. Ethn.*, Pt. I., p. 29.

Coça in what is now Talladega County, Alabama,[1] as far as the Choctaw territory of Tuscaloosa in Alabama.[2] This plan he was now compelled to abandon, but one of his soldiers with a party of friendly natives went a distance of five days' journey from Satapo to Coça, bringing back a report that it was a town of one hundred and fifty householders,[3] the largest and richest that had yet been visited.

Pardo remained several days at Chiaha, where he strengthened the fort already built by Boyano, and left a corporal in charge with thirty soldiers. At Cauchi[4] another blockhouse was constructed and garrisoned with a corporal and twelve soldiers, at the request of the chief, who, under the guise of asking for Christians to teach his people, probably desired their assistance against his neighbours. Juada was reinforced by his sub-lieutenant, Alberto Escudero, and thirty soldiers, and at Guatari, through which Pardo also passed, a blockhouse was constructed and left in charge of another corporal and seventeen soldiers. From there Pardo returned to San Felipe at Santa Elena.[5] Of the fate which ultimately overtook these isolated settlements we have but a very brief record to the effect that the natives upon whom they were

[1] See *Spanish Settlements*, vol. i., p. 232 and note 3. Shea (in "Pardo's Exploration of South Carolina and Georgia," *Historical Magazine*, 1860, p. 232), Gatschet (*Migration Legend of the Creek Indians*, vol. i., p. 191), and Mooney (in "Myths of the Cherokee," *19 Ann. Rep. Bu. Ethn.*, Pt. I., p. 29) all identify it with Soto's Coça.

[2] *Spanish Settlements*, vol. i., pp. 60, 61.

[3] "Vecinos."

[4] Shea, *ibid.*, *Historical Magazine*, 1860, p. 232. "The word Chattahoochee is not much abridged in Ca-u-chi."

[5] "Relación de la entrada y de la conquista que por mandado de Pero Menéndez de Avilés hizo en 1565 [*sic*] en el interior de la Florida el Capitán Juan Pardo, escrita por él mismo," in Ruidíaz, *La Florida*, tomo ii., pp. 469–473. "Relación escrita por Juan de la Vandera," in *ibid.*, tomo ii., pp. 484–486. Herrera in his "Descripción de las Indias," (in vol. i. of the *Decades*, p. 15) says Pardo went from New Spain to Florida in less than two years! See Appendix Z, Pardo's Second Expedition.

quartered finally rose and killed them all, only a fifer, his wife, and daughter escaping from the general massacre.[1]

The reduction of the garrison at San Felipe brought little relief to its starving soldiers, and with the opening of 1568 the familiar conditions were again rife. Towards the end of the winter, supplies reached St. Augustine from Campeche, but previous to their arrival the price of corn had risen to one hundred and fifty reales a bushel and to more than twenty ducats at San Mateo. The garrison at the former place had been subsisting for days on a ration of four ounces of corn,—a quantity of which had been found in the rat-holes in the sand,—on the roots of palms, and on oysters, which Las Alas collected by the boatload. He had, however, carried out the instructions of Avilés as far as it lay in his power, and by the end of March two blockhouses had been built within sight of each other at the mouth of the St. John's, one on the south shore, near the bar, probably on the Mayport Peninsula, and the other across the river on the island of Alimacany, Fort George Island, and a third at Old St. Augustine.[2] The war with Saturiba dragged along, and on the 31st of March, shortly after the completion of the blockhouses, four hundred Indians attacked the fort of San Mateo, and entering it by a breach in the palisade caused by a flood in the river, killed one soldier and severely wounded Castellon, who was in command. On receipt of the news Las Alas at once sent Captain Francisco Nuñez, with fifty of his best men, to the relief of the fort. On their arrival the stockade was restored and

[1] Relación de las cosas que han pasado en la Florida tocantes al servicio de Dios y del Rey. Vino con carta de Juan Mendez, 6 de Abril, 1584. MS. Arch. Gen. de Indias, Seville, est. 54, caj. 5, leg. 16, p. 2.

[2] Las Alas to ———, St. Augustine, March 23, 1568. *Brooks MSS.*, Library of Congress, Washington. Fairbanks in his *History of St. Augustine* (New York, 1858, pp. 61, 103), thinks the blockhouses at the mouth of the St. John's were located the one at Batten Island and the other at Mayport.

Castellon was rapidly recovering from his wound when, like a thunderbolt out of a clear sky, the French avenger descended upon the devoted garrison.[1]

[1] Estevan de la sala en san agustin cinco de mayo mil quinientos sesenta y nueve cuenta como se perdio el fuerte de san mateo. MS. Arch. Gen. de Indias, Seville, est. 2, caj. 5, leg. 1/9. See Appendix BB, The Spanish Account of Gourgues's Attack on San Mateo, where it is shown that the date 1569 is probably a mistake for 1568.

CHAPTER VII

PHILIP NOTIFIES FRANCE OF THE MASSACRE

WHILE Avilés was achieving his conquest and settlement of the transatlantic peninsula, the negotiations pending between France and Spain had reached an acute stage. Only the dependence of Catherine on the assistance her Catholic neighbour might afford her in case the intrigues she was hatching with the antagonistic religious elements in her own country should turn to her own disadvantage had prevented her from coming to an open breach with Philip over the question of Florida. De Thou[1] has accused the Catholic leaders of having betrayed to Philip the departure of Jean Ribaut's final expedition, but we have seen with what accuracy the King was kept informed by his diplomatic agents of every step taken by the French. In the ignorance of the Protestant party concerning the true sources from which Spain derived its information it may well be that in the heat of the moment the rumours current at the time among the Huguenots made the Roman Catholics the scapegoats for the want of caution of the Protestants.

It is not improbable that at the very time when Alava was conveying the final warning to Catherine at Tours,

[1]*Histoire Universelle*, 1620, vol. ii., p. 536; Gaffarel, *Hist. de la Floride Française*, p. 231. Haag says many Frenchmen thought the Guises had advised the Spaniards of the departure of the Protestant colony for Florida. "Un glorieux épisode maritime et colonial," by Maurice Delpeuch in *Revue Maritime*, Oct., 1902, tome clv., p. 1900.

Valdes had already arrived at Court with the information of the capture of Fort Caroline and the final catastrophe which had befallen Ribaut's fleet; for he had left St. Augustine with Avilés's dispatch of October 15th, and had probably reached his destination by the opening of December.[1]

No breath of the result of the expedition had yet reached France, where Catherine was still playing her rôle of injured innocence and writing her daughter and Fourquevaux that neither she nor the King had ever sent a subject of theirs to usurp the estates of the King of Spain, but to the *Terre des Bretons*, and that they would severely punish any of their vassals who should attempt it. "May it please God," she piously concludes in her letter to her daughter, "that Florida may never cause you to believe that which is not so." [2] Jacques Ribaut arrived in France about the middle of December, and with two of his captains had gone post-haste to Coligny, to whom he had related the sack of Fort Caroline and the loss of his vessels, but the news was not yet known even in France.[3]

At Madrid, as well, Fourquevaux was still in complete ignorance. Shortly before Christmas, in an interview with Alba, the Duke had complained to him of the French aggression in a region which had belonged to Spain since the time of Ferdinand; and which was of too much importance for Spain to have neglected it. Had the French taken possession before or during the wars, it would have been mentioned in the treaty of peace[4] ob-

[1] Avilés to Philip II., Dec. 5, 1565, Ruidíaz, *La Florida*, tomo ii., p. 105.

[2] Catherine de' Medici to the Queen of Spain, received Dec. 13, 1565. MS. Arch. Nat., Paris, K, 1504 (84). Catherine de' Medici to Fourquevaux, Dec. 30, 1565, extract in Gaffarel, *Hist. de la Floride*, p. 415 ; Jan. 20, 1566, *ibid.*, p. 418.

[3] Alava to Philip II., Dec. 21, 1565, MS. Arch. Nat., Paris, K, 1504 (88); Jan. 6, 1566, MS., *ibid.*, K, 1505 (64).

[4] Cateau Cambrésis, April, 1559.

served Alba. Fourquevaux retorted that sea charts thirty years old showed that the coast, where Florida was said to lie, was called the *Coste des Bretons;* that it lay a great distance from Hispaniola, Cuba, and New Spain, so that its occupation by the French could not impede Spanish navigation, and concluded by saying that if Florida was not mentioned in the treaty it was their own fault, and proved that at the time of its making the Spaniards had not yet gone there. This drew from Alba the intimation that Philip would employ all of his resources to recover its possession, and that French affairs in Florida were already in a bad way owing to the arrival of the Spaniards who had been sent there the previous summer. But the hint dropped by Alba failed of its desired effect, for Fourquevaux had received reports from Lisbon and Seville that Avilés was awaiting reinforcements at Santo Domingo. In a subsequent audience with Philip, Fourquevaux was unable to gain any further information, although he had expected that the King would refer to Alava's complaints to Catherine.[1]

With the complete success which had attended the expedition of Avilés, Philip at last felt that he could treat Catherine with ungloved hands and, wishing to deal with her directly, he passed over the French ambassador at Madrid, and instructed Alava to take a high tone in speaking with her about Florida. Indeed he had taken the matter so to heart that his Queen informed her mother of her fear lest any attempt to vindicate the French aggression would bring about a change in the friendly relations between the two countries.[2]

When Jacques Ribaut and his companions reached Moulins, where Catherine was at the time, his bearing was so retiring that Alava suspected he had received orders not to talk about the matter until a favourable

[1] Fourquevaux to Charles IX., Dec. 24, 1565, *Dépêches*, pp. 17, 18.

[2] Fourquevaux to Catherine de' Medici, Dec. 25, 1565, *ibid.*, p. 34.

opportunity presented itself to Catherine to lay it before Philip.[1] For all that, it was impossible for Ribaut and his friends to avoid some show of feeling, which was all the more intense from its enforced repression, and meeting Doctor Enveja, one of Philip's agents, in the palace one day they threatened him and all the Spaniards in Normandy with death.

Ribaut had been at least two weeks at Moulins, when, on January 15th, Alava had his interview with Catherine, and broached the question of Florida. He adhered closely to his master's instructions, and according to his report the conversation did not lack spice. When Alava informed her that her actions were not in accordance with the treaty of peace, she ingenuously replied that she believed the men who had gone to the *Isles des Bretons* had returned." "I know of no *Isles des Bretons*," retorted the ambassador; "you can baptise the country *Isles des Bretons*, and call Peru *Tierra firme des Bretons*, as you like, but I heard the order given to your captain to go to New France by way of Florida, in which the name Florida was used." To this Catherine vouchsafed no reply, and, changing the subject, asked Alava not to address her son in so crude a manner, because he was too great to admit of it. "I shall not hesitate to speak to him," said Alava, "for though he is too young to treat of such matters, God has given him a good understanding. I am convinced that had he been old enough His Majesty would have sent some one to address him more urgently some time ago; that as for his greatness His Majesty has upheld it at a time when it was about to tumble to the ground, and will continue to promote it; and as you are regent, you ought to consider it." Catherine's only reply was to indicate her displeasure by a gesture with her head. Then Alava told her of Ribaut's threats to Enveja, at which she professed to be

[1] Alava to Philip II., Jan. 6, 1566, MS. Arch. Nat., Paris, K, 1505 (64).

greatly surprised and said the offenders would be punished, but he added in cipher that nothing had been said to them. The interview was terminated, so far as Florida was concerned, with the routine promises on the Queen's part to prevent the further sailing of vessels in defiance of Spain.[1]

By the middle of January rumours began to reach Fourquevaux of the French defeat in Florida.[2] With the dissemination of the news the delight of the Spaniards had at first been tempered with a judicious fear lest Jean Ribaut might have avenged the attack on Fort Caroline. But early in February a detailed account, not only of the capture of the fort but also of the shipwreck and massacre of Ribaut, was generally known in the Spanish Court, and had reached Fourquevaux in its horrible completeness. It was received with great rejoicing.

> "This Court," wrote Fourquevaux, "were more gladdened than if it had been a victory over the Turks. For they have also said that Florida was of greater importance to them than Malta. And as a reward for Menéndez's massacre of your poor subjects the said Florida will be erected into a marquisate, of which he will be appointed the Marquis."[3]

The hour for further concealment of the facts had now passed, and the time had come for the official announcement to France of the punishment Philip had meted out to the French adventurers. But Philip, while he continued to maintain the same haughty tone towards the French Crown, determined to turn the incident to the advantage of his friends, the Catholic party in France. Although fully informed of the countenance which Catherine had given to the aggression on his territory, he

[1] Alava to Philip II., Jan. 19, 1566, MS. Arch. Nat., Paris, K, 1505 (67).

[2] Fourquevaux to Charles IX., Jan. 22, 1566, *Dépêches*, p. 48.

[3] Fourquevaux to Charles IX., Feb. 11, 1566, *Dépêches*, p. 52; Feb. 18, 1566, *ibid.*, p. 54.

centred all of his attack upon the leader of the Protestant party, the much-hated Coligny. By this proceeding he hoped to compel the Queen to choose between the alternatives of forfeiting his support or of disavowing her unfriendly act by making the Admiral the scapegoat for her Florida policy, and to force her, in the interest of the Catholic religion, to renounce the double part she was acting towards both parties.

Accordingly Fourquevaux was summoned to an interview with the Duke of Alba, and the ambassador was kept impatiently waiting while two fruitless attempts were made to set the time for the meeting. The audience was at last held at Alba's palace after the dinner hour. Alba informed him that he was charged by the King to explain how Philip had learned of the French occupation of Florida, of which he had complained through his ambassador, begging Charles to withdraw his people and not to constrain him to send his forces there, which he otherwise would be compelled to do; that he had so done, advising the French King of the fact in his desire to proceed openly in the matter; that Charles had answered as a prince, brother, and friend of Philip, to the effect that if any of his subjects had gone to Florida, it had not been by his orders. And thereupon the Spanish army had gone thither, seized the fort, and punished the corsairs, pirates, and settlers of the country, who had built a fort, pillaged the Spaniards sailing to and from the Indies, and even sunk two vessels with their crews after robbing them, which the Spaniards had verified when they captured the fort. Alba then told him of the killing of the French, that Ribaut and Courset had confessed having sailed for Florida under orders from Coligny; and that the Spaniards had subsequently found Ribaut's commissions, letters, and instructions, by which it appeared that he had also intended to seize Havana. And Alba ended by saying that Philip begged and required of

Charles that he should visit Coligny with an exemplary punishment as a perturber of the peace and cause of the disorder.

Fourquevaux replied that owing to the absence of instructions from his Government he was unprepared to answer Alba's representations. At the same time, while he denied that there had been any discussion of the Florida question at the date of his leaving France, he admitted that Charles had no designs upon Spanish territory, and could only repeat the argument already used at Moulins respecting the right of his Sovereign to the *Terre des Bretons* in which he claimed that Florida was included. He then asked Alba to explain a report spread by Diego Flores, that Ribaut, when he surrendered, had told Avilés he was waging a fair war, as was the custom among soldiers; to which Avilés had answered that he was no soldier, but a corsair, whereupon Ribaut had said that he could show him his royal patents by which it would appear he had come there in obedience to the orders of his King. Alba answered that Flores had drawn upon his imagination if he had really said such a thing; and assured him that such an idea had never crossed his mind, for had such been the case, Avilés would have so informed Philip.

Then Fourquevaux indignantly protested against the great cruelty with which the prisoners had been treated in putting so many soldiers to death, after their surrender, which was not customary on such occasions, as the Duke well knew. With Alba's answer we are already familiar. The French were no soldiers, he said, for they drew no pay from their prince, but thieving pirates, and were punished according to their deserts; and they were heretics as well, preaching their perverse doctrines and pernicious sects; and had not such evil roots been extirpated, the great harm of it would soon have become apparent. Had Avilés spared them, his own people would have perished from hunger, as there was not sufficient to feed them all. The Spaniards were too few to retain them as prisoners. As Avilés was compelled to go elsewhere, leaving but part of his force in the forts, they would have risen against their captors and killed them. The ships he had were too small to contain them, nor could he safely provide them with ships, which would have enabled them to attack him elsewhere, and that, given all of these conditions, "the Duke knew of no man, however pious he might be, who would have resorted to other means and expedients than those followed by Pedro Menéndez." Finally, Fourquevaux complained of the threatening language with which Alava had addressed the Queen in the Moulins interview, at which she had been greatly disturbed and had observed "that it was not the path by which the King her son was to be led." [1] When the interview was over Fourquevaux at once advised his sovereigns of its purport and of Philip's intention to palliate his dastardly treatment of the French prisoners under cover of an attack on Coligny.[2]

Simultaneously with Fourquevaux's dispatch Philip informed Alava of Alba's conversation with the French ambassador, and of the arguments which had been used to justify the massacre; directed him to tell the Queen that in view of certain papers found in Florida and confessions of prisoners "taken alive" it very clearly appeared that the Admiral was responsible for the enterprise and had harboured designs upon Spanish ports and towns in the West Indies; asked that his punishment should be equal to the offence, as he himself would have acted under similar circumstances, and enclosed to him a relation of

[1] Fourquevaux to Charles IX., Feb. 22, 1566, *Dépêches*, p. 59; Philip II. to Alava, Feb. 23, 1566, MS. Arch. Nat., Paris, K, 1505 (75). There can be no doubt that both letters refer to the same interview.

[2] Fourquevaux to Charles IX., Feb. 22, 1566, *Dépêches*, p. 59; same to Catherine de' Medici, Feb. 23, 1566, *ibid.*, p. 63.

the expulsion of the French. While commanding him to press this matter with the greatest urgency, he charged him at the same time to make it apparent to the Queen and her son that he harboured "no suspicion or thought that the site where the heretics had been found was occupied by their order, but rather that it was reasonable to suppose that they were displeased at their action, as was due to their brotherly relations." [1]

The French Court was still at Moulins, and Catherine with her courtiers was in attendance upon her son, who was in bed, very weak from a recent illness, when on the 16th of March [2] Alava had his audience. No sooner had he touched on the Florida matter, than the Queen cut him short like an enraged "lioness," and turning her face in order that she might be heard by Montmorenci, the Bishop of Valencia, and others of her courtiers whose curiosity had been at once aroused, exclaimed: "Neither Turks nor Moors would have been guilty of so great a cruelty as the Spaniards have practised on the subjects of my son." It was a queenly speech, the gist of which her artistic Italian wit had filched from Fourquevaux's dispatch. [3] "Raising my voice slightly I asked her to listen to what she called the inexplicable cruelty, for the punishment of those who were there was well deserved," wrote Alava in his account to Philip. He related to her the story probably much in the form in which we have it in Avilés's letters, and pressed the moral home with the incisive abruptness which Philip had ordered him to observe, repeating in substance the language used by Alba, and centring his attack on Coligny.

[1] Philip II. to Alava, Feb. 23, 1566, MS. Arch. Nat., Paris, K, 1505 (75), and see same to same, Feb. 25, 1566, MS., *ibid.*, K, 1505 (76).

[2] Catherine de' Medici to Fourquevaux, March 17, 1566, Gaffarel, *Hist. de la Floride*, p. 427.

[3] "Laquelle inhumanité ne fut pas usée par les Turcs aux vieulx soldatz qu'ilz prindrent à Castelnovo et aux Gerbes, ne jamais barbares uzèrent de telle cruaulté." Fourquevaux to Charles IX., Feb. 22, 1566, *Dépêches*, p. 61.

As the covert threats against her, and the malicious insinuations respecting Coligny fell from the lips of the ambassador, mingled with the vindictive and cold-blooded account of the killing of her subjects, her anger kindled and she interrupted him incessantly. Under the lash of his tongue her eyes filled with tears of rage, and at last, casting aside all prudence, her nobler nature came momentarily to her rescue and she exclaimed, her face trembling with agitation, "that the Admiral was guiltless; the armada had been equipped under her orders and that of her son; that in the performance of his duty as a minister the Admiral had done what the King had commanded; that he was not to be blamed and therefore was not deserving of punishment . . . for the armada had gone to their own land, the *Isles des Bretons*, where they had a fort with its garrison, and what would the world say when it learned that in a season of such brotherly love so cruel a war had been waged?"

"I answered," continues Alava, "that your Majesty would not fail to be greatly surprised and pained on learning that the said armada had gone to occupy the said site at her command and that of her son, for Your Majesty had written me to tell them both that he entertained no suspicion or thought that by her order the armada had gone directly to the said site, where that people had been found, having heard quite the contrary, as I had told them. That when the world, as she called it, should hear the facts it would not fail to be scandalised that in a season of such friendship and brotherly love, when they had received so many benefits from Your Majesty, they should send the greatest and most infamous heretics of France to usurp his territories, and the more so when it learned that from the least to the greatest they were all notable Huguenots. . . . If this was the office of the Most Christian King, let them judge. And if, in order to extenuate the Admiral, from whom they received such marked disservice and injury, the Most Christian King and she chose to burden themselves in this wise before the world, let her see to it. Like a mad woman, not allowing me to speak, she returned to the Admiral, saying that it was not his fault . . . and that she regretted that all of the Huguenots were not there." "But be that as it may," continued Catherine, "it was not for you to punish our subjects, and we will not discuss their religion, but the murder you committed." "I said, please God that no Huguenots enter the country of the King my Master, except they be cut in pieces." [1]

Then the audience degenerated into a wordy combat in which the Queen, still labouring under great excitement, harked back two or three times to the *Isles des Bretons*, at which the King, from whom Catherine had concealed the defeat on account of his illness, exclaimed, "Look at the map, look at the map! Have you seen it?" "Yes," answered Alava, "and that must be the title-deed which your Mother holds." Then she returned to the cruelty of the punishment inflicted upon her subjects and with renewed ardour took up the defence of Coligny. But Alava, although he admitted that Avilés had chastised the French with a little more severity than his master had intended, relentlessly pursuing his cross-questioning, asked her, "If the armament was that of your son and the men were in his pay, how comes it that no money was found on them and no papers such as you say, but that everything came from the Admiral?" "You deceived yourselves," she replied. "When you committed that cruelty and carnage, cutting off the heads of Jean Ribaut and of those with him in the ship, he showed his patents from my son and myself." Then Alava dwelt upon the absence of any information to that effect,

[1] Catherine de' Medici to Fourquevaux, March 17, 1566, Gaffarel, *Hist. de la Floride*, p. 428.

reverted to the attack on Enveja, and demanded the punishment of the offenders, which subject Catherine again evaded.

But the importance of continuing friendly relations with Philip was too great for her to maintain for any length of time, so brave a front. When, in reply to her remark that each must go his own course, Alava answered that what she had said would relieve Philip, whose desire had ever been for that which would best serve the interests of her son, she became very grave and replied: "I do not say that." "What then do you mean when you say that from now on each shall look to what concerns him? Would to God it could be so!" exclaimed Alava, "but I see no way to it." And so the interview ended. "She was very angry because I did not answer to the point," concludes Alava in his dispatch, "because she was provided with answers prepared by her council, for which reason it is not advisable to say anything to the King's ambassador in Your Majesty's Court, since it amounts to advising them here, so that this Queen has her answers ready. When she is taken by surprise, her embarrassment is great, and more is learned of their intentions." [1]

At the same time that Alava was ordered to make the formal announcement of Philip's victory in Florida to their Most Christian Majesties, the King and Queen of France, his ambassadors in Austria and England were instructed to convey the same information to their respective Governments. The letters to Silva in England and Chantone in Austria were couched in substantially the same language as to the material facts which they recited, and were both accompanied by a relation of the event for the private instruction of the ambassadors, but

[1] Alava to Philip II., March 16, 1566, MS. Arch. Nat., Paris, K, 1505 80); Catherine de' Medici to Fourquevaux, March 17, 1566, Gaffarel, *Hist. de la Floride*, p. 427.

there was a signal divergence between them in the stress which was laid upon the religious aspect of the question. To the Catholic Emperor and Empress of Austria the ambassador was bidden to relate that the French who had gone to Florida were not only pirates but heretics as well, who had taken with them preachers and quantities of books belonging to their perverse sect, to plant it in that land. The Admiral of France was declared, with some little reservation, to be the prime mover of the enterprise, and the ambassador was informed that the French Queen had been asked to visit him with a punishment commensurate with his offence,

"since it is so notorious that he is the venom of that kingdom; the inventor and promoter of all the evil which they contrive and commit, especially in matters of religion. We shall see how they will take it in France," continued Philip in his instructions. "We have small hope that it will be in a reasonable way. I will inform you of their answer that you may tell my brothers, as I now wish you to give them an account of all this in particular, and that they may understand that the occurrence in Florida has been for the great service of God, our Lord, since in killing those heretics, a stop has been put to the perverse doctrine which they wished and had already begun to sow. The sound and holy doctrine will be shown to the natives of that land, and the true path of salvation, which is that which we chiefly desire and profess." [1]

In Philip's letter to Silva, no reference whatever was made to the heretical religion of the French colonists, and stress was laid solely on the unauthorised invasion of his territory, the danger which it threatened to the

[1] Philip II. to Chantone, Feb. 28, 1566, *Col. Doc. Inedit. España*, tomo ci., p. 126. There is a French translation of this letter in the *Bulletin de la Société de l'Histoire du Protestantisme française* of Dec. 15, 1894, which is reproduced by Maurice Delpeuch in "Un glorieux épisode maritime et colonial," *Revue Maritime*, Oct., 1902, tome clv., p. 1023.

commerce and navigation of the West Indies, and the complicity of Coligny, whose evil influence on French affairs he stigmatised in identically the same terms which he had employed in his letter to Chantone, save that all reference to his religion was omitted.[1] On the 28th of March Silva, in accordance with his instructions, notified the Queen, who was at Greenwich, of the defeat of the French. Elizabeth expressed much pleasure at Philip's success, and bade Silva convey her thanks to his King for having advised her of the event. But the crafty Queen had not forgotten her own intrigues with Ribaut some two years before, and she expressed her surprise at learning that Florida had been previously discovered and occupied by Spain. In her ignorance of Philip's right "she had always believed that Captain Ribaut had been the first to have discovered it, for he had come to her with the news of its discovery, and she had determined to conquer it herself," and she asked Philip's pardon for having treated of the matter. "As for the Admiral," observed Elizabeth, "she understood the French, and did not care to treat of their affairs nor even to answer for them, for they were old enough to attend to themselves." Although she expressed no opinion to the ambassador on the action taken by Coligny, Silva learned that she condemned his invasion of Florida, after the promise of the French sovereigns not to occupy Spanish territory, and in the subsequent interview with Cecil the secretary agreed that he deserved an exemplary punishment and thought that Philip ought to proclaim his discovery of Florida in order that it might be generally known.[2]

[1] Philip II. to Silva, March 2, 1566, *Correspondencia de Felipe II. con sus Embajadores en la Corte de Inglaterra*, tomo ii., p. 275. English translation in *Spanish State Papers*, 1558–67, I. Elizabeth, 527.

[2] Silva to Philip II., March 30, 1566, *Correspondencia*, tomo ii., p. 292. English translation in *Spanish State Papers*, 1558–67, I. Elizabeth, 536.

The news had also reached Rome in the latter part of February,[1] but as we are not yet in possession of Philip's letter, which he undoubtedly addressed to his ambassador there, we can only infer that its tone was similar to the one he sent to Austria.

[1] "News from Rome dated Feb. 23, 1566, with intelligence from Spain of Feb. 15th, of the defeat of certain Frenchmen in Florida," MS. Record Office, London, *Elizabeth State Papers*, 1566–68, Foreign, No. 127, MS.

CHAPTER VIII

THE FRENCH REVENGE

ABOUT the middle of March, five and a half months after his departure from Florida, Laudonnière reached Moulins, where the French Court was gathered. As stated in a previous chapter he had been driven out of his course by bad weather, delayed by illness, and had passed through London on his way to Paris, from whence he had come to Moulins. Events which subsequently occurred seem to indicate that these were not the only reasons for his prolonged delay in presenting himself before his master. He had left Florida while he was still chafing under the disgrace of his recall. The mortification consequent upon his ignominious surprise and the loss of Fort Caroline, joined with his evident ill-health, had made him querulous and discontented,[1] a disposition to which he had given vent in his quarrel with Jacques Ribaut on the eve of his return to France,[2] and the accusations which had given rise to his recall were still unexplained. He was accompanied by an unfortunate Spaniard, who, after various vicissitudes, had ended by becoming an interpreter for the French at Fort Caroline. On the approach of Avilés he had been removed from the

[1] The whole tone of Laudonnière's relation subsequent to the loss of Fort Caroline shows a defensive attitude and a disposition to exculpate himself from blame for the catastrophe.

[2] *Histoire Notable*, Basanier, p. 112; *Hak.*, vol. ii., p. 521.

fort and kept under guard for fear lest he should take flight to his own countrymen. He returned with Laudonnière to France, and upon arriving at Moulins at once became a tool of Alava, who used him to ferret out the designs of the defeated Frenchmen.[1]

On reaching Moulins Laudonnière found Jacques Ribaut the hero of the hour and himself the scapegoat for the disaster which had overtaken the French colony. Ribaut had improved the interval between his own arrival and that of Laudonnière to cast the responsibility of the defeat on the latter, and in the conferences which took place at the house of the Admiral Laudonnière was censured for his neglect in the defence of Fort Caroline, his failure to maintain a sufficient garrison when he could have procured at least two hundred men for its defence, and his carelessness in allowing himself to be surprised during his sleep.

At these meetings, which were conducted with the greatest secrecy, the Florida disaster filled all mouths, and the talk was already of vengeance and of the sinking of all Spanish ships that should be encountered.[2] A number of French adventurers, including Laudonnière, Ribaut, and Sandoval,[3] the piratical governor of Belle-Isle-en-Mer, off the Brittany coast, a man of considerable wealth in ships and in moneys which he had obtained by plundering Spanish commerce, were among the chief conspirators.[4] Laudonnière's interpreter was caressed and cajoled and taken to see the Queen, where in her presence and that of the Cardinal de Bourbon he was made to confirm the French reports, and give them what information he could concerning the gold and pearls that were

[1] Alava to Perez, March 18, 1566, MS. Arch. Nat., Paris, K, 1505 (82).

[2] Alava to Philip II., Jan. 19, 1566, MS., *ibid.*, K, 1505 (67).

[3] See also Alava to Philip II., March 23, 1566, MS., *ibid.*, K, 1505 (95); April 28, 1566, MS., *ibid.*, K, 1505 (96).

[4] Alava to Perez, March 18, 1566, MS., *ibid.*, K, 1505 (82).

found in Florida and of its capacity for the cultivation of the vine and of wheat.[1]

These mutterings, of which Alava was informed through Laudonnière's interpreter, and which the ambassador faithfully reported to his master, could not but alarm Philip, whose suspicions were now aroused so that he looked upon every movement of the French as a covert vengeance, big with further designs upon Florida.[2] Enveja was therefore sent to remonstrate with Catherine against the machinations of Sandoval and his companions.[3] To the complaint of Philip's agent Catherine laughingly replied that she did not see how Laudonnière, who was so poor that she had herself given him fifty crowns, or Ribaut, who, on his arrival, had been ignorant of the massacre, could be arming ships against Florida. As for the interpreter, he was but a poor beggar who had been cared for in the Moulins hospital out of pure charity, and whom she had never seen.[4] Alava also had an audience with the Queen with the object of learning what designs she was harbouring. Meanwhile the rumours of French preparations continued, and now began to assume a more definite shape and to centre about Montluc,[5] who was in reality preparing for his attack upon Madeira, with the object of punishing the Portuguese, whom Fourquevaux had accused of assisting Menéndez in his conquest of Florida.[6] But so haunted was Spain by the one idea of a French descent in that region that she continued to attribute to every ship that sailed from a French

[1] Alava to Philip II., March 23, 1566, MS., *ibid.*, K, 1505 (95).

[2] Philip II. to Alava, March 29, 1566, MS., *ibid.*, K, 1505 (86).

[3] Alava to Philip II., March 23, 1566, MS., *ibid.*, K, 1505 (95).

[4] Précis d'une réponse donnée par la Reine mère de France au Deur Enveja, 1566, MS., *ibid.*, K, 1505 (59).

[5] Alava to Philip II., April 21, 1566, MS., *ibid.*, K, 1505 (93); April 28, 1566, MS., *ibid.*, K, 1505 (96).

[6] Gaffarel, *Hist. de la Floride Française*, p. 255.

port, and to every gathering of French seamen, some secret design against her territory.

During the month of May Alava was at last in a position to assure Philip of his firm conviction that Florida was safe for that year. The information carried with it every evidence of being authoritative, for it came from a man whose opportunities for learning the most intimate councils of the adventurers appeared to be beyond dispute. After a short stay at Moulins, Laudonnière had left the Court at so low an ebb in his pocket that, as we have seen, Catherine had given him money to pay for his food. The accusations of incompetency heaped upon him by his former companions in arms had soured his soul, and the commander of the second French expedition to Florida had finally come to Alava in Paris and had offered his services to the Spanish King. Some qualms of conscience still possessed him at the unworthy office to which he was aspiring, and Alava found it necessary to hold out to him the hope of securing an appointment in Philip's employ, but in the meantime Laudonnière assured the ambassador that no fleet would sail for Florida during that year, especially as the news had reached the French of the departure of Arciniega with a large complement of men to the assistance of Avilés.[1]

Meanwhile the indignation in France had reached the highest possible pitch.[2] Following their return home, Ribaut, Laudonnière, and Le Challeux, whose account, published in May, went through two editions in the same year,[3] had disseminated abroad, and more particularly among the friends and relatives of the murdered French,

[1] Alava to Philip II., May 7, 1566, MS. Arch. Nat., Paris, K, 1505 (98); May 19, 1566, MS., *ibid.*, K, 1505 (101).

[2] Fourquevaux to Charles IX., August 18, 1566, *Dépêches*, p. 105, and see all of his correspondence as well as that of Alava. *La Reprise de la Floride* . . . par M. Ph. Tamizey de Larroque, Bordeaux, 1867, p. 27.

[3] Gaffarel, *Hist. de la Floride Française*, p. 339.

their version of the massacre, and had stirred the deepest feelings of anger and hatred against the Spaniards. A deputation of the widows of the victims went to Paris, probably during the month of May, and raised such an outcry in the city that it had called for a Spanish protest.[1] This was followed by a second deputation of one hundred and twenty widows, who journeyed all the way from Normandy to Paris during the month of August to address the Queen on the same subject.[2] It is probable that at this time was published the stirring and passionate "Petition to the King Charles IX. in the form of a complaint by the widowed women and orphaned children, relatives, and friends of his subjects, who were slain in the said country of Florida."[3] But though the hearts of both Catherine and her son were in keen sympathy with those of their outraged subjects and burning with a like indignation,[4] their interests were so involved with those of Spain that they had been compelled to give the deputation an unfriendly reception and to send the widows back to their homes in order not to appear to countenance a public demonstration against their ally.[5]

It was an inglorious situation for the Most Christian Queen. The massacre of her subjects had been like a stab in the back, to which she was compelled to submit without even lifting her hand, and Catherine sought what relief she could find for her outraged feelings in continued and repeated complaints in which she persistently dwelt upon the unusual cruelty of Philip's action and pressed

[1] Alava to Philip II., June 5, 1566, MS. Arch. Nat., Paris, K, 1506 (5).

[2] Alava to Philip II., Aug. 23, 1566, MS., *ibid.*, K, 1506 (39). The date of their arrival at Paris was August 19th.

[3] See p. 426, in this volume.

[4] See Alava to Philip II., April 21, 1566, MS. Arch. Nat., Paris, K, 1505 (93); April 28, 1566, MS., *ibid.*, K, 1505 (96); May 7, 1566, MS., *ibid.*, K, 1505 (98).

[5] Alava to Philip II., April 21, 1566, MS., *ibid.*, K, 1505 (93); Résumé des lettres de François de Alava, Feb. 13–Apr. 9, 1566, MS., *ibid.*, K, 1507 (104); Alava to Philip II., Aug. 23, 1566, MS., *ibid.*, K, 1506 (39).

her demand for the punishment of Avilés. But Philip was too assured of her weakness to give the slightest weight to her protests, meeting them at first with the same arguments which had been already presented, and then with that policy of procrastination of which he was a master. No means were left untried to work upon Philip, and Catherine sent Fourquevaux to her daughter, who informed her mother that she "did not think that the slaughter of your subjects would be so bitterly felt"; nearly burst into tears "for fear some change should intervene between the two Kings," and finally promised to urge Philip to "execute justice upon murderers who had exceeded their commission by so execrable a massacre." Three days later, the Spanish Queen informed the ambassador that she had spoken to her husband, and had shown him the contents of Catherine's letter, to which his answer had been that his armada had not gone to Florida until after he had first notified Charles and Catherine; that he could not tolerate the usurpation of his territories by any nation in the world, and least of all by the adversaries and enemies of his religion.

In the audience with Philip which followed this communication from the Queen, Fourquevaux went over his conversation with the Duke of Alba, and Alava's representations to Catherine and her response, observing that during the forty-one years he had borne arms, in the course of which the two Crowns had been frequently at war with each other, "so execrable a deed had never occurred"; reiterated the assertion that the French had gone to the *Terre des Bretons;* demanded the punishment of Avilés, and, seeking to touch Philip in the interests which he had most at heart, observed that "it was the best news in the world for the Huguenots, to find that where the French Sovereigns had looked for friendship and alliance and assistance in all of their great undertakings, their subjects had been murdered, overthrown, and hunted out." This should have been the most telling of Fourquevaux's arguments, for French sentiment was outraged at the insult irrespective of party.[1]

Philip answered that if he had allowed such an invasion of his dominions it would have encouraged the natives to rebel and rendered the country uninhabitable for Spaniards; that he could suffer no descent of foreigners upon the Florida coast because it was the most important locality in the Indies for the navigation of his vessels; that France had been warned beforehand at Bayonne; that the French in Florida had captured and sunk Spanish vessels; that Avilés was too weak to have held so large a body of Frenchmen prisoners, and that it had been set down in the treaties of peace that each party should kill pirates, for which reason there was no occasion to have summoned the French before the attack on Fort Caroline. Fourquevaux insisted that they bore patents from the Admiral who represented the person of the King, but Philip put him off with the remark that he would consult with the Duke of Alba. "But I am convinced that it was to get rid of me," writes the ambassador in his dispatch, "for the said Duke will never contradict himself, for it is said that he advised the massacre of all those who should be found in the said Florida, if there were no better way." With a covert threat that not in Spain only were there ministers eager for war, Fourquevaux ended the colloquy and took his leave. His interview with Alba, which took place the following morning, was a mere repetition of that with the King, and Fourquevaux, finally convinced of Philip's inflexible determination to maintain his haughty attitude, wrote Catherine that "there could be no hope of any reparation of the said massacre."[2]

The interview between Fourquevaux and Philip had occurred during the first week in April, and throughout

[1] Alava to Philip II., Sept. 1, 1566, MS. Arch. Nat., Paris, K, 1506 (44).
[2] Fourquevaux to Catherine de' Medici, April 9, 1566, *Dépêches*, p. 69.

the following months the controversy dragged slowly along, once stimulated by the sending of a memorial by Charles and Catherine,[1] and at other times by occasional returns to the subject in Fourquevaux's audiences with Philip.[2] Only in December, ten months after the inception of the negotiations, came a formal reply of the Spanish Government to the French complaints, a not unexpected delay, for Ruy Gomez, Prince of Eboli, whom Fourquevaux had visited in the pleasant Bosque de Segovia, under the shadow of the mountains, had told him "that it was the custom of this Court to proceed slowly in all matters, and with great negligence or delay."[3] The Spanish reply is a brief paragraph only, and as it practically brought the issue to a close, it is here transcribed in full because it affords a complete and accurate summary of the Spanish attitude and is notable for the absence of any reference to the religious aspect of the question. The words read: "To all the articles which treat of the Florida incident there is little new to answer other than what has been previously said, that the Adelantado, Pero Menéndez de Avilés did not chastise the men he found there as vassals of the Most Christian King, but as pirates and infractors of the public peace, having possessed themselves of that country, which so properly and rightly belongs to his Catholic Majesty, as is understood, and therefore there can be no doubt that, given the prudence and sense of justice of the Most Christian King, he will be satisfied once for all with what is here said, since it is the unvarnished truth."[4]

[1] "Mémoire envoyée par Charles IX. et Catherine de Médicis à Fourquevaux," May 12, 1566, in Gaffarel, *Hist. de la Floride*, p. 437.

[2] Fourquevaux to Charles IX., July 5, 1566, *Dépêches*, p. 93; Aug. 11, 1566, *ibid.*, p. 103; Aug. 18, 1566, *ibid.*, p. 104; same to Catherine de' Medici, Aug. 23, 1566, *ibid.*, p. 116.

[3] Fourquevaux to Catherine de' Medici, Aug. 23, 1566, *Dépêches*, p. 116.

[4] "La pura verdad." "Réponse du Roi Catholique," Dec., 1566, *Dépêches*, p. 163.

One point, however, was achieved. The women and the children under fourteen years of age taken at Fort Caroline, to the number of forty-eight in all, who had been sent to Santiago de Cuba, were set at liberty, and the balance of the French prisoners were to be forwarded to the Casa de Contratación at Seville and to be detained there until their cause had been heard.[1] This was followed in the course of two months by the release of at least one of the men who had been captured at the fort.[2]

Notwithstanding the submissive attitude of the French Government and the chilling reception which it gave to the public demonstrations of the widows and orphans of the Florida victims, the annual treasure fleet delayed its sailing through fear of the French,[3] and Catherine continued in her favourable attitude towards Coligny.[4] With the successful outcome of Montluc's descent upon Madeira in conjunction with the English, the hope for vengeance was revived, and "the pirates, openly favoured, moved freely about the towns," where none dared forbid them in spite of the King's order to apprehend them.[5] Their activity on the high seas was continued with unabated vigour, and some of them, like Captain Mymy, of La Rochelle, and Sandoval, of Belle-Isle-en-Mer, wreaked

[1] Fourquevaux to Charles IX., Feb. 22, 1566, *Dépêches*, p. 61, where he says there were 30 women and 18 children. "Réponse du Roi Catholique," Dec., 1566, *ibid.*, p. 163. In the "Plaintes et Suppliques de l'Ambassadeur de France au Roi d'Espagne, Philippe II.," July 20, 1566, fol. 3, MS. Arch. Nat., Paris, K, 1506 (23), and in "Memento pour l'Ambassadeur de France en Espagne," June 10, 1568, MS., *ibid.*, K, 1506 (104), there is mention of 8 men and some children at Puerto Rico and Santo Domingo.

[2] Fourquevaux to Charles IX., Feb. 13, 1567, *Dépêches*, p. 179; Feb. 23, 1567, *ibid.*, p. 186.

[3] Fourquevaux to Charles IX., July 5, 1566, *Dépêches*, p. 97.

[4] Alava to Philip II., June 5, 1566, MS. Arch. Nat., Paris, K, 1506 (5).

[5] Alava to Philip II., Nov. 20, 1566, MS. Arch. Nat., Paris, K, 1506 (80); Nov. 26, 1566, MS., *ibid.*, K, 1506 (81); Fourquevaux to Charles IX., Feb. 23, 1567, *Dépêches*, p. 182.

their vengeance on the unfortunate Spaniards by drowning the crews of the vessels they captured.[1]

With the opening of 1567 Fourquevaux, who during the early stage of the negotiations had advised his masters of what little he could learn concerning the poverty and destitution of the Spanish settlements in Florida and the ease with which the French could overcome them,[2] now wrote that the Florida garrisons had risen several times against Avilés and had even attempted to kill him[3]; that the soldiers, driven to desperation by starvation and the failure of their pay, had scattered abroad through the country, and were thought to have fallen victims to the Indians; that but one hundred men remained in the fort, thirty of whom were Frenchmen saved from the wreck of Ribaut, who had pledged themselves to Menéndez; that Fort Caroline had been burnt to the ground and that Avilés had gone to the Canaries, where he was awaiting the arrival of two companies of foot soldiers from Seville.[4] Although Avilés at the time of this writing was actually at Havana, the account was substantially correct. The time was so opportune for giving vent to the pent-up spirit of revenge which was still slumbering in the bosom of every honest Frenchman that it seems more than a mere coincidence that at this

[1] Fourquevaux to Charles IX., 1566? MS. Arch. Nat., Paris, K, 1507 (4); Raport du Docteur Enveja sur la situation des choses en France au moment de son départ pour revenir en Espagne, Feb. 22, 1567, MS., *ibid.*, K, 1507 (61); Fourquevaux to Charles IX., March 24, 1567, *Dépêches*, p. 193; Eraso to Philip II., May 13, 1567, MS. Direc. de Hidrog., Madrid, *Col. Navarrete*, tomo xxi., Doc. No. 81; Alava to Philip II., Aug. 3, 1567, MS. Arch. Nat., Paris, K, 1508 (42); Aug. 12, 1567, MS., *ibid.*, K, 1508 (45); Aug. 19, 1567, MS., *ibid.*, K, 1508 (47); Aug. 25, 1567, MS., *ibid.*, K, 1508 (49); Aug. 28, 1567, MS., *ibid.*, K, 1508 (50); Catherine de' Medici to Alava, Aug. 30, 1567, MS., *ibid.*, K, 1508 (51).

[2] Fourquevaux to Charles IX., April 30, 1566, *Dépêches*, p. 81.

[3] Fontanedo in his "Memoria," *Col. Doc. Inedit. Indias*, tomo v., p. 540, mentions the plot of a Basque to sell Avilés to the Indians.

[4] Fourquevaux to Catherine de' Medici, Jan. 4, 1567, *Dépêches*, p. 159.

very moment when the hour was found the man had also presented himself. There is not a scrap of evidence that has yet been produced to connect Gourgues with this timely warning addressed to the French sovereigns, but he himself says that "in the beginning of the year 1567 . . . [he] resolved to go to Florida to attempt to revenge the insult offered to the King and to all France."[1] If the French Queen and her royal son actually did lend their aid to the enterprise, there were the weightiest of political reasons why their participation should have been kept profoundly secret.

Dominique de Gourgues was born at Mont de Marsan, in the Landes, about 1530.[2] He came of a distinguished Roman Catholic family, and was himself in all probability of the Roman Catholic religion.[3] He had seen service in Italy, where he had been captured by the Spaniards, and had served them chained to the bank of one of their galleys,[4] and he now set about collecting a small fleet with which to punish the affront put upon his countrymen. Although conducted with the greatest secrecy, it appears that these preparations did not entirely escape the sharp eyes of the Spanish agent, Dr. Enveja, who informed his Government in February that the French,

[1] *La Reprise de la Floride* . . . publiée par M. Ph. Tamizey de Larroque, Paris, Bordeaux, 1867, p. 29.

[2] Gaffarel, *Histoire de la Floride Française*, p. 263.

[3] M. le Vicomte A. de Gourgues in the *Bulletin du Comité d'Archéologie de la Province Ecclésiastique d'Auch*, 1861, tome ii., pp. 466–490, establishes that Gourgues's Protestantism is not mentioned by early historians, but is first asserted by Haag in 1853. That both his parents were Roman Catholics; that his brother, who aided the expedition, was a Roman Catholic; that Gourgues's intimacies and affiliations were with the Roman Catholics and that he was subsequently employed by the King against them. While the Vicomte does not absolutely establish that Gourgues was not of the Reformed religion, he certainly creates a very strong presumption that he was a Roman Catholic. Writers who accept the evidence as conclusive have gone too far.

[4] Gaffarel, *Histoire de la Floride Française*, p. 264.

whose "dissimulation, malice, deceit, and treachery had never reached so high a pitch as at that moment," were equipping another fleet "for the slave trade, under colour of which they are arming to commit robberies . . . for they bear the Florida affair as fresh before their eyes as if it had occurred to-day."[1] The true object of Gourgues's expedition had evidently escaped him, for its apparent purpose was the slave trade, as Enveja had reported, and its real destination was not revealed, even to the crew, until the vessels were well on their way.[2]

Gourgues was largely assisted in his preparations by his brother Ogier,[3] who had served as prisoner in the Spanish galleys during the Florentine war, and he set sail August 2d from Bordeaux in a large vessel of not more than two hundred and fifty tons and two smaller ones of one hundred and twenty and of fifty tons respectively, with a complement of one hundred arquebusiers and eighty sailors, all well armed. So cautious was he that his commission made no mention of Florida, but authorised him to visit the African coast in order to make war on the negroes. Forced by contrary winds to put into the mouth of the Charente, he did not finally leave the coast of France until the 22nd of August. The first rendezvous was on the Barbary coast, whence Gourgues sailed to Cape Blanco, where he had two encounters with the negro chiefs, incited to attack him by the Portuguese, who had a stronghold in that vicinity. From

[1] Raport du Docteur Enveja sur la situation des choses en France, etc., Feb. 22, 1567, MS. Arch. Nat., Paris, K, 1507 (61).

[2] Dr. Shea (in *Narr. and Crit. Hist. Am.*, vol. ii., p. 297) states: "That Gourgues was merely a slaver is evident from this full French account." He overlooks the existing relations between the French and Spanish Governments and the treatment openly accorded the widows of the Florida victims by their own Government, which rendered a subterfuge of primary importance.

[3] Barcia, *Ensayo*, Año MDLXVII., p. 133, *Bulletin du Comité d'Archéologie de la Province Ecclésiastique d'Auch*, tome ii., p. 479.

there he ran to the West Indies and visited the islands of Dominica, Puerto Rico, Mona, and Santo Domingo. In the West Indies he was delayed by bad weather and drove a little trade with the natives in order to revictual his ships.[1]

A long time must have been spent in wandering among the West Indies, for the following year had already set in, when, off Cape San Antonio, at the western end of Cuba, Gourgues assembled his people and finally declared to them the real object of his enterprise, and by the light of a full moon the fleet, increased by two small vessels, which he had probably captured during his voyage, entered the Straits of Florida and soon discovered the shore. While he was coasting along to the north the Spaniards at St. Augustine discovered the ships and fired a gun to inform them of the vicinity of a harbour and a settlement in case they were Spaniards, and to warn them off if they proved to be pirates. Gourgues replied to the signal, which he interpreted to be a salute, but, fearing discovery, he at once put out from shore and did not return till the night had fallen, when he landed on an island within fifteen leagues of San Mateo. His good fortune had favoured him, for the island was that of Tacatacuru,[2] where Father Martinez and Captain Pedro de la Rando with his company had been killed by the Indians, and whose chief was a close ally of the warlike Saturiba. Gourgues found the Indians drawn up under arms along

[1] Dr. Shea (*Narr. and Crit. Hist. Am.*, vol. ii., p. 280) says he sold the slaves he had captured on the African coast. As Dr. Shea in his notes (*ibid.*, p. 297) says "there are no Spanish accounts whatever" of Gourgues's expedition, and bases his own account on the *Reprise de la Floride*, in which there is no mention of any such traffic, it would be interesting to know on what authority he makes the statement. Neither is there any mention of a trade in slaves in Barcia quoted by Dr. Shea. It is true that the relation in *La Reprise* arouses the suspicion that such may have been the case, but not to the extent to admit of so positive a statement as he makes.

[2] See Appendix AA, Tacatacuru.

the shore to prevent his landing. He had brought with him a trumpeter, who, having been in that region with the French colony when Fort Caroline was built, spoke the native language. He sent the trumpeter ashore, and as soon as the latter was recognised by the natives the French were allowed to land and were received with the greatest demonstrations of joy.

Gourgues, who was in ignorance of the hostile attitude the natives had assumed towards the Spaniards, did not at once disclose his projects to them, but, by tactful questions and suggestions, sought to learn their temper and to what extent he could rely upon their support in his designs upon the fort. Friendly and at last confidential relations were speedily established, for the natives attempted no disguise of their hatred of the Spaniards; and when Gourgues, having ascertained their disposition, finally revealed to them his purpose to deliver them from the tyranny of their oppressors, he found them ready and anxious to render him all of the assistance in their power. Saturiba, who with other chiefs visited the French on the day following their arrival, presented Gourgues with a French lad, sixteen years old, named Pierre Debray,[1] who was found in the woods by the Indians after the capture of Fort Caroline, and had been brought up by them. From Debray Gourgues learned of the situation of the two blockhouses at the mouth of the St. John's, and, having sent a party to reconnoitre them, directed the Indians to prepare for the attack.

In the course of three days the scouting party returned, and Saturiba, having assembled his forces, departed by night for the mouth of a river which the French thought was the Alimacany, where he was rejoined at daybreak by Gourgues in two boats with all of his soldiers and sixty sailors. François Lague was left in charge of the ships, which he was to put in condition for

[1] Probably the Pedro Breu of Barcia, *Ensayo*, Año MDLXVIII., p. 135.

an immediate departure. Crossing the river the march was continued from eight o'clock in the morning until five in the evening, through the marshes and water, to the river Sarabay,[1] Gourgues carrying his cuirass on his back. At the river he was reinforced by three more parties of Indians, and learning that the blockhouses were now but two leagues distant, he determined to reconnoitre them in person, although he had eaten nothing during the entire day. Crossing the river with a little company of soldiers he again waded through marshes, and creeks, and in great darkness, to the neighbourhood of the first fort, where he was halted by a small stream rendered impassable by the rising tide. Greatly disappointed, for he had hoped to begin the attack on the following morning, he was retracing his steps when an Indian offered to conduct him to the neighbourhood of the fort by a longer but better path along the shore. Without giving his weary soldiers time to rest, he set out again with his entire force, marched all night, and at daybreak came out at the creek again. The tide was full, and on the failure of his men to discover a ford, he was obliged to abandon his intention of surprising the Spaniards during their sleep, and withdrew to a neighbouring wood to wait for low water. He had scarcely reached the wood when it began to rain so hard that with the greatest difficulty his soldiers could keep their matches alight.

With the increasing daylight Gourgues observed that the intrenchments about the blockhouse had been just begun, and he soon saw the Spaniards at work on the fort, which caused him some anxiety lest his presence had been discovered. At ten o'clock the tide had fallen sufficiently to allow the passage of the creek, and selecting a spot where a grove of trees intervened between the creek and the fort and concealed the approach, the men

[1] Parkman suggests Talbot Inlet, *Pioneers of France in the New World*, Boston, 1893, p. 168.

waded across, with the water waist-deep, their ammunition tied to their morions, and carrying their arquebuses and matches in one hand and their swords in the other. Most of the men had their shoes cut through and their feet wounded by the sharp edges of the oyster shells which covered the bed of the creek. Behind the grove they re-formed, still unperceived by the Spaniards, who were peacefully digging for water. A lieutenant was told off with a party of soldiers and sailors who carried fire-pots and fire-lances with which to burn down the door of the fort, and Gourgues made them a brief harangue. Pointing to the fort, which was visible between the trees, he exclaimed: "Yonder are the thieves who have stolen this land from our King. Yonder are the murderers who have massacred our French. On! on! let us avenge our King! let us show that we are Frenchmen!" And he at once commanded his lieutenant to attack the entrance with his company, while he with the remainder of his troops advanced to a low platform alongside of the fort, where there was the beginning of a trench.

The Spaniards had just dined, "and were still picking their teeth," says the account, which M. Larroque attributes to Gourgues himself.[1] A Spanish gunner had ascended the platform, when he suddenly perceived the French approaching head down and with long strides. "To arms! to arms!" he shouted. "Here are the French," and he let fly at them twice with a big culverin which stood upon the terrace towards which Gourgues had directed his attack. As he was about to load it for the third time, Olotoraca,[2] an Indian chief who had attached himself to Gourgues and served him as guide, sprang upon the platform and transfixed the gunner with his pike. The Spaniards, who had rushed to arms at the

[1] *La Reprise de la Floride*, p. 12.

[2] Gatschet in his *Migration Legend of the Creek Indians*, vol. i., p. 62 says that the Creek *olataraca* signifies "great leader."

first alarm, now poured out of the fort, still uncertain whether to fight or to retreat. Then Gourgues's lieutenant, fearing they would slip through his fingers, called out to the Captain that they were escaping, and Gourgues, who with his men had already reached the terrace, which he was about to ascend, turned to one side, and the unfortunate Spaniards found themselves caught between the two bands. Not one of the sixty members of the garrison escaped death except those who were captured. "As many as possible were taken alive, by Captain Gourgues's order, *to do to them what they had done to the French,*" continues the account.

The fort taken, Gourgues immediately turned his attention to the second fort, which had greatly impeded the attack by keeping up a continual artillery fire from across the river. The French had discovered four pieces of artillery in the blockhouse, one of which, the culverin which had been fired at their approach, was marked with the armorial bearing of Henry II., having probably been captured from the French at the time of the massacre, and the sight of it only served to increase their irritation. These guns they trained on the second fort, while Gourgues, crossing the St. John's, took up a position between the blockhouse and a grove of trees, close at hand, to which he thought the Spaniards would attempt to escape in order to retreat to Fort Mateo, which was but a league distant. According to the French account Gourgues had scarcely touched the other shore, when his Indian allies, unable longer to restrain their impatience and wait for the boat, plunged into the stream, swimming with one arm and carrying their bows aloft with the other. At the sight of such numbers, the Spaniards, greatly terrified and altogether unable to discern between the white men and the savages, took flight for the woods, where they found themselves caught between the Indians and the French. In their panic the fugitives were all mercilessly slaughtered except some fifteen, which Gourgues, with great difficulty, succeeded in saving alive, in order to mete out to them the same fate which he had reserved for the prisoners taken at the first fort. Las Alas with much greater probability relates that when the Spaniards in the second blockhouse had seen the slaughter of their companions and had exhausted their ammunition in firing at the French across the river, they spiked their guns and withdrew to St. Augustine. The date of this victory was April 12th, the eve of Quasimodo, the first Sunday after Easter.[1]

Returning to the first blockhouse, Gourgues fortified his position and rested over Sunday, while he considered how he should next proceed against San Mateo. From one of his prisoners he learned the plan of the fort and the size of the rampart, and had eight ladders made of sufficient height to scale it. Monday he captured a Spanish spy disguised as an Indian, who had been sent out by Nuñez to learn what the French were about. Interrogated by Gourgues, the spy informed him that the Spanish garrison did not exceed two hundred men, and were so surprised that they were at a loss what to do, for the French had been reported to them as two thousand strong. So encouraged was Gourgues by this information that he immediately began his preparations for the attack. The blockhouse was placed in charge of a captain with fifteen soldiers, and the following night the Indians were stationed in ambuscade around San Mateo, while he himself set out in the morning with part of his men, and with the prisoner, who had given him the description, and the spy tied together to conduct him to the fort, and to verify their statements.

The garrison at San Mateo, however, were not as entirely unprepared as the Spanish spy had led Gourgues to believe. On seeing the strange vessels put out to sea

[1] Gaffarel, *Hist. de la Floride Française*, p. 295.

in place of entering the harbour in reply to his signal Las Alas had advised Nuñez of their presence, warned him to be on his guard against a descent of the pirates, for such he took them to be, and had sent the garrison a boat-load of provisions. Sunday following the capture of the two blockhouses he had despatched two soldiers by land to Outina, from where with half a dozen Indians they were to reach San Mateo by river and deliver a second letter of warning to Nuñez and the commander, Castellon; but this reinforcement was destined to arrive too late.[1]

On approaching San Mateo the garrison soon discovered the French and opened upon them with their artillery, which commanded the banks of the river. Gourgues ascended the wooded hill at the foot of which the fort was situated, perhaps the very height from which Le Challeux had looked back and seen the massacre of his companions in the court. Advancing amidst the trees, which concealed and protected him from the Spaniards, he drew as close to the fort as he wished, where he halted, intending to attack it the following morning. But the impatient Spaniards could brook no delay and made a sortie with sixty soldiers to reconnoitre his forces. It was a fatal mistake. From his commanding position Gourgues saw them advance along the trench, crouching low to escape observation. He at once sent his lieutenant with twenty men to place themselves in their rear, between them and the fort, and then charged them in person, having ordered his troops to hold their fire until they were close to the enemy, and then to draw their swords. On reaching the foot of the hill where the French were concealed, the Spaniards were received with a volley, and then followed a hand-to-hand combat in which the French used their swords so well that the Spaniards turned to withdraw

[1] See Appendix BB, The Spanish Account of Gourgues's Attack on San Mateo.

into the fort; but their retreat was cut off by the lieutenant and they were all slain.

On seeing the reception their comrades had met with, those who had remained in the fort attempted to escape into the forest only to fall a prey to the Indians, by whom they were shot down and cut to pieces. Gourgues, who had followed after them, succeeded in saving a few of them alive, but the majority were killed, with the exception of the commander, and several of his companions, who finally managed to make their escape,[1] cutting their way through with their swords. A large quantity of arms was found in the captured fort; but a fatality seemed to haunt the place, and for the second time the magazines and houses were consumed by a fire accidentally lighted by an Indian. The artillery was saved, carried on board the vessels, and brought back to France.

There now remained but one more act to complete the drama.

"The Spaniards captured alive in the last fort were conducted to the place where they had hanged the French, after that Captain Gourgues had shown them the affront they had put upon the King. . . . 'And though you cannot suffer the punishment you deserve,' he said, 'it is necessary that you undergo that which the enemy can honestly inflict upon you, that by your example others may learn to preserve the peace and alliance, which you have violated in so wicked and unfortunate a way.' Having said this, they are swung from the branches of the same trees on which they had hung the French, and in place of the inscription which Pedro Menéndez had put up containing these words in Spanish: *I do this not as to Frenchmen but as to Lutherans*, Captain Gourgues causes to be inscribed with a hot iron on a pine tablet: *I do this not as to Spaniards, nor as to Marranos, but as to traitors, robbers and murderers.*"

[1] Barcia, *Ensayo*, Año MDLXVIII., p. 136.

His work now completed, and the insult to France wiped out in blood, Gourgues turned his face for home. Before his departure he assembled his men and offered thanks to God for his victory, and on Monday, May 3d, set sail for France. Bartolomé Menéndez, on his return to Spain in 1569, informed Avilés that Gourgues left three or four of his men among the Indians friendly to the French to preach their evil sect to them.[1] But from the character of the French raid, it is much more probable that these men, if they really belonged to the company of Gourgues and were not survivors of the Fort Caroline massacre, were deserters rather than missionaries (!) left behind by the French adventurer. On his way back he captured three Spanish vessels, the crews of which were thrown into the sea, and on the 6th of June reached the harbour of La Rochelle with his captured cannon and a large booty of gold, silver, pearls, and merchandise which his soldiers declared had been found at San Mateo, but which the Spanish ambassador, with far greater probability, thought to be the proceeds of his robberies on the high seas.[2] From La Rochelle he proceeded to Bordeaux, barely escaping a Spanish fleet sent out to burn his vessels,[3] and in that city he almost immediately sold the captured artillery.[4] So great was the enthusiasm aroused by his return that Spes, the Spanish ambassador to England, who was passing through Bordeaux at the time on his way from Spain to Paris, was mobbed and threatened, and on crossing the

[1] Avilés to Philip II., November 20, 1569, Ruidíaz, *La Florida*, tomo ii., p. 188.

[2] *La Reprise de la Floride*, pp. 29–65; Alava to Philip II., June 25, 1568, MS. Arch. Nat., Paris, K, 1511 (56); June 28, 1568, MS., *ibid.*, K, 1511 (59).

[3] *La Reprise de la Floride*, p. 67.

[4] "Estimation des pièces d'artillerie rapportées par Dominique de Gourgues de la Floride," Aug. 27, 1568, in *La Reprise de la Floride*, p. 71; Gaffarel, *Hist. de la Floride Française*, p. 317.

river the ships were pointed out to him with which the French "had avenged their friends dead in Florida."[1]

Alava notified Philip II. as early as the 25th of June of the defeat of the Spaniards in Florida, and four days later the news reached the Spanish Court.[2] Alava at Paris protested at once against the outrage committed by the French, to which Catherine merely remarked: "See how they have only just written me that they have taken Florida!" "I assure your Majesty," he wrote, "that she said it with a manner which showed her great joy."[3] To Spes, who also protested on his arrival in Paris, she observed, that "the Florida affair has been without my knowledge or wish," and Spes in his report to Philip, added that "the artillery, which is known to belong to Your Majesty, has been ordered to be returned to Spain."[4]

The Gourgues incident practically terminated the contest between Spain and France for the possession of American territory south of Canada, until the curious attempt of Don Diego de Peñalosa, more than a century later, to enlist the French Government in the conquest of New Biscay, which probably paved the way for La Salle's colony in Texas. The subsequent careers of the protagonists of the French colonies, Laudonnière and Gourgues, do not belong to this history. With regard to the latter, circumstances were such that a public expression of approval on the part of his government was quite out of the question, however much the report of his achievement had quickened the heart-beats of his King

[1] Spes to Philip II., July 19, 1568, *Correspondencia*, tomo iii., p. 127. English translation in *Spanish State Papers*, 1568–79, II. Elizabeth, 68, where the letter is dated July 10th.

[2] Fourquevaux to Catherine de' Medici, July 2, 1568, *Dépêches*, p. 367.

[3] Alava to Phillp II., June 25, 1568, MS. Arch. Nat., Paris, K, 1511 (56); June 28, 1568, MS., *ibid.*, K, 1511 (59); see also same to same, July 27, 1568, MS., *ibid.*, K, 1510 (12), fol. 3b.

[4] Spes to Philip II., July 19, 1568, *Correspondencia*, tomo iii., p. 127. English translation in *Spanish State Papers*, 1568–79, II. Elizabeth, 68.

and Queen, but that he ultimately received the recognition which he deserved of his country there is no longer any doubt. [1] As for Laudonnière, apparently disappointed in his hopes of obtaining anything from Philip, we only know that in June, 1567, he was still lingering about the French Court in company with some of the Normans who had been to Florida.[2]

[1] Gaffarel, *Hist. de la Floride Française*, p. 314 *et seq.*

[2] Alava to Philip II., June 20, 1567, MS. Arch. Nat., Paris, K, 1508 (24).

BOOK III

THE GUALE AND VIRGINIA MISSIONS; CONDITION OF THE COLONY

CHAPTER I

THE GUALE MISSION—DESTITUTION OF THE COLONY

THE task which had fallen to the lot of Father Rogel proved arduous and thankless. Despite his efforts to acquire the language of the Caloosas, he still found it necessary to employ interpreters in preaching among them and in explaining to them the principal articles of the Christian religion. The instruction was of the simplest kind and probably consisted in teaching them to recite the Pater Noster, the Ave Maria, the Credo, Salve, and the Commandments. Together with this the attempt was made to inculcate into their savage hearts the first principles of Christian morals. It was a difficult task to turn them from their ancient customs. He succeeded in gathering about him a great number of the children on whom he hoped to make some impression, using every effort to attract them, and distributing among them for a time the corn-meal which Fr. Francisco de Toral, the Franciscan Bishop of Yucatan, had sent him, when he learned of his missionary labours. But "the children who assembled to chant the doctrine recited only the call of hunger," and their interest ceased when the corn-meal became exhausted.

With the adults he fared no better. Like Fray Luis Descalona in Cicuye, he only succeeded in arousing the jealousy of the shamans, who directed all of their endeavours to create a breach between the natives and the Spaniards. One day, while conducting a masked procession, the shamans resolved to ascend to the fort with their idols, either with the intention of compelling the Spaniards to worship them, or of arousing the indignation of the Christians and providing a motive for killing Father Rogel. In this they were partly successful, for, as the procession approached, Father Rogel reprehended them and ordered them to return to the town. As the shamans, regardless of his warning, continued to advance, Captain Reynoso rushed upon them and with the shaft of his lance gave one of the masked priests so severe a blow that he wounded him in the head. The enraged savages rushed at once to their huts, where they armed themselves with their clubs and staves, and some fifty Indians returned to the fort, but they found the Spanish garrison already under arms, and concluded not to attack it.

At Tegesta Brother Villareal found the natives far more docile. He made much progress with their language, confirmed many of the adults in the faith, baptised some of the children and even a few of the older people, among others an old chieftainess on the point of death. Large crosses were also erected, around which the natives gathered for instruction. But on the whole the labours of the missionaries bore little fruit, for the older converts soon fell away and returned to their idols.

The Spaniards had been settled for a year at San Antonio when it was discovered that Carlos was plotting their death, and, their patience being exhausted, he was killed to make place for his successor, Don Felipe. The new chieftain showed himself so friendly to the Spaniards that hopes were entertained that on the return of Avilés he and his family would submit to baptism and that he would carry the entire tribe with him. But again Father Rogel came into conflict with rooted custom, which put his teachings at defiance. Don Felipe wished to marry his sister, and when the Father sought to impress upon him the enormity of such a sin committed on the very verge of his baptism, the Indian coldly replied that when he should be baptised he would repudiate his sister, but that in the meantime he was compelled to conform to the customs of his country, the laws of which not only countenanced such a marriage, but even considered it necessary. With the absence of Avilés matters had now reached such a pass that the Spanish garrison was subject to the same privations as were the Indians, and Father Rogel left for Havana to collect alms for his mission and to seek assistance for the settlement.[1] Here he appears to have remained until the arrival of Father Segura and his company at St. Augustine in June, 1568.

Among the first matters to which the Adelantado had turned his attention on reaching Spain was the increase of the number of missionaries among his Florida Indians, and in no wise discouraged by the sad fate which had befallen Father Martinez, Francisco Borgia readily lent him his assistance. Father Juan Bautista de Segura with three other priests and ten brothers[2] were selected

[1] Francisco Javier Alegre, *Historia de la Compañía de Jesus en Nueva España*, México, 1842, tomo i., pp. 14–17.

[2] Their names were Fathers Juan Bautista de Segura, Gonzalo del Alamo, Antonio Sedeño, and Luis de Quiros, and Brothers Juan de la Carrera, Pedro Linares, Domingo Augustin, otherwise called Domingo Vaez, Pedro Ruiz de Salvatierra, Juan Salcedo, Gabriel Gomez, Sancho Cevallos, Juan Bautista Mendez, Gabriel de Solis, and Cristobal Redondo. Alegre (tomo i., p. 17), says three fathers and three coadjutors were appointed, but in the course of his account he gives a number of other names (see pp. 18, 21,

to renew the spiritual conquest of the country. With them went a number of Florida Indians who had been baptised. Father Segura, who was appointed the Vice-Provincial, was a native of Toledo, and after his entrance into the Society had been named rector of the College of Villimar by Francisco Borgia. From Villimar he had been transferred to the College of Monterey and subsequently to Valladolid, where he was stationed at the time when he was selected for the Florida mission. On the 13th of March the company set sail from the port of San Lucar. Touching at the Canaries and Puerto Rico, at each of which places a brief stay was made, St. Augustine was reached on the 29th of June.[1]

The missionaries found the colony in a sad condition, a veritable wave of misfortune having overwhelmed it. Gourgues had but just sailed away on his return to France, leaving San Mateo a heap of ruins. Tocobaga was deserted, for the Indians had fallen upon the garrison and slain them all. At Tegesta the soldiers were in the greatest extremity. They had killed an uncle of the chieftain for some trifling reason, and the infuriated sav-

24). Father Luis de Quiros replaced Father Alamo, who was subsequently ordered to return to Europe. Philip Alegambe in his *Mortes Illustres* (Romæ, 1567, pp. 62, 63), gives only the list of the names of the Fathers who accompanied Father Segura to Axacan, which agrees with the corresponding list given by Alegre (*ibid.*, p. 25), except that Alegre mentions an additional Brother, Juan Bautista Mendez. Garcilaso in *La Florida del Inca* (Madrid, 1723, lib. vi., cap. 22, p. 267), also gives a list of their names.

[1] Barcia (*Ensayo*, Año MDLXVIII., p. 137) states that Avilés sailed March 13, 1568, with Segura for Florida. In this error he has been followed by Alegre in his *Historia de la Compañía de Jesus en Nueva España* (México, 1842, tomo i., p. 22), who states that Avilés came over with Segura; by Fairbanks in his *History of Florida* (Philadelphia, 1871, p. 156), who gives the date of March 17, 1568, for his sailing, and by Shea in his *The Catholic Church in Colonial Days* (New York, 1886, p. 143), and in his "Ancient Florida" (*Narr. and Crit. Hist. Am.*, vol. ii., p. 281), who gives the same date. Avilés was, however, still in Spain two months subsequent to the sailing of Segura: see his letter dated at Santander, May 12, 1568 (Ruidíaz, *La Florida*, tomo ii., p. 171).

ages had torn down the crosses which Brother Villareal had set up, burned their huts, and withdrawn into the forest. There they held the path by which the Spaniards went to draw water, killed a large number of the colonists, and drove the survivors to take refuge with the garrison at Santa Lucia. This unexpected increase of its population created so great a famine at Santa Lucia that the unfortunate colonists had been driven to the practice of cannibalism, in order to keep alive.[1] Of the settlements so laboriously founded by Avilés only St. Augustine and San Antonio remained, with the fort of San Felipe at Santa Elena.

At St. Augustine the half-naked soldiers and the settlers were pallid with exhaustion and hunger, say the Jesuit accounts, for Avilés, stirred by the alarming rumours which reached him of the destruction of his colonists and the miserable plight of his garrisons,[2] notwithstanding all of his efforts to assist them in time, had found it impossible to hasten the departure of relief owing to the vexations and delays of his old enemy, the Casa de Contratación.[3] Father Segura distributed among them the garments and provisions which he had brought with him, and the soldiers, being "attracted by these temporal bene-

[1] Velasco, *Geografía de las Indias*, *1571–1574*, p. 161. Francisco Sacchini, *Hist. Societatis Jesu*, Pars tertia, Romæ, 1650, p. 200. Alegre, *Historia de la Compañía de Jesus en Nueva España*, tomo i., p. 18. Relación que da Juan de Velasco cosmografo mayor de Su Majestad de lo sucedido en el descubrimiento de la Florida desde el año de 14 hasta el de 65. MS. Arch. Gen. de Indias, Seville, Patronato, est. 1, caj. 1, leg. 1/19, ramo 23. Relación de las cosas que han pasado en la Florida tocantes al servicio de Dios y del Rey. Vino con carta de Juan Mendez 6 de Abril, 1584, MS., *ibid.*, est. 54, caj. 5, leg. 16, fol. 1.

[2] Fourquevaux to Charles IX., Nov. 19, 1567, *Dépêches*, p. 295. Advis au Roi par le Prebtre, Nov. 30, 1567, *ibid.*, p. 305; Fourquevaux to Charles IX., March 9, 1568, *ibid.*, p. 336; April 6, 1568, *ibid.*, p. 345.

[3] Avilés to Philip II., Sept. 23, 1567, Ruidíaz, *La Florida*, tomo ii., p. 170; Deposition of the Adelantado Pero Menendez [de Avilés], March 28, 1568, Brit. Mus. Add. MSS., 33, 983, fol. 328.

fits, it became an easy matter to make them recognise the hand of the Lord which was afflicting them, and to turn them to Him by confession, with which they all prepared themselves to merit the Jubilee which was immediately promulgated."[1]

Father Segura shortly realised how impossible it was for the depleted colony to maintain all of the missionaries in his company, a conclusion confirmed by the experience of Father Rogel, who had come to him from Havana. He cherished in his mind the plan of founding a Jesuit college in that city, not only for the Spanish colonists but also for the instruction of the sons of the Floridian chiefs, a plan which had its inception with Father Rogel during one of his previous visits there, and the opportunity appeared to be most favourable for its execution. Brothers Domingo Augustin and Pedro Ruiz de Salvatierra were sent to Guale,[2] and with Father Rogel and the balance of his companions Father Segura proceeded to Havana, where it would appear that the winter was spent in establishing the college and in work among the Spaniards and negroes.[3] Both Barcia and Pulgar[4] relate an incident of the voyage to Havana. On the way over a violent storm arose, which so provoked the pilot that he swore it was wholly due to the Jesuits he had on board; for nothing of the kind had ever happened to him in his many crossings "with Lutherans, and even with Turks." The Fathers succeeded in calming the

[1] Alegre, tomo i., p. 18.

[2] Alegre (tomo i., p. 18) says the two brothers were sent "to Sutariva . . . near Santa Elena," referring probably to the Indian village of Saturiba at the mouth of the St. John's, but on p. 22 he says they were both at Guale when Father Segura returned the following year. Sacchini, p. 200.

[3] Alegre, tomo i., pp. 18–21.

[4] Barcia, *Ensayo*, Año MDLXVIII., p. 137. Pulgar, *Historia general de la Florida*, Biblioteca Nacional, Madrid, MSS. 2999, fol. 173.

storm by their prayers, but the unfortunate pilot, on his return to Florida "without the Jesuits," was shortly after lost with all of his belongings at the very place where he had blasphemed.

It was during this visit of Father Segura to Havana that Avilés, who had been appointed Governor of Cuba, arrived there on his second visit to Florida. We have no reliable record and no details of this visit, and his presence in Florida is largely a matter of conjecture. We have no knowledge of the date of his sailing, but it was some time after May 22, 1568, and possibly at the end of June or early in July, after Philip had received the news of the Spanish defeat in Florida. He was in Havana in April of the following year awaiting the arrival of the fleet from New Spain, which he was to accompany on its return home,[1] and is said to have visited Tegesta with Father Segura.[2] By the month of September he was back again in Spain.

In the following year (1569), probably in the early spring, Father Gonzalo del Alamo and Brother Villareal were sent to San Antonio, and Father Sedeño joined the missionaries at Guale. The Vice-Provincial, leaving Father Rogel and three brothers at Havana, himself departed for Tegesta with one of the neophytes, a brother of the cacique of Tegesta, who had accompanied the Jesuits on their journey from Spain.[3] The return of their tribesman, whom the natives had long thought to have died at the hands of the Spaniards, secured a peaceful reception for the missionaries. Laying aside their former suspicions, they renewed their alliances with the Spaniards and restored the crosses. But this peaceful condition of affairs lasted only for a time and, the

[1] See Appendix CC, The Second Voyage of Avilés to Florida.

[2] Alegre, tomo i., p. 22.

[3] Sacchini, p. 201, calls him Jacob; Alegre, tomo i., p. 32, Santiago.

difficulties with the natives reviving, the Spanish garrison was finally withdrawn in 1570.[1]

The settlement at San Antonio was likewise doomed. The crafty Don Felipe had easily imposed upon the missionaries, whom he allowed to destroy his venerated idols, while he showed a ready compliance with their teaching. But Reynoso was not so easily deceived, and, another plot being soon discovered, Don Felipe and fourteen of the chief accomplices were all put to death by order of Pedro Menéndez Marqués. The execution of so many of their principal men struck a final blow at any further understanding between the Spaniards and the Caloosas. The Indians suddenly rose, burned their village, and fled to the forest. The Spaniards, who had largely depended upon the natives for their subsistence, now found themselves utterly helpless; the attempt to maintain the settlement was finally abandoned, the mission was withdrawn, the fort destroyed, and the garrison transferred to St. Augustine.[2]

Such was the condition of affairs on the Peninsula, when Father Segura, despairing of the success of his college at Havana, which he found it impossible to maintain on account of the insufficiency of the alms of the faithful, determined to remove the missionaries to Florida. The first difficulty which presented itself was the distribution of his spiritual forces. With a keen appreciation of the situation, the Vice-Provincial sought to isolate his missions as far as possible from the Spanish settlements. We have already seen enough of the habits of the soldiers

[1] Velasco, *Geografía de las Indias*, *1571–1574*, p. 162.

[2] Alegre, tomo i., p. 22. Relación que da Juan de Velasco cosmografo mayor de Su Majestad de lo sucedido en el descubrimiento de la Florida desde el año de 14 hasta el de 65. MS. Arch. Gen. de Indias, Seville, Patronato, est. 1, caj. 1, leg. 1/19, ramo 23. In this Velasco appears to set the date in 1568, but in his *Geografía de las Indias*, *1571–1574*, p. 161, he says the settlement continued until 1571. Sacchini, p. 266, says the Carlos garrison was withdrawn in 1569.

to understand that they had not endeared themselves to the natives. In their frequent extremities for food they had been compelled to wrest from the Indians by force what supplies they could, and the hostile environment thus created was an unpromising field for missionary labours. Another object, which it was equally desirable to attain, was the avoidance of any friction with the civil authorities. The missionaries were officially the protectors of the Indians, the governor and his subordinates were their rulers. The method pursued in all of the Roman Catholic missions among the natives was such as to render the slightest interference of the secular arm subversive of all missionary authority and prestige. Nor were the civil authorities less jealous of the protection which the missionaries afforded the natives against their rapacity. To what serious conflicts between the two authorities these mutual jealousies led we shall see in the course of this history.

St. Augustine and San Mateo, where the savages were in a state of revolt, seeming to be entirely out of the question, the provinces of Santa Elena and Guale were selected as the field for the further labours of the missionaries. Father Rogel and Brother Juan Carrera were appointed to Santa Elena, where they arrived during the month of June,[1] and Brother Villareal joined the three Jesuits who were labouring in Guale.[2] The Vice-Provin-

[1] Rogel to Avilés, Dec. 9, 1570, Ruidíaz, *La Florida*, tomo ii., p. 301. In his letter to Hinestrosa of Dec. 11, 1569 (*Col. Doc. Inedit. Indias*, tomo xiii., p. 302), Rogel says "A mediado Agosto."

[2] Brinton (*Notes on the Floridian Peninsula*, p. 152), Gatschet (*Migration Legend of the Creek Indians*, vol. i., p. 11), Shipp (*Hernando de Soto and Florida*, p. 560), Shea ("Ancient Florida," *Narr. and Crit. Hist. Am.*, vol. ii., p. 282), and Fairbanks (*History of St. Augustine*, p. 125) all incorrectly identify the Guale of the Segura mission with Amelia Island. There can be no question that it was the Guale previously visited by Avilés in the province of Santa Elena, situated on a river in the interior flowing into Port Royal and but a few leagues distant from San Felipe and Orista. In addition to the proof offered by the story as told in the text, the identity of

cial accompanied them, and after he had stationed Father Rogel at Orista, but five leagues distant from San Felipe, proceeded himself to Guale, where he remained for some time to study the expediency of distributing the missionaries singly among the natives. The Indians at Orista, which consisted of about twenty houses, built the Father a church and a dwelling, where he lived with only three lads as companions, one of them a little boy named Juan, of so sweet and obedient a disposition that the Father was at a loss to find an occasion to whip him "in order that he should not forget the wholesome fear of the discipline."[1]

Father Rogel lost no time in applying himself to learn the native language, and at the end of six months had made sufficient progress both to converse and to preach in it, and he began his instruction by teaching them "the unity of God, His power and Majesty; that He was the Cause and Creator of all things; His love of the good; His horror of evil . . . the rewards and punishment of the next life, the immortality of the soul, and the resurrection of the dead." He found the savages about him far more tractable and moral than those he had known among the Caloosas. After three months spent at Orista he enthusiastically exclaims that "their manner of living was so well ordered and regulated that there was not a single thing to touch or to change among them

the languages of Orista and of Guale proved by the recognition by Father Rogel at Orista of the utility of the grammar prepared by Brother Agostino at Guale is further evidence. That the name Guale Island may at a later date have been applied to Amelia Island, see Velasco, *Geografía de las Indias, 1571–1574*, p. 169, "La barra de Guale."

[1] Rogel to Hinestrosa, Dec. 11, 1569, *Col. Doc. Inedit.*, tomo xiii., p. 305. This is the letter dated Dec. 2, 1569, by Dr. Shea ("Ancient Florida," *Narr. and Crit. Hist. Am.*, vol. ii., p. 282, note 2), a date which he probably obtained from the Buckingham Smith *North American MS., 1561, 1593*, pp. 337–341, in the New York Historical Society, where it is written "á IJ de Dizie de 1569 años."

even if they become Christians." Each Indian had but one wife, worked hard at his planting, and the children were carefully trained. They were neither cruel nor thievish, and unnatural crimes were entirely unknown. They were great traders, expert at barter, carrying their merchandise into the interior. The elders met in the council house, where the affairs of the tribe were ordered. The Indians were truthful, dwelt peaceably among themselves, and were given to but one vice,—they were great gamblers and would stake all that they possessed at a game of dice. During the year they passed but two and a half months at their village, planting their corn in the spring; but when the acorn season arrived they scattered through the forests to gather them and other wild fruits in their season, and only met together at intervals of two months to celebrate their festivals, now at one locality, now at another. Their provisions were held in common, and it was their custom to give away their food without demanding anything in return.

From Guale Father Gonzalo de Alamo, a talented preacher, but ungifted for the work of the missions, was ordered back to Europe after four months' service, and his place was filled by Father Luis de Quiros. Brother Domingo Augustin made such progress in the language that in six months he had translated the catechism and prepared a grammar that proved of great service to his companions,[1] the first instance of the reduction to a system of one of our native languages. But he was not destined to continue in his useful employment. Towards the close of the first year which the missionaries had spent in the country about Santa Elena an epidemic broke out among the natives, and the Fathers, exhausted by their unceasing care of the sick and dying, were successively attacked by it. Fortunately they all recovered

[1] Alegre, tomo i., pp. 23, 24; Rogel to Avilés, Dec. 9, 1570, Ruidíaz, *La Florida*, tomo ii., p. 307.

except Brother Domingo, who fell a victim to his duty, after a year's service among the savages.[1]

Meanwhile Father Rogel continued with his instruction, to which the natives listened with some attention, plying him with curious questions, such as their simple understanding suggested. Particularly were they impressed with the punishment of the wicked, "for I assure you, sir," writes Father Rogel to Hinestrosa,[2] "that I have seen them shed tears at the terrors of hell, when they were told that their souls would burn in hell like a firebrand if they did not die Christians." But it was a difficult matter to reach them, and although the Father attended their feasts and assemblies in order to hasten their conversion, the interruption caused by their nine-months' migrations in search of provisions made his ministrations of little effect, and his teaching was met with a constantly growing spirit of mockery. In vain he sought to cultivate among them more domestic habits, and gave them hoes to aid them in making larger plantings, in order that their wandering should not be so prolonged. The natives gladly accepted the gift, but their inherited customs were incorrigible, and they persisted in spreading over the surrounding country in every direction, making their plantings at distances of six, ten, and even twenty leagues from the village, while only two of the villagers cultivated fields in the immediate neighbourhood. The reason was not far to seek, and Father Rogel, a sensible and intelligent man, as well as a devoted one, was quick to recognise it. The soil was so poor that it soon became exhausted, and it was necessary that the cultivators go elsewhere.

At the expiration of eight months Father Rogel had brought them to the belief in the Trinity and to under-

[1] Alegre, tomo i., p. 23; Rogel to Avilés, Dec. 9, 1570, Ruidíaz, *La Florida*, tomo ii., p. 307, who, however, does not mention the pestilence.

[2] Letter of Dec. 11, 1569, *Col. Doc. Inedit. Indias*, tomo xiii., p. 303.

stand the significance of the Roman Catholic veneration of the Cross, and had, as it seemed to him, gained their good-will so that they had grown to love him. Then "I began to declare to them how, in order to be the sons of God, it was needful for them to be enemies of the devil, for the devil is evil, and loves all evil things; and God is good and loves all good things," says Father Rogel. To his consternation and alarm the effect produced by this teaching was altogether the reverse of that which he had intended, while not wanting in a ludicrous side. "When I began to treat of this," he continues, "so great was the vexation and hatred which they conceived at my words, that never again would they come to listen to me; and they said to my people that they were very angry and did not believe a thing I said, since I spoke ill of the devil." And even the two remaining dwellers in the village abandoned him for the same reason. It is permissible to think that the good Father was here the innocent victim of a foreign vocabulary, and that in his choice of names with which to designate the Spirit of Evil he had fallen upon that of some beneficent Indian deity, whose office he imperfectly understood, and to whom in his ignorance he had attributed all of the qualities of the arch-fiend.

Undismayed by the discouraging result of his labours, and with that consummate devotion to his vocation which has everywhere distinguished the missionaries of the Society, the Jesuit Father journeyed from chief to chief, offering to live in their midst that he might teach them the Divine Word, provided they honestly wished to become Christians; otherwise he would depart from them and return to Spain. But he met with no response whatever. At last, at a great council of Orista's vassals, after he had repeated his offer, the Indians sadly observed: "How can you say that you love us so greatly when you say you wish to leave us?" "From that time on," continues the Father, "I certainly expected to lose my skin,[1] and as soon as I saw it I changed my language and praised them like children, and was thus able to return in safety to my post."

Father Rogel's work was brought to an end in July, 1570, by the occurrence of one of the very incidents which the Vice-Provincial had taken so many precautions to avoid. There was a small settlement of twenty married men at Santa Elena,[2] consisting of farmers who had been colonised there by Avilés,[3] but the land was poor, and fear of the natives prevented them from going any distance to establish their farms. The fort was falling into decay, the soldiers were half naked and poorly armed,[4] and hunger was again staring the garrison in the face, for their supplies had become greatly reduced. Their only resource was to obtain relief from the Indians. Towards the end of June Juan de la Vandera, who still remained in command at San Felipe, attended an Indian festival at Escamacu, and ordered four of the chiefs, among whom were Orista, Hoya, and Escamacu, to send some canoe-loads of corn to the fort. At the same time, in order to reduce the number of mouths at San Felipe, he quartered forty of his soldiers among the natives to await the arrival of supplies. The necessary consequence was not slow to follow. Shortly after the arrival of the soldiers the Indians rose in revolt, and the disturbance continued until the arrival of Marqués and Las Alas, who finally succeeded in restoring order.

As soon as Father Rogel learned of Vandera's intention he foresaw what would come of it, its evil effect upon his work, and the false position in which it would

[1] "Dar la piel" (to be killed).

[2] "Diligencias hechas en Sevilla con motivo de la venida de Esteban de las Alas, de la Florida, 1570," Ruidíaz, *La Florida*, tomo ii., pp. 572, 579.

[3] Avilés to Philip II., Nov. 24, 1569, *ibid.*, tomo ii., p. 190.

[4] "Diligencias," 1570, *ibid.*, tomo ii., pp. 576, 580, 583, 584.

place him. If he remained among the Indians, they would turn to him for a protection which he could not give, for he realised the stern necessity under which the Spanish commander was acting. If they rose in insurrection they would visit their vengeance upon him, and in every event the ill-will stirred up among the natives would bring his labours to an end. The Vice-Provincial had ordered him to withdraw to Santa Elena in case his life was threatened, and with sorrowful heart he determined to abandon his mission. He commended his little flock to God, and, eight or ten days before the arrival of the soldiers at Orista, pulled down his house and his church, and on the 13th of July departed for Santa Elena, leaving word that whenever the Indians should have need of him they were to call on him and he would return to live among them.

Father Sedeño and probably all of the other missionaries were withdrawn from Guale, where their work had borne but little fruit,—seven baptisms in all, administered when the recipients, four of whom were children, were on the point of death. The instruction of the missionaries concerning the devil had met with a reception similar to that accorded to it at Orista. Father Rogel was ordered back to Havana and Father Sedeño to instruct the native children collected at St. Augustine from the villages of Saturiba and Tacatacuru; but the Jesuits found the fort so poorly garrisoned and in so bad a condition and the Indians so turbulent that the plan was given up, and Father Sedeño accompanied Father Rogel to Havana.

Father Rogel had rightly apprehended one of the chief causes of his failure to produce any lasting impression upon the Indians when he ascribed it to their migratory habits, and the impossibility of obtaining any permanent ascendency over their minds during two or three months, when for the balance of the year they roamed the forest in search of food like wild beasts. As a result of his experience he included in his letter to Avilés some suggestions as to the proper course to pursue in such circumstances, and his observations are highly interesting, as they embody for the first time the method which the missionaries subsequently adopted throughout the length and breadth of our land irrespective of the Order to which they belonged, a method which may be studied in some of its most interesting phases in the California missions more than two centuries later.

"In order to obtain fruit in the blind and sad souls of these provinces, it is necessary first of all to order the Indians to come together, and live in towns and cultivate the earth, collecting sustenance for the entire year; and after they have thus become very settled, then to begin the preaching. Unless this is done, although the religious remain among them for fifty years, they will have no more fruit than we in our four years among them, which is none at all, nor even a hope, nor the semblance of it."

And even then it will be a most severe labour of many years,

"for it must be done rightly, as our Lord God commands, neither by compelling them nor with a mailed hand. And this for two reasons: the first that they have been accustomed to live in this manner for thousands of years, and to take them out of it is like death to them; the second, that even were they willing, the poverty of the soil and its rapid exhaustion will not admit of it; and so it is that they themselves give this reason for their scattering and change of boundaries." [1]

[1] Rogel to Avilés, Dec. 9, 1570, *ibid.*, tomo ii., pp. 301–308. There is a translation of this letter by Daniel G. Brinton in the *Historical Magazine*, 1861, p. 327. See also his *Notes on the Floridian Peninsula*, pp. 152, 153. There is an unimportant reference to Rogel made by Mooney in *19 Ann. Rep. Bu. Ethn.*, Pt. I., p. 201.

The deplorable state of the San Felipe garrison, which had driven Vandera to the necessity of quartering part of his forces on the Indians, and thus compelled the withdrawal of Father Rogel, was but one instance of the conditions reigning throughout the settlements. At St. Augustine the suffering was so great that on the arrival of a vessel to receive the military accounts it had been compelled to anchor outside of the harbour for fear the colonists would seize it and abandon the town.[1] The soldiers were almost naked, some going about in a shirt, which was all they possessed; others dressed only in the wadded cotton armour, which had been adopted from the Mexicans as a protection against the arrows of the Indians. Their weapons were in as miserable a condition: the arquebuses worn out or burst, the swords, which only some of them had, old and damaged, and no means were at hand with which to repair them. But one married man was left in the settlement in addition to the soldiers forming the garrison. A few horses still survived, some fifteen or sixteen, but it was a difficult matter to keep them alive, for they were devoured by mosquitoes[2] or killed by the Indians, and no fodder had been raised for their food. As the Indian war still continued,[3] the colonists were exposed to the greatest risks in leaving the fort in search of food. For this reason they went without fish or meat and were compelled to subsist on corn and inferior meal. The fort, which, in the absence of more enduring material, was constructed

[1] Avilés to Philip II., Nov. 24, 1569, Ruidíaz, *La Florida*, tomo ii., p. 190.

[2] Both Le Challeux in the "Histoire Mémorable" (reprint in Gaffarel, *Hist. de la Floride*, p. 461), and Meleneche in his deposition (Noriega to Philip II., March 29, 1565, MS. Direc. de Hidrog., Madrid, *Col. Navarrete*, tomo xiv., Doc. No. 33, fol. 4b), mention the plague of mosquitoes about the St. John's.

[3] Avilés to Philip II., Nov. 24, 1569, Ruidíaz, *La Florida*, tomo ii., p. 190.

of wood and sand, was rotting away on account of its age and the great humidity of the climate, and had even fallen down in places so as to afford hardly any protection against the descent of pirates or the attacks of the natives.[1]

The conditions at San Pedro on the island of Tacatacuru, where most probably was the blockhouse which Avilés had ordered built, were equally bad. The soldiers were naked, half-armed, and famished, and the fort was falling into decay.[2] It would appear that in April, 1569, succour had been sent to Las Alas from Spain,[3] but it had also brought with it more mouths to feed, and during the summer Avilés's brother, Bartolomé, had himself departed for Spain, taking with him the renewed complaints of the unpaid soldiers.[4] He probably also bore with him the demands of Las Alas and Governor Marqués for their salaries as Accountant and Treasurer of Florida respectively, offices to which they had been appointed by Avilés, since payments to them had been stopped owing to some Court intrigue.[5]

Patiently the sorely tried colony waited for the arrival of the much-needed help, while Avilés in Spain pressed the necessity of sending reinforcements to protect the farmers from the natives and urged the fear of a descent upon the coast by Hawkins, who was reported to be preparing a great armada, and predicted the imminent abandonment of the forts by the desperate soldiery,[6] unless help was

[1] "Diligencias hechas en Sevilla con motivo de la venida de Esteban de las Alas de la Florida, 1570," *ibid.*, tomo ii., pp. 572, 578, 579, 580, 582–584, 587, 588.

[2] "Diligencias," 1570, *ibid.*, tomo ii., pp. 578–580, 583, 584, 587.

[3] Barcia, *Ensayo*, Año MDLXIX., p. 138.

[4] Avilés to Philip II., Nov. 20, 1569, Ruidíaz, *La Florida*, tomo ii., p. 185.

[5] Avilés to Philip II., May 12, 1568, *ibid.*, tomo ii., p. 178.

[6] Avilés to Philip II., Dec. 4, 1569, *ibid.*, tomo ii., p. 195; Dec. 31, 1569, *ibid.*, tomo ii., p. 199; Jan. 4, 1570, *ibid.*, tomo ii., p. 201.

soon forthcoming. But his old enemy, the Casa de Contratación, and other obstacles impeded the sailing of the fleet.[1] At last the patience of Las Alas became exhausted and he determined to take matters into his own hands, to reduce the garrisons of the three remaining forts, and, after abandoning Ays and Carlos, to sail himself for Spain with the troops he had withdrawn from the colony.

In the month of June he equipped a vessel named the *Espiritu Santo*, and embarking with most of the garrison at St. Augustine, where he left but fifty soldiers in charge of Pedro Menéndez Avilés, a nephew of the Adelantado, he proceeded to Tacatacuru, where he reduced the garrison to the same number, leaving Antonio Fernandez in command and taking with him Juan Gutierrez and the balance of the soldiers. At Santa Elena the same measures were repeated; Vandera was left in command, and the lieutenant-governor, Marqués, who happened to be at San Felipe at the time, left for Havana,[2] where he had been appointed to a similar office during the absence of Avilés. August 13, 1570, Las Alas set sail from Santa Elena and reached Cadiz on the 20th of October with about one hundred and twenty men, including a number of officers and officials. It was virtually an abandonment of the country, for only one hundred and fifty soldiers had been left there, with barely sufficient food and ammunition to sustain them a few months. It is probable that such was also the opinion of the King, for Las Alas had been but two weeks in Spain when Philip ordered a secret investigation[3] to be made into the reason of his return. The result was the pitiable showing which we have just reviewed. But no further consequences seem

[1] Avilés to Philip II., Sept. 22, 1569, *ibid.*, tomo ii., p. 180; Nov. 27, 1569, *ibid.*, tomo ii., p. 191; Dec. 31, 1569, *ibid.*, tomo ii., p. 196.

[2] "Diligencias," 1570, *ibid.*, tomo ii., p. 572.

[3] "Diligencias," 1570, *ibid.*, tomo ii., p. 569, Nov. 3, 1570.

to have followed Las Alas's desertion of his post, owing either to the imperative necessity under which he had acted, or, what is much more likely, to the powerful influence which Avilés was able to exert at Court in his favour.

CHAPTER II

THE VIRGINIA MISSION

DURING his brief visit to Havana Marqués wrote to Spain an account of the condition of affairs in Florida, and then returned to San Mateo, which for the third time had been put in a state of defence. On his arrival he was greeted with the news that shortly after the departure of Las Alas from St. Augustine the soldiers there had mutinied. Their intention was to seize a boat lying in the harbour and to put to sea in her without a pilot, sailors, anchors, or any equipment whatever, so eager were they to abandon the fort and escape from that fateful region. Marqués's only resource was to temporise, and he wrote from San Mateo to the mutineers, that in case assistance did not arrive by the following month of March he would himself come to St. Augustine in April with his ships and transport them to Havana, together with all of the armament of the fort. From there he promised them that they should have leave to return to Spain to obtain their pay. He even authorised them to leave in any vessel they could secure in the event of his own failure to arrive at the time he had set, offering to meet a deputation of the garrison on board his ship to discuss the matter, and stating his willingness to lend them money with which to send one of their number to Havana to purchase provisions. To this low ebb had discipline fallen.[1]

[1] Traslado autorizado de una carta que escribió el Gobernador de la Florida Pedro Menéndez Marqués desde San Mateo á los soldados de el

The failure of the Santa Elena missions had brought no abatement in the zeal of the Vice-Provincial, and at the very time when he had withdrawn the missionaries from Guale and Orista he was contemplating his departure for new fields in the country about Chesapeake Bay, to which his attention had been turned by an Indian of that region, whom the Jesuits had found in Havana. This was Don Luis, who, it will be remembered, had accompanied the Dominican friars, sent by Avilés prior to his departure for Spain to visit that neighbourhood, and who had returned with them to Spain when they abandoned the enterprise.[1] On his arrival at Court Don Luis, who was intelligent and of an agreeable address, ingratiated himself to such an extent into the good-will of Philip II. that he lived at the royal expense during all of his stay. From Spain he had gone to Havana in company with some Dominicans, who were on their way to Florida to assist them in their work, but, the mission having been abandoned, Don Luis, in his apparent zeal to convert his countrymen, joined the Jesuits under Father Segura on their departure for Florida.[2] He was a valuable accession to their party on account of his rank among the natives, and his ability to act as interpreter.

On the 5th of August, 1570, Father Segura sailed from Santa Elena for Chesapeake Bay with seven companions,[3] the Indian Don Luis, and a small boy named Alonso,

fuerte de San Agustin de la Florida, Sept. 7, 1570, MS. Arch. Gen. de Indias, Seville, est. 54, caj. 5, leg. 9.

[1] Barcia, *Ensayo*, Año MDLXVI., p. 123.

[2] Alegre, *Historia de la Compañía de Jesus en Nueva España*, México, 1842, tomo i., p. 25.

[3] Father Luis de Quiros, Brothers Gabriel Gomez, Sancho Cevallos, Juan Bautista Mendez, Pedro de Limares, Gabriel de Solis, who was related to Avilés, and Cristobal Redondo (Alegre, tomo i., p. 25). Quiros and Segura to [Hinestrosa ?], Dec. 12, 1570. Buckingham Smith, *Florida MSS., 1526, 1743*, p. 255, MS. New York Historical Society.

son of a settler at Santa Elena, who had been trained by the Fathers to serve at mass.[1] The journey was prolonged owing to bad weather and difficulties in finding the region of which they were in search, and the Jesuits were compelled to share their provisions with the crew of the ship, so that on reaching their destination they had consumed all of their flour and two of the four barrels of biscuit with which they had provided themselves for the voyage. Finally they discovered the bay, up which they ascended, and on the 10th of September reached the province of Axacan,[2] in Virginia, where they entered a river and landed. They found the country poor and sparsely inhabited owing to a prolonged drought of six years, and the famine which had followed in its wake had killed some of the inhabitants and driven others to change their abode. All the corn of the scant harvests had been eaten; the forest fruits had perished, as well as the roots upon which the natives subsisted, and what little food could still be found was obtained with great difficulty on account of the severity of the winter and the deep snow. Only a small number of the principal men of the tribe remained, "that they might die where their fathers had died." Some of these proved to be relatives of Don Luis, whom they received "as if he had risen from the dead and had come from heaven," and in their gratitude they gave the Fathers "the only thing the Indians had to offer," their "good will," writes Father Quiros. The Jesuits began their ministrations at once, and hearing that a three-year-old son of a chief, a brother of Don Luis, living seven or eight leagues from their landing-place, lay at the point of death, sent one of their number the night of their arrival to baptise him.

On account of the low state of its supplies, it was

[1] Pedro Fernandez de Pulgar, *Historia general de la Florida*, Biblioteca Nacional, Madrid, MSS. 2999, fol. 176.

[2] See Appendix DD, Axacan.

impossible for the vessel which had brought the Fathers to remain any length of time at the harbour where the landing had been made, and on the following morning it departed on its return voyage, bearing a letter written by Father Quiros under the direction of the Vice-Provincial, who added a short postscript. This was the last message that was ever received from them. It described the desolate condition of the country, and showed in a pathetic way the utter dependence of the Jesuits in their isolated and distant mission upon the precarious assistance of the Indians for the very food they had to eat. Both Fathers pleadingly insisted upon the absolute necessity of dispatching a vessel to their succour with corn for the Indians to plant not later than the beginning of April of the following year, if it was found impracticable to send it during the winter. As the Fathers proposed to establish their mission on a stream not far from the landing-place, they directed that the relief ship on reaching the river signal its presence by a bonfire at night or a column of smoke by day, and added a brief and indefinite description of the place to which they were going and of what little they had been able to learn from the natives of "the entrance through the mountains and China." "Three or four days' journey from yonder," wrote Father Quiros, referring to the lower reach of the river which they had ascended, "were the mountains, and two of these days' journey were by a river, and one or two days' travel beyond the mountains another sea is observed."

Father Quiros concluded his letter with the remark that the Indians freely gave the Jesuits food from their own impoverished stores without expecting any return, and in order not to awaken their cupidity he requested that the crew of the relief ship be forbidden to trade with them, and that all articles of barter which the sailors might bring be deposited with Don Luis, who would pay them its equivalent, all bartering to be conducted only in accordance with the judgment of the Fathers.[1] Brief as the letter is, it is highly interesting, for it illustrates the spirit which has always distinguished the Society, the unselfish devotion of its missionaries, their bent for scientific investigation, and the policy which Father Segura probably intended to follow in the mission of the complete dependence of the natives upon the will of the missionaries, even in matters of trade.

With the departure of the vessel, the Jesuits, conducted by the Indians, who carried their baggage for them, proceeded to a neighbouring stream,[2] which was but two leagues distant, and ascending it in canoes, fixed their settlement near a village governed by a younger brother of Don Luis. The Fathers erected there a hut and a small chapel, where mass was celebrated, and for some time Don Luis remained in their company, serving them as interpreter and preacher. Patiently they waited for the return of the vessel which was to bring succour from their compatriots; and when the winter sped by and nothing came, Don Luis, lured back to his native customs, abandoned them under the pretence of preparing a place for their reception at another village. The Fathers were now reduced to providing for themselves, and searched the forest for herbs and roots on which to subsist.

On the 2nd of February, 1571, four months having passed since their arrival in the Virginia wilderness, Father Segura determined to send Father Luis de Quiros with Brothers Gabriel de Solis and Juan Bautista Mendez to induce Don Luis to return, and the embassy started on its perilous mission. But they were marching to their martyrdom. Don Luis, completely alienated, had already planned their death. He received them with a

[1] Quiros and Segura to [Hinestrosa?], Dec. 12, 1570, Buckingham Smith, *Florida MSS., 1526, 1643*, pp. 355 *et seq.*

[2] See Appendix EE, The Site of the Segura Mission.

show of great friendship, promising to return on the following day, and the Father with his two companions, believing his word, retraced his steps to the little cabin. The same night Don Luis collected a band of Indians, followed them, and, overtaking them on the way, received a friendly salutation from Father Quiros, who supposed him to be alone, for the darkness concealed the presence of his companions. The answer to the kindly greeting was a shower of arrows, which pierced the heart of the Jesuit, and he fell dead.[1] Then Don Luis stripped him of his possessions, while his companions with their clubs made an end of the two Brothers.

But the savage purpose of the renegade was not yet fully attained, and in the course of a few days Don Luis again prepared to exterminate the surviving ministers of the faith which he had either professed as a mask to his evil intentions or else had been weaned from by his return to his native wilds. There still remained to the missionaries a few hatchets and knives, which served them in their daily offices, and Don Luis, fearing that they would defend themselves with these, employed a transparent strategy to disarm them. On the morning of the 8th of February[2] some Indians were sent to borrow the hatchets of the Fathers in order to chop wood, and the simple Jesuits fell into the trap. Then Don Luis and his party descended upon them. On the way they encountered Brother Cevallos, who had gone to cut wood in the forest, and killed him. Then they attacked Father Segura and killed him with a blow on the head with an ax, and the remaining missionaries shared his fate.

Only one person escaped, the little boy Alonso, who

[1] Father Luis de Quiros was of a noble family of Xerez de la Frontera, and in 1566 had been rector of a college at the Albaycin at Granada. Pulgar, *Historia general de la Florida*, Bib. Nac., Madrid, MSS. 2999, fol. 175.

[2] Tanner, *Societas Militans*, pp. 449–451.

was saved by the brother of Don Luis, and upon whose account rests the story of the martyrdom of the Virginia missionaries. He was finally rescued from the Indians by Avilés, when, in 1571, the latter visited Axacan to wreak vengeance on the natives for the murder they had committed. Father Rogel has left us a legend of an incident which followed the death of the Jesuits typical of the stories which surround the career of the early missionaries to the Indians:

"It happened that an Indian, coveting the spoils, went to a coffer in which there was a crucifix, and wishing to open it or break into it, in order to extract its contents, fell dead on the spot as he began to unlock it. Then another Indian possessed with the same covetousness, sought to follow the same intent, and likewise the same thing occurred. Then none dared further approach the coffer, but they preserve it to this day with much veneration and fear, without daring to approach it. And this was told me by some old soldiers who came from Florida of those who had been to Axacan, to whom it was told by the Indians how the coffer was still in the country and no one dares approach it, even now, after the lapse of forty years." [1]

[1] Alegre, tomo ii., p. 32; Andres Perez de Ribas, *Historia de los Trivmphos de nvestra Santa Fee*, etc., Madrid, 1645, lib. xii., cap. 14, pp. 746–749. There was a tradition that the crucifix was preserved in the Jesuit College at Guaraca (*ibid.*, p. 749). Francisco Sacchini, *Historia Societatis Jesu*, Pars tertia, Romæ, MDCL., pp. 323, 324; Pedro de Ribadeneyra, *Vida del P. Franciso de Borja*, Madrid, 1592, fol. 141b–143; *Vita Francisi Borgiæ* . . . a P. Ribadeneira Hispanice scripta; Latine vero ab And. Schotto Antverp, Moguntiæ, 1603, lib. iii., cap. 6, p. 257. (This is a translation of the preceding.) John Gilmary Shea, "The Segura Mission" in the *United States Catholic Magazine*, 1846, vol. v., p. 604. This is based on the accounts given by Barcia and Garcilaso de la Vega. "The Spanish in the Chesapeake," in the *Historical Magazine*, 1859, vol. iii., p. 268. This is based on the accounts of Barcia, Algambe, and Tanner. "The Log Chapel on the Rappahannock," in *The Catholic World*, March, 1875, p. 847, a much more mature production than the two preceding, but, unfortunately, without references.

Father Rogel had been enjoined to send a ship to the assistance of the Virginia missionaries after the expiration of four months, and had made every effort to follow out his instructions. As soon as he could find a pilot acquainted with the coast he set sail for the Bay of Santa Maria in company with Brother Juan de Salcedo in a vessel commanded by Vincente Gonzalo. On reaching the harbour where the Jesuits were to have met him the absence of the signal which had been agreed upon between them awakened his suspicions, and he did not land. The savages, in order to induce him to come ashore, disguised some of their companions in the garments they had stolen from their victims, and, causing them to walk along the shore in sight of the ship, shouted out: "Come, here are the Fathers you seek." This grotesque stratagem failed to deceive the rescuers, but rather confirmed their suspicions. At the same time two of the natives, casting themselves into the water, swam out to the ship, where they were seized and dragged aboard. Then, raising the anchor, Father Rogel immediately set sail for Havana, carrying the two Indians with him. In order to avoid the full force of the Gulf Stream the vessel returned along the coast, close to the land, an opportunity which one of the Indians improved to make his escape, throwing himself into the water and swimming ashore. The other Indian was secured and taken to Havana, where every effort was made to learn from him the final fate of the missionaries, but without success. The party appears to have reached Havana about the time of the arrival of Avilés in July.[1]

[1] Pulgar, *Historia*, fol. 176; Alegre, tomo i., p. 33; Ribas, lib. xii., cap. 14, p. 748.

CHAPTER III

THE LAST VISIT OF AVILÉS TO FLORIDA

IN addition to the unremitting care which he continued to bestow on his colony, Avilés took advantage of his presence in Spain to present Philip the plans of the extended exploration and conquest which he had first conceived shortly after his arrival in Florida. Not even the disheartening news which reached him from time to time of starvation and mutiny, Indian wars, and French revenge could curb his enterprising and self-reliant temperament. Four months after his return from his first expedition to Florida he was already maintaining his favourite theory of a passage to the Pacific and to China by way of Chesapeake Bay,[1] and Fourquevaux informed Catherine that Philip was so taken with the proposition that he had advanced two hundred and thirty thousand crowns for the undertaking.[2] Avilés also called the attention of his master to the Portuguese settlements "on the coast of Florida in Newfoundland, the discovery of which was under his charge." According to his account the Portuguese had been fortifying themselves for two years at a place in the interior near some large Indian towns two hundred leagues away, and reached from Newfoundland by an arm of the sea, and were threatening the passage to China and the Moluccas, unless they were driven out.[3]

[1] Advis au roi par le Prebtre, Nov. 30, 1567, *Dépêches*, p. 305.

[2] Fourquevaux to Catherine de' Medici, May 8, 1568, *ibid.*, p. 358.

[3] Deposition by Pedro Menendez (de Avilés) relating, among other matters, to Portuguese settlements in Florida, and the urgent necessity of

As if these considerations were not enough for his unbounded ambition, Avilés had also conceived the design of extending his domain to the confines of Mexico, and applied to the King for a licence to settle in the northern part of Pánuco, "which was in Florida," giving as one of his titles to its possession the proximity of the country to the region he had already conquered, and in compliance with his suggestion a royal cédula [1] was dispatched to the Audiencia of Mexico for its opinion. The Audiencia, jealous of his pretensions, reported adversely.

"For measured by an air line from the corner of Pánuco to the corner of Santa Elena," it said, "there are four hundred and fifty leagues, and it is a common practice among cosmographers to add a third more of the way by land, on account of the sinuosities of the mountains, lagoons, and valleys which usually occur. And we are informed that they exist there in great number, and it is more difficult to conduct the road by the mountains, on account of the great ravines, and hollows and valleys, and the excessively mountainous condition of the county, so that the distance is not the eighty leagues which Pedro Menéndez says, but six hundred according to this computation."

Another reason for discountenancing the grant, and one more especially intended to appeal to the royal purse, was that the colonists "would extract silver there to mint for foreign kingdoms, or for where they chose, and would introduce all kinds of merchandise, without its being subject to the proper accounting." The Audiencia also insisted that all of the turbulent element of the country

provisioning the soldiers in Florida, March 28, 1568, Brit. Mus. Add. MSS., 33,983, fol. 324. Avilés apparently thought that the Portuguese were in the vicinity of the range of mountains eighty leagues to the north of Chesapeake Bay (see p. 212 in this volume), and not a great distance from the channel connecting the bay with the South Sea.

[1] Dated Madrid, July 21, 1568.

would gather about the new colony, and it would become a source of trouble to New Spain.

"The site he lays claim to settle is sixty leagues from Mexico, and in case the Rio del Espiritu Santo should have to be discovered in order to go to the point of Santa Elena, it would have to be done from this New Spain in order to avoid these inconveniences, and in no way does it profit the service of Your Majesty and the peace of this land, to accede to the pretensions of Pero Menéndez,"

concludes the Audiencia.[1]

The opinion is interesting as showing the extent of the geographical knowledge of the time among those having the best opportunities to be correctly informed. The concluding paragraph, relating to the short distance from the City of Mexico to the proposed Pánuco settlement, raises more than a mere suspicion that the Audiencia seriously dreaded the presence of the enterprising Avilés in its neighbourhood, and was still mindful of Cortés's dreams of independent conquest. And perhaps its caution was well advised, for the atmosphere of Mexico has possessed the peculiar property of disturbing the imagination of soldiers from the time of Cortés to that of Bazaine. The protest of the Audiencia, however, could not check a man of such determination as the Adelantado, although it may have served the purpose of somewhat delaying the execution of his plan. Four years later his request was granted and the limits of his Florida grant were extended west to the Rio Pánuco "eighty leagues," and to the north to the confines of Mexico, and east, north-east, and north from Santa Elena.[2]

[1] "Parecer que da á S. M. la Audiencia de Nueva España, sobre lo propuesto por Pero Menéndez de Abiles, de poblar en el rio de Panuco que es en la Florida," Mexico, Jan. 19, 1569. MS. Direc. de Hidrog. Madrid, *Col. Navarrete*, tomo xiv, Doc. No. 42.

[2] "Real Cédula ordenando al Adelantado Pero Menéndez de Avilés la continuación de la conquista de la Florida por la parte de Panuco," Madrid, Feb. 23, 1573, Ruidíaz, *La Florida*, tomo ii., p. 368.

Throughout the month of February, 1568, Avilés was in Biscay preparing the fleet that was to sail for Flanders, which at the time it was thought that he would himself command.[1] In the summer he appears to have made his fifth voyage to the Indies, returning in the summer or early fall of the following year, between which terms it is among the possibilities that he made one visit to Florida as recorded in a previous chapter.[2] On reaching Spain he found a letter from the austere Pius V., a man of deep but rigid religious convictions, congratulating him upon his appointment as Governor of Florida, and enjoining upon him "the good sense and discretion" which he should observe in his government of the Indians, "to effect the increase of our holy Catholic faith, and gain more souls to God." With the same sound sense which he recommended to the observation of the Adelantado, the Pope dwells upon the moral standard to be maintained among the colonists.

> "But nothing is more important in the conversion of these Indians and idolaters," he observes, "than to endeavour by all means to prevent scandal being given by the vices and immoralities of such as go to those western parts. This is the key of this holy work, in which is included the whole essence of your charge."[3]

During most of 1570 Avilés appears to have been at sea, protecting the arriving and departing fleets from the depredations of pirates, probably accompanying the outgoing India squadrons on their way to the Canaries, and

[1] Fourquevaux to Charles IX., Feb. 18, 1568, *Dépêches*, p. 328.

[2] See Appendix CC, The Second Voyage of Avilés to Florida, p. 457, in this volume.

[3] Pius V. to Avilés, Aug. 18, 1569, Ruidíaz, *La Florida*, tomo ii., p. 299. English version in Shea's *The Catholic Church in Colonial Days*. New York, 1886, p. 145.

returning with the treasure ships.[1] On land his time was actively occupied with his Cuban Government in addition to his other cares.

Ever since the arrival of Avilés in Spain rumours had been afloat of his impending return to Florida, mostly in connection with the discovery of the Northwest Passage,[2] but his various occupations had so far prevented his departure. With the arrival of Las Alas, the knowledge of the defenceless and desperate condition of his colony must have pressed heavily upon him, but it was only in the spring of 1571 that he was enabled again to visit his conquest, and, as it happened, for the last time. May 15th he was at San Lucar to hasten the sailing of his fleet, which had been delayed by the weather, the sinking of one of his ships, and the unremitting meddling of the officials of the Casa de Contratación.[3] On the 17th of the month he set sail with seven galleons, two hundred and fifty sailors and soldiers, and four hundred persons in addition.[4] So great was the danger from pirates to which a small fleet was exposed that secret instructions appointing a meeting-place were left for Diego Flores, who was to follow him with two galleons, and Las Alas remained in Spain to afford Flores his assistance.[5]

[1] See Appendix CC, The Second Voyage of Avilés to Florida, p. 457, in this volume.

[2] Fourquevaux to Charles IX., Aug., 1567, *Dépêches*, p. 263. Gaffarel, p. 452, dates this letter Sept. 12, 1567. Same to same, Oct. 15, 1567, *Dépêches*, p. 280; Apr. 6, 1568, *ibid.*, p. 345. Same to Catherine de' Medici, May 8, 1568, *ibid.*, p. 358. Advis au Roi par le Prebtre, Nov. 30, 1567, *ibid.*, p. 305.

[3] Avilés to Philip II., May 15, 1571, Ruidíaz, *La Florida*, tomo ii, pp. 222, 224.

[4] Avilés to Philip II., July 22, 1571, *ibid.*, tomo ii., pp. 228, 235. This letter (p. 235) contains a statement that "mi muger y casa" were in a vessel of the fleet which sailed for Carthagena. It must be an error of the copyist, for Avilés intended to return shortly to Spain and could not have taken his family with him.

[5] Avilés to Philip II., May 16, 1571, Ruidíaz, *La Florida*, tomo ii., p. 226.

July 3rd Avilés reached Havana, where he spent a few days attending to the sailing of the armada, which was to escort the returning treasure fleet. During his stay he lost some men by desertion, and as a considerable number of his company had fallen ill, he was obliged to put the sick ashore. Here he found his nephew, Pedro Menéndez de Avilés, whom Las Alas had left in charge of St. Augustine, and who had fallen very ill,[1] and he learned from Father Rogel the fate which had overwhelmed the Segura mission. His resolution was quickly taken, and he determined to visit Axacan and verify the details of the death of the missionaries. Taking with him Father Rogel and two Brothers,[2] he promptly set sail for Santa Elena, which he reached on the 22nd of July. He found the small garrison at San Felipe in a satisfactory condition, and the natives "humble and obedient," but engaged in war with "the Indians friendly to the French."[3] "For the Indians, as a rule," he observes, "are better friends of the French, who leave them to live in freedom, than to my people and the Teatines (monks), who restrict their way of living; and the French can accomplish more [with them] in one day than I in a year." To increase the attachment of the natives to his interests he sent to Campeche for supplies to distribute among them.[4]

Having reinforced the garrison at San Felipe, his next step was to proceed to Axacan. On his arrival he found that the Indians had fled to the mountains. Avilés, who was determined to read the savages a lesson which they should not forget, disembarked with a company of soldiers

[1] Avilés to Philip II., July 22, 1571, *ibid.*, tomo ii., p. 228.

[2] Alegre, tomo i., p. 34.

[3] It does not appear what Avilés means by this expression, unless he attributed the continuance of the Indian war to French influence.

[4] Avilés to Philip II., July 22, 1571, Ruidíaz, *La Florida*, tomo ii., p. 228 *et seq.*

to go in search of them, but only succeeded in capturing eight. He had, however, the good fortune to rescue the lad Alonso, and from him he learned the details of the cruel death that had overtaken the missionaries. The boy also informed him that the prisoners which he had taken were among their murderers, and the Adelantado hung them all from the yard-arms of his ship, after they had been converted and baptised by Father Rogel. Father Rogel asked Avilés for a company of soldiers to search for the bodies of the martyred missionaries and to give them burial, but the season was far advanced, Avilés anxious to return, and the request of the Father had to be denied.[1] This was the last of the Jesuit missions on our eastern coast. In July, 1572, Father Sedeño went to Mexico to prepare the way for the first Jesuit mission to that country, and from there he was sent to the Philippines, where he passed the remainder of his life.[2] Father Rogel lived to a ripe old age, for the legend of the crucifix related by him was written forty years after the martyrdom of Father Segura and his companions.

It was late in the fall when Avilés arrived at St. Augustine, and after attending to the necessities of the garrison he set sail on the 20th of December for Havana, with the Jesuits and Alonso, whom Father Rogel had taken with him, in two small tenders and a bark. While pursuing the usual course along the coast the vessels were overtaken by a storm which separated them. The bark succeeded in making Havana. A second boat was driven

[1] Pulgar, *Historia general de la Florida*, fol. 176b, Biblioteca Nacional, Madrid, MSS. 2999. Ribas, *Historia de los Trivmphos de nvestra Santa Fee*, etc., Madrid, 1645, lib. xii., cap. ii., pp. 748, 749. Alegre, tomo i., p. 34. *Labor Evangelica, Ministerios Apostolicos de los Obreros de la Compañía de Jesvs*, Fvndación y Progressos de sv Provincia en las Islas Filipinos. Historiadores por el Padre Francisco Colin. Parte primera, Madrid, MDCLXIII., lib. ii., cap. i., p. 168.

[2] Alegre, tomo i., p. 50. *Geographia Historica*, El P. Pedro Murillo Velarde, Madrid, 1752, lib. ix., cap. ii., p. 80.

ashore in the province of Ays,[1] where the crew was attacked by the natives. Unable to defend themselves because the water had rendered their arquebuses useless, they were all killed and their boat was burned.

The boat containing Avilés and the Jesuits was cast ashore near Cape Canaveral, probably not far from the locality where Ribaut had suffered a like fate; its occupants, some thirty in number, escaped to the land, constructed a kind of fort with the wreckage, and with a few arquebuses, which were still uninjured by the wet, defended themselves from the attacks of the Indians until nightfall, when they set out in the direction of St. Augustine, a distance of thirty-one leagues. Struggling onward through the forest, crossing the streams in canoes, in great danger from the sea, from which they managed to escape "by means of some reliques which the companion of Father [Rogel] cast upon the waters,"[2] and, fighting the Indians, they accomplished the entire distance, finally reaching St. Augustine without the loss of a single member of the company. They came as a timely reinforcement, for a few days after their arrival three large English vessels, fully manned, attacked the town, but were successfully driven off.

The boat which escaped to Havana had announced that the other two vessels would arrive the following day. As time passed without news of them or of the Adelantado, the report spread that he had been lost. At the end of four months a small vessel set sail on the 10th of April, 1572, in search of Avilés, and finally found him at St. Augustine, where he embarked in time to reach Havana on Good Friday. Here he remained but two weeks, and, having sent the news of his arrival to New Spain, set out again in the same vessel for Puerto de

[1] Osorio in his letter of May 24, 1572 (Ruidíaz, *La Florida*, tomo ii., p. 487) says "Ris." This is in all probability a misprint for "Ais."

[2] Pulgar, *Historia general de la Florida*, fol. 173b.

Plata, in Hispaniola. The date of his return to Spain does not appear, but it is not improbable that he sailed with the treasure fleet during the summer of 1572, leaving Pedro Menéndez Marqués in charge of his government. At the time of his arrival at Havana Las Alas was already on his way to Florida and the West Indies.[1]

As this was the last visit of Avilés to the country which he had undertaken to subdue and colonise, it will be of interest to learn the condition in which he finally left it and to consider what profit he derived from the enormous expense to which he and his friends had been put in its conquest and maintenance. We have seen that Avilés, who at the outset had so keenly appreciated the importance of cultivating the soil,[2] sent out farmers at different times to colonise his province.[3] These were settled for the most part on the little island at Santa Elena, on which was situated Fort San Felipe. There are two accounts of the condition of the colony, of particular interest because they emanate from the colonists themselves, and as a consequence present their side of the story, which has an unhappy ring of truth about it, despite what may be some inevitable exaggeration.

In 1572 the settlement on the island, in addition to soldiers in the garrison, consisted of some twenty-odd farmers with their families, most of whom had been

[1] Osorio to ———, May 24, 1572, Ruidíaz, *La Florida*, tomo ii., p. 487. In the "Declaración de Juan de Saravia vecino de Sevilla sobre las nuevas de la Armada y flota de Indias que se apresaba del cargo del General Dn Cristoval de Eraso," Seville, Oct. 19, 1572 (MS. Direc. de Hidrog., Madrid, *Col. Navarrete*, tomo xxii., Doc. No. 7), it appears that Avilés had ordered the Governor of Havana to notify him in Florida of the arrival of the galleons in order that he might return to Spain with Eraso's armada.

[2] Avilés to Philip II., Sept. 11, 1565, Ruidíaz, *La Florida*, tomo ii., p. 83.

[3] Avilés to Philip II., Dec. 3, 1570, *ibid.*, tomo ii., p. 208, in which he says he has sent out 200 farmers. Same to same, Nov. 27, 1569, *ibid.*, tomo ii., p. 190, where he mentions the presence of farmers in Guale. Same to same, Nov. 29, 1566, *ibid.*, tomo ii., p. 170, where he refers to the farmers in Florida.

farmers and raisers of stock in Spain. These the Adelantado had induced to emigrate to Florida by representing to them the fertility of the country, "as good as the plain of Carmona," says one of the Andalusians, the memory of that beautiful valley watered by the Guadalquivir and dotted with olive groves and orange trees rising before his eyes. The farmers were promised an assignment of good farming land and twelve head of stock apiece, and some of them had even brought cows and sheep of their own. They were soon at work planting corn and wheat, oats and pumpkins, chick-peas and beans, and perhaps the sugar-cane, as Fontanedo[1] informs us; and cows, horses, sheep, and goats were brought to the fort for their use. Pigs were given to them with the curious condition, according to one of the deponents, that they were not to be slaughtered for ten years, after the expiration of which the increase was to be divided between the settlers and Avilés.

As already stated, the island was small and low, subject to be flooded by the sea at the high tides, and the soil sandy and unproductive. The frost and cold of winter proved extremely trying to the crops. During April and May it rained continually. The wheat failed entirely; worms, rats, and moles devoured the seed which had been planted, and the only vegetables that gave any results were the pumpkins and melons. The cattle, roaming at large over the island, got into what little corn that grew and ate it up. The cows and sheep perished, owing, as the settlers thought, to the extensive marshes. The Indians killed the pigs, and as starvation pressed upon them the balance of the stock was consumed by the soldiers and the wretched settlers. For a while, on the arrival of relief at St. Augustine or Santa Elena, rations of corn and wine, oil and vinegar were regularly distributed among them, and, as we have seen, pigs were sent

[1] "Memoria," *Col. Doc. Inedit. Indias*, tomo v., p. 544.

to them a second time on the arrival of Avilés in June, 1566.[1] But these soon shared the fate of the other pigs, and as the other garrisons felt the pressure of necessity, the supplies became less frequent. Then the settlers, driven by hunger, hunted the shores for oysters, sea-food, and herbs. What little corn could be obtained was laboriously pounded in a mortar, but the sick were unable to eat it, and some of the settlers died from starvation.

Nor was this the only misfortune which befell them. Juan de la Vandera, who was in charge of the fort and beyond the reach of control, exercised the office of a tyrant and plundered the colonists without mercy. He sold the provisions to his own advantage. When a settler refused him anything that he wished he caused him to be beaten, and when his permission was asked to leave the country and go to Havana, he had the petitioner seized and imprisoned in the fort and condemned to the payment of penalties which enabled him to get possession of his property, and he took from the settlers all of their arms. It was a virtual slavery, and only by trickery and stratagem was it possible to leave the island. One of the exiles relates how he escaped from Santa Elena on the pretence of returning to Spain for more colonists. Four years later, after frequent and useless applications to Avilés for permission to abandon Santa Elena, the inhabitants of the settlement, "ruined, aged, weary, and full of sickness," "maltreated and insulted by the governors," petitioned the King to the number of twenty-three for leave to return to Spain and for a vessel in which to make the voyage. The conditions were still unchanged, and the notary public was an inexperienced boy under the legal age.

At St. Augustine there appear to have been in the neighbourhood of a dozen farmers. The supplies which Arciniega had brought from Spain had profited them

[1] Avilés to Philip II., Jan. 30, 1566, Ruidíaz, *La Florida*, tomo ii., p. 144.

little, for peculation had been rife, and it was said that the officials in charge of the settlement had reloaded them on the very vessels in which they had come and sent them to be sold on their own account in the Windward Islands and elsewhere in the Indies. It is true that the land at St. Augustine was better than at Santa Elena, and the plantings which the settlers had made were more successful. But though stock was distributed to the farmers, as had been done at Santa Elena, it suffered the same fate as elsewhere, for many of the pigs were killed by the Indians, and the balance was given no time for natural increase, being eaten up by the colonists and the soldiery in their extremity. At San Mateo and at San Pedro on Cumberland Island there appear to have been no colonists.[1]

So far as the discovery of mineral wealth was concerned, an equal want of success had attended the conquest. Fourquevaux, it is true, had reported the finding of a gold mine thirty or forty leagues beyond San Mateo, on the authority of one of the captains who had accompanied Avilés; and also the discovery of a mine of azurite of the finest quality.[2] But these stories find no confirmation in any of Menéndez's letters; and as the only expedition made into the gold-bearing region of the country, that of Juan Pardo, occurred subsequent to Fourquevaux's report and was without results, the alleged discoveries may be dismissed as merest rumours. The anticipated pearl fisheries had proved as illusory. As a consequence

[1] Información hecha en Madrid por el Licenciado Gamboa sobre cosas tocantes á la Florida, Madrid, Feb. 4, 1573, MS. Arch. Gen. de Indias, est. 2, caj. 1, leg. 1/27; Instancia á S. M. de Francisco Ruiz en nombre de los vecinos y pobladores de la Florida solicitando cambiar de residencia acompañada de información de testigos, MS., *ibid.*, est. 54, caj. 5, leg. 16; Relación de las cosas que han pasado en la Florida tocantes al servicio de Dios y del Rey. Vinó con carta de Juan Mendez, 6 de Abril, 1584, MS., *ibid.*, est. 54, caj. 5, leg. 16, p. 1.

[2] Advis au Roi par le Prebtre, Nov. 30, 1567, *Dépêches*, p. 305.

trade and commerce were non-existent, and the vast conquest, undertaken at such an expense of lives and money, reduced itself to two or three miserable outposts containing a handful of starving and naked soldiers, stationed in the neighbourhood of the Florida Straits to protect the passage of the treasure fleets and to prevent the descent of foreign powers upon its shore. How utterly inadequate these outposts were for the latter purpose we see by the ease with which Drake sacked the city of St. Augustine but a few years later. It will be recalled that the salary of the Adelantado was to be paid out of the produce of the country without recourse to the King in event of his failure[1] to find it, and that some, at least, of the royal officials in Florida were in the same case,[2] so the anxiety of Avilés on his own account, as well as on theirs, will be easily understood.

The Spanish occupation had led to the discovery of two plants—the sassafras and the nut grass. The deprivation of food to which the soldiers were subjected, the roots and herbs which they were driven to eat, coupled with the drinking of impure water, caused much sickness, which the Spaniards alleviated to a considerable extent by the use of the sassafras, whose virtues they had learned from the French. A decoction of the root was prepared, which was drunk in and out of season, at every meal and even when fasting, the well using it in place of wine. The Florida soldiers who arrived in Spain in 1569 were strong and healthy, which they attributed to the use of the root. Dr. Nicolas Monardes, who wrote at the time a treatise upon the medicinal plants of the West Indies, relates that

"these [Florida] soldiours doeth trust so muche in this woodde, that I beyng one daie emongest many of them, informing my

[1] "Asiento," March 30, 1565, Ruidíaz, *La Florida*, tomo ii., p. 420.

[2] Avilés to Philip II., May 12, 1568, *ibid.*, tomo ii., p. 178.

self of the thynges of this Tree, that moste parte of them tooke out of their pokettes, a good peece of this woodd, and said; Maister, doe you see here the woodde, that euery one of vs doth bryng for to heale vs with all if we do fall sicke, as we haue been there; and thei began to praise so muche, to confirme the meruelous workes of it, with so many examples of them that were there that surely I gaue greate credite vnto it."

The Indians, he says, called it *pauame*, and he informs us, in the curious medical terminology of the period, that it is cold and dry in the second degree, although its bark reaches the third degree; and among its marvellous properties it relieves the liver, drives fevers away, restores the appetite, voids the stone, quiets toothache, cures gout, preserves from pest, and is most serviceable in all cold sicknesses.[1]

The nut grass, a plant resembling the galanga, was described by the Spaniards at the time as having roots which presented the appearance of a string of beads, and the nodules when cut apart were dry and hard as pebbles, black without and white within, and of an aromatic flavour. The Indians crushed the herb into a powder, with which they rubbed their bodies when they bathed, saying it refreshed the skin, and they also used the powder for the stomach-ache. The plant grew plentifully about Santa Elena, and the Spaniards used it for the

[1] Nicolas Monardes, *Historia medicinal de las cosas que se traen de nuestras Indias occidentales, que sirven en medicina*, Sevilla, 1565–1574. The translation given in the text is that of the English version, entitled: *Ioyfvll Nevves ovt of the newe founde worlde* . . . Englished by John Frampton, London, 1577, fol. 47. There is a cut of the tree in Frampton's version on fol. 45b, which is reproduced by De Laet in his *Histoire du Nouveau Monde*, Leide, 1640, p. 127, where he gives an account of its properties. The 2nd edition of the Latin version of Monardes's work is entitled: *Simplicium medicamentorum ex novo orbe delatorum, quorum in medica usus est, historia* . . . Latino . . . donata . . . a Carolo Clusio, Antverpiæ, 1579.

same purpose as did the Indians, besides discovering other virtues which it possessed, and held it in such esteem that all the soldiers carried rosaries of beads made from the roots.[1]

In 1573, a year after the protest of the Santa Elena colonists, Pedro Menéndez Marqués made an extended reconnaissance of the entire coast, from the head of the Florida Keys to Chesapeake Bay. Unfortunately there was no cosmographer in the party, so the report of Marqués was unaccompanied by maps. The original extensive and detailed report which he prepared for the Council of the Indies was given to the cosmographer, Juan López de Velasco, who probably received it after he had completed his *Geografía y Descripción Universal de las Indias*,[2] since his great work gives no details whatever of this discovery. The report was subsequently lost, and we are indebted to the historian Barcia for a brief of the original which escaped a similar fate. The coast was carefully examined and its trend noted. Depths and distances were recorded. Shoals and bars, bays, rivers, and headlands were set down, with conspicuous objects by which the entrance of the harbours could be recognised, and sailing directions were also given. Marqués also appears to have entered the Bay of Santa Maria and explored it for some distance. It is not improbable that he was accompanied in this expedition by the pilot Vincente Gonzalo, on account of his previous familiarity with the coast, for we find Gonzalo again visiting the Chesapeake at a later date. During the course of his expedition Marqués rescued a number of Christian captives from the Indians and brought them back with him to

[1] Barcia, *Ensayo*, Año MDLXVII., p. 131. Mr. Frederick V. Coville, Botanist of the Department of Agriculture, thinks the plant is in all probability the nut grass, *Cyperus rotundus*, which has an aromatic odour, similar to but less pronounced than that of the true Asiatic galanga.

[2] First published at Madrid in 1894 by the learned Don Justo Zaragoza.

Santa Elena. Avilés had in the meantime exerted himself to send missionaries in the place of those who had withdrawn from the province, and on the arrival of Marqués at Santa Elena he found there a number of Franciscan friars who had been sent out to him from Spain.[1]

Pedro Menéndez de Avilés has filled too prominent a place in this part of our history to be dismissed without casting a glance at the few remaining years of his eventful career. On his return to Spain he continued his active employment in naval affairs, his attention being particularly given to the equipment of a fleet directed against the English corsairs and Cimarron negroes,[2] and on the 10th of February, 1574, he was appointed Captain-General of the formidable armada which Philip was forming ostensibly with the view of clearing the western coast and the Flanders channel of pirates, an armada of one hundred and fifty sail and twelve thousand men according to some, of three hundred sail and twenty thousand men according to others.[3] Not on this account did Avilés neglect his Florida interests, for in the early spring of 1573 he obtained a royal licence to send fifty families from the Asturias to Florida, an undertaking he was in haste to put into execution,[4] while his remarkable versatility is shown in his invention of an instrument for

[1] Barcia, *Ensayo*, Año MDLXIII., p. 146. On p. 149 he says nine monks, but note that the two following references mention only six. "Real orden a los officiales de Sevilla que prouean de lo necesario a seis religiosos q̄ uan a la florida." "Real orden al comisario general de s̄ franco que nombre seis religiosos que uayan a la florida." Both dated Madrid, Feb. 23, 1573, MSS. Arch. Gen. de Indias, Seville, est. 154, caj. 1, leg. 18, tomo i., fol. 82.

[2] Vigil, *Noticias*, pp. 31, 177–179.

[3] *Ibid.*, pp. 31, 32; Ruidíaz, *La Florida*, tomo i., pp. ccvi, ccix.

[4] "Real licencia concedida á Pero Menéndez de Avilés para llevar, previa información, cinquenta familias asturianas á la Florida," Madrid, March 3, 1573, Ruidíaz, *ibid.*, tomo ii., p. 373; Avilés to Marqués, Sept. 8, 1574, *ibid.*, tomo ii., pp. 290, 291.

measuring longitude,[1] for which he was conceded a ten-years' patent.

In the midst of these various and engrossing occupations his heart yearned for the white sands and palmetto groves of Florida, brilliant amidst her torrid waters. Almost his last thoughts and last words were for her. September 8, 1574, he wrote to his nephew and lieutenant, Marqués:

"Expressing to His Majesty my discontent at finding myself separated from Florida, he has graciously told me that as often as it is possible to allow me to return he will very gladly do so. And I hope to God he will do so in the spring, for I do not doubt that the affair of Flanders will be arranged this winter. And with that I shall be free to go at once to Florida, not to leave it for the rest of my life; for that is the sum of my longings and happiness. May our Lord permit it, if possible, and if He sees fit."[2]

Whether the armada assembled at Santander was really intended for Flanders, or, as has been supposed,[3] was to attack England, Avilés was not destined to lead it, nor to see his beloved Florida again. Nine days after writing the letter just quoted he died at Santander from an attack of indigestion.[4] He was buried first at Llanes, but his body was transferred in 1591 to the Church of St. Nicholas in his native city of Avilés, where it now reposes in a niche on the Gospel side of the altar, with this inscription:

"Here lies interred the very illustrious cavalier Pedro Mene^z^ de Avilés, native of this town, Adelantado of the Provinces of Florida, Commander of the Holy Cross of La Çarça

[1] Real cédula of Feb. 17, 1573, Pardo, *ibid.*, tomo ii., p. 366.

[2] Avilés to Marqués, Sept. 8, 1574, *ibid.*, tomo ii., p. 288.

[3] Ruidíaz, *La Florida*, tomo i., p. ccix, and see Avilés to Marqués, Sept. 8, 1574, *ibid.*, tomo ii., p. 290.

[4] *Ibid.*, tomo ii., p. 513.

of the Order of Santiago and Cn. Genal of the Ocean Sea and of the Catholic Armada which the Lord Philip II. assembled against England in the year 1574, at Santander, where he died on the 17th of September of the said year being fifty-five years of age." [1]

The only ornament on the tomb is his coat-of-arms, placed above the chest which contains his remains.

The testimony of his companions in arms goes to confirm the statement made by his biographers that Avilés died poor.[2] He left two daughters, Doña Catalina, who married Hernando de Miranda, and after his death Hernando de las Alas; and Doña Maria, who married Diego de Velasco. All of his Florida interests, except the marquisate, were bequeathed to his daughter Catalina, who also inherited his title of Adelantado of Florida, while Pedro Menéndez Marqués was authorised to prosecute the Pánuco conquest. The marquisate was left to his daughter Doña Maria,[3] wife of Diego de Velasco, and her sons, with the singular condition that in the event of male issue the heir, on reaching twenty years of age, was to reside with his wife and household in Florida for a period of ten years, "for my ultimate object and desire is to procure that Florida be settled in perpetuity, that the Holy Gospel be extended and planted in those provinces." The same condition was imposed upon the Pánuco inheritance.[4]

[1] Barcia, *Ensayo*, Año MDLXXIV, p. 151; Ruidíaz, *La Florida*, tomo i., p. ccxxiv, and tomo ii, p. 337, on which he gives a cut of his tomb reproduced from a photograph.

[2] Barcia, *Ensayo*, Año MDLXXIV., p. 151. And see p. 126, note 3 in this volume.

[3] Ruidíaz (*La Florida*, tomo i., p. ccxxvi.) says she was a professed nun at Avila, but the will specifically speaks of her as married at the time to Diego Velasco (*ibid.*, vol. ii., p. 518).

[4] "Testamento del Adelantado Pedro Menéndez de Avilés otorgado en Sanlúcar de Barrameda el 7 de Enero de 1574," *ibid.*, tomo ii., p. 516. Further details will be found in Ruidíaz, who at the end of the second

Avilés was unquestionably a man of unusual talent, enterprise, and courage, of indomitable energy and will, of remarkable self-control and tact. Every emergency was anticipated, every obstacle was surmounted with promptness and dexterity. Fatigue and weariness, hesitation, doubt, perplexity were alike unknown to him. However strange the circumstances in which he found himself he was never at a loss for one moment as to how they should be met. His experience in naval affairs and more particularly in the West Indies exceeded that of any captain of the day. His loyalty to his King and to his religion were without question, "for he considered nothing but the service of God and of his Majesty, without looking to human interests," said one of his soldiers.[1] He could descend to the consideration of the smallest details and order them with practical common-sense while indulging in dreams of the conquest of a continent. He shared with his soldiers their privations, and led them in person in their most dangerous undertakings. For their sakes he could receive an insult with a bow, and pawn his own clothes. As a result "he was much loved, feared, prized, and respected."[2]

There is but one blot on his fame, that of the Matanzas massacre, nor is the shame of it palliated when it is ascribed not to fanaticism or bigotry, but to the reasons assigned by his master,—the desire not to risk the lives of his own people. If this was, indeed, his motive, it was a worthy one. But when the genius and resourcefulness of Avilés are considered it is reasonable to believe that had he but sought it some other expedient would have presented itself rather than the bloody one to which he

volume (p. 627) gives a list of the Adelantados of Florida. Barcia in his *Ensayo* gives a plate (facing p. 1) of the "Casa de los Adelantados de la Florida," and Vigil in his *Noticias* gives a variety of genealogical data.

[1] Grauiel Justiniano, Ruidíaz, *La Florida*, tomo ii., p. 622.

[2] Merás in *ibid.*, tomo i., p. 131.

resorted. But we must not allow our judgment to be so outraged by this cold-blooded murder as to blind us to his signal merits, and Pedro Menéndez de Avilés surely deserves to take rank among the greatest and most gifted of the early discoverers and conquerors of the New World.

APPENDIX A

REGISTERED GOLD AND SILVER IMPORTED INTO SPAIN FROM THE WEST INDIES, 1560–1569

ROYAL REVENUES FROM THE INDIES.—In 1561 the royal revenues from the Indies are said to have averaged, one year with another, 600,000 ducats. ("Memoria de las riendas y patrimonio del rey de Españia [*sic*] dell año 1561." Brit. Mus. Add. MSS., *Cotton Vesp. C.*, vii., fol. 216.) In 1564 the royal revenues from the Indies were 225 "cuentos" (Brit. Mus. Add. MSS. *Eg.*, 1873, fol. 225); that is to say, 225,-000,000 maravedis. (See Relación Breue, etc., Brit. Mus. Add. MSS., 8691, fol. 36b, which says: "Contados al uso, que se asientan todos en los libros Reales, que es a cuentos, y marauedis. Cada cuento son diez uezes cien mil marauedis.") In 1564 a ducat was still approximately 350 maravedis, so that we have about 600,000 ducats for the total revenue.

The following table shows the royal revenue from Mexico for the years 1560–69 inclusive. So far as can be determined from the data here given Mexico paid a minimum of about two-fifths of the total revenue from the Indies.

1560—268,702 pesos	1565—424,409 pesos
1561—252,937 "	1566—480,597 "
1562—284,457 "	1567—517,394 "
1563—315,218 "	1568—931,463 "
1564—333,209 "	1569—338,737 "

(Relación de la Plata Reales Oro I oias que se a lleuado a su magestad desta nueua españa a los Reinos de Castilla desde el año de mil y quinientos y veinte dos . . . hasta el año presente de mil y quiniētos y nouenta y nueue. Brit. Mus. Add. MSS., 13,964, fol. 196.)

GOLD AND SILVER IMPORTED INTO SPAIN.—Alava, writing from Lyons, July 22, 1564, reports that the banks "tienen abisso que han llegado a seuilla seis nabios y esperan otros quatro que la Voz es que traen para registrar de V. Md. y particulares Vn million y docientos mil escudos y callado dos milliones mas" (MS. Arch. Nat., Paris, K, 1502 (10), fol. 2b). Fourquevaux writes to the King, Sept. 17, 1566, that the fleet from the Indies, consisting of thirty-seven ships, has probably arrived at San Lucar "et porte quatre millions XLVII mil escuz d'or" (*Dépêches*, p. 126), which is confirmed by a letter of Saint Sulpice to the King of October 17th of the same year, in which he says: "La flotte des Indes arrivée a Seville porte quatre millions et demy d'or ou d'argent sans le secret, et porte une grande richesse de perles, pierreries et drogues pour taingdre en cramoisy, et autres choses" (*Dépêches*, p. 133). Writing Aug. 2, 1567, to the King, Fourquevaux says that Menéndez brings the report of the Governor of Cuba that the fleet from New Spain carries two millions of gold (*Dépêches*, p. 242). June 25, 1568, Fourquevaux again writes the King that "la flotte du Peru est arrivée à Seville; et ne s'y parle plus de peste, puisqu'ilz ont ce qu'ilz attendoient: ce sont trois millions et demy d'or, desquelz l'un million est por le Roy Catholique. On parle de trois esmeraudes de grande valleur que lad. flotte a portée, dont l'une est si grande et belle pezant XXVI caratz, qu'on ne luy scait mectre pris. Autre flotte attendant de la Neufve Espagne par tout juillet; laquelle porte pour deux millions et demy d'or en argent et peu d'or" (*Dépêches*, p. 365). This gives a total of 15,247,000 ducats for the four years specified imported for the King and private individuals, two millions of which were smuggled.

Excluding the smuggled gold we have an average for the four years of about 3,312,000 ducats a year; and if we take this as an average of the entire amount annually imported, exclusive of the smuggled gold, which necessarily cannot be estimated, we have the enormous importation for the ten years of thirty-three millions of ducats. How fallacious all such estimates as the above are liable to be is best realised by comparing the two statements quoted in the text, and written within a very few years of each other and of the period of which they treat. Moncada, covering the earlier years, and therefore those of less development of the mines, gives for about the same extent of time five hundred millions more revenue than Navarette!

APPENDIX B

THE "RIVIÈRE DE MAI"

Ribaut, in "The true and last discoverie," chap. 3 (reprinted in the *Hist. Col. of Louisiana and Florida*, by B. F. French, 2nd series, "Historical Memoirs and Narratives," p. 179), places the "Rivière de Mai" in 30 degrees, and this may very well have been the river referred to by Chantone in his correspondence, and in the instructions of Manrique de Rojas under its Spanish name of "Ribera de las Corrientes" in 30 degrees. (Chantone to Philip II., Jan. 24, 1563, MS. Arch. Nat., Paris, K, 1500 (43), and Relación e información de los franceses que han ido a poblar en la costa de la Florida. San Cristóbal de la Habana, 9 de Julio de 1564, MS. Arch. Gen. de Indias, Seville, est. 54, caj. 1, leg. 15, p. 5.)

When Manrique visited the locality he found that three vessels loaded with Christians had been there recently (see p. 46 in this volume), and it is probable that these were Ribaut's fleet of two ships and a large sloop, for the two smaller boats intended for the shallow Florida waters were carried aboard the large vessel while at sea (*Relación e información*, MS., pp. 10, 18, 19). Hawkins, who visited Laudonnière's settlement on the River of May in 1564, found the river "standing in 30 degrees and better." ("The voyage made by M. John Hawkins Esquire . . . to the coast of Guinea, and the Indies of Noua Hispania, begun in An. Dom. 1564," *Hakluyt*, Edinburgh, 1889, vol. iv., p. 240.)

Rojomonte, one of the Frenchmen who escaped from Laudonnière's colony, and was captured by the Spaniards, mentions the river in his deposition as: "La ribera de mayo que esta segun dizen en treynta y un grados de altura." (Noticia de la población que habian hecho los Franceses á la Florida, 1564. MS. Arch. Gen. de Indias, Seville, Patronato, est. 1, caj. 1, leg. 1/19, ramo 4, p. 1.) Meleneche, another Frenchman, who also escaped from Fort Caroline and was captured by the Spaniards, says in his deposition that Laudonnière's fleet "baxaron a veinte y nueve y medio, donde hallaron un rio que tiene de ancho por la boca un tiro de verso," and he describes the river as "entrando por la tierra al Sudueste, poco mas o menos," a description which can only apply to the St. John's. ("Relación del suceso de la Armada Francesa que fue a poblar la tierra de la Florida" in "Carta escrita al Rey por Juan Rodriguez de Noriega, Sevilla, á 29 de Marzo de 1565." MS. Direc. de Hidrog., Madrid, *Col. Navarrete*, tomo 14, Doc. No. 33, fols. 3b and 5b.)

Menéndez, in his "Carta al Rey, 15 de Octubre de 1565" (Ruidíaz, *La Florida*, tomo ii., p. 92), says: "El rio que esta en el fuerte de Sant Mateo, que tomamos a los franceses [*i. e.*, Fort Caroline], va sesenta leguas por la tierra dentro, y no se llegó al cabo dél la buelta del Sudueste, á salir casi á la baia de Juan Ponce"; and in the same letter, p. 93, he says: "El [puerto] del fuerte de Sant Mateo que ganamos está en treynta y un quarto; porque los franceses y sus pilotos se engañavan, é yo he hecho tomar el sol en tierra y averiguarlo." This and the similar description given by Meleneche appear to establish the identity of the "Rivière de Mai" with the St. John's beyond a doubt.

OTHER IDENTIFICATIONS.—Jean de Laet, in his *Histoire du Nouveau Monde*, Leyde, 1640, liv. iv., chap. xvii., p. 129, identifies it with the River of St. Augustine.

The Altamaha: Guillaume De l'Isle, in his "Carte et Cours du Mississipi . . ." Paris . . . 1718, identifies it with the "Riviere des Cavuitas," the Altamaha, as does also Io. Bapt. Homann in his map: "Amplissima regionis Mississipi seu Provinciae Ludovicianae . . ." (1763).

Mr. George F. Becker, in a carefully prepared note to his "Reconnaissance of the Gold Fields of the Southern Appalachians," p. 8 (Extract from the *Sixteenth Annual Report, U. S. Geological Survey*, 1894–95, Part II.), argues that the "Rivière de Mai" is the Altamaha, because "Lemoyne's map shows it as the largest river of the South, its main branch extending to the north-west into the Montes Apalatci, and placed much farther north than one would expect to find the St. John's. Laudonnière also speaks of the Mai as one of the three great rivers rising in the Appalachian Mountains and as being navigable for small boats from the mountains to the sea." Mr. Becker cites the De l'Isle map above referred to in which the mouth of the "Caouitas or May . . . is shown at a distance north of St. Augustine almost exactly corresponding to the real position of the Altamaha"; he also cites "A new and accurate map of the province of Georgia in North America" of 1760 (?) (No. 92, *Col. of American Maps made in England*, Lib. U. S. Geological Survey), in which the river is labelled, "Formerly river of May, now Altamaha or St. George's River."

Mr. Becker's error lies in placing too great confidence in Le Moyne's map, which can be accurate only in respect to the country which the French actually explored, the balance being put in from Indian reports imperfectly understood, if not copied from other and equally unreliable sources. The French at no time went farther up the river than Lake George. They ascended no northerly arm to the mountains, and Laudonnière may well have thought that in a vague Indian account of the Altamaha he recognised a description of a northerly branch of the River of May. The later maps have no force, because they merely copied the error made by Mercator in his map of 1606 (see Appendix J, Maps of the French Colonies in Florida and South Carolina), and naturally identified his River of May with the Altamaha, when the course of the latter became known. Moreover, it has already been shown that Menéndez and Meleneche both state that the River of May flowed southwest.

The first map subsequent to that of Le Moyne to show the St. John's flowing southward is "A Map of the West Indies or the Islands of America in the South Sea; with ye adjacent

Countries," etc., by Herman Moll, Geographer, London, for Thos. Bowles and John Bowles. It is dated 1710 by the British Museum and 1715 (?) by P. Lee Phillips in his *A List of Maps of America*, Washington, 1901. But see Brinton, *Notes on the Floridian Peninsula*, p. 85.

IDENTIFIED WITH THE ST. MARY'S.—N. Bellin, in "Carte des costes de la Floride Française," in Charlevoix, *Hist. de la Nouvelle France*, Paris, 1744, tome i., between pp. 24, 25. François-Xavier Martin, in his *Hist. of Louisiana* (1st edit., 1827), New Orleans, 1882, chap. 1, p. 39. John W. Monette, in his *Hist. of the Valley of the Mississippi* (New York, 1846), vol. i., p. 67 and p. 69, note. J. G. Kohl, "A History of the Discovery of the East Coast of North America," Portland, 1869, vol. i., pp. 425, 436 (*Col. Maine Hist. Soc.*, 2nd series).

The general consensus of modern opinion, however, identifies the "Rivière de Mai" with the St. John's. *Descripción Historica . . . de la Florida*, MS. Anonymous, undated (end of 18th century?), fol. 24b, note. In the possession of the writer. Holmes's *Annals*, London, 1813, vol. i., p. 79, note 3, and p. 80, note 1. *Memoir of Florida*, by William Darby, Philadelphia, 1821, p. 47. *Historical Collections of South Carolina*, by B. R. Carroll, New York, 1836, vol. i., pp. xxxiii. and xxxiv. *The Territory of Florida*, by John Lee Williams, New York, 1837, p. 170. *History of Georgia*, by William B. Stevens, New York, 1847, vol. i., pp. 32, 33, 37. *History of the United States*, by George Bancroft (15th edit.), Boston, 1855, vol. i., p. 61. "Map of Florida, 1565," in the *History of St. Augustine*, by George R. Fairbanks, New York, 1858, between pp. 14, 15, and text on p. 16. This map is reproduced by John Gilmary Shea in "Ancient Florida," in *Narr. and Crit. Hist. Am.*, New York, 1886, vol. ii., p. 264. *History of Florida*, by George R. Fairbanks, Philadelphia, 1871, p. 93. *Historical Collections of Louisiana and Florida*, by B. F. French, 2nd series. "Historical Memoirs and Narratives," New York, 1875, p. 170, note. "Carte de la Floride Française (1562, 1568)," in *Histoire de la Floride Française*, par Paul Gaffarel, Paris, 1875. *History of Hernando de Soto and Florida*, by Barnard Shipp, Philadelphia, 1881, p. 499, note. *The Catholic Church in Colonial Days*, by John Gilmary Shea, New York, 1886, p. 134. *The Pioneers of France in the New World*, by Francis Parkman, Boston, 1893, p. 38, and in the map "Florida 1565," between pp. 96, 97. *Memoirs of Florida*, by Roland H. Rerick, edited by Francis P. Fleming, Atlanta, Ga., 1902, p. 39, note.

Laudonnière, in 1564, on the second French expedition, established Fort Caroline on the "Rivière de Mai" (see p. 57 in this volume). From this he was driven out by Menéndez de Avilés, who changed the name of the fort to that of San Mateo, which name was in consequence given to the river; and the Spanish settlement of San Mateo, which grew up on the right bank of the river, near its mouth, has retained its name down through the first quarter of the nineteenth century. See the following maps: "East Florida, from Surveys made since the last Peace, adapted to Dr. Stork's History of that Country," by Thomas Jefferys, Geographer to the King, in *A Description of Florida*, by William Stork, 3rd edit., London, 1769. "A New Map of the British Colonies in North America," by John Andrews, London, 1777. "The West Indies," Jno. Cary, London, 1783. "The West Indies," G. G. and J. Robinson, London, 1799. "Map of Florida," published by Wm. Darby, 1821, in his *Memoir of the Geography and Natural and Civil History of Florida*, Philadelphia, 1821. Bernard Romans tells us that the Indians called the St. John's River the Ylacco, a name which conveys an indecent meaning, which he nowhere explains. *A concise Natural History of East and West Florida*, New York, 1775, vol. i., pp. 1, 259–273. Daniel G. Brinton, in his *Floridian Peninsula*, p. 154, note 1, gives a list of the various names of the St. John's River, both English, Spanish, and native.

APPENDIX C

THE PILLAR SET UP BY RIBAUT

Hist. Notable, Basanier, p. 8; *Hak.*, vol. ii., p. 417. Chantone to Philip II., Jan. 24, 1563, MS. Arch. Nat., Paris, K, 1500 (43).

The Frenchman Rufin, left at Port Royal by the small force Ribaut had settled at Charlesfort, thus describes the pillar: "El qual dicho mojon es de piedra blanca é de alto y grueso como un hombre poco más ó menos y en lo alto del esta debuxado un escudo con una corona ençima y dentro del tres flores de lis é mas abajo una IR . . . e mas abajo quatro numeros de guarismo que dizen 1561." Relación e información de los franceses que han ido a poblar en la costa de la Florida, 1564, MS. Arch. Gen. de Indias, Seville, est. 54, caj. 1, leg. 15, p. 27. Le Moyne, in Plate VIII. of his "Indorum Floridam provinciam inhabitantium eicones," forming part of the De Bry *Brevis Narratio*, Frankforti ad Moenum, 1591, shows a column in substantial accordance with the above description, *i. e.*, a crown with the coat of arms, and below them an oval, which probably contained the cypher, which he does not give. Neither does he give the inscribed name and date. The pillars were brought out from France ready to set up. *Relación e información de los franceses*, etc., p. 21.

APPENDIX D

THE RIVERS BETWEEN THE "RIVIÈRE DE MAI" AND PORT ROYAL

There are three independent sources from which we learn the names of the rivers visited or seen by Ribaut in his first expedition along the Florida coast. The first is Ribaut's *The true and last discoverie of Florida*, published in 1563; the second is Laudonnière, in his *Histoire Notable*, published in 1586, and the third is Le Moyne's map in De Bry's *Brevis Narratio*, published in 1591. From two of these accounts we also learn the order in which the rivers were discovered. Laudonnière accompanied Ribaut on this first expedition, of which he gives a detailed account. Ribaut, in addition to his relation, made "maps or sea-cards," which appear to have formed part of it. ("The true and last discoverie of Florida," reprint in *Hist. Col. Louisiana and Florida*, by B. F. French, 2nd series, "Historical Memoirs and Narratives," p. 183.) Le Moyne accompanied Laudonnière on the second expedition and subsequently prepared the only contemporary map which we now have of the country colonised by the French. All three authorities agree in the names of several of the rivers, and two of them in the order in which they were visited; but disagree as to the number of them between the "Rivière de Mai" and Port Royal. Thus there are in all fifteen different names of rivers, of which Le Moyne gives fourteen, Laudonnière twelve, and Ribaut ten. Ribaut omits two rivers given by Laudonnière, and places another north of Port Royal which Laudonnière has placed to the south of it. Ribaut also omits five of Le Moyne's rivers. Laudonnière omits three of Le Moyne's rivers, but substitutes another of a different name in place of the one last omitted.

The following table best illustrates the superficial agreement, but real confusion, that exists in the list of names given by the three authorities mentioned:

Le Moyne[1]	Laudonnière	Ribaut
1. Maij	1. May	1. May
2. Sarvauahi	———	———
3. Aij	———	———
4. Sequana	2. Seine	2. Seine
5. Axona Iracana	3. Somme	3. Somme
6. Ligeris	4. Loire	4. Loire
7. Charenta	5. Charente	5. Charnet
8. Garumna	6. Garonne	6. Caro
9. Gironda	7. Gironde	———
10. Bellum	8. Belle	7. Belle
11. Magnum	9. Grande	8. Grande
12. S. Helenæ	———	———
———	10. Belle a veoir	———
13. Portus Regalis	11. Port Royale	9. Port Royale
———	———	10. Belle voir
14. Humilde	12. Basse	———

[1] In the list of these rivers given by Le Moyne in Plates III., IV., and V. of his *Eicones* he omits 2 and 3; 11 is called "Grandis," 12 "The River Jordan," after which comes the "Conspectu bellum," and then "Port Royal."

Questions of the following nature at once suggest themselves: Is the "Seine" of Laudonnière and Ribaut the same river as the "Sequana" of Le Moyne, or was the name given by them to one or the other of Le Moyne's second and third rivers? If the latter be the case the relation of the other rivers is altered. Was Ribaut right as to the location of the "Belle voir," or was Laudonnière? Is "S. Helenæ" Le Moyne's name for Laudonnière's "Belle a veoir"? And if so, must it be accepted as against Ribaut, although Ribaut's account was written within a few months of his return and the others twenty-four and twenty-nine years after? Why did Ribaut, commander and map-maker of the expedition, omit the "Gironde"? Until these and similar questions can be answered it seems futile to attempt any identification of these names with rivers known to us to-day in that region. Charlevoix says of these various names: "On reconnut dans la suite qu'il avoit pris plusieurs anses pour des embouchures de Rivières" (*Hist. de la Nouvelle France*, Paris, 1744, p. 25). And Barcia also makes the same statement (*Ensayo Cronologico*, Año MDLXII., p. 44).

The attempt at identification has been made by various historians and map-makers, as follows:

The Seine corresponds, perhaps, to the St. Mary's. Holmes's *Annals*, London, 1813, vol. i., p. 80, note 1; *Hist. Col. South Carolina*, by B. R. Carroll, New York, 1836, vol. i., p. 567; *Hist. of Georgia*, by William B. Stevens, New York, 1847, vol. i., p. 33; *Hist. Col. of Louisiana and Florida*, by B. F. French, New York, 1875, 2nd series, "Historical Memoirs and Narratives," p. 184, note; *Hist. of Hernando de Soto and Florida*, by Barnard Shipp, Philadelphia, 1881, p. 499, note; *Pioneers of France in the New World*, by Francis Parkman, Boston, 1893, p. 39.

The Seine is identified with the river named by the Indians Tacatacuru in: Gourgues, 1567, *Reprise de la Floride*, Larroque, Bordeaux, 1867, p. 47; Guillaume De l'Isle, "Carte et Cours du Mississipi . . ." Paris . . . 1718; Io. Bapt. Homann, "Amplissima regionis Mississipi seu Provinciæ Ludovicianæ . . ." (1763). Shipp, *De Soto*, 1881, p. 571, and John Gilmary Shea, in his "Ancient Florida," in *Narr. and Crit. Hist. Am.*, vol. ii. (1886), p. 280, identify the Tacatacuru with the St. Mary's.

To the Altamaha: N. Bellin, "Carte des costes de la Floride Française," 1744, in Charlevoix, *Hist. de la Nouvelle France*, 1744, tome i., between pp. 24, 25; Tamizey de Larroque, *La Reprise de la Floride*, Bordeaux, 1867, p. 47, note; "Carte de la Floride Française (1562, 1568)," in Gaffarel, *Hist. de la Floride Française*, Paris, 1875.

The Somme corresponds, perhaps, to the Satilla: Holmes's *Annals*, vol. i., p. 80, note 1; Carroll, *ibid.*, p. xxxiv., note; Stevens, *ibid.*, vol. i., p. 33; French, *ibid.*, p. 182, "and Jykill or St. Andrew's Sound"; Gaffarel's map, *ibid.*; Shipp, *ibid.*, p. 499, note.

To the St. Mary's: *Hist. of St. Augustine*, by George R. Fairbanks, New York, 1858, p. 103.

The Somme is identified with the river named by the Indians the Alimacany: Gourgues, 1567, *Reprise de la Floride*, Larroque, Bordeaux, 1867, p. 48; Shipp, *De Soto*, 1881, p. 571, note; Laudonnière, on the other hand, says the Somme was the river "which the Sauages call Iracana" ("A Notable History," in *Hakluyt*, Edinburgh, 1889, vol. ii., p. 502, and *Basanier*, p. 93), and Larroque identifies "L'Iracana des Espagnoles" with the Alimacany (*Reprise de la Floride*, p. 48, note). From this it appears to have had two Indian names, for Larroque's "des Espagnoles" is merely a slip of the pen. Gatschet "The Timucua Language," in *Proceedings of the American Philosophical Society*, vol. xviii., p. 500, says the Iracana, "also called Salinacana," was probably in Georgia.

The Loire corresponds, perhaps, to the Savannah: Holmes's *Annals*, vol. i., p. 80, note 1.

To the Altamaha: Carroll, *ibid.*, p. 567; Stevens, *ibid.*, vol. i., p. 33; French, *ibid.*, p. 184, note; Shipp, *ibid.*, p. 499, note.

To the Sapello: Gaffarel's map, *ibid.*, 1875.

The Charente corresponds, perhaps, to the Newport: Holmes's *Annals*, vol. i., p. 80; Carroll, *ibid.*, p. xxxiv., note; Stevens, *ibid.*, vol. i., p. 33; French, *ibid.*, p 184, note; Shipp, *ibid.*, p. 499, note.

To the Ogeechee: N. Bellin's map, *ibid.*, 1744; Gaffarel's map, *ibid.*, 1875.

The Garonne corresponds, perhaps, to the Ogeechee: Holmes's *Annals*, vol. i., p. 80, note 1; Carroll, *ibid.*, p. xxxiv., note; French, *ibid.*, p. 184, note; Shipp, *ibid.*, p. 499, note.

To the Savannah: Gaffarel's map, 1875.

To St. Catherine's Inlet: Stevens, *ibid.*, vol. i., p. 33.

The Gironde corresponds, perhaps, to the Savannah: Holmes's *Annals*, vol. i., p. 80, note 1; Carroll, *ibid.*, p. xxxiv., note; French, *ibid.*, p. 184, note; Shipp, *ibid.*, p. 499, note.

To the Ogeechee: Stevens, *ibid.*, vol. i., p. 33.

To the Santa Helena (?): Gaffarel's map, *ibid.*, 1875.

To the "Riviere des Chaouanes" or Edisto: Guillaume De l'Isle's map, *ibid.*, 1718; Io. Bapt. Homann's map, *ibid.*, 1763.

The Belle corresponds, perhaps, to the May in South Carolina: Holmes's *Annals*, vol. i., p. 80, note 1; Carroll, *ibid.*, p. xxxiv., note; French, *ibid.*, p. 184, note.

To the South Edisto (?): Gaffarel's map, *ibid.*, 1875.

Laudonnière, in 1564, looking from the top of a bluff near the mouth of the "Rivière de Mai" (the St. John's), says: "And more than sixe leagues off, neere the Riuer Belle, a man may behold the medowes diuided asunder into Iles and Islets enterlacing one another" ("A Notable Historie," in *Hakluyt*, vol. ii., p. 450, *Basanier*, p. 41). The position of the Belle in the other relations and in Le Moyne's map is quite irreconcilable with this statement.

The Grande corresponds perhaps, to the Broad River: Holmes's *Annals* vol. i. p. 80, note 1; Carroll, *ibid.*, p. xxxiv., note; Johnson, quoted by Carroll, *ibid.*, p. xxxvii., note; French, *ibid.*, p. 184, note; Shipp, *ibid.*, p. 499 note. Le Moyne places the S. Helenæ, and Laudonnière the Belle a veoir, between the Grande and Port Royal, which is quite inconsistent with the theory that the Grande is the Broad River. Only in Ribaut, *The true and last discoverie*, is the Grande immediately followed by Port Royal.

To the Edisto: François-Xavier Martin, *ibid.*, 1882, chap. i., p. 39.

To the Savannah: Stevens, *ibid.*, vol. i., p. 33.

The Belle a veoir is probably the May in South Carolina: Shipp, *ibid.*, p. 499, note.

The Basse is probably the Edisto of the English: Holmes's *Annals*, vol. i., p. 411.

The Libourne is identified with Skull Creek: Parkman, *ibid.*, p. 39.

APPENDIX E

PORT ROYAL

DESCRIPTION OF PORT ROYAL.—Its entrance is three French leagues wide (*Hist. Notable*, Basanier, pp. 11, 12; *Hak.*, vol. ii., p. 421. Le Moyne's "Eicones" in De Bry's *Brevis Narratio*, Plate V.). It is divided into two arms (Basanier, Le Moyne, Plate V.). The Relación e información de los franceses que han ido a poblar en la costa de la Florida, San Cristóbal de la Habana, 9 de Julio de 1564 (MS. Arch. Gen. de Indias, Seville, est. 54, caj. 1., leg. 15, p. 16), describes it as having "dos bocas de puertos que estan juntos una con otra," and as the fifth harbour visited by Manrique de Rojas after leaving the "Rio de Sancta Elena" in 32 degrees and sailing north, and again as "un puerto grande de dos," (*ibid.*, p. 26). One arm extends to the north (Basanier, Le Moyne), nearly ten or twelve leagues up into the country ("The true and last discoverie of Florida by Captain John Ribaut," reprint in *Hist. Col. Louisiana and Florida*, by B. F. French, 2nd series, "Historical Memoirs and Narratives," 1527–1702, p. 185). The other branch extends west for twelve leagues and runs into the sea. The two arms are two leagues wide, with an island in the centre having its point towards the great river's mouth (*Hist. Notable*, Basanier, pp. 12, 13; *Hak.*, vol. ii., pp. 421, 422; Le Moyne, *ibid.*, Plate V., and map).

There is a discrepancy between the statements of Laudonnière and Ribaut in respect to the distance sailed up these arms. Laudonnière says that Ribaut sailed twelve leagues up the *western* arm, and then returned to his ships, and the next day sailed three leagues west and discovered the island where the pillar was set up (*Hak.*, vol. ii., pp. 422, 423). Ribaut, as above noted, says he went up the *northern* arm ten or twelve leagues.

The western arm has an affluent from the east (*Hist. Notable*, Basanier, pp. 12, 13; *Hak.*, vol. ii., p. 422; Le Moyne, map), which Le Moyne shows as uniting the western and eastern branches.

Le Moyne appears to have derived all of the data for the legend of Plate V. from the *Histoire Notable*, of which it is almost a translation, and Port Royal, as shown on his map, is in agreement with this description, and Le Moyne is therefore of no value in determining whether Ribaut or Laudonnière is correct in this particular.

The fort built by Ribaut was situated "sobre un braço de un rrio que esta en un puerto grande de dos que estan junto a la banda del sur" of the harbour in 32° 20′, where Manrique de Rojas anchored, from which it was but three leagues distant "por el rrio arriba sin salir a la mar," where it was found (*Relación e información de los franceses*, pp. 17, 21, 26, 27).

Its Location.—Port Royal is in 32 degrees (Chantone to Philip II., Jan. 24, 1563, MS. Arch. Nat., Paris, K, 1500 [43]; Instructions to Manrique, *Relación e información de los franceses*, p. 5, and the French observations in Rufin's deposition, *ibid.*, p. 21). But it was not found there by Manrique, who visited a harbour in 32 degrees (*ibid.*, pp. 10, 11). It is in 32 degrees and 15 minutes (Observations of Ribaut's Spanish pilot in Rufin's deposition, *ibid.*, p. 21). Manrique finds it a little south of a port in 32 degrees and 20 minutes (*ibid.*, pp. 26, 27).

The Coast to the South of Port Royal.—One league to the south of Port Royal, that is to say, of the harbour where Manrique found the pillar, are (*a*) "dos puertos . . . junto de uno." One league from (*a*) is (*b*) "otro puerto . . . que tiene dos rrios." Two leagues from (*b*) is (*c*) "otro puerto." —[1] leagues from (*c*) is (*d*) "otro puerto." Three or four leagues from (*d*) is Manrique's Santa Elena in 32 degrees. (*Relación e información de los franceses*, *passim.*)

THE COAST TO THE NORTH OF PORT ROYAL.—Two or three leagues to the north of Port Royal, that is to say, of the harbour where Manrique found the pillar, is a harbour in 32° 20′, which has "un rrio que esta sobre la vanda del norueste" (*ibid.*).

CONCLUSION.—The latitude of Port Royal Sound is 32° 15′, which corresponds accurately to that observed by Ribaut's Spanish or Portuguese pilot, *i. e.*, 32¼°, as reported by Rufin. The latitude of Fripp's Inlet to the north-east is 32° 20′, which corresponds accurately with that observed by Manrique, *i. e.*, "treinta y dos y un tercio." Fripp's Inlet has a small creek, unnamed in the Coast Survey Chart, near its mouth on the south side, also a stream on the north-west bank, not far from its mouth, and Port Royal Sound can be reached by going up Story River in a small boat, without going to sea; all of which agrees very closely with Manrique's description of his harbour. It is also to be noted that Port Royal, *i. e.*, where the pillar was found, was unquestionably beyond the harbour in 32 degrees where Manrique first entered. Too much stress must not be laid upon the coincidence of the latitudes, as observed by Manrique, with those determined by the Coast Survey, as, in view of the imperfect means by which the observations were made at that time, it may be entirely fortuitous. The correspondence of the harbours to the south of Port Royal, *i. e.*, Tybee Roads, Wassaw Sound, Ossaba Sound, and so on, to the harbours visited by Manrique prior to reaching Port Royal, where he found the pillar, is only a very general one and is, perhaps, rather forced.

In direct conflict with this identification of Ribaut's Port Royal with the present harbour of the same name is the statement made by Menéndez in his letter to Philip II. of October 15, 1565, before he had visited the locality. Writing from St. Augustine, Florida, he says: "Y para el Maio convendra que . . . yr á poblar á Santa Elena, que está cinquenta leguas de aquí, y en tres leguas tiene tres puertos y rios, y el mayor

[1] The distance is not given in the manuscript.

tiene seys brazas de agua y el otro quatro puertos admirables; y el que nos llamamos Santa Elena, que es el tercero donde los franceses estaban, es muy ruin, y todos tres se navegan por dentro del uno al otro" (Ruidíaz, *La Florida*, tomo ii., p. 94). This seems to indicate Santa Helena Sound as that of the French settlement.

Port Royal has been identified with the Edisto (*i. e.*, the South Edisto) by J. Oldmixton, "History of Carolina" (London, 1708, cap. i., reprinted in *Hist. Col. South Carolina* by B. R. Carroll, vol. ii., p. 394), where he calls it "The Albemarle River." Charlevoix, *Hist. de la Nouvelle France*, Paris, 1744, tome i., livre i., p. 25. N. Bellin, "Carte des costes de la Floride Françoise . . ." in Charlevoix, *ibid.*, between pp. 24, 25. Dr. Hewit, "History of the Rise and Progress of the Colonies of South Carolina and Georgia" (London, 1779, cap. i. reprinted in *Hist. Col. South Carolina and Georgia* by B. R. Carroll, vol. i., p. 23), calls it the "Albemarle River." Geo. Chalmers "Political Annals of the United Colonies, Carolina" (printed in London, 1780, reprinted in *Hist. Col. South Carolina* by B. R. Carroll, vol. ii., p. 275), makes it the Edisto. John W. Monette (*Hist. of the Valley of the Mississippi River*, New York, 1846, vol. i., p. 67) says it was "above the St. Helena Sound, south of the Combahee River." Dr. Belknap identifies it with the St. John's (cited by B. R. Carroll in *Hist. Col. South Carolina*, vol. i., p. xxxvi., note).

Modern writers are generally agreed to place it at Port Royal Sound, South Carolina. Brigstock, who travelled through that region in 1653 (and not in 1623, as erroneously stated by French in his note to Ribaut's "The true and last discoverie," in *Hist. Col. Louisiana and Florida*, 2nd series, "Historical Memoirs and Narratives," p. 184), is cited to this effect by French (*ibid.*). Holmes's *Annals*, London, 1813, vol. i., p. 80, note 1. Dr. Holmes, according to Carroll (*Hist. Col. S. C.*, vol. i., p. xxxvi.), addressed several interrogations to his friends in Beaufort, South Carolina, on the subject of the situation of Charlesfort. *Memoir of Florida*, by William Darby, Philadelphia, 1821, pp. 47, 48. *History of Louisiana*, by François-Xavier Martin (first edition, 1827), New Orleans, 1882, p. 39. *Historical Collection of South Carolina*, by B. R. Carroll, New York, 1836, vol. i., pp. xxxiv., xxxvi. Mr. Carroll personally conducted investigations to determine the site of Charlesfort, and a search was made to find the pillar erected by Ribaut, which we now know had been removed by the Spaniards. On page xxxvii. he relates a tradition of the South Carolina Indians in West Georgia, where they had been compelled to retire by the influx of the whites, that "the first place at which they ever saw the whites, was at Coosawhatchie, in South Carolina," which is the principal stream that flows into the Broad River, "and was no doubt among the first that were explored by Ribault's men."

Bancroft, in his *History of the United States* (15th edit., Boston, 1855, vol. i., cap. 2, p. 61), referring to Laudonnière's account, says: "The description is sufficiently minute and accurate; removing all doubt" as to its not being Port Royal Sound, South Carolina. *History of St. Augustine*, by George R. Fairbanks, New York, 1858, p. 15. J. G. Kohl, "A History of the Discovery of the East Coast of North America," Portland, 1869, vol. i., p. 427 (*Col. Maine Hist. Soc.*, 2nd series). *History of Florida*, by George R. Fairbanks, Philadelphia, 1871, p. 94. *Historical Collection of Louisiana and Florida*, by B. F. French, 2nd series, "Historical Memoirs and Narratives," New York, 1875, p. 184, note. *History of Hernando de Soto and Florida*, by Barnard Shipp, Philadelphia, 1881, p. 499, note. *The Catholic Church in Colonial Days*, by John Gilmary Shea, New York, 1886, p. 134, and in his "Ancient Florida," in *Narr. and Crit. Hist. Am.*, New York, 1886, vol. ii., p. 260, where it is identified with Villafañe's Santa Elena. *Pioneers of France in the New World*, by Francis Parkman, Boston, 1893, p. 39.

APPENDIX F

CHARLESFORT

Ribaut, in "The true and last discoverie" (reprint in *Hist. Col. Louisiana and Florida*, by B. F. French, 2nd series, "Hist.

Memoirs and Narratives," p. 188), says Charlesfort was situated "on the north side of an island . . . upon a river, which we called Chenonceau." Laudonnière writes, "ayant navigué dans la grande rivière du costé du septentrion [that is, having ascended the northerly arm of the Port Royal], en costoyant une isle qui finit en pointe vers l'embouchure de la rivière . . . il découvrit une petite rivière, qui entroit pars le dedans de l'isle," on which the fort was built (*Hist. Notable*, Basanier, p. 19; *Hak.*, vol. ii., p. 429). Le Moyne (*Eicones*, Plate VII.) says: "qui in Charles-fort propugnaculo supra fluviolum insulam, quæ in majore Portus Regalis alveo Septentrionem spectante sita est." The Frenchman Rufin deposes that it could be reached from a harbour in 32° 20′, "por el rrio arriba sin salir a la mar" (see p. 400, antea in this volume), and Manrique reported "que es sobre un braço de un rrio que esta en un puerto grande de dos que estan junto a la vanda del sur del susodicho [harbour in 32° 20′] hasta tres leguas," where he afterwards found it. This description is too indefinite to permit of determining its location. Nevertheless the following attempts have been made:

On or near Beaufort Island, Port Royal: Carroll, *Hist. Col. South Carolina*, 1836, vol. i., p. xxxvi.; Stevens, *Hist. of Georgia*, 1847, vol. i., p. 34. J. G. Kohl, "A History of the Discovery of the East Coast of North America," Portland, 1869, vol. i., p. 427 (*Col. Maine Hist. Soc.*, 2nd series). French, in his note to "The true and last discoverie" (in *Hist. Col. Louisiana and Florida*, 2nd series, "Historical Memoirs and Narratives," 1875, p. 188), says on the "island named in the old Spanish maps Santa Cruz, and near the present beautiful town of Beaufort." Parkman, *Pioneers of France in the New World*, 1893, p. 41.

On the Edisto: Chalmers, "Political Annals of the Province of Carolina," London, 1780, reprint in Carroll's *Hist. Col. South Carolina*, vol. ii., p. 275.

Beaufort or Edisto: Gaffarel, *Hist. de la Floride Française*, 1875, p. 22.

Mouth of the Albemarle River: Oldmixton, "Hist. of Georgia," 1708, reprint in Carroll's *Hist. Col. South Carolina*, vol. ii., p. 394. Monette (*Hist. of the Valley of the Mississippi*, New York, 1846, vol. i., p. 67) places it "a few miles above the St. Helena Sound, south of the Combahee River." Both Barcia, in his *Ensayo Cronologico*, (año MDLXII., p. 44), and John Lee Williams, in his *Florida* (New York, 1837, p. 169), confuse the Charlesfort of Ribaut with Fort Caroline, built in 1564 by Laudonnière.

The Chenonceau is identified with Pilot's Creek, which empties into the Port Royal, in the note to "The Port Royal Discovery," in *Hist. Col. South Carolina*, vol. v., p. 75. Parkman (in *The Pioneers of France in the New World*, p. 41) and French (in *Hist. Col. Louisiana and Florida*, 2nd series, "Hist. Memoirs and Narratives," p. 184, note) identify it with Archer's Creek, about six miles from the present town of Beaufort, to which French also gives the name of Skull Creek.

APPENDIX G

FORT CAROLINE

Rojomonte, in his deposition (*Noticias de la Población*, etc., p. 3), says of the situation of Fort Caroline: "Puede estar de la boca del dicho Rio dos leguas y sobre una barranca alta sobre un braço del dicho Rio á la banda del Sudueste." Meleneche, in his deposition ("Relación del suceso," etc., in Noriega to Philip II., March 29, 1565, fol. 3b, MS.), says: "Entrado de la barra adentro hay muchos bancos . . . y estos bancos los hay quatro ó cinco leguas por el rio adentro, al fin de los quales han fundado un Pueblo la gente de esta Armada," and farther on he repeats: "Fundaron un fuerte de madera y faxina, quatro ó cinco leguas á dentro de la boca deste rio, passados los bancos que estan dichos." The writer of the "Coppie d'une lettre venant de la Floride" (*Recueil de Pièces sur la Floride*, p. 241) says: "Lequel fort est sur la dicte riuiere de May, enuiron six lieues dās la riuiere loign de la mer." Velasco, in his *Geografía* (p. 168), says: "San Mateo [the name given by Menéndez to Fort Caroline] tiene por señas una tierra mas alta que todas, que está una legua por la tierra, adonde solia estar el fuerte que los franceses hicieron." Laudonnière, in his *Histoire Notable* (Basanier, p. 44; *Hak.*, vol. ii., p. 453), says: "This place is ioyning a mountaine." Menéndez, in his letter of September 11, 1565 (Ruidíaz, *La Florida*, tomo ii., p. 75), says of the French: "Tiene hecha su fuerça cinco leguas por el rio adentro"; but this information he had probably derived from the three French mutineers he took with him, as he had not yet been to the fort.

Some confusion exists in the above descriptions, but four of the authorities agree in placing the fort on or near a high hill, and it was unquestionably situated on a river, probably where a small stream flowed into it. It is not at all unlikely that it was at the head of the sand-bars in the river; and if Rojomonte indicates the distance by land, he is in substantial agreement with Velasco.

George R. Fairbanks, in his *History of St. Augustine* (New York, 1858, p. 16), places Fort Caroline "about two leagues" above the mouth of the St. John's, and between pages 50 and 51 he gives an interesting map entitled, "Entrance of the St. John's River," showing the nature of the neighbouring region, which goes far to prove the correctness of his conclusion. In chapter vi., pp. 51–59, he gives an excellent discussion on the subject of its site, although he was not in command of some of the data which we now have. Mr. Fairbanks adheres to this location in his *History of Florida* (p. 100), and is followed by Parkman in his *Pioneers of France in the New World* (Boston, 1893, p. 55, note 1), and by John Gilmary Shea in his "Ancient Florida" (in *Narr. and Crit. Hist. Am.*, vol. ii., p. 265), who reproduces the above-mentioned Fairbanks map with a note that "his view of the site is open to question." Charles B. Reynolds, in his *Old St. Augustine* (St. Augustine, Florida, 5th edition), in the map given on p. 21 and elsewhere in his book, places the fort in the bight in the river to the south of the location given by Fairbanks. Le Page Du Pratz, in the English version of his *History of Louisiana* (London, 1763, vol. i., p. 3), says the ruins of Fort Caroline "are still to be seen above the fort at Pensacola"(!). His translator, in a foot-note to the author's remark, places it at St. Augustine. As Dr. Shea has observed, the location at St. John's Bluff does not altogether satisfy the requirements; but in the course of years the topography of the river may have greatly changed, and St. John's Bluff cannot be far out of the way.

APPENDIX H

TIMUQUA

The name is variously written Timoqua, Timuca, Timucua, Tymangona, Tymangoua, Thimogona, Thimogoa, Thimagoa, Timogona, Timoga, and, by the English, Tomoco and Alimuca. It contains the word *atimoqua*, signifying "lord, ruler," which occurs in Father Pareja's *Confessionario En lengua Castellana y Timuquana*, Mexico, 1613, p. 205, and elsewhere in his works. Albert S. Gatschet in "The Timucua Language," in *Proceedings of the American Philosophical Society*, Philadelphia, 1877, vol. xvi., p. 627.

For the region inhabited by the Timuquanans see: Albert S. Gatschet, *ibid.*, 1877, vol. xvi., p. 626; *ibid.*, 1878, vol. xvii., p. 490; *ibid.*, 1880, vol. xviii., p. 465. The final article in Mr. Gatschet's interesting and exhaustive essay contains on page 475 a bibliography of the titles of Father Pareja's works in the Library of the Historical Society of New York consulted by him. The *Zeitschrift fur Ethnologie* for 1877, pp. 245–260, and for 1881, pp. 189–200, contains an abridgment in German of his essay published in *The Proceedings of the American Philosophical Society* above mentioned. J. W. Powell, "Indian Linguistic Families," *Seventh Ann. Rep. Bu. Ethn.*, 1885–86, p. 123. Cyrus Thomas, "The Indians in North America in Historic Times," in Lee's *Hist. of North America*, Philadelphia, vol. ii., p. 58. Bernard Romans, in *A concise Natural History of East and West Florida* (New York, 1775, vol. i., pp. 37, 267), gives an account of their last home.

For the Timuquanan language, in addition to the essay of Mr. Gatschet above cited, see: *Arte de la Lengua Timuquana*, compuesto en 1614 por el P^e^ Francisco Pareja y publicado conforme al original único por Lucien Adam y Julien Vinson, Paris, 1886.

Some idea of the numerous Timuquanan villages can be gathered from Laudonnière's relation in the *Histoire Notable.* Menéndez, writing of the St. John's River, says: "En este rio ay grandes poblaciones de yndios" (Avilés to Philip II., Oct. 15, 1565, Ruidíaz, *La Florida*, tomo ii., p. 92). Le Moyne shows "Timoga" on his map on the right bank of the St. John's shortly before it turns south, opposite the mouth of the mythical northern branch of the river, which may perhaps correspond to Trout Creek.

Timuqua also appears on various maps as follows: Lescarbot (Marc), "Figure et description de la terre reconue et habitée par les François en la Floride et audeça, gisante par les 30, 31, et 32 degrez," in Lescarbot's *Histoire de la Nouvelle France*, Paris, 1611, facing p. 596. De Laet (Jean), "Florida et Regiones Vicinae," in *Histoire du Nouveau Monde* . . . par le Sieur Iean de Laet . . . A Leyde, 1640, p. 102. Sanson d'Abbeville, "Le Nouveau Mexique et la Floride," Paris, 1656. Du Val (P.), "La Floride Françoise Dressée sur La Relation des Voyages que Ribaut, Laudonier, et Gourgues y ont faits en 1562, 1564 et 1567," in *Diverses Cartes et Tables pour la Géographie Ancienne* . . . Par O. Du Val . . . Paris, 1665. Sanson d'Abbeville, "Le Nouveau Mexique et la Floride," Paris, 1679 (a reprint of the 1656 map). De l'Isle (Guillaume), "Carte du Mexique et de la Floride," Paris, 1703. Senex and Maxwell, "North America," London, 1710. Châtelain (H. A.), "Carte contenant le Royaume du Mexique et de la Floride," in Gueudeville, *Atlas Historique* (1705–1719), tome vi. (1719), No. 27, p. 101. De l'Isle (Guillaume), "Carte du Mexique et de la Floride," etc., Amsterdam, 1722. Renier & Ottens, "Insulæ Americanæ," etc. (1730?). Seutter (Matthaeus), "Mapa Geographica Regionam Mexicanam et Floridam," etc. (1740–1760). De l'Isle (Guillaume), "Carta Geografica della Florida Nell' America Settentrionale" (1750), in *Atlante Novissimo* del Sig[r] Guglielmo de l'Isle, Venezia, 1740–1750, vol. ii. (1750). In this last map, as well as in all the preceding ones, the location of "Timogoa" follows that given it in the Le Moyne map, or varies only slightly from it. Martin (Benjamin), "A Map of the British and

French Settlements in North America" (second part), in his *Miscellaneous Correspondence*, 1755–1756, London, vol. i., p. 88, where the name Timooquas is applied to the northern section of the Peninsula of Florida. Homann (Joh. Baptista), "Regni Mexicani seu Novæ Hispaniæ," etc. (1763), in his *Atlas Geographicus Major*, tomus i. (published 1763). Romans (Bernard), "A General Map of the Southern British Colonies in America," by B. Romans, 1776. He shows the "Ancient Timookas" in about northern Alabama. Pownall, "A New Map of North America with the West India Islands," 1783, and Albert and Lotter, "A New and Correct Map of North America with the West India Islands," 1784, show the country of the "Ancient Timookas" in southern Georgia.

Recent maps are: "The Linguistic Families of the Gulf States," by Albert S. Gatschet, in his *A Migration Legend of the Creek Indians*, vol. i. Philadelphia, 1884, between pp. 48, 49. "Florida, 1565," in Parkman, *Pioneers of France in the New World*, Boston, 1893, between pp. 96, 97.

APPENDIX I

LAUDONNIÈRE'S STORY OF THE NOVEMBER MUTINY

Laudonnière, Le Moyne, and Hawkins, who obtained his information from the French, give a much more dramatic account of the mutiny than that recorded by the Spaniards. It is evidently derived from the mutineers, who returned to Fort Caroline, and who, faithful to the traditions of their country, make their ill-luck turn upon the cleverness of a woman. Their story, which we have only at second and third hand, runs as follows: The vessel captured off Cape Tiburon proved to have a rich prize on board, for it contained no less a personage than the Governor of Jamaica (Le Moyne, *Brevis Narratio*, p. 19, says, Governor of Havana), together with a great store of gold and silver, merchandise and wines. Having agreed with the Governor upon a ransom, which, sailor-like, was to include some monkeys called sanguines, natives of the island, they set sail for Jamaica. Arrived off the island, the Governor persuaded them to allow his two little boys, who had been captured with him, to go ashore and advise his wife to send him some provisions. At the same time he forwarded secret instructions by the lads as to where his captors were and asked that vessels be sent to his rescue. The lady proved equal to the occasion, and at daybreak next morning the pirates were surprised by the descent upon them of three Spanish ships, which chased them for three leagues and succeeded in recapturing their own vessel, but allowed the brigantine to escape with the larger part of the pirates. (See also Hawkins's account in *Hak.*, vol. iv., p. 242.)

APPENDIX J

MAPS OF THE FRENCH COLONIES IN FLORIDA AND SOUTH CAROLINA

The earliest map of the French settlements is:

(1) Le Moyne de Morgues (Jacques), "Floridae Americae Provinciae Recens & exactissima descriptio Auctore Iacobo le Moyne cui cognomen de Morgues, Qui Laudonierum, Altera Gallorum in eam Prouinciam Nauigatione comitat^{s} est, Atque adhibitis aliquot militibus, Ob pericula, Regionis illius interiora & maritima diligentissime Lustrauit, & Exactissime dimensus est, Obseruata etiam singulorum Fluminum inter se distantia, ut ipsemet redux Carolo IX Galliarum Regi, demonstrauit." In Part II. of T. De Bry's *Historia Americæ*, Francoforti ad Moenum, 1591. There are good reproductions of the map in *Narrative of Le Moyne* . . . translated from the Latin of De Bry, Boston, 1875. Shipp's *History of Hernando de Soto and Florida*. Gaffarel's *Histoire de la Floride Française*. Ruidíaz's *La Florida*, tomo i. Winsor's *Narr. and Crit. Hist. Am.*, vol. ii., p. 274.

Generally speaking, the Atlantic coast-line runs north-east and south-west. On the northern margin of the map is shown the southern section of a great body of water without any legend, Verrazano's sea according to Winsor (*The Kohl Collection*, by Justin Winsor, with Index by Philip Lee Phillips.

Library of Congress, Washington, 1904, p. 89), probably the Pacific, as in the Münster map of 1540 and others of a similar type. Directly south of this body of water are the "Montes Apalatci," with a small lake at their foot fed by a spring gushing out of the mountains. Along the north-eastern Atlantic coast two nameless rivers, one coming from the north and the other from the north-west, unite to form Port Royal Sound. Two streams connect the rivers together at some distance from their confluence, which gives them somewhat the appearance of an inverted V. Farther down the coast the "F. Maij" (the St. John's) flows north-westerly for about a third of its length, and then sends a branch abruptly to the south-west in a direction approximately parallel with the coast. It surrounds in its course an island named Edelano (*Hist. Notable*, Basanier, p. 75; *Hak.*, vol. ii., p. 485; De Bry, *Brevis Narratio*, pp. 15, 19), identified by Mr. Fairbanks with Drayton Island (*Hist. of Florida*, Philadelphia, 1871, p. 105), and terminates in a nameless lake bearing a legend to the effect that one shore cannot be seen from the other (*Hist. Notable*, Basanier, p. 75; *Hak.*, vol. ii., p. 485). This was the highest point on the river reached by the French and is identified by Mr. Fairbanks (*ibid.*, p. 105) with Lake George, a body of water twenty miles long and twelve broad, distant about a hundred miles from the mouth of the river (*Memoir . . . of Florida*, by William Darby, Philadelphia, 1821, p. 17).

Still farther south is a small lake called "Sarrope" (*Hist. Notable*, Basanier, p. 73; *Hak.*, vol. ii., p. 483; De Bry, *Brevis Narratio*, p. 17), which Brinton (*Notes on the Floridian Peninsula*, Philadelphia, 1859, p. 117), and after him Parkman (*Pioneers of France in the New World*, Boston, 1893, p. 80), think may be Lake Ware in Marion County; but it is far more probable that it is an echo of Lake Okeechobee, as identified by Powell ("Indian Linguistic Families," in *Seventh Ann. Rep. Bu. Ethn.*, 1885–1886, p. 123), the Lake Mayaimi of Fontanedo ("Memoria de las cosas y costa y indios de la Florida," *Col. Doc. Inedit. Indias*, tomo v., p. 534). A second arm of the "F. Maij" extends to the north and terminates in the vicinity of the great unnamed body of water.

The map embodies data derived from three different sources of information. The first and most reliable are those within the sphere of Le Moyne's personal observation, which includes, so far as we are aware, the region immediately around Fort Caroline, such as the countries of Saturiba and Alimacany. Le Moyne says that he was wounded in an expedition against Outina, consequently he went a certain distance up the river, and villages such as Malica, Casti, Melona, and Timoga, are probably correctly placed. Data of the second class are those derived from Le Moyne's companions. Thus Port Royal was previously known to Laudonnière, and during Le Moyne's residence in Florida a captain was sent to Audusta to renew the relations between him and the French. An expedition was also sent up the St. John's to the island of Edelano and to the edge of the lake of the unseen shore, Lake George. "Calos" was heard of from the escaped Spaniards, but the vagueness of the information which they gave is indicated by the location which Le Moyne has given to Lake Sarrope (Lake Okeechobee). These data also are deserving of a varying degree of credit. Belonging to the same class, but of inferior credibility, are the data obtained from the Indians, which we can determine by a process of exclusion to include all of the remaining indications on the map relating to the *interior* of the country. The third class consists of data derived from prior records, such as the shape of the Peninsula, and the names along the coast of foreign origin, such as Sinus Ioannis Ponce, F. Canotes, F. Pacis, Aquatio, and the names along the Carolina coast, which, according to Winsor (*The Kohl Collection*, p. 89), indicate that Le Moyne used Spanish drafts of the coast.

This map has exerted a great influence upon the subsequent cartography of this region. One or more of the features just described reappear in Dutch, French, and English maps for over a century and a quarter subsequent to its publication, either as laid down by Le Moyne or in the modified form given them by Mercator. To this influence Dr. Shea has given a very brief reference in his "Ancient Florida," in *Narr. and Crit. Hist. Am.*, vol. ii., p. 274, note 1. But André Thevet's map of "Le Nouveau Monde descovvert et illvstre de nostre temps," in his *La Cosmographie Universelle*, Paris, 1575, to which Dr. Shea refers, is on too small a scale to be of interest, and shows the Florida Peninsula without details and without the French names.

(2) With (John), also styled John White, "Map of southern part of the Atlantic coast of North America, showing the strait leading from Port Royal to the South Sea," 1585, MS. Brit. Museum. First published in reduced facsimile in "The Beginnings of a Nation," by Edward Eggleston, in the *Century Illustrated Monthly Magazine*, Nov., 1882, vol. xxv., pp. 66, 67, where it is accidentally dated 1685. There is a larger reproduction entitled "Chart of Virginia and Florida, by John White," in *The Principal Navigations . . . of the English Nation* . . . by Richard Hakluyt, Glasgow, MCMIV., vol. viii., between pp. 400, 401. It is also reproduced on a smaller scale, and with most of the names omitted, by Justin Winsor in his *Christopher Columbus*, Boston and New York, 1891, p. 589.

The Atlantic coast outline of the Florida portion of this map corresponding to that shown by Le Moyne differs materially from the latter. The trend of the coast from the Cape of Florida to Port Royal is substantially north and south. The promontory formed by the River of May and the River of Dolphins in Le Moyne is here a peninsula projecting due east far into the Atlantic, and Cape Canaveral has undergone a like change. The two rivers which unite to form Port Royal flow, the one east and the other nearly west, in place of south and south-east, as in Le Moyne, and the stream from the west is a strait connecting the Atlantic with the Pacific. The River of May rises in a western lake and flows due east, without turning to the south or having any northern affluent, as in Le Moyne. All of the names are in French, and the names of the rivers are those given by Laudonnière, and follow in the same order, with the exception of the "Belle a veoir," which is omitted. They also correspond in name and order to Ribaut's list, but include the Gironde, which he omits. The "Montes Apalatci" of Le Moyne become the "Montagnei

Pallassi," but retain substantially the same position as in Le Moyne's map. The Indian names, "Vlina," "Machiaca," "Satvriona," "Oatchaqva," and "Catos," correspond to Le Moyne's "Vtina," "Mathiaca," "Saturnva," "Oathkaqua," and "Calos"; but are placed in different locations from those given by Le Moyne, except for Satvriona and Catos, which have the same position in both maps. Le Moyne's "lake of the unseen shore" has been moved north and becomes the western source of the River of May, but it is without any legend. Le Moyne's "Sarrope" is "Sieropea," and remains in substantially the same position in both maps, but his crescent-shaped lake and the lake of the gushing spring are omitted.

These differences are too pronounced for the map to have been based upon the Le Moyne map, to which With might have had access prior to its publication by De Bry in 1591. The supposition that the information was obtained from Ribaut's relation published in 1563, and the maps Ribaut says he transmitted with his report, is excluded, because the data therein contained relate to his first voyage and the founding of Charlesfort. Laudonnière's relation was first published in the following year, 1586, and Le Challeux's *Discours*, printed at Dieppe in 1566, is not sufficiently definite in its descriptions of the country. The evidence as a whole appears to point to an independent French source for the new data given by the map, to a person familiar with Laudonnière's exploration of the St. John's, the escape of the Spaniards from the Caloosas, and the report of the rivers seen by Ribaut on his first voyage. If a suggestion may be ventured it is possible that the information upon which With based his map, in so far as the Florida portion of it is concerned, was furnished him by a member of Laudonnière's colony who had escaped the massacre. The name of the map-maker, John With, in place of John White, as it is usually written, is here used in view of the lucid argument in its favour made by Mr. P. Lee Phillips in his "Virginia Cartography," *Smithsonian Miscellaneous Collections*, Washington, 1896, p. 3.

(3.) Mercator (Gerard). "Virginiae item et Floridae Americanæ Provinciarum, nova descriptio." In Gerardi Mercatoris, *Atlas sive cosmographicæ meditationes de fabrica mundi et fabricati figura* . . . auctus et illustratus a Iudoco Hondio . . . aditæ . . . descriptiones novæ; studio et opera Pet. Montani. Dispensis Cornelli Nicolai Amsterodami, 1606, p. 347. The legend affixed to the map says: "Verum nos eam solummodo Floridæ partem hic apposiuim[s] cujus pleniorem notitiam habemus ex ipso autographo illius qui hanc nomine regis Galliæ accuratissime descripsit." This probably refers to Laudonnière's *Histoire Notable*, Paris, 1586, and put into English by Hakluyt in the following year (1587), for the data given in Ribaut's *True and last discoverie* of 1563 are insufficient to form the basis of a map. Le Moyne's map, however, has very largely influenced him, for the Port Royal River is reproduced as in the Le Moyne map; the Appalachian Mountains with the lake and gushing spring, the lake to the south, and the small lake Sarrope. But the River of May has become much more tortuous. Its northerly arm now takes its rise in the lake of the unseen shores, which is here placed immediately south-west of the mountains, while its south-westerly arm has been changed into a small western extension without any lake. In a word, while all of the main features of Le Moyne have been retained, a transposition has taken place as to the lake, and consequently in the direction of the course of the River of May, which flows from it.

For the entire seventeenth century this map of Mercator became the source from which the mapmakers drew all of their information concerning the territory occupied by the French.

(4.) Hondius (Henricus) in his "Virginiae item et Floridae Americæ Provinciarum Nova Descriptio," 1633, reprints it bodily.

(5.) Jansson (Joannes) in his "Virginiæ partis australis, et Floridæ partis orientalis, interjacentiumq; regionum nova descriptio" (In *Le Noveau Theatre du Monde ou Novvel Atlas*, Amstelodami. Apud Ioan Ianssonium, 1642, vol. iii., pt. 2) puts it in a more finished dress. (6) Guillaume Bleau in *Le Theatre du Monde ou Novvel Atlas*, Mis en lumiere par Gvillavme et Iean Blaev. Segonde partie (Amsterdam, 1644),

Amerique, between pp. 10, 11; (7) Joannes Blaeu in his *Atlas major, sive cosmographia Blaviana* (Amst., J. Blaeu, 1662) vol. ii., "America," between pp. 41, 42, and in other editions; (8) Carel Allard in his *Atlas Minor* (Amstelodami ex officina Caroli Allard [1696?] No. 141); and (9) Gerard Valk and Peter Schenk (Amstelodami), [1710?], all reprint the map with the same title and apparently from the same plates with an occasional insignificant change of some of the lettering and the addition or removal of an ornamental design. And (10) Arnoldus Montanus in his *De Nieuwe en Onbekende Weereld of Beschryving van America en t Zuid-land* . . . Door Arnoldus Montanus (t'Amsterdam . . . 1671) between pp. 142, 143 reproduces it with the same title in smaller size.

(11.) Lescarbot (Marc), "Figure et description de la terre reconue et habitée par les François en la Floride et audeça, gisante par les 30, 31 et 32 degrez." De la main de M. Marc Lescarbot. (In his *Histoire de la Nouvelle France*, Paris, 1611, facing p. 596.) This map, while very different in outline from the Mercator of 1606, still plainly shows its influence. But the "R. Loire" has extended northward until it takes its rise in the lake of the gushing spring. The lake of the unseen shores has moved farther north, and the "R. des Dauphins" has at last found its source in Lake "Saropé."

(12.) Dudley (Robert), "La Florida," in *Del l'Arcano del Mare*, di D. Rvberto Dvdleo Dvca di Nortvmbria et conte di Warvich. . . . Firenze . . . 1630. Dudley gives in two instances Spanish equivalents for French names which appear on Le Moyne's map, whose influence he shows.

(13.) Laet (Jean de), "Florida et Regiones Vicinae." In *L'Histoire du Nouveau Monde* . . . Par le Sieur Iean de Laet . . . A Leyde, 1640, p. 102, follows the 1606 Mercator.

(14.) Sanson d'Abbeville (N.), "Le Nouveau Mexique et la Floride . . ." Paris . . . 1656. (This map was republished in 1679 with a change in the date and an unimportant addition to the title.) This map shows the Mercator influence as does (15) Du Val (P). "La Floride Françoise Dressée sur La Relation des Voyages que Ribaut, Laudonier, et Gourgues y ont faits en 1562, 1564 et 1567." Par P. Du Val, Géographe du Roy, in *Diverses Cartes et Tables pour la Géographie Ancienne*. . . . Par P. Du Val . . . Paris . . . 1665. And (16) Speed (John), "A New Description of Carolina," in *The Theatre of the Empire of Great Britain*, by John Speed, London, 1676, between pp. 49, 50.

With the opening of the eighteenth century and the gradual advance of the English to the south the country became better known, as may be seen in (17) Guillaume de l'Isle's "Carte du Mexique et de la Floride" of 1703, where the French names begin to disappear and are replaced by Indian names known to the English. But the influence of the Mercator map continued to show itself, on occasion, far into the century, as in (18) Nicolas de Fer's "Partie Méridionale de la Rivière du Mississippi" of 1718, where a "Rivière de Mai" still flows from north to south, and in (19) Guillaume de l'Isle's "Amerique Septentrionale" (Chez Covens & Mortier) of about 1730, and in (20) Johannes Keulen's "Pas Kaart van West Indien," of about 1735, where the French names for the rivers are still retained. It may be said in conclusion that the Le Moyne and Mercator maps and those of the preceding list give the location of a great number of Indian villages mentioned in the Relations; but they appear to be largely the result of mere guesswork and quite undeserving of serious consideration until better evidence of their accuracy can be secured than can be commanded in the present state of our knowledge.

APPENDIX K

LA TERRE DES BRETONS

The Portuguese Portolano, dated 1514 by Kunstmann and 1520 by Kohl (*Discovery of Maine*, p. 179), reproduced in *Narr. and Crit. Hist. Am.*, vol. iii., p. 56, shows Nova Scotia with the legend: "Tera que foij descuberta por bertomas." Ribero's chart of 1529, a section of which is reproduced in *Narr. and Crit. Hist. Am.*, vol. iv., p. 38, shows the legend "Trra de Bretõ" on the Nova Scotia coast. The legend on the mainland to the west of it reads: "Tiera de Esteva Gomez la qual descubrio por mandado de su mag. el año de 1525" etc. The Münster map of 1540 (See *Narr. and Crit. Hist. Am.*, vol. iii., p. 201, and iv., p. 41) shows Nova Scotia with the legend: "C. Britonum," and on the mainland to the west, "Francisca." The section of the Ulpius Globe of 1542, reproduced in *Narr. and Crit. Hist. Am.*, vol. iv., pp. 42 and 82, shows the "Cavo de Brettoni" with the legend appended to the mainland: "Verrazana sive Nova Gallia aver razano florentino comperta anno sal, M.D." The Henri II. map of 1546 by the Abbé Desceliers (*Narr. and Crit. Hist. Am.*, vol. iv., pp. 85, 86) shows Nova Scotia with the legend: "Terre des Bretons." The map by the same author, No. 9814 of the British Museum, dated 1550, and reproduced in *Narr. and Crit. Hist. Am.*, vol. iv., p. 87, has the legend "Tierra de los Bretones" on the mainland, west of what is now Nova Scotia. The map in Baptista Agnese's Venetian atlas of 1554 (*Narr. and Crit. Hist. Am.*, vol. iv., p. 90) shows Nova Scotia with the legend: "Tarra de los bertoms." Ruscelli in his map of 1561, reproduced in *Narr. and Crit. Hist. Am.*, vol. iv., p. 92, shows Nova Scotia with the legend: "Tierra de los Breton." The sketch of the Des Liens map of 1566 in *Narr. and Crit. Hist. Am.*, vol. iv., p. 79, shows Nova Scotia with the legend "Cap aux Bretons," and to the west of it, on the continent: "La nouv. France."

APPENDIX L

PORTRAITS OF PEDRO MENÉNDEZ DE AVILÉS

There is a copperplate engraving published in *Retratos de los Españoles Ilustres con un Epitome de sus Vidas.* De Orden Superior. En la Imprenta Real de Madrid. Siendo su Regente D. Lâzaro Gayguer. 1791." It is entitled: "Pedro Menéndez de Avilés, Natural de Avilés en Asturias, Comendador de la orden de Santiago, Conquistador de la Florida, nombrado Gral de la Armada contra Jnglaterra. Murió en Santander A° 1574, á los 55, de edad." It is drawn by Josef Camaron, and engraved by Franco de Paula Marte, 1791. It measures 23 x 17 cms. It is said in the Biblioteca Nacional, Madrid, Sec. de Bellas Artes, Dibujos Originales, that the portraits in this work are not all of equal authority.

This portrait, a reduced photogravure facsimile of which is given in the frontispiece of this volume, has been frequently reproduced in whole or in part. There is a copy in Ruidíaz, *La Florida*, tomo i. Mr. Parkman has engraved the head for his *Pioneers of France in the New World*. Dr. Shea used the plate for his *Charlevoix*, and it also appears in Charles B. Reynolds's *Old St. Augustine* (St. Augustine, Florida, 5th Edit., p. 45). The head has also been reproduced in *La Ilustración Española y Americana* of Nov. 15, 1880, in *La Ilustración Gallega y Asturiana*, of March 10, 1879, and in Duro's *Armada Española*, tomo ii., p. 214. It is apparent that the date of the likeness is subsequent to January 19, 1568, at about which time he was appointed to the Commandery of the Holy Cross of Zarza, the insignia of which, a crimson cross in the shape of an antique sword, appears in the portrait. (See p. 292, note 3, in this volume.)

Ruidíaz, in the preface to his *La Florida* (tomo i., p. cxvii., note **) says that according to Canon Posada there was a portrait of Avilés by Titian in the possession of the first Duke of Almodóvar del Rio. He also cites Pezuelo to the effect that there was a good engraving by Coello made after an ancient portrait in the house of Doña Ana Antonia Suárez de Góngora, ninth Adelantado of Florida. In the "Petición de Don Martin Menéndez de Abilés, sobre que se le conceda licencia para ir á México y otras mercedes fundado en los servicios prestados por sus antecesores" (Arch. Gen. de Indias, Seville, est. 54, caj. 5, leg. 18) we learn that Philip II. ordered the portrait of Pedro Menéndez de Avilés to be painted and placed in his gallery among those of other illustrious individuals and conquerors of provinces, and this may be the above mentioned Titian portrait.

COAT OF ARMS OF PEDRO MENÉNDEZ DE AVILÉS

The Coat of Arms of Avilés is given by Ruidíaz in his *La Florida*, tomo i., p. cxviii. It consists of a field gules on which is an armed vessel under sail with a cross on the mainmast and a saw on the bow breaking a large chain suspended between two castles (Vigil, *Noticias*, p. 15). This is in allusion to a deed of an ancestor in an encounter with the Moors on the Guadalquivir.

APPENDIX M

THE DEPOSITION OF JEAN MEMYN

Jean Memyn was from La Rochelle and was a member of Ribaut's final expedition. He was made a prisoner on the capture of Fort Caroline, but, coming to Spain with his captor, escaped from him, and on October 16, 1566, made a deposition at the request of M. de Fourquevaux, the French Ambassador at Madrid. The deposition is a curious jumble of fact and fancy. He says that on Ribaut's arrival in Florida he was attacked by a combined fleet consisting of twenty-five Spanish and Portuguese vessels from which Ribaut fled in his six ships. Memyn gives a confused account of Ribaut's shipwreck; tells of the surprise of Fort Caroline, in which the Portuguese were as many, if not more in number than the Spaniards, and were the more cruel of the two; says the women and children were sent to Puerto Rico; that 350 men were killed in the attack on the fort and in a neighbouring island, probably the Matanzas massacre, and that Ribaut's beard was cut off to send to the King of Spain. He adds that seventeen or eighteen sailors were alive and prisoners at Havana (*Dépêches* de M. de Fourquevaux, tome i., pp. 131–133). The curious feature in this relation is the gratuitous and wholesale importation of the Portuguese into the conquest, a statement which so impressed Fourquevaux, that he again refers to it in a subsequent letter of November 2, 1566, to the King.

APPENDIX N

THE CAPTURED FRENCH VESSELS

The six vessels captured at Fort Caroline by the Spaniards were: (1) The one remaining ship of Laudonnière's fleet; (2)

The vessel brought in by the mutineers; (3 and 4) Two small shallops; (5) A galley on the stocks; (6) The vessel purchased from Hawkins. It seems altogether probable from the Spanish account, and in part from the French, that these six ships were up the river, somewhere in the neighbourhood of the fort.

When Avilés attacked the fort he sank one of these vessels. Laudonnière acknowledges (*Histoire Notable*, Basanier, p. 112; *Hak.*, vol. ii., p. 521) that he left the vessel purchased from Hawkins behind. Le Moyne (De Bry, *Brevis Narratio*, p. 27) says that Laudonnière scuttled (1) his own ship and (6) the vessel purchased from Hawkins. If we accept the assumption that the ships which he scuttled were at Fort Caroline, it is difficult to understand how Laudonnière could have accomplished it, considering his own story of his escape; and if he had really scuttled them he would have stated it in his account in order to palliate his defeat. Instead of so doing he admits having abandoned one of them to the enemy and does not mention the fate of the others.

Mendoza ("Relacion" in Ruidíaz, *La Florida*, tomo ii., p. 459) says there were six vessels in the river including two which were at the river's mouth, four of which were captured including the vessel sunk or disabled by Avilés. Thus the evidence, although conflicting, has a tendency to confirm Avilés's statement that five French ships were left behind. Of Ribaut's fleet of seven vessels four were wrecked, one was scuttled, and two returned to France. No reason can be assigned for doubting the statement made by Avilés, and twice repeated in his letter, that in addition to these five he found two other boats stolen by the French.

APPENDIX O

THE OATH OF AVILÉS

Spanish Accounts—The First Massacre.—We have four sources which repeat the terms offered by Avilés to the French. The first is Avilés himself. In his letter of October 15, 1565 (Ruidíaz, *La Florida*, tomo ii., p. 89), he writes that

Laudonnière's lieutenant "abiendo dado y tomado conmigo, ofreciome que me entregarian las armas y se darian con que les otorgase la vida. Respondile que las armas me podian rendir y ponerse debaxo de mi gracia para que yo hiziese dellos aquello que Nuestro Señor me ordenase; y de aquí no me sacó ni sacará, si Dios Nuestro Señor no esperara en mí otra cosa; y ansí se fué con esta respuesta," etc.

The second is Dr. Gonzalo Solís de Merás, his brother-in-law. Merás (in Ruidíaz, *La Florida*, tomo i., p. 114), after repeating in substance the declaration of enmity which has just been quoted in the text (p. 191 in this volume), follows it immediately with the terms of the oath: "que si ellos querían entregarle las banderas é las armas, é ponerse á su misericordia, lo podían hacer, para que él hiciera dellos lo que Dios le diese de gracia, ó que hiciesen lo que quisieren, que otras treguas ni amistades no habían de hacer con él; y aunque el Capitán Francés replicó, no se pudo acabar otra cosa con el Adelantado; é ansí se partió para su gente," etc.

The third is Barrientos (" Hechos," in García, *Dos Antiguas Relaciones de la Florida*, p. 64), who uses almost identically the same language as Merás. After repeating the declaration of enmity, he follows it immediately with the terms: "que si ellos quisieren entregalle las banderas y armas, y ponerse a misericordia, lo podian hacer para q̄ el haga lo q̄ dios le diere de gracia; o determinen lo que quieren: q̄ otras treguas ni amistades no auian de hacer Con el: ansí no se pudo acauar Con el adelantado otra cosa: partiose Con esto para su gente a decilles lo que pasaua," etc.

The fourth is the chaplain Mendoza (Ruidíaz, *La Florida*, tomo ii., p. 464), who was a member of Avilés's council (*ibid.*, tomo ii., p. 454, "deputado para las consultas"), was present at the massacre, and saved the lives of the Roman Catholics among the Frenchmen. He says: "Vino un gentil-hombre francés, sargento, y truxo un mensaje del real de los enemigos en que pedian que se les otorgase la vida, y que rendirian las armas y entregarian las personas; y despues de mucho parlamento entre él y nuestro buen General, respondió y dixo que no les queria dar tal palabra, sino que truxesen las armas y sus personas para que él hiziese á su voluntad; por que si él les diese la vida queria que se lo agradeciesen; y si la muerte, que no se quejasen de abérsela quebranto; visto que no podian hazer otra cosa, se volvió á su real," etc.

THE SECOND MASSACRE.— Avilés in the letter already quoted (*ibid.*, p. 102) says that Ribaut "sobre seguro enbió á su Sargento mayor á hablar conmigo. . . . Respondile lo que á los otros: que yo era enemigo suyo y tenia guerra con ellos á fuego y sangre, por ser luteranos y por venir á plantar á estas tierras de V. M. su mala secta y á doctrinar los yndios della, y desengañarle que su fuerte teniamos ganado; que me entregasen las banderas y las armas y se pusiesen debaxo de mi gracia, para que hiziese de sus personas lo que quisiese, y que otra cosa no avian de hazer ni acabar conmigo. Y aviéndose ydo con este recado el Sargento mayor," etc. Merás, who was present at this massacre, and was one of the two who stabbed Jean Ribaut, says (*ibid.*, p. 123) that when Ribaut came to treat of the terms "el Adelantado le respondió lo que á los primeros franceses de que hizo hacer justicia, é dando é tomando con él, no pudo acabar otra cosa el Juan Ribao con el Adelantado." Barrientos (*ibid.*, p. 68) merely says that in the interview with Ribaut "el adelantado le Respondio lo que a los otros, y con el no pudo acauar otra cosa."

We have thus the concurrent testimony of Mendoza and of Merás to the terms in which Avilés made his promise to the French, one of them having been present at one massacre, and the other at the other. The statement of Barrientos is not of equal importance with that of the two just mentioned because he appears to have drawn his information for this part of his history from a source common to himself and Merás. It is difficult to imagine any connivance between Avilés, the chaplain, and the brother-in-law to misrepresent the words used, because it is not easy to conceive what motive there could be for so doing.

FRENCH ACCOUNTS—SECOND MASSACRE.—We have but two original accounts of the oath of Avilés from the French side, and both of them relate to the second massacre. The first is that given by the Dieppe sailor and reported by Le Moyne, a translation of which appears in the text (p. 202 in this volume). The paragraph describing the promise in the original is: "Ille Caillii oratione audita, non modo conceptis verbis fidem Caillio dedit, quam repetitis multis crucis signis, osculo sancitis, confirmavit, sed etiam juratam corā omni suorum caterva, & scriptam suoq; sigillio obfirmatam tradere voluit, per quam denuo jurabat, & pollicebatur, se sine fraude, fideliter, & ut virum nobilem atque probum decet Ribaldi atque militum ipsius vitam conservaturum: datæ sunt igitur litteræ eleganter scriptæ," etc. (*Brevis Narratio*, pp. 28, 29).

The second is that of Le Challeux ("Histoire Mémorable," reprint in Gaffarel, pp. 474, 475), who has also preserved an account of the same event, but does not positively state its origin. As he ascribes the report of the mutilation of Ribaut's body to the sailor Christophe le Breton, from Havre de Grace, one of the persons saved from the massacre, it is possible that he learned it from him. It is as follows: "Les déléguez [of Ribaut] furent reçus de prime face assez humainement. Le capitaine de ceste compagnie espagnole, lequel se faisoit nommer Vallemande, protesta en foy de gentilhomme, chevalier et chrestien, de sa bienveillance envers les François, mesmement que c'estoit la façon qui avoit esté de tout temps pratiquée en la guerre que l'Espagnole victorieux se contentast, à l'endroit du François principalement, sans passer plus outre: exhortant en truchement, afin q'tous fussent persuadez de ceste belle promesse, que iamais il ne voudroit faire faire en ceste endroit, de quoy les nations se puissent en après ressentir, et prestement fist accoustrer une barque," etc. Fourquevaux in his letter to Charles IX. of July 5, 1566, says: "qu'il m'a esté dict que led. Menendes avoit receu vosd. subjectz la vie sauve et promis de les fere mener en Espagne pour y attendre l'adveu ou desadveu de Votred. Majesté" (*Dépêches*, p. 93).

This is the evidence on the French side. Its characteristics are that it reaches us indirectly, neither Le Moyne nor Le Challeux having been present at the massacre; that the two sailors were not of a rank, nor in a position to be informed as to what were the exact terms of the promise made by Avilés to Ribaut, but knew only the construction put upon it in the form in which it was announced to them. Stripped of all religious prejudice and racial hatred, the credibility of the two contradictory accounts resolves itself into a question of the relative weight of the evidence. On the one hand is the direct testimony of Merás and Mendoza, each witness of one of the massacres, each confirming the statement made by Avilés, and each in a position which enabled him to obtain correct information; and opposed to this, on the other hand, are the two concurrent accounts, reaching us at second hand, of two sailors, each present at the massacre, from which one escaped, and where the other is pardoned, and neither of them in a position to obtain direct information. Gaffarel in his *Histoire de la Floride Française* (pp. 222, 223) accepts the Spanish version as to the form of Avilés's promise at the first massacre, and gives both versions of the promise made at the second massacre (*ibid.*, pp. 225, 226) without deciding between the two. Parkman in his *Pioneers of France in the New World* (pp. 137 and 142) accepts the Spanish version for both massacres, and adds: "That they contain an implied assurance of mercy has been held, not only by Protestants, but by Catholics and Spaniards"; and he cites in support of his statement Salazar, *Cricis del Ensayo*, p. 23; and Padre Felipe Briet, *Anales.*

The theory has been advanced by Gaffarel (p. 225) that Vallemande of Le Challeux was an officer of Avilés, upon whom the Adelantado had imposed the burden of perjuring himself in the Spanish interest. No corresponding name, or one approximately like it, appears among the names of officers of the conquest given by Barrientos or by Merás. Neither was it in the nature of Avilés to compel another to do that which he would not do himself.

APPENDIX P

THE DEATH OF RIBAUT

French Accounts.—Le Challeux in his *Histoire Mémorable*, which was printed at Dieppe in 1566 (*Narr. and Crit. Hist. Am.*, vol. ii., p. 296) agrees substantially with the details given by Barrientos, as related in the text, except as to the nature of the promise given by Avilés,—a subject which has already been considered in Appendix O (p. 421 in this volume),—and as to the subsequent treatment of Ribaut's body. He relates on the authority of Christophe le Breton, a French sailor spared by Avilés, and who on being sent to Seville, had escaped from there to Dieppe, "et pour combler leur cruauté et barbarie: ils ont rasé la barbe du lieutenant du Roy, pour faire monstre de leur expédition et l'on bien tost après envoyée à Civile, . . . et pour le trophée de leur renommée et victoire, démembrèrent le corps de ce bon et fidèle serviteur du Roy, et firent de sa teste quatre quartiers lesquels ils fichèrent en quatre picques, et puis les plantèrent aux quatre coings du fort" (reprint in Gaffarel, *Hist. de la Floride Française*, p. 476). There is a simplicity and a ring of truth about the Le Challeux Relation, the sincerity of which is confirmed by his giving the source of this latter report. It will be noted, however, that the story comes through Le Breton, who had been pardoned by the Spaniards, had been for a short time in their service, and whose interest it was to appease the suspicions his pardon would naturally excite among his compatriots by exaggerating the ferocity of the Spaniards.

October 16th of the same year Jehan Memyn, a French sailor also spared by the Spaniards and who had remained in Florida for some time subsequent to Ribaut's death, deposed that the Spaniards "couppèrent plustost la barbe aud. cap^{ne} Ribbault disant la vouloir envoyer au Roy d'Espagne" (*Dépêches de M. Fourquevaux*, p. 132), but says nothing of his head being cut off.

The *Requeste au Roy*, the approximate date of which is probably August, 1566 (see p. 318 in this volume), and which is full of exaggeration, relates (reprint in Gaffarel, p. 478) that after Ribaut was killed "ledit soldat luy coupa la teste, luy raza le poil de la barbe et partit la teste en quatre quartiers, qui furent plantez sur quatre picques au milieu de la place où les François estoyent morts. Finalement ledit capitaine Hespagnol envoya une lettre au Roy d'Hespagne, et fit enclore dedans ladite lettre le poil de la barbe dudit

Ribaut." It conveys the impression that all the women and children were killed, which was incorrect. It says that "seven or eight hundred" Frenchmen were killed. The name of Pedro or Pero Menéndez, as it was frequently written in the Spanish of that time, is transformed to Pétremclaud. Finally, the description of Ribaut's death has a curious resemblance to that given by Le Challeux, with the exception that the head is now erected in a different place. And the beard story is almost identical with that told by Memyn. The *Requeste* breathes a spirit of intense excitement and a fierce desire for revenge, which, however righteous it was, does not inspire the reader with the conviction that the composition of the *Requeste* was governed by a nice weighing of the truth of the particular statements which it contains. As the number of Frenchmen spared by the Spaniards was very few, and those who finally escaped and returned to France were fewer still, it is highly probable that the *Requeste* derived this information from Le Challeux and Memyn.

La Popelinière, in *Les trois Mondes* (1582, liv. ii., p. 34), reported that the Spaniards "escorchèrent la peau du visage avec la longue barbe de Ribaut, les yeux, le nez et oreilles, et envoyèrent ainsi le masque défiguré au Pérou, pour en faire des montres." Lescarbot in his *Histoire de la Nouvelle France* (1611, p. 120), relates that "after several tortures they cruelly skinned him (contrary to all the laws of war that ever were) and sent his skin to Europe." De Thou adds nothing further to this catalogue of atrocities.

It thus appears that the only contemporary French evidence which we have of the indignities inflicted on Ribaut's body is that of Le Challeux and Memyn. It is to be noted that Barrientos, who finished the writing of his history December 30, 1568, explicitly states that Ribaut's head was cut off, a fact passed over by Merás and Avilés. When we bear in mind that Philip spoke of the French in Florida as pirates and corsairs, who should be treated as such, and recall the customs of that age, there would be nothing unusual in the proceeding had Avilés caused the head of a pirate to be cut off and exhibited on the point of a spear at Fort St. Augustine. The legend of the shaven beard sent to Spain is too puerile to deserve consideration. Avilés was a nobleman of high rank and of acknowledged courage, and the man who wrote the modest and business-like reports of September and October would be far above such pettiness. The French are an excitable people of vivid imagination, and although of an eminently artistic temperament, lose all sense of proportion the moment their antipathy is aroused, and lend a willing ear to the wildest rumours. The ready acceptance given within the last decade to the reported correspondence of a German emperor with an alleged spy furnishes us with a recent parallel.

Spanish Accounts of Ribaut's Death.—Vasalenque, who appears to have been present on this occasion, for he served in the company of Diego de Amaya which was sent to the scene of the massacre by Avilés (Ruidíaz, *La Florida*, tomo ii., pp. 615 and 616), gives a somewhat different account of the death of Ribaut. He relates that after a demonstration of banners and music on each side, Jean Ribaut came over alone, at about noon in an Indian canoe, "and the first thing he did was to take off his sword and dagger, and some keys, which he took out of his pocket and surrendered them and the said fort to the said Adelantado; and the said Adelantado told him that he had already captured the fort; and the said Juan Ribao asked after his son, and the said Adelantado told him he had escaped in a boat; and thereupon there was a long conversation between them alone; and after that the said Adelantado said that the said Juan Ribao be given something to eat, and it was given him; and wishing to return to his people, for it was already late, he was given two bags of biscuits and other things. And all that night there was a great stir among the French, on account of which Pedro Menéndez and his soldiers remained under arms all night, and at dawn all of the French came unarmed to the river bank, asking to be taken across, and they were taken over in boats; and when they had arrived where the said Pedro Menéndez was, they were given something to eat, and within an hour they [*i. e.*, the Spaniards] began to march with them according to a certain command which the said Adelantado gave, and on turning a point of land the Spanish soldiers began to cut off the heads of all of them, without one of them escaping, nor the said Juan Ribao, except a few lads mechanics of the said Juan Ribao and some calkers." This deposition was made thirty years after the event ("Información de algunos servicios prestados por el Adelantado Pedro Menéndez de Avilés," México, 3 de Abril de 1595, in Ruidíaz, *ibid.*, tomo ii., pp. 615–617).

Silva in his letter to Philip II. of May 18, 1566 (*Correspondencia de Felipe II. con sus Enbajadores en la Corte de Inglaterra 1558 á 1584*, tomo ii., p. 319; English translation in *Spanish State Papers, 1558–67*, I. Elizabeth, 551), gives a paragraph to the wreck of Ribaut and his death, as it was related to him by an English sailor who had been taken in a vessel captured by Avilés before the Florida incident, and who claimed to have been present at the death of Ribaut.

APPENDIX Q

THE SITUATION OF AVILÉS AT THE TIME OF THE MASSACRE

Philip II., in his letter to Alava of February 23, 1566 (MS. Arch. Nat., Paris, K, 1505 (75), fol. 2b), tells him that when Fourquevaux complained "that a great cruelty had been committed in putting so many soldiers to the knife after they had surrendered," one of the explanations given him in extenuation of the act of Avilés was the following: "In no other way in the world could Pero Menéndez secure himself against the said pirates than in the way he did, for he had nothing to give them to eat, and if he had so done, his own people would have perished and died of hunger; besides, being as they were so many French, and those of Menéndez so few, he could place them nowhere, where he and his people could be safe, and that besides Pero Menéndez was obliged to go to other parts, and necessarily was compelled to leave part of his people in the fort. And leaving the French, who were so many more in number, with them, it was evident they would kill our people and take the fort. And as to putting them in the ships, they would not hold them, because they were so small, neither could he go away in safety. That as to giving them ships in which to go to France, he had none, and even should he have had them, it would evidently be providing them with ships and facility to disturb him elsewhere." See also Ruidíaz's observations in *La Florida*, tomo i., pp. clxxvi.-clxxvii.

RELATIVE NUMBER OF THE FRENCH AND SPANIARDS.—Avilés, in his letter of October 15, 1565 (Ruidíaz, *La Florida*, tomo ii., pp. 88, 102), sets the minimum number of Frenchmen who escaped from the wreck of Ribaut's fleet at 440. Merás, in his "Jornadas" (*ibid.*, tomo i., pp. 116, 121), says 558. The total number of the French, at the lowest estimate, including the 50 women and children saved (letter of October 15, 1565, *ibid.*, p. 87) and the few prisoners spared at Fort Caroline, was 500, of whom over 440 were men. Avilés in his letter of September 11, 1565 (*ibid.*, tomo ii., p. 75) gives 800 as the total number of the Spaniards, of whom 500 were soldiers and 200 sailors. The sailors must necessarily have remained with the fleet. Of the 500 soldiers, 300 were already in garrison at San Mateo (Merás, in Ruidíaz, *ibid.*, tomo i., p. 104) and in November, subsequent to the massacre, 200 were left at Ays (Avilés to Philip II., December 5, 1565, *ibid.* tomo ii., p. 107).

THE FOOD-SUPPLY.—Avilés, in his letter of September 11, 1565 (Ruidíaz, *La Florida*, tomo ii., p. 79), wrote that he had sufficient biscuit to last him till December, but that he could make it go through January. In his letter of October 15, 1565 (*ibid.*, tomo ii., p. 104), he says: "With the burning of the fort we are suffering very greatly from hunger, because the meal was burnt up, and the biscuit I landed here is spoiling and being consumed, and unless we are succoured very shortly we will be in suffering and many will depart this world from starvation." Merás states (in *ibid.*, tomo i., p. 178) that after the burning of Fort Caroline over a hundred casks of flour still remained, and although many of the soldiers voluntarily reduced their rations, the supply was exhausted by the middle of February. The news of the burning of the extensive food-supply captured from the French at Fort Caroline here referred to reached Avilés in the interval between the first and the second massacres.

SHIPS.—In the interview preceding the first massacre, when Avilés was asked to furnish a ship to convey the French back to France, he made the following answer, according to Merás (in *ibid.*, tomo i., p. 113): "That he would gladly do so were they Catholics and had he ships for such a purpose, but that he did not have them, for he had sent two to San Mateo with the artillery and to transport the French women and the children to Santo Domingo, and to obtain supplies; and the other was to go with dispatches to His Majesty of what had so far occurred in these parts." He does not mention the *San Pelayo* and the *San Salvador*, which had sailed some time previously. The reply was, however, disingenuous, to say the least, for according to his own statement he had found eight vessels at Fort Caroline (letter of October 15, 1565, *ibid.*, tomo ii., pp. 90, 91), of which two or three at the least were available.

APPENDIX R

AYS

Juan López de Velasco (*Geografía y Descripción Universal de las Indias, 1571–1574*, Madrid, 1894, p. 167) places "el Rio Asis" in 27 degrees north latitude, south of Cape Canaveral. Hernando de Escalante Fontanedo refers to the "Ais" Indians and the "coast of Ais" in his "Memoria" (*Col. Doc. Inedit. Indias*, tomo v., pp. 541–543). He mentions Mayaca and Mayajuaca as in the country of Ays, in the direction of Cape Canaveral (pp. 540, 545). His account was written in Spain about 1575 (*Narr. and Crit. Hist. Am.*, vol. ii., p. 291, note 1). Herrera, in his "Descripción de las Indias" (in his *Decadas*, Madrid, 1730, tomo i., cap. viii., p. 15), places it south of Cape Canaveral and mentions the settlement made there by Avilés. Barcia, in his *Ensayo* (Año MDLXVI., p. 118), places it twenty leagues up the St. John's, beyond Macoya, possibly the Mayaca of Fontanedo. In this he merely copies the statement made by Merás (in Ruidíaz, *La Florida*, tomo i., p. 253). Brinton, in his *Notes on the Floridian Peninsula* (Philadelphia, 1859, p. 116, note 3), questions Barcia's statement, saying "distances given by the Spanish historians are often mere guesses, quite untrustworthy."

There can be no doubt that the Rio de Ays, Ais, Is, Ys, Days, Asis, Aiz, is Indian River. William Roberts, in his *History of Florida* (London, 1763, p. 22), mentions the "Rio de Ays, three leagues north of Rio Santa Cruz," which he also calls Santa Lucia on the same page, "and in latitude 27 deg. 45 min.," etc. William Stork in *A Description of East-Florida* (London, 3d ed., 1769, p. 10), says, "We are as yet unacquainted with the sources . . . of Hillsborough River; it is generally believed to have a communication with an Indian inlet, called by the Spaniards Rio Days, sixty miles to the south, where there is such another harbour as Musquito, with eight feet water; it is said to communicate with St. John's River." Bernard Romans, in his *A concise Natural History of East and West Florida* (New York, 1775, vol. i., p. 2), says: "On the East side [of Florida] is . . . the Lagoon, known by the name of Aïsa Hatcha, Rio d'ais or Indian River" (see also p. 282) and on p. 273 he refers to the names of South-hillsborough and Hysweestake given it by De Brahm. Both he (p. 273) and Brinton (*Floridian Peninsula*, p. 116) derive the name from a native word, *aïsa*, deer. Grant Forbes, in his *Sketches, Historical and Topographical, of the Floridas* (New York, 1821, p. 93), says "the lagoon of Aise or Indian River" and on p. 102 he quotes Romans on the "Aïsa Hatcha." George William Lee in his *Florida* (New York, 1857, p. 51), says "Indian River . . . formerly called Ys." George R. Fairbanks in his *History of St. Augustine* (New York, 1858, p. 125) says "Indian River was the province of Ys." Daniel G. Brinton, in his *Floridian Peninsula* (Philadelphia, 1859, p. 116) is disposed to think "Ais" was the northern extremity of the province of Tegesta, in which he is probably mistaken. He adds: "The residence of the chief was near Cape Cañaveral, probably on Indian River." Barnard Shipp, in his *Hernando de Soto and Florida* (Philadelphia, 1881, p. 560) says "Province of Ais or St. Lucia," but in his note, p. 587, he incorrectly locates it at the southern extremity of the peninsula.

Albert S. Gatschet in his "The Timucua Language" (*Proceedings of the American Philosophical Society*, Philadelphia, 1880, vol. xviii., p. 469) says "the northern portion of this section of land [*i. e.*, of the "Province of Tequesta," which he locates south of Cape Canaveral] was called in later epochs Ais, Ays, Is, and Santa Lucia by the Spaniards. *Ais* is interpreted by aïsa, *deer*, a term not belonging to the Timucua language, but identifiable with itcho, *deer*, in Seminole, or itchi, itche in Hitchiti and Mikasuke." In his *Migration Legend of the Creek Indians* (Philadelphia, 1884, vol. i., p. 12) he adheres to the same location and places the "Ais" Indians "from Cape Canaveral, where the Spaniards had the post Santa Lucia, to a lagoon once called Aïsahatcha." "They formed the northern portion of the Tequesta domains" (p. 15). It is to be noted, however, that Santa Lucia was not at Cape Canaveral, but south of it at the second inlet into the Rio de Ais. In this respect Williams in his *Florida* (pp. 52, 53) observes that Indian Lagoon undergoes frequent changes. (See Appendix S, Santa Lucia.) It is to be observed that most of the authorities quoted subsequent to Romans base their conclusions on and quote liberally from him, with and without acknowledging their source.

Ays appears on the following maps: "Derrotero util y provechoso y en todo verdadero de Rios, caños, lagunas, montes, poblaciones, envarcaderos, baradereos, rancherias, el qual reza desde la ciudad de San Agustin hasta la varra de Ais por Albaro Mexia." MS. Arch., Gen. de Indias, Seville, Patronato, est. 1, caj. 1, leg. 1/19, ramo 29. It is accompanied by a Relation of 1605 in which "Aiz el biejo" is situated on the northern extremity of what is probably Hutchinson Island, between the lagoon and the sea. "Mapa de la Florida y Laguna de Maimi donde se ha de hacer un fuerte." MS. Undated, (1595–1600?), Arch. Gen. de Indias, Seville, est. 145, caj. 7, leg. 7. In this "Ais" is shown as a lagoon. Jean de Laet, "Florida et Regiones Vicinæ," in his *L'Histoire dv*

Nouveau Monde, Leyde, 1640, between pp. 102, 103. In this "R Ayz" is shown as a lagoon. Ioannes Jansson, "America Septentrionalis," in his *Nuevo Atlas*, Amsterdam, 1653, vol. ii. In this it appears as "Enseada [*sic*] de Ays." Nicolas Bellin, "Carte reduite des Costes de la Louisiane et de la Floride," 1764. In this the "R. de Ays" is shown approximately correct in position. Fernando Martinez, "Descripción geographica de la parte que los Españoles poseen actualmente en el continente de la Florida," 1765. Brit. Mus. Add. MSS. 17,648A, and in Ruidíaz, *La Florida*, tomo i., between pp. xliii., xliv. In this "Rio Ais" is shown as a river and not as a lagoon. Thomas Jefferys, "The Peninsula and Gulf of Florida or Channel of Bahama with the Bahama Islands," 1775, in the *North American Atlas*, London, 1777, No. 34. Bernard Romans, "The Seat of War in the South British Colonies," 1776, in *The American Military Pocket Atlas*, London (1776), No. 5. John Andrews, "A New Map of the British Colonies in North America . . ," 1777. Pownall, "A New Map of North America with the West India Islands . . ," 1783. All of these three show "Ays Inlet." Tomas Lopez, map of Florida, inset to his "Plano de la Ciudad y Puerto de San Agustin de la Florida," 1783. In this it is shown as "Barra de Ays." George Frederic Lotter, "A New and Correct Map of North America with the West India Islands . . . ," 1784. This shows "Ays Inlet" into the "St. Lucia R." Joseph Purcell, "A Map of the States of Virginia . . . comprehending the Spanish Provinces of East and West Florida. . . ," 1792. This shows "Rio Ays or Indian R." John Walsh, "Tabvla Geographica maximæ partis Ameriæ Mediæ sive Indiæ Occidentalis," 1798. This shows "River Ays od. Indian."

APPENDIX S

SANTA LUCIA

The Spaniards named this settlement Santa Lucia (Merás in Ruidíaz, *La Florida*, tomo i., p. 169). The name is preserved in that of the St. Lucia River, called on some maps Rio Santa Cruz, and "river of St. Luz," probably an abbreviation of Santa Lucia, according to Roberts (*History of Florida*, London, 1763, pp. 22, 286), who places it three leagues south of the "Rio de Ays" (p. 22). It is to be noted, however, that the inlets between the sea and Indian River (Ays) have been subject to many changes in the past. John Lee Williams in his *Florida* (New York, 1837, p. 43, and see p. 51), says: "A few years since the high waters of St. Lucia River forced a passage through the coast at a place called the Gap." "Jupiter Inlet has opened and closed three times within seventy years" (pp. 52, 53), and: "There is every reason to believe that at some period [Indian Lagoon] discharged a great column of water at Cape Cañaveral" (*ibid.*). "St. Lucia Island was formerly connected with Jupiter. . . . In 1831 a mile in front of the north end of the island was torn away by storms" (p. 43). The name of "New Inlet" opening into "Sharks Head and Tail River" (Lake Worth?) in Thomas Jefferys's map of "East Florida" appended to *A Description of East Florida* by William Stork, 3rd edition, London, 1769, indicates a recent inroad of the sea similar to that mentioned by Williams. In the Mexia map referred to below there was a second inlet to the Matanzas River, named Barreta de Ribao, south of the present Matanzas Inlet. Bernard Romans (*A concise Natural History of East and West Florida*, New York, 1775, vol. i., pp. 34, 284–286) merely describes the river and has nothing of interest to add.

The cartography is somewhat curious. In Mexia's map of 1605 (MS. Arch. Gen. de Indias, Seville, Patronato, est. 1, caj. 1, leg. 1/19, ramo 29) the name of "Rio de Sta. Luzia" is given to the lagoon between the "Barra de Ays," Indian River Inlet, and Gilbert's Bar. "S iozia" appears on "Mapa de la Florida y Laguna de Maimi done se ha de hacer un fuerte" (MS. Arch. Gen. de Indias, Seville, est. 145, caj. 7, leg. 7. Undated, 1595–1600?), south of "Ays" lagoon, and is probably intended for S. lozia, *i. e.*, Santa Lucia. Guillaume Blaeu, "Insulæ Americanæ in Oceano Septentrionalis cum Terris adiacentibus" (in *Le Theatre dv Monde ou Novvel*

Atlas, Mis en lumiere par Gvillavme & Iean Blaev. Segonde Partie. A Amsterdam Chez Iean Blaev. 1644. Amerique, pp. 5, 6) has a "p^{ta} S. Luzia" which reoccurs in the majority of the Dutch, French, and Spanish maps. The latest of these is Mentelle et Chanlaire, "Carte de la Floride et de la Georgie," in *Atlas Universelle de Géographie Physique et Politique*, Paris, An six de la République [1798]. The name was probably applied to Cape Malabar. John Senex, "A New Map of the English Empire in America," etc., 1719 (in *A New General Atlas* . . . London, 1719), places "S. Lucia" at the southern extremity of the peninsula. Covens et Mortier, "Archipelague du Mexique ou sont les Isles de Cuba," etc. (*ca.* 1757?), has "S. Lucia" on the west coast. Nicolas Bellin, "Carte reduite des Costes de la Louisiane et de la Floride," 1764, has "R Ste Lucie" in an approximately correct position. Fernando Martinez, "Descripción Geographica de la parte que los Españoles poseen actualmente en el continente de la Florida," 1765 (Brit. Mus. Add. MSS. 17,648A, and in Ruidíaz, *La Florida*, tomo i., between pp. xliii., xliv.) has "Rio Sta Lucia." Pownall's "A New Map of North America with the West India Islands . . ." 1783. George Frederic Lotter, "A New and Correct Map of North America with the West India Islands," 1784, and Laurie and Whittle, "West Indies," 1794, all have "St. Lucia" as a river.

APPENDIX T

CALOOSA

For the early accounts of the Caloosas and their country see: "Memoria de las cosas y costa y indios de la Florida" . . . por Hernando de Escalante Fontanedo. *Col. Doc. Inedit. Indias*, tomo v., pp. 532, 535, 538, 539, in which a list of the names of the Caloosa villages is given. Ternaux-Compans's translation in *Recueil de Pièces sur la Floride* (Paris, 1841, p. 13) is inaccurate, and Barnard Shipp's English translation in his *Hernando de Soto and Florida* (Philadelphia, 1881), which is apparently based on that of Ternaux-Compans, is incomplete, see p. 584, where he omits an entire sentence, which he supplies in a note with the Ternaux-Compans rendering added. Le Moyne in De Bry's *Brevis Narratio*, Francoforti ad Moenum, 1591, p. 17. *Histoire Notable*, Basanier, Paris, 1586, pp. 72–74; English translation in *Hakluyt*, Edinburgh, 1889, vol. ii., pp. 481–483. *Geografía de las Indias* por Juan López de Velasco, 1571–1574, Madrid, 1894, p. 164. Barrientos, "Vida y Hechos," in *Dos Antiguas Relaciones de la Florida*, Genaro García, Mexico, 1902, pp. 87–95. Merás, "Jornadas" in Ruidíaz, *La Florida*, tomo i., pp. 149–168. Herrera in his "Descripción de las Indias" (*Decadas*, Madrid, 1730, cap. viii., tomo i., p. 15), refers only to Carlos Bay.

The recent history is given in: *History of Florida*, by William Roberts, London, 1763, p. 17. *A concise Natural History of East and West Florida*, by Captain Bernard Romans, New York, 1775, vol. i., pp. 289, 290, 291. Appendix, p. lxxvi. *et seq.* Captain Romans's history, of which only the first volume was ever published, is the source from which most subsequent writers have derived their information. *Journal of Andrew Ellicott*, Philadelphia, 1814, pp. 246, 247. Forbes's *Florida*, New York, 1821, pp. 100, 108. *Observations upon the Floridas*, by Charles Vignoles, New York, 1823, pp. 53, 81. John Lee Williams's *Florida*, New York, 1837, pp. 25, 32, 36. Daniel G. Brinton's *Notes on the Floridian Peninsula*, Philadelphia, 1859, pp. 112, 113. *A Migration Legend of the Creek Indians*, by Albert S. Gatschet, Philadelphia, 1884, vol. i., p. 13. "Indian Linguistic Families" by J. W. Powell, *7th Ann. Rep. Bu. Ethn.*, 1885–1886, p. 123.

Caloosa is shown in the following maps; John With's map, 1585, in the *Century Magazine*, vol. xxv., pp. 66, 67. The name "Catos," probably intended for "Calos," appears on the southern end of the peninsula. Le Moyne's map in De Bry, 1591, previously cited. Guillaume de l'Isle, "Carte de la Louisiane et du Cours du Mississipi" (1718?) shows "Les Carlos Antropophages" correctly located. John Senex, "A Map of Louisiana and the River Mississipi" (in *A New*

General Atlas, etc., London, 1719), is probably copied from De l'Isle and shows "The Carlos Man-eaters." Matthaeus Seutter, "Mappa Geographica Regionem Mexicanam et Floridam Terrasque adjacentes ut et Anteriores Americæ Insulas," etc., 1731–1760. Johann Baptista Homann, "Amplissima regionis Mississipi seu Provinciæ Ludovicianæ," etc. (1763), and his "Regni Mexicani seu Novæ Hispaniæ . . . Tabula" (1763, in *Atlas Geographicus Major*, Norimbergæ, 1763, Nos. 139 and 147), both show "Les Carlos" in about the correct location. Fernando Martinez, "Descripción geographica de la parte que los Españoles poseen actualmente en el continente de la Florida" (1765, Brit. Mus. Add. MSS. 17,648A, and in Ruidíaz, *La Florida*, tomo i., between pp. xliii., xliv). Jnº. Cary, "The West Indies," 1783, and Joseph Purcell, "A Map of the States of Virginia, . . . comprehending the Spanish Provinces of East and West Florida," 1792, both show "Carlos" island. See also *Spanish Settlements*, 1513–1561, p. 441, Appendix G, "The Bay of Juan Ponce."

APPENDIX U

SAN FELIPE

Barrientos in García, *Dos Antiguas Relaciones de la Florida*, p. 179) says San Felipe was "En Vna ysla de quatro leguas . . . Estando de la baRa Vna legua." Velasco in his *Geografía de las Indias, 1571–1574*, p. 161, says San Felipe was the island settled by the French five years before and abandoned by them when they learned of the victory of Avilés. But there was no French settlement at Santa Elena prior or subsequent to that of Charlesfort in 1562, to which it is possible that he refers. It is noticeable that Pardo, who went to Cufitatchiqui on the Savannah twice, once across country and once along the coast, mentions no large river between it and San Felipe from where he started (see pp. 275, 294, 445, in this volume). Avilés, in his letter to Philip II. of October 15, 1565, written before he had visited the locality (see p. 401

in this volume), placed Santa Elena fifty leagues from St. Augustine, "and in a distance of three leagues it has three ports and rivers, and the largest has six fathoms of water and the other four admirable harbours; and that which we call Santa Elena, which is the third where the French are, is very bad, and all three can be navigated inside from one to the other."

In the "Relación de la Costa de la Florida" of Joan de Herrera of 1576, forming part of the *Derrotero hecho Por el ynsigne y sabido piloto ysidro de la puebla . . . 1578* (Biblioteca Nacional, Madrid, MSS. 4541, fol. 87), the writer, after giving the latitudes of St. Augustine in 29°, of San Mateo in 30°, of Santa Elena in 32°, and of Guale, "which is between San Mateo and Santa Elena," in 32° 20′, "according to the Reportorio [*sic*] of Chabes," continues "from Santa Elena to the north-east is the Point of Santa Elena itself, and it is an island in itself, for the sea washes between it and the land. . . . To the north-east of the cape of Santa Elena is a very good river . . . and these shoals extend fully three leagues from the land into the sea. . . . It has three or four entrances. . . . In the midst [medio] of the bay you will find within it an island in the middle [en mitad] of the river which is like a galley. . . . To reach the port you must hug the east shore; there is a shoal there, along which the waves break, for in the morning by the full tide (?) and by the roar of the water the current tells you where the bottom lies until you see the houses. To the north-east of the Cape of Santa Elena is another river, which has a good bar, where is the first Indian village . . . and there is a beech beyond, the which is a sweet water river. And the land is more than fifteen leagues, more than any of these rivers. And between one river and the other there are many shoals. . . . This river of sweet water, which is in 32° 20′ *largos* for the River Jordan the coast runs east north-east. . . . From here to the River Jordan is the same east north-east coast. . . . Four leagues beyond the River Jordan is a sand bar which projects into the sea (sale a la mar) nine leagues, all white water."

Mr. Herbert C. Graves, of the Coast and Geodetic Survey, to whom Herrera's description was submitted for his opinion, identifies the Punta de Santa Elena with Hilton Head, in view of J. G. Kohl, "A History of the Discovery of the Coast of North America," vol. i., pp. 309, 399 (*Collection of the Maine Historical Society*, 2nd series), the Ribero map of 1529, facing p. 299, Winsor, *Narr. and Crit. Hist. Am.*, vol. ii., pp. 256, 260, and Le Moyne's map on p. 274. Mr. O. H. Tittmann, Superintendent of the Coast and Geodetic Survey, through whose kindly assistance the report of Mr. Graves was obtained, adds that "Herrera's description and sailing directions answer well to Port Royal and its entrance, and Hilton Head then follows of necessity as Cape St. Helena."

It appears highly probable that the Point of Santa Elena was Hilton Head, and that San Felipe was therefore in the immediate neighbourhood of Charlesfort. As bearing on this conclusion, Mr. Graves calls attention in his report to the similarity of Herrera's galley-shaped island to that of the largest of the islands shown on Le Moyne's map at Portus Regalis, although it should not be forgotten that Le Moyne did not himself visit this region. The Fort of San Felipe may have been on St. Phillip's Island or perhaps on Paris Island.

APPENDIX V

TEGESTA

After describing the island of Metacumbe at the northern extremity of the Martyr Islands (the Florida Keys) Velasco writes (*Geografía de las Indias*, 1571–1574, Madrid, 1894, p. 166): "En la mesma punta de Tequesta, entra en la mar un rio dulce, que viene de la tierra adentro y al parecer corre del oeste al leste . . . junto á el, de la parte del norte, está el pueblo de indios que se dice Tequesta, de donde se dice asi la punta; poblóse aquí un pueblo de Españoles año de 67, que después se despobló año de 70. . . . La Costa va corriendo desde Tequesta al norte, declinando al norueste hasta ponerse en 27 grados: desde la dicha punta hasta rio Dulce que serán seis leguas, hay tres islas al lungo de la costa norte sur, que tendrán todas tres de largo las dichas seis leguas." Fontanedo (" Memoria," *Col. Doc. Inedit Indias*, tomo v., p. 534) writing in 1575 (*Narr. and Crit. Hist. Am.*, vol. ii., p. 291, note 1), says: " Voy á lo que trataba del cabo de las islas de los Mártires hácia el Norte. Fenecen estas islas junto a un lugar de indios, que han por nombre Teguesta, que está á un lado de un rio que entra hácia la tierra dentro; este rio corre hasta quince leguas, y sale á otra laguna, que dicen algunos indios que la han andado más que yo, que es un brazo de la laguna de Mayaimi."

Romans in his *A concise Natural History of East and West Florida* (New York, 1775, vol. i., pp. 296 and 299) knows nothing of the name Tegesta, and ridicules De Brahm's use of the name in his *Atlantic Pilot* (London, 1772). Forbes, in his *Florida* (New York, 1821, p. 103), applies the name Tegesta to the southern extremity of the peninsula. Brinton in his *Notes on the Floridian Peninsula* (Philadelphia, 1859, p. 112) places the province of Tegesta at the southern extremity of the peninsula, and (p. 116) speaks of it as a part of the province of "Ais," in which he is followed by Albert S. Gatschet in his *Migration Legend of the Creek Indians* (Philadelphia, 1884, vol. i., p. 15), who places the village of Tequesta "on a river coming from Lake Mayaimi." J. W. Powell in his " Indian Linguistic Families " (*7th Ann. Rep. Bu. Ethn.*, p. 123) is even less definite.

It is to be noted that both the descriptions of Fontanedo and Velasco mention a point of land with three islands at the head of the Florida Keys and a river of sweet water flowing east and west from an arm of Lake Miami. They point with much probability to Biscayne Bay and Miami River, the large river of sweet water flowing east and west in that neighbourhood, and which finds its source in a sweet water lagoon in the interior. Snake River, to the north of it, does not flow in the same direction, although it is also a sweet-water river.

In the maps the name " Province of Tegesta " has been applied at different times to the southern extremity of the peninsula, to its northern part, and to the entire peninsula.

The most interesting and typical of these maps are: Jean de Laet, "Florida et Regiones Vicinae," 1640, in his *L'Histoire dv Nouveau Monde*, Leyde, 1640, between pp. 102, 103. Ioannes Jansson, "America Septentrionalis," in his *Nuevo Atlas*, Amsterdam, 1653, vol. ii. Sanson d'Abbeville, "Le Nouveau Mexique et la Floride," 1679. Nicolaus Visscher, "Insulæ Americanæ in Oceano Septentrionali," etc. (1680?), in his *Atlas Minor*, Amst. All four of these maps give "Tegesta Provincia." Edward Wells, "A New Map of North America," etc. (in his *A New Sett of Maps both of Antient and Present Geography*, Oxford, 1701), shows the "Peninsula of Tegesta." Matthieu Albert Lotter, "Carte Nouvelle de l'Amerique Angloise," etc., 1720 (?) shows "Tegeste" applied to part of the peninsula. Matthaeus Seutter, "Novus Orbis," etc., 1725–1760. Renier & Ottens, "Insulæ Americanæ," etc., 1730 (?) Matthaeus Seutter, "Mappa Geographica Regionem Mexicanam et Floridam," etc., 1731–1760. All three of these maps show "Tegesta Prov." Covens et Mortier, "Archipelague du Mexique ou sont les Isles de Cuba," etc., *ca.* 1757, shows "Tegeste Province." Johann Baptista Homann, "Totius Americæ Septentrionalis et Meridionalis," etc., 1765, shows the name "Tegesta Provincia," applied to the southern end of the peninsula. Johann Baptista Homann, "Regni Mexicani seu Novæ Hispaniæ," etc., 1763, shows "Tegesta Prov." Fernando Martinez, "Descripción Geographica de la parte que los Españoles poseen actualmente en el continente de la Florida," 1765 (Brit. Mus. Add. MSS. 17,468, and in Ruidíaz, *La Florida*, tomo i.), has the legend: "Tequesta que oy se dicen Indios Costas." John Grear de Brahm, "The Ancient Tegesta, now Promontory of East Florida," in his *The American Pilot*, London, 1772. De Brahm has been copied by the following maps, all of which represent Tegesta across the southern end of the Peninsula: Thos. Jefferys, "The Peninsula and Gulf of Florida or Channel of Bahama with the Bahama Islands," 1775. Bernard Romans, "A General Map of the Southern British Colonies in America," 1776. John Andrews, "A Map of the British Colonies in North America," 1779. Jno. Cary, "The West Indies," 1783.

APPENDIX W

DATE OF PARDO'S FIRST EXPEDITION

There is a conflict between the dates given in the Relation of Martinez and that of Pardo, for the inception of the various expeditions of the latter. Pardo in his undated report says he was sent to Santa Elena, " donde desde á pocos dias que ay estábamos llegó el Adelantado pero Menéndez de Avilés . . . y . . . me mandó que yo entrase el dia de Santo Andrés, primo venidero, la tierra adentro . . . y ansí, benido el dia de Santo Andrés, yo me partí " (" Relación de la entrada," Ruidíaz, *La Florida*, tomo ii., p. 466). He then proceeds with the report of this expedition or *entrada*, which ends with the words: " Esto es lo de la primera jornada " (p. 469). These are immediately followed by the words: " Llegó el Adelantado Pero Menéndez de Avilés el año 1566 á la cibdad de Santa Elena, á donde me mando yo tornase á proseguir la jornada . . . y así yo me partí el primer dia de Setiembre" (p. 469). Martinez in his Relation dated July 11, 1567, says that: " De la civdad de Santa Elena salío el Capitan Juan Pardo el primer dia de Nobienbre año de 1566, para entrar la tierra dentro á descubrilla y conquistalla dende aqui hasta México" (Ruidíaz, *La Florida*, tomo ii., p. 477). Pardo went as far as " Juada," where, finding his progress impeded by snow upon the mountains, he returned to San Felipe, leaving his sergeant at Juada The sergeant subsequently made a reconnoissance as far as Chiaha, " dondc aguardó al dicho Capitan que ha de partir deste fuerte mediado Agosto " (p. 479) *i. e.*, during August, 1567. Vandera in the opening of his narrative refers indefinitely to expeditions in 1566 and 1567 (see the copy given by Buckingham Smith, *Col. Doc. Flo.*, tomo i., p. 15, which begins with these dates, given only in the title by Ruidíaz), and neither he nor Barcia gives dates nor distinguishes the entradas.

It thus appears from the Pardo Relation that Avilés was twice at Santa Elena in 1566 and that Pardo's second entrada was made in September subsequent to Avilés's second visit. But Avilés, in fact, made but one visit to Santa Elena during the year 1566, leaving San Mateo April 1st, and returning May 15th, or in August, according to Merás. He returned a second time in 1567, sailing from there for Spain on the 18th of May. It is therefore altogether probable that the date 1566 in Pardo's Relation is a misprint or error of the copyist for 1567, in which latter case all of Pardo's statements will substantially conform with the dates given by Martinez and by Vandera. Thus we will have two entradas, the first November 1, 1566, the date given by Martinez, and subsequent to Avilés's first visit according to Pardo, and a second entrada on the 1st of September, 1567, the year given by Martinez and Vandera, the month that of Pardo in approximate agreement with Martinez's statement that an entrada was to be made in August of 1567, and also subsequent to the second visit of Avilés according to Pardo. There is also the mistake of a year in the printed title of the Pardo Relation, 1565 being given for 1566.

APPENDIX X

PARDO'S FIRST EXPEDITION

Pardo's Rel. Ruidíaz, *La Florida*, tomo ii., pp. 465–473.	Vandera in Buck. Smith, *Col. Doc. Flo.*, pp. 15–17.	Vandera in Ruidíaz, *La Florida*, tomo ii., pp. 481–486.
———	———	Uscamacu
———	———	Ahoya

Vandera (Ruidíaz, tomo ii., p. 481) describes it as an island. In "Mapa de la Florida y Laguna de Maimi donde se ha de hacer un fuerte" (MS. Undated, 1595–1600? Arch. Gen de Indias, Seville, est. 145, caj. 7, leg. 7), it is shown as an island directly south of Santa Elena. Albert S. Gatschet in his *Migration Legend of the Creek Indians* (vol. i., p. 62) derives the name from a Creek word signifying "two going," and says it was a Creek village along the Savannah River. This is incorrect, as Pardo had not yet reached the Savannah. Ahoya is probably only another form of "Hoya," on page 352 of this volume. The prefix "a" in names of persons and places was frequently dropped by the Spaniards (see Maya and Amaya, p. 225, note 2, in this volume).

Pardo's Rel. Ruidíaz, *La Florida*, tomo ii., pp. 465–473	Vandera in Buck. Smith, *Col. Doc. Flo.*, pp. 15–17.	Vandera in Ruidíaz, *La Florida*, tomo ii., pp 481–486.
———	———	Ahoyabe
———	Coçao, Cozao	Cozao

J. G. Shea in a note to his "Pardo's Exploration of South Carolina and Georgia in 1566–67" (*Historical Magazine*, August, 1860, p. 231) suggests the Coosawatchee(?)

———	———	Enfrenado
(Guiomae?)	Guiomaer	Guiomaez

Vandera (p. 482) places it on a large river. Both Vandera (*ibid.*) and Pardo (p. 469) say forty leagues from Santa Elena.

Canos	Cofetaçque	Canos, Canosi, Cofetazque

Pardo (p. 466) says: "Tyene un rio cavdal." Vandera (p. 482) describes it as "Canos, que los indios llaman Canosi, y por otro nombre Cofetazque. . . . Hay hasta Sancta Elena cinquenta leguas y hasta la mar como veinte leguas; puédese ir hasta el por el rio dicho, cursando la tierra, y por mucho mas adelante por el mismo rio." James Mooney in his "Myths of the Cherokee" (*19 Ann. Rep. Bu. Ethn.*, pt. i., p. 28) and Shea (*ibid.*, p. 231) identify Canos with De Soto's Cufitatchiqui. Gatschet in his *Migration Legend of the Creek Indians* (vol. i., p. 20) with the Cannouchee River at the head of which lived the Yuchees. He derives Canosi from the Creek *ikano'dshi* signifying, "graves are there" (*ibid.*, p. 63).

Tagaya	Jagaya	Tagaya
Tagaya el Chico	———	———
———	———	Gueza
———	Arauchi, Aracuchi.	Aracuchi.
Ysa	Issa	(4) Isa [1]

[1] The numbers indicate the order in which these names are given by Vandera, who describes them in the order in which they were visited on the second entrada, *i. e.*, from south to north.

Gatschet (p. 62) derives Issa from the Creek *idshu*, deer, and locates it on the Savannah. But it is to be noted that neither Pardo nor Vandera states that Ysa was on the same river as Canos. In fact, Pardo says of Canos: " Tyene *un* rio cavdal " (p. 466) and of Ysa " tiene *un* rio cavdal " (p. 467), from which it does not necessarily follow that both were on the same river. Had he ascended the river to Ysa he would have said: " Pasa *el* rio cavdal por él," as he does in the case of Quihanaqui, which was on the same stream as Juada, below it (p. 467). Shea (*ibid.*, p. 230) derives the name from the " Chahta," *íssi*, a deer, and says it is apparently identical with Ays, which Romans describes as on the Indian River. The mistake in the location is too apparent to require comment.

Pardo's Rel. Ruidíaz, *La Florida*, tomo ii., pp. 465–473.	Vandera in Buck. Smith, *Col. Doc. Flo.*, pp. 15–17.	Vandera in Ruidíaz, *La Florida*, tomo ii., pp. 481–486.
Juada	———	(6) Joara

This is the " Toana " of Barrientos (" Hechos " in *Dos Antiguas Relaciones de la Florida*, p. 140). Mooney identifies this with the Xuala of De Soto (see *Spanish Settlements*, 1513–1561, p. 230, and note 3), which he locates in the territory of the Suwali Indians about the head of the Broad River in North Carolina (see "Xuala and Guaxule" by Cyrus Thomas and J. N. B. Hewitt in *Science*, N. S., vol. xxi, p. 863, for a different location). But the distance, fifty or sixty miles from the nearest point on the Savannah, is excessive for a two-days' march. Shea (*ibid.*, p. 231) also notes its similarity to De Soto's Xuala.

———	———	Aguaquiri

Mooney (*ibid.*, p. 28) thinks it the "Guiaquili" of De Soto.

Quihanaqui	———	(3) Quinahaqui

Pardo (p. 467) says it was a large river, and the context appears to indicate that it was the same river which flowed by Juada. Vandera (p. 483), who mentions the localities in the reverse order, *i. e.*, from south to north, says it was a large river other than the river on which Guatary was situated, and Ysa lay twelve leagues to the left (*i. e.*, the East? See p. 450 in this volume).

Pardo's Rel. Ruidíaz, *La Florida*, tomo ii., pp. 465–473.	Vandera in Buck. Smith, *Col. Doc. Flo.*, pp. 15–17.	Vandera in Ruidíaz, *La Florida*, tomo ii., pp. 481–486.
Guatari	Guatari	(2) Guatary

Vandera (p. 483) says of it: "que viene á dar á Sauapa y Usi, donde se hace sal, junto con la mar sesenta leguas de Sancta Elena. Desde este Sancta Elena á este Guatari hay ochenta leguas, y por este mismo rio puede entrar mas de veinte, segun dicen, cualquier navio." Mooney (*ibid.*, p. 28) identifies it with the Wateree. He says Usi is Ushery or Catawba, and Sauapa is Waxhaw or Sissipahaw(?) It is to be noted, however, that Vandera locates them in the region where the river becomes salt.

Guatariatiqui (Quatariaatiqui of 2d Entrada)	Otariyatiqui	(1) Otariatiqui Otari.

James Adair in *The History of the American Indians* (London, 1775, p. 226) says the Cherokees call the mountain portion of their territory *Ottare*, signifying "mountainous." Mooney (*ibid.*, p. 28) suggests that it may have been a frontier Cherokee settlement. Perhaps the Cherokee *â tărĭ* or *â tálí*—"mountain." Gatschet (*ibid.*, p. 24) places the Cherokee villages of the Overhill Settlements, *Otari*, *Otali*, signifying "up, above," north-west of the "Smoky Mountains," along the Great and Little Tennessee rivers and their tributaries.

Pardo's return was by the same route, *i. e.*, Tagaya Chiquito (Chico), Tagaya, Cajucos, Guiomae, and Santa Elena. George R. Fairbanks in his *History of St. Augustine* (New York, 1858, p. 101) think Pardo probably visited the up-country of Georgia, in the neighbourhood of Rome. Luys de Paez (Expediente del Sargento Pedro Luys de Paez, 1579, MS. Arch. Gen.

Indias, Seville, est. 51, caj. 5, leg. 16) relates that Pardo on his expedition into the interior constructed "three or four" forts named "Zuara," "Aguatira," and "Orista." These are Juada and Aguaquiri.

APPENDIX Y

TOCOBAGA

Velasco in his *Geografía de las Indias*, *1571–1574*, pp. 162, 163, gives the following description: "La bahía de *Tocobaga*, por otro nombre del *Espíritu-Santo ó de Miruelo*, está en 29 grados y 1/2 de altura: la entrada tiene por travesía el oeste; tendrá tres leguas de boca, y en ella tres isletas pequeñas en que no hay cosa ninguna sino arena y pájaros; por la parte del norte corre la costa dentro della como dos leguas del oeste al leste y luego vuelve un brazo de mar de tres leguas de ancho derecho al norte, diez y ocho leguas la tierra adentro, hasta el mesmo pueblo de Tocobaga, pueblo de indios donde se acaba: para navegarse, se ha de arrimar siempre á la costa del este, por que la otra es todo bajo; en pasando el dicho brazo vuelve otro brazo más ancho que el sobredicho; al es nordeste no se ha navegado; por esto no se sabe donde va á parar." Fontanedo ("Memoria," *Col. Doc. Inedit. Indias*, tomo v., p. 537), writing in about 1575 (*Narr. and Crit. Hist. Am.*, vol. ii., p. 291, note 1), places "Toco-baja," in which town "esta el Rey casi mayor de aquella comarca," near a river on the west Florida coast called "Guavaca-Esgui" by the Indians. The river is between "Abalache" and "Ogale," locations which he does not describe. The chief's residence "llámase Toco-baja Chile . . . á cabo posterior del rio, hácia la tierra adentro, que hay de rio más de quarenta leguas." "Desde Tocovaga hasta Santa Elena, que habrá de costa seiscientos leguas" (p. 546). It can be reached from "Saravay, que esta cinquenta ó sesenta leguas la tierra adentro del rio (St. John's?) arriba, ó á la provincia de Utina," and then west, "tomando por arriba de pueblo en pueblo, y dar consigo á la Cañogacola, vasallos de Tocovaga, y de allí al lugar mismo de Tocovaga, en que esta otro rio muy grande, donde Soto estuvo y murió" (p. 545). Herrera in his "Descripción de las Indias" (*Decadas de Indias*, Madrid, 1730, tomo i., cap. viii., p. 15) places Tocobaga thirty-three leagues to the north of Tampa Bay. Barcia in his *Ensayo* (Año MDLXVII., p. 127) says, "Avilés entro por el Puerto y un Indio . . . guió al Pueblo de Tocobaga, que estaba 20 Leguas la Tierra adentro, sobre vn Braço de Agua salada." William Roberts in his *History of Florida* (London, 1763, p. 16), says: "Between Rio Pedro and the Rio Amasura are the two small rivers of St. Martin and Tocobogas. Between these rivers reside the tribe of Tocobogas." He places the Rio Amasura or Masura in latitude 28 deg. 25 min. (*ibid.*, p. 16). The Rio Pedro is "almost S.E. from Apalache River." Williams's *Florida* (New York, 1837, pp. 31, 32) writes: "Helley's Keys are a range of sandy islands extending in front of Tocobagos, or St. Joseph's Bay. From Tocobagos to Tampa there is a boat channel behind these keys, but at some places it is very shoal at low water." Daniel G. Brinton in his *Notes on the Floridian Peninsula* (Philadelphia, 1859, p. 118) says: "In later times the cacique dwelt in a village on Old Tampa Bay, twenty leagues from the main, called Tocobaga or Togabaga, whence the province derived its name, and was reputed to be the most potent in Florida. A large mound still seen in the vicinity marks the spot." Fairbanks in his *History of Florida* (Philadelphia, 1871, p. 139) places "Tocobayo" about Cape Canaveral. Cyrus Thomas in his "The Indians of North America in Historic Times" (Lee, *Hist. of North America*, Philadelphia, vol. ii., p. 57) places Tocobaga on Old Tampa Bay.

Velasco's description evidently refers to Tampa Bay. The first bay within three leagues of the mouth and eighteen leagues deep, extending directly north, is Old Tampa, where the village of Tocobaga is correctly placed, according to the independent observations of subsequent authorities to whom his description was unknown. The second wider arm, which extends east north-east (incorrectly punctuated in Velasco's text), is Hillsborough Bay. It is to be noted that Velasco does not locate Tampa Bay, showing a confusion existing in his mind between it and Tocobaga, and that the only two other localities which he gives on the west coast, "Bahia de Carlos" and "la punta de Muspa," are correctly located.

"Mapa de la Florida y Laguna de Maimi donde se ha de hacer un fuerte" (Undated, 1595–1600? MS. Arch. Gen. de Indias, Seville, est. 145, caj. 7, leg. 7), shows the "b[a] de tacabaga" in about the correct position. Tocobaga is also shown on the following maps, which have been already referred to in previous notes: De Laet, 1640; Sanson d'Abbeville, 1656 and 1679; Visscher, 1680. It reappears with Reinier & Ottens, 1730, and Jno. Cary, "West Indies," 1783, who gives it in approximately the correct position. The river of Tocobaga referred to by William Roberts appears on the following map, as well as elsewhere: "East Florida, from Surveys made since the last Peace," adapted to Dr. Stork's History of that country, by Thomas Jefferys, Geographer to the King, in *A Description of East-Florida*, by William Stork, 3rd edit., London, 1769. In "The Bay of Espiritu Santo, in East Florida," by Tho. Jefferys, facing Bartram's "Journal," which is published by Dr. Stork in the work just referred to, the north-west arm of the bay is named "Tampa Bay According to the Spaniards."

APPENDIX Z

PARDO'S SECOND EXPEDITION

On reference to Appendix W in this volume it will be noted that Vandera gives the villages between Joara (Pardo's Juada) and Otariatiqui (Pardo's Guatariatiqui) in the reverse order from that followed by Pardo. On collating this list of Vandera with that in Pardo's second expedition the order will be found to be substantially the same in both, indicating that Vandera described the route followed on the second expedition. For this reason it is necessary only to give the names of the towns beyond Juada in the order in which they are given by Pardo and by Vandera.

Pardo's Rel. Ruidíaz, *La Florida*, tomo ii., p. 465.	Vandera in Buck. Smith, *Col. Doc. Flo.*, pp. 15–17.	Vandera in Ruidíaz, *La Florida*, tomo ii., pp. 481–486.
Juada Tocalques, Tocae.	——— Tocax	Joara Tocar

See p. 295 in this volume.

Canche, Cauchi,	———	Cauchi

Pardo (p. 470) says it has a large river. Mooney, in "Myths of the Cherokee" (*19 Ann. Rep. Bu. Ethn.*, pt. i., p. 29), suggests Nacoochee, apparently a Creek town. And see p. 296, note 4 in this volume.

Tanasqui	———	Tanasqui

Pardo (*ibid.*, p. 470) says, "It has a large river." Mooney (*ibid.*, p. 29) says apparently a Creek town.

Chihaque, Lameco Chiaha	———	Solameco, Chiaha

See p. 286 note 1 in this volume.

———	———	Chalahume
Satapo	———	Satapo, Tasqui.

From Satapo Pardo returned to San Felipe at Santa Elena.

Fourquevaux, under date of November 30, 1567 (*Dépêches*, p. 305) forwarded to Charles IX. a curious account of an expedition which probably relates to this entrada, furnished him by an usher of Philip II. It gives a few interesting details of the country, although it contains some exaggeration and appears to be somewhat confused with the events of the first entrada made during the winter. It reads as follows: "The captain Jehean Pardo, governor of the point of Santa Elena in Florida has written that he has sent thirty soldiers in a brigantine one hundred leagues up the said river of Santa Elena, and some of them having landed on the north side, they went thirty leagues over land away from the said river, and have found at the foot of the mountains an open town, the houses built of stone, and a small castle also of stone where there was a tower. The inhabitants are peaceable and appear to be good people. They are dressed in cotton shirts and the furs of various beasts. They sow corn and other seed. There are oxen, but they are small. The land is fertile and they have trees bearing various fruits which are good to eat. There are mines of gold and silver. And they told the said soldiers that several days' distance farther on there was a population of bearded men; they were unable to learn if they were Frenchmen or Spaniards, neither were they allowed to proceed farther; the said Indians, however, gave them food and provisions for their return to the brigantine, and thus they returned to the said fort."

The ascent of the Savannah in boats, according to this account, is not inconsistent with Pardo's Relation, for he may have followed the coast to the mouth of the Savannah River, visiting Ahoya on his way. The silver mines suggest the second entrada in which the fumes of silver were perceived (see p. 295 in this volume). The refusal to allow the Spaniards to advance may refer to their return from Chiaha on account of the hostile Indians farther on; and the report of the white settlement may have arisen from the imperfect understanding by the Spaniards of a reference made by the Indians to De Luna's settlement of a few years before.

APPENDIX AA

TACATACURU

"El fuerte de San Pedro, que es en la isla de Tacatacoru." Disposición de cuatro fuertes que ha de haber en la Florida y guarnición que debe tener cada uno de ellos. (In Ruidíaz, *La*

Florida, tomo ii., p. 507. Ruidíaz dates this document 1566, see *ibid.*, p. 713. The date of 1569 given it in *Col. Doc. Inedit. Indias*, tomo xiii., p. 307, is probably correct). Velasco in his *Geografía de las Indias, 1571–1574*, pp. 168, 169 does not mention the island by this name, but, describing the coast to the north-east, in the direction of Santa Elena, which is filled with islands both large and small, he says: "La primera de las más señaladas es, en pasando la boca del rio de San Mateo, la que se llama *Carabay*, que es una barra muy chiquita, y así no puede servir sino para chalupas; dos leguas más adelante está otra que llaman la *Revuelta*, con dos bocas por una isleta que tiene en la entrada; y más adelante otras dos leguas está la barra de *Seña*, adonde solía estar el fuerte de San Pedro; es barra que, si aguardan marea, pueden entrar navíos de docientos toneles. Más adelante cuatro leguas, está *Bahia de Ballenas*, que es una bahía muy grande y ancha; pero no tiene buena barra, porque es todo bajío: arriba de la tierra, un rio muy poderoso de agua dulce, que se llama el rio del *Marqués*, está muy poblado de indios al luengo dél de una y de otra parte. Más adelante de esta bahía dos leguas, está otra barra pequeña que se dice *Gualequeni*, adonde no pueden entrar sino con chalupas." And see also p. 161, where he says: "El fuerte de San Pedro estuvo en la barra de Seña."

According to the "Plano de la Entrada de Gualiquini Rio de San Simon situado á 31° 17′ de latitud Septentrional" (MS. Dep. de la Guerra, Madrid, Arch. de Mapas, L. M. 8a–1a–a, No. 43, and of which there appears to be another MS. copy dated May 15, 1757, in the Archives of the Indies, Seville, *Relación Descriptiva de los Mapas, Planos, & [sic] de México y Florida existentes en el Archivo General de Indias* por Pedro Torres Lanzas, Sevilla, 1900, tomo i., No. 131), there can be little doubt that Gualiquini is Jykill Island, which is substantially in agreement with the conclusion reached by Dr. Shea in *The Catholic Church in Colonial Days* (New York, 1886, pp. 142, 143, note 1, p. 178, note 1) from independent observation. Accordingly the island of San Pedro is Cumberland Island ; la barra de Seña is Cumberland Sound; La Revuelta is Nassau Sound, and Carabay is Fort George Inlet.

William B. Stevens in his *History of Georgia* (New York, 1847, vol. i., p. 135), says: "Missoe is the Indian name, meaning sassafras, of the island called San Pedro by the Spaniards and by the English Cumberland." Fairbanks in his *History of Florida* (Philadelphia, 1871, p. 143) identifies the harbour of Fernandina with Tacatacuru. This is substantially in agreement with the above, for the entrance to the harbour of Fernandina is through Cumberland Sound, although it appears that he is disposed to consider Amelia Island as Tacatacuru. William W. Dewhurst, in his *History of St. Augustine* (New York, 1881, p. 60), and Shea in his "Ancient Florida" (*Narr. and Crit. Hist. Am.*, vol. ii., p. 280), identify Tacatacuru with St. Mary's River. It is to be noted that the name "Seña" used by Velasco for this harbour bears a curious resemblance to the French name "Seine," by which the French are said to have called the Tacatacuru River (*La Reprise de la Floride*, p. 47). The Spanish form of "Seine" is "Sequena." Gatschet says the name Tacatacuru contains the Timucuanan word *taca*, fire, probably in a redoubled form. "The Timucua Language" in *Proceedings of the American Philosophical Society*, vol. xviii., p. 502.

APPENDIX BB

THE SPANISH ACCOUNT OF GOURGUES'S ATTACK ON SAN MATEO

A careful collation of the incomplete manuscript letter of Las Alas entitled: "estevan de la sala en san agustin cinco de mayo mil quinientos sesenta y nueve cuenta como se perdio el fuerte de sant mateo" (Arch. Gen. de Indias, Seville, est. 2, caj. 5, leg. 1/9) with Gourgues's Relation in *La Reprise de la Floride* (Larroque, Paris, Bordeaux, 1867) raises so strong a presumption that we have here part of the original Spanish version of the French attack upon San Mateo, that the events which it relates have been incorporated into the narrative in the text in the belief that the date of 1569 appended to the document is a clerical error. The letter appears from its context as well as from its title to have been written from St.

Augustine. So much of it as is essential to a comparison of the two accounts is as follows: "Good Friday at three o'clock in the afternoon five ships appeared upon the bar three of which were of reasonable size and the other two smaller and they were about a league from the fort a gun was fired to inform them that there were people and a harbour here thinking they were Spanish ships and if they were enemies that they might also know we were here. hearing the gun . . . they took the direction of San Mateo . . . the first Sunday after Easter [el domingo de pasquilla] in the morning the sergeant of San Mateo arrived at this fort with thirty persons who had been with thirty men in one of two houses which had been built at the bar of San Mateo and said that the Saturday before at midday he had seen from this house where he was which is on this side of the river of San Mateo towards this fort many Indians approach and another band of persons armed with guns and corselets and arquebuses and four field banners and their trumpets and drums and at once they closed in on the house which is on the other side of the Island of Alimacani in which there were thirty other soldiers who became so confused that they abandoned the house and he who could fly fled but only a few for of all of them only five escaped the sergeant continued firing from this house to where they were with two guns which he had in it until the ammunition gave out and perceiving that succour could not reach him speedily from San Mateo because the tide would not permit of it and the weather which was very fierce from the north east he spiked the guns and came as I have said to this fort."

The fragment of the letter contains no hint as to the nationality of the ships, and only from its title do we know that the missing portion, which probably bore the date and the signature of the writer, relates the fall of Fort San Mateo. The result of a comparison of the two accounts is as follows: Gourgues states that he had three vessels (*La Reprise de la Floride*, p. 29). Las Alas mentions five. This difference in numbers is not material, since Gourgues had captured Spanish vessels during his voyage (Alava to Alba, June 25, 1568, MS. Arch. Nat., Paris, K, 1511 [56], fol. 2; Alava to Philip II.,

June 28, 1568, *ibid.*, [59]). Eight days prior to his capture of the blockhouses (*La Reprise*, pp. 38, 40, 44, 46, 47, 49, 50) Gourgues, who was sailing in a northerly direction, passed a Spanish fort which saluted him with two guns, to which he replied (*ibid.*, p. 38). Las Alas relates that on Good Friday, nine days before the capture of the blockhouses according to his own dates, he fired a gun to signal five ships, which were discovered off St. Augustine. Thereupon Gourgues sails away until out of sight of land, but returns at night and lands within fifteen leagues of the fort. Las Alas says the ships took the direction of Fort San Mateo.

Gourgues says it rained hard the morning of the attack and that it blew a north-east wind the previous day (*ibid.*, pp. 49, 50). Las Alas says that on the day of the attack there was a strong north-east wind. Gourgues attacked first the blockhouse on the left (north) bank of the St. John's with a force of Indians and of armed men. Las Alas says the same. Gourgues attacked the first blockhouse after ten o'clock in the morning (*ibid.*, p. 52). Las Alas says at midday. Gourgues says the south fort incommoded the French attack on the north fort by firing cannon at them (*ibid.*, p. 54). Las Alas says the south fort fired at the party attacking the north fort until its ammunition was expended. According to Gourgues the two forts were captured on "the eve of Quasimodo," *i. e.*, the Saturday preceding the first Sunday after Easter. Las Alas says the same. Gourgues says there were sixty Spaniards in the south fort (p. 54), and does not mention the number in the first fort. Las Alas says there were sixty men in both forts.

The coincidences are remarkable. The salute on first seeing the ships, the direction taken by the ships after being sighted, the direction from which comes the attack on the first blockhouse, the character of the attacking force, the weather, the fort first captured, the defence made by the second fort, the locality, and finally the ecclesiastical date. Against the probability, raised by this similarity in the two accounts, that they are both describing the same event, is to be set the remote possibility of an event's repeating itself for two years in succession with all of these characteristics in common and occurring in the same order. The mistake of one figure in the date of the title is not an unusual circumstance, instances of such errors having been noticed in the course of this volume, particularly as the title in which it occurs is in the nature of a caption written in by a clerk.

While this volume was going through the press, Professor William R. Shepherd has, in a recent review, assumed the same position as the author in respect to the authenticity of the Gourgues incident, in view "of the evidence presented by the correspondence of Menéndez de Avilés published in the second volume of Ruidíaz y Caravia's *La Florida*, by the statements of Barrientos in his *Vida y Hechos de Pero Menendez de Auiles*, and by other original authorities recently discovered." (*Political Science Quarterly*, vol. xx., p. 331, June, 1905.)

APPENDIX CC

THE SECOND VOYAGE OF AVILÉS TO FLORIDA

A period of sixteen months intervenes between Avilés's letter of May 12, 1568, from Santander and his next letter from Spain, dated at Seville, September 22, 1569 (Ruidíaz, *La Florida*, tomo ii., p. 180). During this interval he appears to have been at Havana in April (?) of 1569 according to his letter of September 22, 1569, above cited, in which he says: "y aviéndome V. M. mandado por una su Real Cédula, hecha por Febrero de este presente año, recibida en la Habana por este mes de Abril pasado, en que me manda con la armada de mi cargo aconpañe la flota de Nueva España hasta la meter en Sanlucar de Barrameda en salvamiento, . . . y que viniendo la dicha flota sola, quedando yo en las Indias" (*ibid.*, tomo ii., pp. 182, 183). Fourquevaux observes that Avilés was expected at the Azores about June, 1568 (Letter of May 21, 1568, *Dépêches*, p. 360). Gabriel de Cayas wrote Alava that Avilés had sailed from Laredo August 12 to punish pirates (Sept. 4, 1568, Arch. Nat., Paris, K, 1511 [81]). Garcilaso (*La Florida del Inca*, Madrid, 1723, lib. vi., cap. xxii., p. 268), Pulgar (*Historia general de la Florida*, Biblioteca Nacional, Madrid, MSS. 2999, fol. 173), and Barcia (*Ensayo*, Año MDLXX., p. 141) insist upon three voyages of Avilés to Florida, although Barcia attributes a wrong date to this voyage, as stated in note 1, p. 342, in this volume. The date of Avilés's return to Spain was prior to that of his letter of September 22, 1569, above referred to. He remained in Spain until after January 4, 1570. (See letters dated Escalona, November 12, 1569, Ruidíaz, *La Florida*, tomo ii., p. 184; Seville, November 20th, *ibid.*, p. 185; Seville, November 24th, *ibid.*, p. 189; Seville, November 27th, *ibid.*, p. 191; Seville, Dec. 4th, *ibid.*, p. 193; Cadiz, December 31st, *ibid.*, p. 196, and Cadiz, January 4, 1570, *ibid.*, p. 201). It follows that Shea's statement that Avilés returned to Spain after hearing of Segura's landing, September 11, 1570, at Axacan, is incorrect.

It is true that a period of eleven months intervenes between Avilés's letter of January 4, 1570, and his next letter dated at Seville, December 3, 1570 (*ibid.*, tomo ii., p. 203). But during this interval Avilés appears to have been at sea protecting the treasure fleets on their voyage between the Canaries and Spain from Pie de Palo and other pirates (*ibid.*, tomo ii., p. 205, of this same letter). Subsequent to December 3, 1570, he remained in Spain until he sailed for Florida, May 17, 1571. (See his letters dated San Lucar de Barrameda [Dec.?], 1570, *ibid.*, p. 213; Seville, January 23, 1571, *ibid.*, p. 220; Seville, March 12th, *ibid.*, p. 221; San Lucar de Barrameda, May 15th, *ibid.*, p. 222; Sanflanejos, May 15th, *ibid.*, p. 224; and San Lucar, May 16, 1571, *ibid.*, p. 226).

APPENDIX DD

AXACAN

The first visit of the Spaniards to Axacan was that of the Dominican missionaries in 1559–1560, who are said by Sacchini (*Hist. Soc. Jesu.* Pars tertia, Romæ, 1650, p. 323) to have taken the Indian Don Luis from there eleven years prior to 1570. Avilés refers to Don Luis as being already in Mexico in his letter to the King of October 15, 1565 (Ruidíaz, *La*

Florida, tomo ii., p. 94), and it seems probable that from him the existence of the Bay of Santa Maria of Axacan (Xacan, Jacan, Iacan, Axaca, Axacam) was learned. Avilés in the letter above referred to says of the Bay of "Santa Maria" "que está an treynta y siete grados, ciento y treynta leguas mas adelante de Santa Elena" (p. 94); but in his letter of December 25, 1565 (*ibid.*, p. 131), he places it one hundred leagues to the north of Santa Elena, and elsewhere in the same letter (p. 134) fifty leagues by land from St. Augustine and San Mateo, which shows how indefinite his information was.

There can be little doubt as to its identity with Chesapeake Bay. Velasco in his *Geografía de las Indias, 1571–1574* (p. 172) says: "Cabo de Santiago: [está] al norte del cabo de Arenas [the Cabo de Arenas was in 37° 30′], cerca dél. Bahia de San Cristóbal; más al norte. Bahia de Santa Maria: más al norte. Rio de San Anton: en 42 grados y 1/2 como ochenta leguas al norte del cabo de las Arenas." The Chesapeake was visited in 1588 by Vincente Gonzales, for he entered a bay where the Indians told him there was an English settlement towards the north on a river flowing into it, but Gonzales does not give the name of the bay. ("Relación que dió el Capitan Vizente Gonzales," 1588, MS. Direc. de Hidrog., Madrid, *Col. Navarrete*, tomo xiv., Doc. No. 54, fol. 8.) Juan Menéndez Marqués in his "Relación escrita en el fuerte de San Agustin . . . al P. Comisario General de Indias Fr. Miguel Avengoçar," June 7, 1606 (Ruidíaz, tomo ii., p. 498) refers to this expedition of 1588 as being to the Bay of Jacan. "Y aviendo por el año de 88 ydo al descubrimiento de la baya de la Madre de Dios del Jacan, y tomar lengua de la poblacion del ynglés, juntamente con el Capitan Vincente Gonzales," etc. In 1609 Ecija, Piloto Mayor, was ordered to reconnoitre the coast "hasta allegar a la Altura de 37 grados y medio donde se sospecha estan poblados los primeros yngleses en el sitio que ellos llaman (la Virginia)[1] o cortuan y en nuestra lengua se llama la vaya del Iacan." (Orden del Gobernador D. Pedro de Ibarra a el Capitan Francisco Fernandez de Ecija para reconocer las costas del norte de aquella Provincia, 1609,

[1] Bracketed in the original MS.

MS. Arch. Gen. de Indias, Seville, Patronato, est. 2, caj. 5, leg. 3/16, p. 2.)

In the "Report of the voyage to Virginia made in behalf of Don Diego de Molino, Marco Antonio Perez and Francisco Lembri," enclosed in a letter of the Duke of Lerma of November 13, 1611, there is mention of "the point of Virginia . . . at 37° and 10 minuits N. latitude . . . this aforesaid Bay of Virginia (which is called bay of the Xacan),"[1] (Translation in Alexander Brown, *Genesis of the United States*, Boston and New York, 1890, vol. i., pp. 514, 515), and (on p. 518) "Xacan, since that is the name of Virginia." In the letter of Diego de Molino (to Alonso de Velasco?) of May 28, 1613, he says of the region visited: "This country lies in the midst of thirty-seven degrees and a third, in which lies also the bay which we/they call Santa Maria" (Translation in Alexander Brown, *Genesis of the United States*, vol. ii., p. 650). Francisco Sacchini, in his *Historiæ Societatis Jesu*, Pars tertia (Romæ, 1650, p. 323), says: "Est Axaca Floridæ Prouincia perampla, ab æquatore in Boream erecta triginta septem gradibus, ab Sancta Elenâ leucis centum septuaginta disiuncta." Barcia in his *Ensayo* (Madrid, 1723, Año MDLXVI., p. 119) says: "Baía de Santa Maria, que está en 37 Grados," and (Año MDLXIII., p. 148) "en 37 Grados y medio." Alegre in his *Historia de la Compañía de Jesus en Nueva España* (México, 1842, tomo i., p. 26), says Father Segura and his companions "llegaron á la provincia de Axacan, que hoy . . . hace parte de la nueva Georgía y la Virginia, á los 11 de setiembre, y dieron fondo en el mismo puerto de Santa María (hoy S. George), patria del cacique D. Luis."

Fairbanks in his *History of St. Augustine* (New York, 1858, pp. 100–102) and in his *History of Florida* (Philadelphia, 1871, p. 157) and Shea in his *The Catholic Church in Colonial Days* (New York, 1886, p. 147), in his "Ancient Florida" (*Narr. and Crit. Hist. Am.*, vol. ii., p. 282) and elsewhere in various essays on the Segura mission, both identify the Bay of Santa Maria and Axacan with the Chesapeake. J. G. Kohl in his "A History of the Discovery of the East Coast of North

[1] Bracketed in Alexander Brown's translation.

America," Portland, 1869, vol. i., pp. 309, 399–401 (*Collections of the Maine Historical Society*, 2nd series) identifies the Baya de Santa Maria with Chesapeake Bay. Justin Winsor, in *Narr. and Crit. Hist. Am.*, vol. iii., p. 167, appears to have some doubts as to the identity, while he admits "that there seem to have been visits of the Spaniards to the Chesapeake at an early day (1566–1573)." Dr. Shea in "The Log Chapel on the Rappahannock," in *The Catholic World*, March, 1875, p. 847, suggests the derivation of Axacan from Occoquan, and Alexander Brown in his reference to the Ecija Relation of 1609 (*The First Republic in America*, Boston, 1898, p. 88) repeats this derivation. In his *Genesis of the United States* (1890, vol. ii., p. 947) he admits the identity of Axacan with the Chesapeake, and his conclusion is deserving of great weight. In vol. i., p. 488, of the same work there is a note to the name "Xatamahane," which he has bracketed in the Spelman Relation, and which he thinks may possibly be the Spanish name "Xacan."

APPENDIX EE

THE SITE OF THE SEGURA MISSION

The only knowledge which we have of the locality where the Jesuits established their mission is contained in the very vague description of it given by Father Quiros in the joint letter which he wrote with Father Segura on the 12th of December, 1570, a day or two after the landing, and is as follows: After referring to "la esperanza grande q̄ se tiene de la conversion desta gente . . . y entrada para la sierra y la China" (p. 2), the letter continues on page 3: "de la informacion desta tierra lo que toca a la derota q̄ se ha de traer el piloto la dara porque no conviene q̄ se entre por el rio que nosotros entramos a causa de no tener tambuena informacion quanto convenia de los indios por donde aviamos de entrar y por esso es ydo oy el piloto por la tierra dos buenas leguas de aqui a ver un rio por donde se ha de hazer la entrada quanto con la buena ventura nos vengan a proveer y visitar, pues por aquella parte se puede yr por mar hasta el lugar donde hemos de hazer la habitacion y por aqui ay dos buenas leguas por tierra y otros dos o mas por la mar . . .

"La informacion que hasta ahora se ha podido aver de la tierra adentro es que unos indios que encontramos alla abaxo en este rio nos informaron que tres o quatros jornadas de alli estava la sierra y las dos dellas se yva por un rio y despues de la sierra otra jornada o dos se via otro mar. . . . (p. 6) . . . desque se entienda ser tiempo en que venga la fragata . . . se embiara un indio o dos con una carta a la boca del braço de mar por donde se ha de passar . . ."

This is the sum total of the information conveyed by the letter. It does not mention when land was sighted, nor when the bay was entered. It does not state the distance sailed nor the direction taken by the vessel after entering the bay, nor how many rivers or harbours, if any, were passed before the vessel reached the river up which it sailed. It does not give the direction of the course of the river nor how far up it was ascended. The landing-place is not described, nor are its latitude and longitude mentioned. It does not tell the direction followed by the pilot to reach the other river, nor the direction in which the other river flowed. The way to the mountains was partly by *a* river, but whether by a river flowing into the bay above or below the river the ship had ascended there is nothing to indicate. This is absolutely all that is known of the region visited by the Jesuits, for the only survivor of the party was the boy Alonso, whose account is obscure, and none of the authorities relied on for the subsequent visit of Avilés to avenge the murder of the Fathers gives any details.

It is upon this meagre evidence that Dr. Shea has based his conclusion that the Jesuits ascended the Potomac and ultimately settled on the Rappahannock. ("The Log Chapel on the Rappahannock," in *The Catholic World*, March, 1875, p. 847. *The Catholic Church in Colonial Days*, New York, 1886, pp. 147, 149. "Ancient Florida" in *Narr. and Crit. Hist. Am.*, New York, 1886, vol. ii., p. 282.) In "The Log Chapel" (*ibid.*, p. 848), Dr. Shea observes: "Believing that the Chesapeake, by the rivers running into it, would easily lead to the Western Ocean Menéndez spent the winter of 1565 studying out the subject with the aid of Don Luis de Velasco [*i. e.*, the Axacan Indian] and Father Urdaneta, a missionary just arrived from China by the overland route across Mexico." Both Merás (Ruidíaz, *La Florida*, tomo i., p. 258) and Barrientos (García, *Dos Antiguas Relaciones de la Florida*, p. 126) say Don Luis had been six years with Avilés, and all the information about Axacan which Avilés had obtained from him is probably set out in his letter to Philip II., of October 15, 1565 (Ruidíaz, *ibid.*, tomo ii., pp. 93, 94, 100; see p. 212, in this volume). In the absence of any mention of the presence of Don Luis on the Ays expedition either by Avilés or by his two biographers, it is problematical whether he accompanied the Adelantado on his exploration and was with him in Havana during the winter of 1565–1566. What little we know of the information which Avilés obtained from Father Andres de Urdaneta, concerning the straits leading to China is found in the letter of the former to the King of January 30, 1566 (Ruidíaz, *La Florida*, tomo ii., p. 151). The active occupation of Avilés during this winter could have left him but little time for the study of geographical problems.

While it is probable that the Jesuits were commissioned to inform themselves of the "entrada . . . para la China," the context of the quotation above given indicates that this was not their immediate objective, otherwise they would have followed the directions given by the natives. Their desire was to reach the country of Don Luis, where he could serve them as an interpreter, an object which they appear to have accomplished, for they certainly reached a region the language of which he spoke. As their communication with the natives was entirely through him, his representations as to his relationship with the chiefs is not altogether free from suspicion in view of his subsequent treachery. The only point in favour of the site selected by Dr. Shea lies in his suggestion that Axacan is derived from Occoquan ("The Log Chapel," in *ibid.*, p. 851) in which he is followed by Alexander Brown, who is disposed to accept Dr. Shea's identification of the location (*The*

First Republic in America, p. 88, *Genesis of the United States*, vol. ii., p. 947).

It is only necessary to consult a map of the Chesapeake with its many rivers and creeks, both large and small, flowing into it from the west to see how improbable it is that a vessel delayed in its voyage by stress of weather and short of provisions would ascend it to the Potomac before making harbour, and how readily the vague data of the letter can be applied to any of its numerous affluents, both as to the landing-place, the site of the mission, and the distance to the Alleghanies. In the absence of further particulars the term "braço de mar por donde se ha de passar" can refer to the estuaries of the James, the York, Mobjack Bay, Piankatank River, and the Rappahannock as well as to the Potomac, into some small river either above or below the mouth of any of which the Jesuits may have entered, since no direction is given. While it is equally impossible to assert that the rivers visited by the Jesuits were not the Potomac and the Rappahannock, yet in view of the absence of any substantial evidence to establish their identity the question must remain an open one until more definite information is produced, notwithstanding the high authority of Dr. Shea.

APPENDIX FF

MAPA DE LA FLORIDA Y LAGUNA DE MAIMI DONDE SE HA DE HACER UN FUERTE (ARCH. GEN. DE INDIAS, SEVILLE, EST. 145, CAJ. 7, LEG. 7)

This map is anonymous, undated, and unaccompanied by data of any description.

The coast names on the map, reading from east to west, are: s̃ helena (Santa Elena). ahoya. b de los baxos (Bahia de los Bajos). cofonufo. hospogahe (Espogache of the Relations). asao. Guadalquini. Ballenas. S pedro (San Pedro). Sena. S mateo. S agustin. matancas (Matanzas). moysquitos (Mosquitos). cabo de cañaberal. ays. S iozia (probably san lozia—Santa Lucia). Xega. vocas de migel mora (Bocas de Miguel de Mora). hensenada de niupa. b[a] de carlos (Bahia de Carlos). b[a] de tacabaga (Bahia de Tacabaga, also written Tocobaga). hensenada de carlos. punta de apalahe (Punta de Apalache).

In the centre: laguna de meiymi. The islands are: bahama. mimeres. isla de cuba. havana. martires. tortugas. The inscription endorsed on the map, and reproduced at the bottom of the copy in this volume, is: "Planta de la costa de la florida y en que Paraje esta La LaGuna Maymi y adonde se ha de hacer el fuerte."

The map is No. 94 of D. Pedro Torre Lanzas, *Mapas de Mexico y Florida*, tomo i., p. 71, where he dates it "siglo 17 (?)"

All of the names on this map are found either on earlier maps or in Relations accessible to the writer prior to 1596 with the exception of "hospogahe," which first appears under the form "Espogache" in 1606 (in Marqués's "Relación," Ruidíaz, *La Florida*, tomo ii., p. 506) and "hensenada de niupa," which does not appear elsewhere.

In 1595 Juan Maldonado Barnuevo, Governor of Havana, sent his nephew Juan Maldonado to examine the coast from St. Augustine as far as the southern extremity of the Florida Keys. In the "Derrotero" of the expedition appears for the first time the Florida coast names "jega" (Xega of the map) and "bocas de miguel de mora" (see Barnuevo's letter of July 6, 1595, with the annexed "Derrotero." Arch. Gen. de Indias, Seville, MS., est. 54, caj. 1, leg. 15). At about this date Juan de Posada, who had come to Florida in 1586, where he had spent seven years (Letter of Albaro Flores, November 9, 1586, Direc. de Hidrog., Madrid, *Col. Navarrete*, tomo xxii., Doc. No. 98) wrote to the home government advising the dismantling of all of the forts in Florida, "y que haga hacer uno en la cabeza de los Martires" (see his undated "Relación," Direc. de Hidrog., Madrid, *Col. Navarrete*, Doc. No. 31).

In view of the fact that Posada was probably in Florida at the time of Maldonado's return from his expedition; that the location given the fort on the map corresponds with the description in the "Derrotero"; that these particular legends are identical in both map and "Derrotero," and that the script used on the map and in the endorsed title is of the period in which his letter was written, it is not at all improbable that the map formed part of Posada's letter.

INDEX

S

T

X

Y

Z